AF270391

ORIGINAL FORGIVENESS

Northwestern University

Studies in Phenomenology

and

Existential Philosophy

General Editor Anthony J. Steinbock

ORIGINAL FORGIVENESS

Nicolas de Warren

Northwestern University Press
Evanston, Illinois

Northwestern University Press
www.nupress.northwestern.edu

This title is licensed under the Creative Commons Attribution-NonCommercial 4.0 International License (CC BY-NC). Read the license at https://creativecommons.org/licenses/by-nc/4.0/legalcode.

This book is freely available in an open access edition thanks to TOME (Toward an Open Monograph Ecosystem)—a collaboration of the Association of American Universities, the Association of University Presses, and the Association of Research Libraries—and the generous support of the Pennsylvania State University. Learn more at the TOME website, available at openmonographs.org.

DOI: 10.21985/n2-qzwz-k976

Copyright © 2021 by Northwestern University Press. Published 2021. All rights reserved.

Printed in the United States of America

10 9 8 7 6 5 4 3 2 1

Library of Congress Cataloging-in-Publication Data

Names: Warren, Nicolas de, 1969– author.
Title: Original forgiveness / Nicolas de Warren.
Other titles: Studies in phenomenology and existential philosophy.
Description: Evanston, Illinois : Northwestern University Press, 2020. |
    Series: Northwestern University Studies in phenomenology and existential
    philosophy | Includes bibliographical references and index.
Identifiers: LCCN 2020031402 | ISBN 9780810142787 (paperback) |
    ISBN 9780810142794 (cloth) | ISBN 9780810142800 (ebook)
Subjects: LCSH: Forgiveness. | Trust.
Classification: LCC BJ1476 .W37 2020 | DDC 179.9—dc23
LC record available at https://lccn.loc.gov/2020031402

pour Felix et Cleo

La verité et la vie sont bien ardues, et il me restait d'elles, sans
qu'en somme je les connusse, une impression où la tristesse
était peut-être encore dominée par la fatigue.
—Proust

Contents

Acknowledgments

Along the way, friends and colleagues accompanied the conceiving of this book since its inception. In ways not known even to myself, the writing of this book matured through their participation, inspiration, and challenge: Mette Lebech, Darian Meacham, Esteban Marín Ávila, Tobias Keiling, Patricia Portela, Tomas Šinkūnas, Ignacio Quepons, Anna Yampolskaya, Witold Płotka, Saulius Geniusas, Francesco Tava, Raphael Zagury-Orly, and, last, but not least, i ragazzi di Infinite Task (Claudio, Emiliano, Daniele). For his astute editorial eye and comments, Kyle Barrowman; for the pleasure of learned conversations without end, Basil Vassilicos; for his exemplariness, even from afar, Roland Breeur; for encouragements with an earlier draft, William Remley; for the generosity of his thoughts, Joseph Cohen; for the precious gift of time to rewrite what was most important, Trevor Perri.

Gratitude as well for questions, objections, and suggestions from welcoming audiences in Copenhagen, Gdańsk, Warsaw, Philadelphia, Paris, Wuppertal, Vienna, Bristol, Helsinki, Xalapa, Salzburg, Milan, Landau, Dublin, Moscow, Johannesburg, Würzburg, Hokkaido, and Beijing.

And for Clara:

> *Wege will ich erkiesen,*
> *die selten wer betritt*
> *in blassen Abendwiesen—*
> *und keinen Traum, als diesen:*
> *Du gehst mit.*
> —Rilke

Introduction

C'est que le seul abord convenant à la morale ne saurait être qu'abrupt.
    —Maurice Blanchot

An assumption that unites various conceptions of forgiveness is the thought that forgiveness is a response to an inciting incident: something must have been done against me in order to find myself in the situation of granting or refusing forgiveness. Likewise, you must have done something against me in order to find yourself in the situation of receiving or rejecting forgiveness. Forgiveness enters the scene—the scene of history, the scene of biography, the scene of politics, the scene of thinking—only once, and only once I, or some other, have done some specific harm against you, or you, or some other, have done some specific harm against me. Whether for the aggrieved who forgives or for the transgressor who stands to be forgiven, forgiveness crystallizes around an encounter between both persons in the aftermath of a determinate and contested past: an original sin, an act of violence, a grave offense, an egregious malfeasance, or commonplace wrongdoings. After injury, there can be forgiveness, but never before. This assumption, that forgiveness comes into the picture only after some specific harm has been done against me, appears self-evident. Forgiveness enters into our lives dramatically, whether loudly or quietly, with indignation and incredulity—"Why have you done *this* against me?" "Why *have* you forsaken me?" "How could I ever forgive you for what you *did*?"—and thus remains haunted by the specter of theatricality much as it is gripped by the suspense of promised renewal. We do not originally begin in forgiveness. In the beginning, there was no forgiveness.

Why should I ask for forgiveness if I have done nothing against you? When we meet strangers for the first time or pass one another anonymously on the street, when we greet each other and enter into the concourse of communication and commerce by exchanging our names, making our intentions known, and narrating our lives, we begin by asking everything except for forgiveness. It would indeed be disconcerting if upon meeting you for the first time, I promptly beseeched your forgiveness, or if you implored me for forgiveness, I, who have done nothing against you, and you, who have done nothing against me. It seems impossible to ask for forgiveness in innocence: you would think me either mad, perverse, or ridiculous. What is there for which to ask forgiveness if nothing has happened between us, if a world between has never before existed, if a tale has yet to be told? What is there to gain—is there not everything to lose?—in extending my hand in forgiveness without cause or reason, thus apparently giving you carte blanche for harms yet to be committed? Would the issuing of forgiveness without license not give license to capricious and calculated wrongdoings against me? We do not originally begin in forgiveness. And this would seem commonsensical, since nothing between us has yet begun. Everything is in fact about to begin.

I would like to reconsider this assumption—commonsensical, theological, philosophical—without thereby dismantling or discrediting entirely this largely sensible construal of forgiveness as a responsive beginning anew in the aftermath of moral injury. The depth of forgiveness for human existence, however, is not adequately grasped with this conventional understanding. As developed in these explorations, one cannot arrive at a proper grasp of what is fundamental about forgiveness, as essential for the human condition, without a revision of this assumption in light of which forgiveness becomes more adventurous as well as more precarious. What if there existed an availability of/for forgiveness as well as a responsibility of/for forgiveness—an original forgiveness—that was prior to any act or situation to ostensibly call for it? What if we originally began *in* forgiveness? Not simply as a reactive stance toward antecedent harm, not merely as relative to a determinate past, and not exclusively as concerning reconciliation and regeneration, but also as an absolute beginning of promise without any promises—a beginning without history or theater, an unprecedented beginning? What if I first began in forgiveness without ever having done anything against you? What if I first opened my hand toward you through forgiveness without your ever having done anything against me? Forgiveness not as the restoration of freedom but as its indispensable condition, an original forgiveness that, because it is not reactive, thus could not be manipulated or feigned, nor give me any particular advantage. Because of this originality, such a beginning in forgiveness would remain all the more precious upon being exposed to harms yet unexpected and possibilities yet unimagined—a forgiveness for nothing where everything between us would remain at stake and hang in the balance. Under the designation of "original forgiveness," my aim in this book is to delineate such a conception in terms of which forgiveness as commonly understood and practiced, as responsive to determinate harms, and as rooted in encounters between transgressed and transgressor, is repositioned and rearticulated.

My argument critically hinges on motivating and developing a distinction between "forgiveness as encounter" and "original forgiveness." This distinction does not mark two opposing conceptions of forgiveness, as if I am presenting alternatives from which to choose. Nor does this distinction *decide* how to understand the former, forgiveness as encounter, even though I develop my own account here. The former designation encompasses theological as well as philosophical conceptions of forgiveness in their established forms as a power of new beginning in response to antecedent harms and wrongdoings, while the latter expression designates an original availability *to* the possibility of forgiveness, prior to finding oneself in any specific situation of having (or not having) to forgive, or to be forgiven, as well as an original beseeching *for* forgiveness without ever having first done any specific harm or wrongdoing against someone other. Encounters in forgiveness are "always already" situated within an original forgiveness, even as the meanings of "always" and "already" are not transparent in the terms of encounter with forgiveness—that is, expected and understood in advance. Without original forgiveness, there would be no availing of oneself to the possibility of forgiveness, hence no possibility of forgiveness *tout court*. At the origin of my openness toward the Other, I cannot stand unforgiving toward the possibility of forgiveness, without thereby committing myself in advance to whether in any given future situation of forgiveness (when we encounter each other in the question of forgiveness) I should or must, as duty or virtue, forgive, *or* not forgive. Conversely, at the origin of my openness to the Other, I already find myself beseeching forgiveness in the name of an inexpugnable responsibility that I must bear toward the Other.

What is at stake with these reflections, gravitating around this recasting of forgiveness, is the question of whether forgiveness (asking for forgiveness as well as granting forgiveness, or, conversely, refusing to ask as well as rejecting to forgive) stands at the center and therefore at the beginning of any encounter with others, such that forgiveness in this more original setting underlies the possibility of our encounters, giving them a precariousness and adventure that markedly makes, or unmakes, us human. Rather than consider the possibility or impossibility of forgiveness after injury, and hence within an encounter among persons who have already claimed their own freedom and autonomy with respect to and against each other, I aim to understand the significance and consequence of an original forgiveness within a foregrounding entrustment of responsibility. Within this original configuration, forgiveness already circumscribes openness to the Other and hence the possibility of our encounters, be it in peace or violence, or, as more often is the case, in that indiscernible zone caught between each. Insofar as such an original forgiveness is not yet "to forgive" or "not to forgive" in advance, neither promised nor refused beforehand, we can be said to begin upon our adventures with each other from the "nonplace" of an anarchic beginning, from which we are launched toward the possibility or impossibility of forgiveness, come what may. In forgiveness without anything already to be forgiven or not to be forgiven, *nous sommes embarqués.*

Original forgiveness abides in truthfulness within an originally self-positing ignorance. In this posture of original forgiveness, I must already avail myself to the possibility of encountering the Other in forgiveness without ever being entirely prepared or able beforehand, in knowing or in acting, to live up to the demands placed upon me when called upon the scene of forgiveness (to forgive or not to forgive) in the aftermath of what the Other has done against me. My standing in original forgiveness places me in a suspended time of unknowing and indefinite time of waiting. I am for myself as well as for the Other extended in time without end, of whether I *could ever* still open myself to the drama, and often violence, of the encounter in forgiveness. Such foregrounding availability for forgiveness is structurally connected to an original responsibility for the Other, whose ethical claim on my being assigns to me a responsibility I cannot truthfully bear without an original forgiveness in enduring what I want not to bear, but must, that I am the Other's keeper. Expressed in these terms, original forgiveness does not represent a novel discovery or invention in ethical thought but an original understanding of the *meaningfulness* of ethics as encapsulated in the question "Am I the Other's keeper?" To stand as the Other's keeper is both to remain available to forgiveness when the Other betrays me and to stand in forgiveness toward the Other for a betrayal already under way. Strictly speaking, "I am the Other's keeper" is less a statement or question than a recurring scruple, "Am I the Other's keeper?" in and against which I perpetually risk losing myself once more, only to find myself here again.

Construed in this way, original forgiveness is part and parcel of the indispensability of trust and responsibility for human existence. The impossibility of circling back upon oneself completely, in drawing a circle around oneself, as the place uniquely one's own, attests to the hole within the ethical subject where trust, responsibility, and original forgiveness implacably take hold. Unaccommodated as but poor, bare creatures, we are necessarily dependent on the accommodations of trust. Upon trust, human existence stands, but by that same affordance, risks falling. We are, in this sense, forked creatures of trust. As developed here, insofar as trust in others, trust in myself, and trust in the world are fundamental conditions for the sustained meaningfulness of human concourse, communication, and commerce, in the beginning, I already find myself in the posture of original forgiveness, not for what has been done against me or what will be done to me, or for having done anything in particular against you. In finding oneself with the Other entrusted to me, I must trust in myself that I will not abandon the Other, when the Other abandons me. In having the Other entrusted to me, I find myself in forgiveness toward the Other for this impossible responsibility to which I have been elected. "Am I the Other's keeper?" bespeaks and betrays an original responsibility within which forgiveness finds its proper originality. Inscribed within this original responsibility and investiture of the Good, original forgiveness is not a moral power of restoration or renewal but an originating power in powerlessness, the anarchy of all beginnings. In its anarchical beginning, forgiveness in this existential breach cannot be understood along the lines of instituting reconciliation in the aftermath of rupture, or renewal and regeneration in releasing a novel future from a deranged past. Rather than releasing us from the past toward a future, original forgiveness entrusts the present to the future, for which there is no past not already promised as a future other than what has come to pass between us. Absent of any determinate past, original forgiveness is equally bereft of any grounding past principle. Unleashed is the openness of time to the possibility of forgiveness, of time in its ethical promise as such. Stated in these terms, original forgiveness does not center, as might a reactive conception of forgiveness, on reconciliation and renewal but precariously gauges human existence in the ambit of redemption. Original forgiveness is the anarchy of redemption.

This proposed revision of our understanding of forgiveness as exclusively and exhaustively a reactive beginning anew entails a revision of our understanding of the relation between forgiveness and evil, and hence a revision of our understanding of the sourcing of evil as such. Whether implicitly or explicitly, a reactive understanding of forgiveness acknowledges evil as its necessary precondition and initiating event; without eruptions of evil in the world, there would be no occasions for forgiveness, if by evil we broadly understand a determinate harm or suffering inflicted upon me by another, and thus, within the scope of considerations advanced here, remain within (and retain) a circumscription of evil—and by extension, of forgiveness—vis-à-vis interpersonal, human, interactions. Whether we also stand in an original posture of forgiveness, as availability and responsibility, toward God, Nature, and animals remains here in abeyance, a matter for future consideration. In a conventional story, forgiveness promises to deliver us from evil even as we are first thrust into the situation of forgiveness through evil. Evil gives occasion for forgiveness. This antecedence of evil to forgiveness assumes an original beginning not touched by evil or graced with forgiveness and likewise remains committed to the derivative status of evil, as privation of the Good or inverted relationship between personal maxim and ethical imperative. Evil descends from the Good, while forgiveness reascends to Goodness. Forgiveness enters the scene only reactively and retrospectively; it is not originally originating but originally reoriginating of a tarnished Good, a broken covenant, or a paradise lost. On this conception, forgiveness inaugurates a new beginning from past evils in bringing closure to the arching claim and enduring touch of evil on the present, for the sake of a future no longer beholden to a past that seems to never pass. Evil is said to be "overcome," "over and done with," or "left behind." Forgiveness is a forgoing of the past in remembrance of the future. The unending night of evil, it is said, has given way to a new dawn for eternity.

Under the heading of original forgiveness, once forgiveness is no longer understood exclusively as a reactive response to antecedent harm but considered more originally as standing before any committed evil, forgiveness becomes released from the hostage of evil, while evil in this light becomes more distinctly profiled in its relation to forgiveness. The point is neither to dismiss nor to disavow the conception of forgiveness as a response to antecedent evil; indeed, when perhaps no other response seems possible or meaningful. The point is rather to think anew the relation between evil and the Good from a dramatic grasp of forgiveness within an original responsibility for others. From the posture of original forgiveness, the relation between forgiveness and evil is *reversed*: forgiveness is not originally an upheaval against evil, but, quite the contrary, evil is an upheaval against original forgiveness from within responsibility itself. Rather than falling into forgiveness from an original evil, or original sin, we fall into evil from an original forgiveness. With this insight, evil manifests itself most originally as blasphemy and betrayal; to wit, as rage and revolt against forgiveness itself. As exposed in the explorations of this book, the mystery of Goodness lies with an irrecusable election not only to bear oneself—to endure in patience and forbearance—an original responsibility for the Other, but also to already stand oneself accused of betrayal and blasphemy in this assignment of the Other to one's keep and investiture of the Good.

* * *

It being understood that any advance précis of what is to come must necessarily be imprecise, fall short, and summarily betray, and hence already be forgotten and forgiven, *Original Forgiveness* is divided into eight chapters of unequal length and scope, each taking the time to find its course. In lieu of a conclusion, chapter 8 marks a point of arrival at original forgiveness, from which, in an "Afterwords," a new point of department is signaled, and hence another beginning, by way of a children's story.

In chapter 1, "Upon Trust We Stand, upon Trust We Fall," I begin with an analysis of the foundational significance of trust for human existence. Surprisingly, philosophical accounts—phenomenological or otherwise—of the life-world and intersubjectivity have on the whole neglected the indispensable and largely unspoken dimension of trust in human flourishing. This lack of attention to the constitution of the life-world in trust is just as evident in mainstream discussions of forgiveness. In beginning with the theme of trust, this chapter does not offer a comprehensive account of trust—a task that far exceeds the scope of this book—nor is the endeavor necessary for the argument at hand. The aim of this chapter is to establish, delineate, and explore the foundational significance of trust for the life-world (or "being-in-the-world") and, in this light, situate the theme of forgiveness in the larger context of this book. Through an engagement with the writings of Martin Heidegger, Edmund Husserl, Annette Baier, Knud Ejler Løgstrup, Mikhail Bakhtin, and other thinkers, I argue that an analysis of trust must include an examination of the relations between *three* existential forms of trust: trust in the world, trust in others (or intersubjective trust), and self-trust. Two main insights into trust are developed in this discussion with an eye toward subsequent chapters. First, relations of trust involve an edging, or lining, of the trusted Other in the self and, by the same token, a lining of the self in the entrusted Other. In this manner, the trusted Other is carried within me just as (much as) I am carried within the Other to whom I have entrusted myself. What is to live upon trust with others is for others to necessarily participate and partake in our lives, as much as participate and partake in the lives of others. Beholden thus to others, we are not self-begotten beings. Second, relationships of trust inherently involve a responsibility (or honoring of trust) to which we are committed without knowing what the commitment of trust means or what it demands of us. Trusting gains its meaning from this responsibility for our trusts without yet understanding the rules, meanings, and expectations of our trusts. I further argue that recognizing the foundational sense in which human existence stands upon trust must likewise entail recognition of how human existence also falls upon trust—namely, how trust facilitates our ruin and grief. It is by trusting that we open ourselves up to manipulation, deception, and betrayal. The bivalence of trust, its forked significance, as the ground upon which humans stand *and* fall, points to the anarchic character of trust's foundation for human life. By way of Herman Melville's *The Confidence-Man*, I argue that the foundational character of trust critically implies that if trust (or confidence) resides at the core of being-in-the-world, being-with-others, and being-in-oneself, then all three forms of trust in the life-world are haunted by "nothingness," there being nothing other than or beyond trust upon which we stand and hence into which just as significantly we fall when our trusts are manipulated, deceived, or betrayed. Trust, in other words, can equally be the hole upon which we stand or the hole into which we fall: the issue, or challenge, is one of filling this hole with ground enough for us to stand in relation to the world, to others, and to ourselves. This chapter concludes with the argument, as illustrated through a reading of Emmanuel Carrère's *The Adversary*, that the betrayal of trust in the world, trust in others, and self-trust, as provoked by the impostor of trusts, represents an *ethical* rupture—not merely an ontological rupture—within the life-world. The experience of betrayal in those trusts in which we have invested ourselves reveals the profound ethical sense of what it means to lose trust in the world. As explored in Carrère's narrative, the most extreme manifestation of this ethical rupture of trust takes the form of the impostor of forgiveness who betrays, and thus reveals, an original entrustment of responsibility for others, upon which trusts given and received are predicated.

After having established a frame for my investigation of forgiveness in chapter 1, I turn in chapter 2, "Forgiveness and the Human Condition," to an examination of Hannah Arendt's influential conception of forgiveness and its indispensable significance for human plurality and the life-world. I take Arendt's conception of forgiveness as an exemplary statement of the established casting of forgiveness as an encounter between two parties in the aftermath of a determinate wrongdoing in the past. Given that my argument for original forgiveness does not seek to repudiate or refute the common understanding of forgiveness as encounter but seeks to reposition it with regard to original forgiveness, I endorse and emend Arendt's account with an eye toward revealing how this form of thinking about forgiveness tacitly presupposes an unbroken *trust* in the world, in others, and in oneself, and hence an abiding *availability* to forgiveness. Specifically, I further refine her suggested characterizations of the relationship between forgiveness, narrative, temporality, agency, and—most important—argue that Arendt ascribes a redemptive significance to forgiveness. Despite the importance of her conception, as reconfigured herein, Arendt's exemplary account of forgiveness as encounter presupposes what I call original forgiveness, as broached in the next chapter.

Chapter 3, "The Unforgivable and Forgiving without Forgiveness," turns to Simon Wiesenthal's narrative of his encounter with the request for forgiveness from a dying SS soldier during World War II in *The Sunflower*. Against the background of my discussion of "forgiveness as encounter" in chapter 2, I argue in this chapter that Wiesenthal's narrative introduces an implicit distinction between the possibility or impossibility of forgiving (to forgive or not to forgive in the encounter of forgiveness) and opening oneself to the encounter of forgiveness. As I develop, although Wiesenthal departs from his encounter with the dying German soldier's request for forgiveness in silence, thus suggesting a refusal to forgive, his posture of *listening* to the soldier's narrative and, indeed, the writing of his own narrative of this encounter, represents a not unforgiving availability to the encounter of forgiveness. This attitude toward a nonetheless not forgiven SS soldier turns on an availability to the encounter of forgiveness as already a not unforgiving response to the Other in her despair and evil. This discussion also introduces a further element to the significance of forgiveness: forgiveness as unbinding or release (absolution) from the living in terms of which a life in its passage of death takes stock and measure of itself and restores trust in the world. In the impossibility to forgive, as marked nonetheless by the patience of listening, and hence standing available, the futurity of a forgiveness becomes opened without any promise of reconciliation or, indeed, forgiveness as such. As with the circulation of Wiesenthal's narrative, posing its question of forgiveness to others, even when forgiveness has not occurred, there remain the specters of a forgiveness not given, of forgiveness *yet* to come or *still* never to come. Once the contours of this notion of availability to forgiveness have been established, I consider the opposite of such availability—namely, unavailability to the encounter of forgiveness—through a discussion of Jean Améry's *refoulement* of the very question of forgiveness in his response to Wiesenthal's narrative. As Améry declares to Wiesenthal, "I don't want to hear anything of forgiveness." On the basis of this introduction of the theme of remaining unforgiving, I discuss different forms of *unforgiveness* and *ressentiment* as forms of unavailability in Fyodor Dostoevsky's *Notes from Underground* and Heinrich von Kleist's *Michael Kohlhaas*. In contrast to these manifestations of remaining unforgiving, I suggest that Améry's unforgiving *ressentiment* speaks from a distinct place and event of evil, to which I turn in the next chapter.

In chapter 4, "The Unforgivable and the Inhuman Condition," I develop an interpretation of Améry's argument that torture, as the manifestation of the unforgivable, institutes a threefold loss of trust in the world, in others, and in oneself. My aim here is to understand the nexus of trust, responsibility, and forgiveness negatively: the catastrophic loss of trust in the world results in an abiding condition of *unforgiveness.* I place special emphasis on loss of trust through the suffering of the body in torture and the violation of skin as the border that sets the world at a distance but also sets the terms for the encounter with the world. This constitutional significance of embodiment, and, more specifically, what I term (following Didier Anzieu) the skin-ego (*le moi-peau*), I argue to be critical for the formation of trust and hence, with its loss, the condition of remaining unavailable—unforgiving—to forgiveness. I further examine the various meanings of what Améry calls the fundamental "expectation of assistance," or better, as I propose, the entrustment of oneself to the responsibility of Others, which is betrayed in torture. The unforgivable is produced here through an existential sense of abandonment and isolation from the world and others, that others have failed in their responsibility to stand as one's keeper. A number of themes are developed here that anticipate my conception of original forgiveness in the next set of chapters: *ressentiment* as horror at indifference; the connection between sensibility and language (bodily and verbal acts of torture); the proximity of the Other in the form of responsibility for the Other's suffering and vulnerability; the transformation of the lived-body into "meat" and the visceral annihilation of the "I can" of response; the constitutive significance of sadism for political sovereignty. As Améry proposes, the unforgivable is a condition marked by the absolute—unforgiving—betrayal and abandonment of responsibility for others, and hence, alongside, the availability of forgiveness without which trust in the world, in others, and in oneself becomes voided.

Chapter 5, "I Wonder Men Dare Trust Themselves with Men: The Forked Significance of Trust," and chapter 6, "No Cause, No Cause: Breakages of Trust and the Availability of Forgiveness," develop in tandem a bifocal account of original forgiveness through an interpretation of Shakespeare's *King Lear* and a philosophical elaboration, drawing from Martin Buber, Mikhail Bakhtin, Annette Baier, and Gabriel Marcel, of "availability to forgiveness" and "creative fidelity" as essential to the constitution of trust. As I argue, the intertwining narratives of King Lear and his daughters, and of the Earl of Gloucester and his sons, move across the fractious landscape of three basic forms of trust's unmaking: *betrayal* (Lear's betrayal of Cordelia's love; Edmund's betrayal of his father and half brother); *deceit* (Regan's and Goneril's mutual sisterly deceits; Edmund's deceit of his father); and *abandonment* (Lear's banishment of Cordelia; Edgar's banishment from humanity in the figure of Poor Tom; Gloucester's blind wanderings). I thus return to the conception of trust as trust in the world, trust in Others, and self-trust proposed in chapter 1 in order to resituate my advance toward my conception of original forgiveness more clearly. As I argue, in the tragedy of *King Lear*, the three basic forms of trust's undoing (betrayal, deceit, abandonment) are matched with three forms of *availability* as represented by the three characters who do not abandon Lear when Lear has betrayed their trusts (Cordelia, Kent, the Fool): availability of forgiveness, availability as fidelity, and availability as candor, or confidentiality. I seize on this mapping of availability to develop more fully the dimension of original forgiveness as "availability." I develop this conception through an interpretation and appropriation of Marcel's notions of *disponibilité* and *fidélité créatrice* and Buber's dialogical conception of the I-Thou relation as the ontological foundation for being-in-the-world. Essential to my argument is the articulation of trust as a dialogical relationship where the meaningfulness of trust itself becomes entrusted to the dialogical relationship that transpires between those who trust. Each of us is the keeper of our trust in the triadic structure of its dialogical constitution. In this manner, what is entailed in trusting and being trusted is our availability for each other in the dialogue of trust. I argue that what is entailed in trusting the Other is that I remain available to the Other when the Other betrays my trust. This availing oneself in advance to the encounter with the Other in forgiveness is neither a kind of promise nor a form of contract. Instead, I must trust in myself to become—"create"—the kind of person I need to be in order to do what would seem impossible beforehand: to remain available to forgiveness when the Other has committed the unforgivable in betraying my trust. I conclude this discussion with an extended interpretation of Cordelia's forgiveness of King Lear, her father, as not only her forgiveness for the unforgivable (her banishment) but also as the expiation of his death, so that he might "unburdened crawl toward death." Part of my argument hinges on demonstrating how the drama of Cordelia's forgiveness of her unforgivable father is structured implicitly in terms of a distinction between "original forgiveness" as "availability to forgiveness" and "forgiveness as encounter." To this end, I position my reading in contrast to Jean-Luc Marion's interpretation of Cordelia's forgiveness as an exemplification of forgiveness as "giving once more" the original gift of unconditional love. Contrary to this theologically underwritten conception, I argue for the anarchic setting of Cordelia's heart to her father, without cause, as predicated on an availability to forgiveness, that she is not unforgiving to the possibility *or* impossibility of forgiveness, without which she could not return to her father and allow him to return from the grave of the unforgivable, to find each other again in the encounter of forgiveness and kind nursery of her responsibility toward him. In this manner, I argue that the "fine revolution" of Shakespeare's vision of forgiveness upends the theologically dominant image of the Father's forgiveness of the wayward son. In Cordelia's "no cause, no cause," we witness the daughter's forgiveness of the wayward Father.

Chapter 7, "The Death of the Other as Murder," and chapter 8, "The Trauma of the Good and the Anarchy of Forgiveness," develop a bifocal account of "original forgiveness" as inscribed within an original responsibility for the Other—thus deepening and expanding the argument for an original availability (*disponibilité*) to forgiveness in chapters 5 and 6—through an interpretation of Dostoevsky's *The Brothers Karamazov* and a philosophical elaboration, even at the risk of its betrayal, of Emmanuel Levinas's thinking. At the center of these considerations is the argument that trust in the world, in others, and in ourselves is grounded in the anarchic entrustment of responsibility for the Other. I further argue that central to Levinas's provocative thinking, as encapsulated in the statement "the death of the Other is always in a way a murder," is the rehabilitation and reconfiguration of the significance of being not self-created beings, that, as creatures who are begotten into being, we stand beholden to the Good "beyond and otherwise" than being. In this original binding, or beholdenness, to an entrustment of the Other to my keep, there is an original drama of forgiveness, not for anything that I have or have not done but for that I am. Beginning with an extended exploration of the significance of the statement "the death of the Other is always in a way a murder" through the lens of *The Brothers Karamazov*, I examine the portrayal of different conceptions of the death of children in Dostoevsky's novel, the confrontation between Ivan and Alyosha, and upsurge of responsibility for the Other's death, crystallized in the declaration, "Each of us is guilty before everyone for everyone, and I more than the others." Here, my argument is that Levinas's provocation that the death of the Other is murder leads to the formulation of an original forgiveness inscribed within the assignment and accusation of responsibility for the Other. In tracking the configuration of the idea of "substitution," by which Levinas proposes to rethink the significance of our creaturely existence as ethical subjects ("the subjectivity of the subject"), I emphasize the pronounced word "expiation" with which "substitution" finds its consummate expression. As I demonstrate under the heading of the "trauma of the Good," the assignment of responsibility is unforgiving and merciless; thus "persecuted" by the commandment of the Other, "Thou shall not kill," one stands accused, caught in the lenticular enigma of the Other's face as at once prohibition and temptation. If the face of the Other is the commandment "Thou shall not kill," or, in other words, "You are my keeper," the face is likewise an incitement to murder, a double face without thereby being two-faced. To stand as my brother's keeper is to stand in an original posture of forgiveness for the death of the Other. I argue that the burden of such an original responsibility as "persecution" reveals an unsuspected dimension in the relation between evil and original forgiveness. In finding oneself ashamed before the Other in one's freedom, the self is liable to become ashamed at its own shame, and thus come to hate the persecution to which it has been elected in the assignation of responsibility for the Other's death. I contend that the self becomes ashamed of its shame and thus comes to hate the Other in her persecution—assignment and accusation of responsibility. The enigma of the face of the Other as prohibition and temptation, as assignment and accusation, marks the mysterious navel of responsibility in the enigma of the Good. An impatience with the responsibility for the Other rebounds into what I call rage against the Good—namely, wanting to murder the Other, whereby the outrage undergone by the trauma of the Good rebounds into murderous rage against the Other and divestiture of the Good that has been entrusted unto me. In an original forgiveness, I stand to be forgiven for this original rage against a responsibility entrusted to me as well as forgive the Other for their unforgiving assignment and accusation. To declare, "Here I am" is to stand in forgiveness for wanting to kill you, not as an afterthought but as the condition for an infinite patience required to endure your merciless, and hence unforgiving, entrustment of responsibility (without consent or recourse) to me. As with the brothers Ivan and Alyosha, the mysteriousness of the Good is at the same time the mysteriousness of evil, both sourced from within a confounding anarchy of all beginnings. This mystery is the anarchy of Goodness: to be entrusted with the responsibility of wanting to die for the Other whom you yourself would want to murder, where, in an original forgiveness, we abide within an infinite patience for the Other and infinite postponement of our own murderous being.

In lieu of a conclusion, *Original Forgiveness* ends with a recapitulation of my fundamental contention, crystallized in chapters 7 and 8, through a reading of Maurice Sendak's *Outside Over There.*

* * *

Let me close with the thought that these reflections stand as an attempt at motivating and delineating, however imprecisely and tenuously, "original forgiveness" in its relation to "forgiveness as encounter." The former subtends the latter as the anarchy before and allowing for any situated ground of encounter. Each chapter has been written in a way that searches on its own, even as each chapter is geared into the trajectory of the entire book, thus allowing for an argument and a narrative to take shape around the reliefs of each chapter. Throughout these explorations,

I have been mindful of Levinas's remark that "the word creation designates a signification older than the context woven about this name." In the same vein, the word "forgiveness," I have endeavored to show, designates a signification "older" than the manifold contexts, historical as well as conceptual, woven about this name, and hence, in this sense, be yet spoken anew. Even *this* context woven about this name "forgiveness" cannot claim to speak with any finality of what can (and how) still be designated in its name; hence, its profound anarchy. These reflections should not be received without a bespoken solicitation of forgiveness for what must necessarily remain incomplete, but hopefully not fatally lacking. Every act of writing enacts an assumption of enduring the search for what it cannot meaningfully say, but likewise the presumption of having something enduringly meaningful to say. There is no writing without an implicit promise that at the same time seeks to be forgiven as the very condition for its promised, and hence, unfulfilled intelligibility.

Upon Trust We Stand, upon Trust We Fall

Upon trust human life stands. This hold of trust is immediate; as immediate as the book in your hands, the paper before you, the screen on your desk, or however you are presently reading these very words. When reading, you implicitly subscribe to a network of trusts: trust in the author, whom you most likely have never met and most likely will never have the pleasure of meeting, not only to be the person signed under the author's name but also to have credibly composed these words according to standards of academic honesty and scholarly integrity; trust that these words on the page are more or less meant in their accepted usage, even when terms of art and academic jargon abundantly proliferate; trust that the author intends to be understood and thus, as the reader, that you trust in yourself to sustain an understanding attitude and charity of interpretation, even when your own disagreements and differences become startlingly apparent; trust that the copy currently before you is identical with other copies circulating in the world, not a Borgesian singularity; trust that what you are reading is neither a counterfeit nor a hoax, practiced upon you (and the system of peer reviews that sanctioned this publication) by self-regarding clever folk who seek to air their own grievances against the perceived grievance-ridden or ill-begotten discourses of certain disciplines. We read in an atmosphere of trust, such that reading becomes meaningful as an ethics, an aesthetics, and a practice. This atmosphere of trust permeates the experience of reading with felt assuredness, come what may. You must follow these words with inspired confidence as having something meaningful to say, even if provocative or not at all to your fancy—to say, in short, something that is not a waste of your time or an abuse of your trust.

From this entrustment of reading, other concentric horizons extend outward, embracing ever more diverse forms of trust: that you will be left alone while reading, not bothered by family and friends with frivolous requests; that what has been promised to you earlier in the day by colleagues will be delivered; that supply chains bringing nourishment to your table are not contaminated; that your financial transactions are not compromised; that your spouse's flight will arrive safely this evening after stopovers in distant lands; and countless other instances of trust, the accounting of which would circumscribe the complexity of modern life yet leave us none the wiser for how what passes so unremarked is in fact so remarkable, that we are necessarily so trusting. In its most elemental form, the presentness of trust remains unspoken, unnoticed, and unreflective, without thereby running athwart of our freedom, deliberation, and speaking. This presentness of trust enables mutual flourishing to the degree that entrusted presentness remains inconspicuous and taken for granted, as par for the course of everyday life. Trust serves as the basis for action and conduct in the world as well as a measure for our values, projects, and aspirations.[1] Practical rationality, as exercised and acquired in the world, does not create trust but functions instead as the "caretaker" of an already constituted trust.[2] Anchoring trusts allows for the acquisition of cognitive capacities and the cultivation of talents.[3] We necessarily grow in mind and body in trust. Primarily oriented toward the future in view of a goal, a value, or an affection, we are so necessarily trusting because we are so necessarily creatures of action.[4] In the context of acting, trust operates dominantly in our lives: acting along with others and, hence, living interdependently with others. This ever-present horizon of possible action afforded by trust is likewise a horizon of possible movement. We cannot move about the world without some form of trust; by the same token, we cannot remain stationary and allow others to approach us—to receive others much as we are received by others—without trust. The presentness of trust underwrites mobility as well as having a place in the world that we might claim our own, our home. Not only do we anticipate and remember on the basis of trust but also trust itself must be anticipated and recalled in order for us to move, act, think, and simply be in the world. Were we not at all trusting, we would remain "prey to a vague sense of dread" and "paralyzing fears" such that we would neither be able to formulate any targeted distrust nor adopt any precautionary measures (since such guarded attitudes would require the acceptance of some other forms of trust), or ever get ourselves out of bed in the morning.[5] Or else, we would become a resentful misanthrope, much like the Underground Man, whose paralyzing plunge into corrosive distrust of others ensnares him in spirals of self-mistrust, even as his own mistrust rebounds into accelerated aggression, even rage, against others, and especially against those relationships essentially formed in trust—namely, love and friendship. Without trust, we would not live in the embrace of emotional and cognitive assuredness; we would not restfully sleep or go about our daily lives with that necessary wakeful slumber of vested unthinking. But this, of course, is already familiar to you, and any author who ventures to write on trust and consider trust so thematically must trust that what is elemental about trust is already known to the reader, that every reader would readily accept the truism that, as Locke remarks in a letter, "men live upon trust."[6] From this truism any consideration of trust must begin—and, hence, must trust. As Sissela Bok judiciously remarks, "*whatever* matters to human beings, trust is the atmosphere in which it thrives."[7]

And yet trust is just as much the atmosphere in which humans come to grief and ruin. Just as surely as it is upon trust that human life stands, so, too, is it upon trust that human life falls. As we thrive on trust, so we fall prey to trust. When all too trusting, naive, or charitable, we can become unwittingly duped, manipulated, or led astray. In his letter, Locke's truism is proffered with the reflection that since human knowledge is "nothing but opinion moulded up between custom and interest," we are "left to the uncertainty of these two fickle guides" as the "only lights [to] walk by."[8] We navigate life upon the raft of trust, floating precariously between a lack of knowledge and abundant impostors of knowledge. As Locke remarks, "When did ever any truth settle itself in anyone's mind by the strength and authority of its own evidence? Truths gain admittance to our thoughts as the philosopher did to the tyrant, by their handsome dress and pleasing aspect."[9] We must trust because we cannot know absolutely, but because we are thus entrusted we are exposed to pretensions of knowledge that enter into our lives by that very same allowance. In the conspicuous absence of true beliefs, we conspicuously *want* to truly believe. The fault of Eve was to trust in a context in which she could not truly know, but wanted to; the fault became repeated, and hence sealed into humanity, in Adam's trusting confidence in his only partner. We seldom fall alone.

Living upon trust, we unsuspectingly entrust ourselves to counterfeit truths that, having gained admittance into our domain, cannot easily, if ever, be expelled by argument or demonstration. Once in our hold, such false notions come in turn to possess us, and so become, as explored by Dostoevsky, our demons. Fancy would not rule so effectively and effortlessly as the impostor of reason if not in the guise of trust with its emotional clutch of assuredness. As Sartre avers in *Being and Nothingness*, we succumb in such instances to what he terms "non-persuasive evidence."[10] Trusting such evidence, we are not persuaded *to believe*; rather, we believe in order *not to be persuaded*. That is, we latch on to a belief and thereby short-circuit the possibility of being persuaded to believe something— anything—else. Of beliefs, we have plenty. The challenge, so rarely met, is to acknowledge what we believe, and why we believe it, so as to more properly hold a belief—or, as the case may be, properly let it go. For Locke, as reflected upon in his letter, the predicament of trust is balanced between the absence of knowledge, that rare and precious "Great Diana of the world," and fanciful impostors of knowledge. In this condition, we are pinned between all-too-generous custom and all-too-narrow interest. We must therefore live upon others. Given that custom and interest are "fickle guides," let the "examples of the bravest men direct our opinions and actions; if custom must guide us, let us tread in those steps that lead to virtue and honour."[11]

As Scheler observes, we cannot live without exemplary images (*Vorbilder*) of others as trustworthy guides for our own self-realization and *Bildung*.[12] Within his ethical system, Scheler ascribes a critical function to "exemplariness," not only as a material condition for the shaping and directing of ethical conduct but also in answer to the question regarding the origin of authority, allegiance, and loyalty. Values are manifest through exemplary individuals; we are motivated to adopt such values and act accordingly on the basis of our openness to the persuasiveness of such individuals, which, in turn, presupposes their (perceived) trustworthiness. The force of their persuasiveness depends on the persuasiveness of their inspired trust. Becoming an ethical individual constantly struggles against one's own particularity and selfishness, as pulled back and forth between positive (*Vorbilder*) and negative examples (*Gegenbilder*). Scheler distinguishes between a broader and a narrower concept of *Vorbild*. In its narrower meaning, a *Vorbild* is a force or vitality (*Kraft*) that provides both a schema (*Bild*) and a catalyst for the creative formation of an individual. Given that a *Vorbild* is an affective vitality, there is no affective *Vorbild* without an effective *Nachbild*, where the meaning of *Nachbild* is decidedly not to be understood in any mimetic or reproductive sense, as the mere copy of an original. What distinguishes *Nachbild* from *Nachahmung* is the former's efficaciousness (*Wirksamkeit*) as well as the receptive individual's openness to the affective force of exemplariness. The effectiveness of an exemplary individual (*Vorbild*) is not an issue of "blind submission" or authoritarianism. Efficaciousness operates in the opposite direction: an exemplary individual becomes a force, or catalyst, who enables another individual to emancipate herself from herself in offering a new, and external, point of orientation. This external point of orientation offers a bearing for a process of self-transformation (*Umbildung*) and, in this sense, self-transcendence. A receptive individual becomes taken up by an exemplary individual when she senses that she could grow into a more generous existential space of possibility for her own self-realization. This catalyst to enter into a wider berth of her own individual existence allows her to gain an expanded space of meaning and action, thus opening possibilities that an individual might never have imagined, or that had long seemed extinguished. Stated in these terms, the efficaciousness of a *Vorbild* and affective openness of a *Nachbild* put into play the freedom of an individual to embark upon a new beginning. Receptiveness to a *Vorbild* promises the advent of a new dawn. A moment of vitality breaks (*anbrechende Augenblick*) into life as the upbeat (*Auftakt*) for a new beginning. As Scheler expresses his insight, "Role models are only pioneers in listening to the call of our own person. They are only the dawn of the sun of our individual conscience and law."[13] The openness to such exemplary figures in our lives presupposes trust in those who might lead us to becoming otherwise than ourselves as well as trust in ourselves that we might take up such sources of inspiration in creative ways of self-fashioning.

The Confidence-Man

Upon trust human life stands and falls. Were we not so trusting, we could not live; yet because we are so trusting, we fall game to others who prey upon our trust. Is it therefore true that, as Evert Augustus Duyckinck remarked, "it is a good thing, and speaks well for human nature, that men *can be swindled*"?[14] In Herman Melville's *The Confidence-Man*, passengers board the steamboat *Fidèle* ("truthful," "faithful," "trustworthy," and "steadfast"), the raft of trust upon which we live. Is it a ship of fools or a vessel of ready charity, or both, an enduring that must always suffer its own foolishness?

Recall the opening chapter of Melville's novel, "A Mute Goes Aboard a Boat on the Mississippi." We are introduced to the sudden appearance of a man without a name, a Stranger, who boards the Mississippi steamer *Fidèle* at "sunrise on a first of April."[15] This stranger boards without any luggage, friends, or porter in his train. Even as he boards, while bringing no attention to himself his appearance as a stranger becomes immediately registered in the whispers, murmurings, and wonderings of the crowd aboard the vessel. This Stranger seems to be passing through the world, wandering with no apparent purpose or cause aboard the *Fidèle*, all the while eliciting uneasy regard without himself regarding or shunning others. His presence is neutral and blank. He chances upon a placard next to the ship captain's office, offering a reward for "the capture of a mysterious impostor." This announcement warns of an impostor on board who may have come "from the East" and whose "original vocation" remains obscure. Although this person is known, as the placard reports, to be an impostor and has been previously sighted (the placard speaks of a "careful description of his person"), the precise nature of his vocation remains shrouded. The originality of the impostor is made all the more mysterious. Everyone and no one could be an impostor. Not unexpectedly, suspicion immediately befalls the Stranger, whose sudden appearance on the *Fidèle* coincides with the announcement of the placard, next to which he finds himself standing.

Crowds gather in front of this placard of warning. An impostor thrives upon trust; every impostor is an impostor of trust, imposing on their victims to trust in imposing themselves in trust. With this mysterious impostor from the East, one cannot even trust the announcement of warning. Looks can be deceiving, and in this particular instance the placard gives a description of the impostor without identifying the impostor's fraudulent vocation. Various safeguards against this spectral impostor on board the *Fidèle* are taken by the passengers. One cannot know with any certainty his, or her, vocation: it could be anything, for any human vocation can serve as the mask of and occasion for imposture. Even as books about infamous impostors and precautions are discussed among the crowd, the singularity of each impostor always *surprises* in perpetuating a fraudulent being against which the known history of past impostors, or technologies of safeguarding against imposture, or anticipation and vigilance (the placard) cannot preempt or annul.

The Stranger makes his way to the placard. He does not wear any "badge of authority" and seems to have no recognizable place or standing in society. He appears to be an idiot—a simpleton, a harmless intruder, "wholly unobnoxious," a cause of wonder and curiosity. Deaf and dumb, the Stranger holds up a slate with the words traced upon its surface, CHARITY THINKETH NO EVIL. This provokes a person to flatten down his hat upon his head; unaffected, the Stranger, who is pushed aside and insulted, returns to the front of the crowd with his slate: CHARITY ENDURETH ALL THINGS. More "stares and jeers" from the crowd: CHARITY BELIEVETH ALL THINGS. Finally: CHARITY NEVER FAILETH. Throughout these permutations, the word "Charity" remains constant, always placed next to a blank space in which these different formulations are written, then erased.

The placard announcing the presence of an impostor and the mute scribbling of the Stranger on a slate form a juxtaposition, the implication of which changes depending on one's angle of view. The Stranger inscribes different declinations of charity within a blank space. That blank space is the space wherein inscriptions of identity become traced and erased. Charity is a mute and absolute *assumption*—without constitution. Charity is itself *blank*, an openness that does not speak and does not hear, a kind of original muteness on the basis of which there can be speech and silence. Is the mute Stranger's slate a warning or a response? He holds his slate level with the placard announcing that other mysterious stranger, the impostor. The ambiguity is whether the blankness of charity remains unshakable, the ground upon which we stand, *despite* the impostor, or whether the impostor's vocation exploits the blankness of charity, as that upon which we fall.

In Melville's narrative, this opening scene shifts laterally (the novel is composed of lateral shifts in scene, situation, and individuals). Two doors down from the Captain's Office, the placard, and the stranger, there is a Barber's Shop underneath a Saloon. We are given, in these two locales, a description of the world in miniature, much as the *Fidèle* presents a microcosm of the world. In the Barber's Shop, individuals of different professions come and go. The Barber hangs next to his door a sign: NO TRUST. It is freely offered as worldly wisdom and cultured sophistication, the product of experience and knowledge of human beings.

Melville's *Confidence-Man* presents a "grotesque" vision of human existence: beneath the masks and roles we play for each other, there is apparently "nothing at all."[16] The tension between "Charity" and "No Trust" structures Melville's novel without any dialectical resolution or finality. We must necessarily trust in others, the roles and mask of social and personal identity, although identity is always haunted by a gap, or fissure, between the "mask" and the "self." This gap between the mask and the self, which allows the self to identify itself in or with a mask, and appear to others as a self, is the gap filled by trust and self-trust; one cannot avoid the sentiment of imposture, that we are all impostors in being, or *at being*. Are we not all impostors at being, with that uncanny sense that there is something *other* and *otherwise* than who we assume ourselves to be within us? There is a suffering of the impostor: the impostor plays, or feigns, at fashioning a convincing image that needs to be confirmed and accepted, trusted, by others; yet the image the impostor carries of himself is always doubled: he never coincides with himself, with his own image, which he guards against being exposed as *not himself* even as he convinces himself and others that it is himself.[17] The inscrutability of others requires that we must necessarily trust, and yet our trust remains haunted from within by the "nothingness" of identity itself—the fissure between self and mask. As Melville explores, trust is lodged at the core of identity, not only our own identity but also our identities for others. As a character in Melville's novel remarks, "Confidence is the indispensable basis of all sorts of business transactions. Without it, commerce between man and man, as between country and country, would, like a watch, run down and stop." Within this world geared together in confidence, the Confidence-Man "operates in the shadows of the ambiguity of being" in exploiting "the obscurities of confidence" and "the indeterminate possibilities" of *being otherwise than being,* or what Plato in the *Sophists* calls the *meon*. As Jason Wirth comments, "The confidence man acts like a kind of mirror that allows one to glimpse the back of one's head. That is, he dramatizes what is at stake in one's character, giving it shape, despite one not necessarily being fully aware of it. Character is not who one really is, but rather the role that one plays, the mask that one wears, and the confidence man discerns the shape of the mask more readily than its host."[18]

Dimensions of Trust in the World

Considerations of trust widely recognize trust as indispensable for human concourse, communication, and commerce. When we commonly speak of trust, we principally have in mind the trust that is given, received, and honored among individuals. Philosophical elaborations of trust likewise focus on or ascribe special ("paradigmatic") status to mutual trust between individuals. When we enter into relationships of trust with the Other, we entrust ourselves—our well-being—or something in our care and concern to the Other for safekeeping, sound judgment, and guided conduct in the world without forfeiting our own freedom and responsibility.[19] We enter into relations of trust freely, even if not issuing from extended deliberation, and must confidently entrust ourselves without demanding trust in return, even as trusting relations are more often than not predicated on reciprocity and mutual recognition in trust. If, as Nietzsche remarks, "people who place their full trust in us believe they have a right to ours. This is a false conclusion; through gifts one acquires no rights," to give our trust to the Other who entrusts us is not to give in return or exchange for that trust but to give in attestation of the Other's acceptance as my trusted equal: as friend, lover, companion, spouse, and so forth.[20] While interpersonal trust in this paradigmatic form, around which other forms of trust (collective, institutional, cultural) relations proliferate, undoubtedly represents a central dimension of trust, a consideration of trust must take into view a more complex landscape to include self-trust and trust in the world.[21] A fertile conception of trust must consider these dimensions of trust—interpersonal trust (in its different configurations: social, political, cultural), self-trust, and trust in the world—in their distinct yet interrelated function and significance. Any account of these dimensions of trust in isolation, and especially with the prevalent single-minded focus on interpersonal trust commanding much of the philosophical literature, must be deemed inadequate to the truism that "upon trust men live in the world."

Largely unremarked upon, Heidegger suggestively characterizes in *Being and Time* what he terms *das Worin* (the where-in) of Dasein's understanding of being-in-the-world as *Vertrautheit*. As Heidegger writes, "Worin Dasein in dieser Weise sich je schon versteht, damit ist es ursprünglich vertraut."[22] The fundamental sense of being-there—my being there in the world and there being a world for me—is disclosed in the hold of trust, that "where-in" Dasein understands itself as being-in-the-world. This constitutive trust in the world (*konstitutive Weltvertrautheit*) is neither, strictly speaking, constituted by Dasein nor dependent on any "theoretical transparency," or knowledge. It is originary (*ursprünglich*) in the sense of primordial and unreflective, yet always disclosed in Dasein's manifold ways of being-in-the-world. "What is meant by '*Being-in*'?" Heidegger is quick to reject a metaphorical or literal meaning of "in" based on the presence of physical objects in three-dimensional space. Dasein is not "in" the world in any comparable sense as the chair can be found in the room or water is located in the glass. What characterizes such an understanding of "in" is the determination of beings as present-at-hand. Such objects are located in space next to each other without any object encountering another. As distinct from this object-oriented meaning of "in," the meaning of "being-in" for Dasein is existential. Heidegger calls attention to the etymological roots of "in" in German from the word *innan*: "to reside, to dwell in." The term *an* means "I am accustomed to" or "I am familiar with." The meaning of *in* from *innan* as "to inhabit" must be understood in a "verbal-transitive sense" such that to exist "within" the world is existing within the world in attunement, understanding, and discourse. As Peter Sloterdijk writes, this meaning of inhabitation "does not mean simply attributing domesticity within the gigantic to those who exist: for it is precisely the possibility of being-at-home-in-the-world that is questionable, and to presuppose it as a given would be a relapse into the very physics of containers that is here meant to be overcome."[23] To say that inhabitation is not pregiven domesticity means we must trust in being at home; to be at home in the world is to trust, and hence to be at home in a world that is fundamentally questionable, and thus a question of trust. Being-in is neither a property that Dasein might gain or lose nor is it the "substance" or "subject" of Dasein. For Sloterdijk, this suggests that Dasein is structured through "Inhood," or what one might term holdings of trust." As he writes, "The *subject* or Dasein can only be *there* if it is contained, surrounded, encompassed, disclosed, breathed-upon, resounding-through, attuned and addressed. Before a Dasein assumes the character of being-in-the-world, it already has the constitution of being-in."[24]

In his late writings, Husserl likewise characterized the anchoring dimension of the life-world as an original form of *Vetrautheit*. This form of

Vertrautheit is to be distinguished from *Bekanntheit* (familiarity or acquaintance) as well as dependability, both of which are constituted through the secondary acquisitions of historical sedimentation and habitualities.[25] In speaking of "eine unbestimmt allgemeine Vertrautheit" *in which* "alle weiteren Unterschiede zwischen Bekanntheit und Unbekanntheit verlaufen," Husserl suggests that the distinction between "the known" and "the familiar," on the one hand, and "the unknown" and "the unfamiliar," on the other, presupposes an original and pervading *Vertrautheit* that, despite its "indeterminate" form, is nonetheless singular in its presentness.[26] As implied by Husserl's expression "eine unbestimmt allgemeine Vertrautheit," to be in the world is to be in the presentness of *unknown unknowns*, or, alternatively: *Vertrautheit* characterizes the presentness of unknown unknowns. It is a trust that eludes any pristine conversion into the opposition, and hence dialectic, of known knowns and known unknowns. Yet in a manner more emphatically recognized than by Husserl, what distinguishes the primordial presentness of the world is precisely that it is an issue of *trust, not knowledge.* To face the world in the presentness of unknown unknowns *in which* differentiations between the familiar and the unfamiliar can be constituted and, most significantly, *played out,* is to find oneself from the beginning in the situation of trust. We are entrusted *with* the unknown in finding ourselves in the presentness of the world. It is this presentness of the world in trust that allows and affords any having of the world in view and any comportment toward others and myself. Importantly, however, this original trust in the world, as the presentness of unknown unknowns, does not gain relief against a haunting suspicion of distrust, but on the contrary the presentness of the world, as an *openness into the unknown,* is entrusted to us on account of an original investment, or care for, the truthfulness of the world.

The term *Vertrautheit* in Heidegger's (sparsely employed in *Being and Time*) expressions *Vertrautheit mit der Welt* and *Weltvertrautheit* weaves together different strands of meaning: "familiarity," "nearness," "reliability," and "intimacy." This compactness of what can be subsumed under the designation "trust in the world" does not allow for any strict separation between those strands of meanings, as if "trust" could be entirely divorced from reliability with tools and things (as well as others) or from emotional and cognitive familiarity. And yet this primordial "trust in the world" is likewise not reducible to or accountable merely in terms of reliability and familiarity. Hence the elusiveness of "trust in the world" within the configured world. The elusiveness of trust's presentness is a function of its pervasiveness throughout the configured world of meaning and acting. This hold of trust (*das Worin*) is the hold of the world in which vectors of reliability and contours of familiarity are situated within an embracing whole. Such vectors of reliability and contours of familiarity are braced against this primordial trust in order to remain settled within the whole. Things have place in the world in the hold of the world held in trust.

Weltvertrautheit underpins the weave of references and relations texturing the world in its plural environments of understanding, doing, and speaking. Such environments (*Umwelten*) are built from complexes of references and relations, or connections (*Bezüge*). Within such environments, Dasein's fluency and fluidity in navigating the world becomes underwritten by a trust that permeates, without appearing distinctly, the nexus of what Heidegger calls *Zeugganzheit*. A nexus of tool usage is woven from references to other tools and practices: the pen refers to paper, writing on paper refers to sitting down at a table, and so on. Being-able-to-do-something-with a tool is always inscribed within a system of references (*Verweisungen*) and relations (*Bezüge*). The employment of a tool in the manner of *Zuhandenheit* is essentially an issue of trust in the reliability of the tool's construction and designed purpose as well as our own facility with its usage. We are fluent and fluid in our use of a tool in the manner of *Zuhandenheit*. This "knowing-how," as it is often termed, is not a knowledge (*ein Wissen*) above and beyond doing-something-with the tool but inheres to and becomes expressed in our fluid and fluent employment of the tool in a fitting and affording context. *Zuhandenheit* crystallizes in a nexus of expectations contoured around vectors of reliability: that the material strength of the tool will not fail, that nailed boards are solid, and so forth. The density of this nexus of reliability and expectation is suffused with a sense of familiarity and comprehensibility. This comprehensibility of a tool-nexus and its environment is, in turn, spanned by an overarching *meaningfulness*, or what Heidegger calls *Bedeutsamkeit*. In this primordial sense, trust in the world attests to an understanding of this meaning-fullness of an encompassing whole of meaning (*das Bedeutungsganze*). Trust in the world (*Weltvertrautheit*) is woven into the vectors of reliability and contours of familiarity, without being reducible to the aggregation or sum of such configurations of reliability and familiarity. In turn, the networks of reliability and familiarity hold together only within the "meaning-fullness" of a whole, its *Bedeutsamkeit*, which provides the atmosphere in which Dasein exists in the world. Dasein's being-in-the-world anchors, as condition of possibility, the "discoverability of the wholeness of *Bewandtnis*," the latter tricky term translatable as "involvement," "explanation," "ground," or "characteristic sense."[27] This trust in the meaning-fullness of the world, existing within this meaning-fullness as trust in the world, allows for a condensation of complexity into an atmospheric affordance, or enabling condition, for encountering things and entities in the world. This *Vertrautheit* of *Bedeutsamkeit* provides the condition of possibility for the revealing and encountering of things (and others in the manner of *Besorgnis*) in the world. As Heidegger writes, "Das Dasein ist in seiner Vertrautheit mit der Bedeutsamkeit die ontische Bedingung der Möglichkeit der Entdeckbarkeit von Seiende."[28] This "meaningfulness" with which Dasein is already entrusted provides the "ontological condition" for the possibility of the interpretation of meanings (*Bedeutungen*) in the world, or, in other words, for Dasein to speak about the world.

It is in terms of this unspoken and inconspicuous trust that Dasein "allows ready-at-hand things to be encountered as discovered."[29] We can encounter things in the world only within this encompassing trust in the world as *Verweisungsganze der Bedeutsamkeit.* Our trust in the world as trust in *das Verweisungsganze der Bedeutsamkeit* means that trust facilitates a reduction of referential complexity.[30] The "network" of references is much too fine-grained and complex for us to encounter as such. And it is only when this network of references is taken for granted and inconspicuous that we can relate to objects and encounter them. Trust in this sense is a kind of spacing or distancing: it allows things to be experienced or encountered at a distance, not in the spatial sense of three-dimensionality but in terms of allowing for a space in which we can deal with and handle encountered things. A world in which we lacked this "vorgängig verstehende Vertrautsein" (prior understanding familiarity) would be a world too close to us, that would fall upon us all at once, hence a world in which we would be in the position of the paranoiac: everything would be equidistant from us and too close, too oppressive.

This trust in the world entailed in Dasein's understanding of being-in-the-world is not constituted by Dasein nor does it represent a distinct temperament (or attunement: *Befindlichkeit*), form of talk (*Rede*), or type of understanding as directed and engaged toward inner-worldly entities. As indicated by Heidegger's choice of the term *Verfassung,* trust in the world designates the primordial constitution (*Verfassung*) of Dasein's being-in-the-world, that upon which Dasein lives and breathes, in being entrusted to the "meaningfulness" (*Bedeutsamkeit*) of the world. In this sense, Dasein exists upon and within this fundamental constitution of the world in trust. More fundamental than any emotion, cognition, or desire, this trust in the world underwrites the meaningfulness of every emotion, cognition, and desire. This entrustment of the world opens the world to its discovery and possible encounter. It is on the basis of such trust in the world that Dasein can (in the Heideggerian sense of *Seinskönnen*) act, understand, and speak fluidly and fluently in the world. Moreover, it is when braced against such trust in the world that Dasein can recover its bearings and orientation in the world, when its acting, understanding, and speaking suffer interruptions, breakages, and crises. The world is never fundamentally lost in its meaningfulness despite breakages in its configurations of meaning; unless, of course, the world as such has become ruptured, or withered away, in its fundamental meaningfulness, in which case Dasein would find itself in the throes of a catastrophe befalling its anchoring trust in the world, expelled into transcendental homelessness.

Trust in the world as the "where-in" of Dasein's understanding of being-in-the-world is neither a trust *given* to the world by Dasein nor a trust *received* by Dasein from the world. Dasein neither constitutes for itself, as one of its projects, this anchoring trust in the world nor does trust in the world simply issue from the world, as if the world, or God, as with the biblical creation narrative, entrusted the world to Dasein. Dasein is always "referred" to or "reliant" (*angewiesen*) on this constitutive trust in the world in the sense that Dasein always *confers* itself to the world in trust. Dasein becomes entrusted to the world such that Dasein can navigate the world with fluency and fluidity or, when breakages upsurge in the world, recover itself in the world. *Bedeutsamkeit* confers a trust upon Dasein, entrusts Dasein to the world, and, in turn, Dasein lives upon this trust, so that it can encounter things in the world in a nexus of reliability and familiarity. We understand *from the world,* or upon the world, and in this sense the world confers trust upon us; we are thus entrusted by the world and so trust in the world.

Constitutive trust in the world (*Weltvertrautheit*) is suffused with an ontological familiarity. Dasein is at home in the world in trust. We feel a sense of belonging to the world as held in trust. We are self-possessed or "have" ourselves in the possession of an intimacy with the world. And yet since trust in the world is conferred upon Dasein such that Dasein lives and understands *from the world,* this entrustment to the world is both a conduit into the world and at the same time, in Heidegger's vocabulary, a falling away from ourselves. Held in trust, we fall into the world; we fall into a trust of the world in being lulled away from ourselves; we become insouciant toward ourselves in shaping ourselves through our care and concern for the world. The ambiguity of trust is present here in an ontologically pronounced manner: entrusting itself to the world, and hence defining itself *from the world* (as well as *from others,* or what Heidegger calls *Fürsorge*), Dasein loses itself and becomes unknown to itself, or "inauthentic," in Heidegger's parlance. We are *Benommen* by the world: captivated and caught up in the world, fascinated by it, much as with a theater spectacle. We are *taken in* by the world in trust. I live more of myself *from the world* rather than *from myself.* In living upon trust, I fall away from myself, unless I am able to recuperate myself in an attitude of self-regard and resolution—"authenticity"—which can be understood as an authentic mode of self-trust and self-attestation toward my trust in the world as well as my trusts in others. Constancy in oneself as a matter of self-trust and truthfulness toward oneself, and, in this sense, what Heidegger calls *Ständigkeit,* underlies Dasein's "one-ness" or "singularity" (*Selbstheit*) in such a manner that allows Dasein to distinguish itself from manifold ways (its roles or personae) in which it is not itself.

Trust in Others

When we enter into relations of trust, we become entrusted not only to the Other but also to the determinate relation of trust to which we have subscribed along with the Other. Trust is not simply given and received; it must be honored, and in honoring our trusts we must continually attest to ourselves as entrusted as well as to our trusting relationship. In its interpersonal form, trust is not simply a binding—to be bound to the Other in trust. It is also an accompanying: when we trust the Other, we are bound to her, much as she is bound, in cases of mutual trust, to us (in friendship, in love, in collegiality, etc.). I become the Other's keeper much as the Other becomes my keeper. We are both the keepers of our trust. In this bond of trust along with the Other (to the Other as well as to our bond of trust), I am also bound to myself in the company of the Other's trust in me. There is no binding to and with the Other that is not also a binding to and with myself. My trustworthiness, on the basis of which the Other trusts me, engages and requires truthfulness toward myself as well as the Other. Self-attestation, and hence self-trust, are inseparable yet distinct from trust in Others.[31] In attesting to myself as being truthful, I stand truthfully toward the Other. The formation of the self in self-truthfulness and self-attestation, as entrusted to oneself, is critical for discourse and collaborative action. Without this assumption of truthfulness, discourse would collapse into either blatant hypocrisy or sheer rhetorical performance. To be truthful to oneself is to be authentic to oneself in cultivating a distance within oneself that only oneself can know and, in this sense, *own.*

As Alfred Schutz stresses, the life-world necessarily assumes the "truthfulness" or "creditability" (*die Wahrhaftigkeit*) of others.[32] This assumption of truthfulness, without which we would not entrust others (either give, receive, or honor trusts), entails not only a trust that others speak truthfully and take responsibility for their speaking; we would not be disappointed at the person who lies to us were it not for an underlying trust and hence demand that others speak truthfully. This assumption of the Other's truthfulness bespeaks a general attitude of trust in others that underwrites the possibility of sustained and meaningful conversation. We accept the stranger's words in trust and fall into mistrust and suspicion only when provoked or caused to do so. To speak is always implicitly to give you my word that I am promising you my words truthfully. In giving you words, I give you my word, that I will keep my word, or, in other words, that when my words are returned to me I will still uphold these words as having been minted genuinely.[33] As Knud Ejler Løgstrup develops, trust as the condition for conversation and discourse is not only a function of giving one's word but also a "self-surrender" by which I place myself in the hands of the Other and, hence, open myself up to risk and vulnerability. This basic trust, without which "human life could hardly exist if it were otherwise," expresses a "basic trust in life itself, in the ongoing renewal of life."[34] In "surrendering" myself to the care and keep of the trusted Other, there issues an implicit demand that we protect the life of the person who has placed her trust in me. For Løgstrup, trust makes possible human encounters: "In every encounter between human beings there is an unarticulated demand, irrespective of the circumstances in which the encounter takes place and irrespective of the nature of the encounter"—namely, that we take care of the life that trust has placed in our hands.[35] Such an implicit demand in the assumption of trust underwrites social conventions, cultural grammars, and political institutions. Indeed, social norms often reduce and tailor the force of this implicit demand, just as, on the contrary, social norms might amplify and enhance the force of this implicit demand. Among those institutions, where the tension between the implicit demand in trust and its social institutionalization is arguably the most volatile and yet the most imperative for the life-world, is the world of finance. As Georg Simmel examined, money and, more broadly, economic exchange and value are institutions of trust: both institute a network of trusts as well as depend on a basic trust, or original institution of trust. As Simmel writes, "Without the general trust that people have in each other, society itself would disintegrate, for very few relationships are based entirely upon what is known with certainty about another person, and very few relationships would endure if trust were not as strong, or stronger than, rational proof or personal observation."[36] This "general trust" (or "basic trust") is inseparable from yet irreducible to the plurality of trust networks, or institutions of trust, structuring the life-world.

In its elemental form, trust is both a binding and an accompanying. When we trust the Other, we are bound to the Other and she is bound to us (in friendship, in love, in collegiality, etc.). These bindings are edgings, or linings, of the self in a dual sense: a boundary of inclusion becomes circumscribed around the trusting parties that at once internally distinguishes a schema of mutual recognition as those in whom we trust as well as externally forming a schema of discrimination as those outside the bounds of our trust, toward whom we are more readily, if not by default, distrustful. Bound in trust, we accompany and, in this sense, participate in the lives of others, much as those others accompany and, in this sense, participate in our lives. Trust constitutes an elemental form of participation, or involvement. In trust, that is, we do not simply live *with others*: we live with others *in us* much as we live *in* others.[37] Persons in whom we trust line our sense of self from within; the inner lining of the Self is the Other in whom I trust. We are involved in their lives in an emotional atmosphere of assuredness from the inside, from within their own lives in the allowance of their trust. Such intimate involvement *in* the lives of others (in contrast to involvement *with* lives of others) fosters an assured form of identification and emotional attachment: we identify more assuredly with those in whom we trust, much as we come to identify ourselves more assuredly in our entrustments by others. Such "trust networks" (family, community, parish, army, nation-state, etc.) reflect the social structuring and modal specification of trust that compose the various institutions of trust in the life-world.[38] Institutions of trust are bound to modal specifications: we trust a given person in her capacity as a doctor, as a professor, and so forth.[39] On the flip side, we more readily distrust others, or simply distrust by default, in terms of modal specifications measured by a respective distance, or exclusion, from our self-invested trust networks. Trust networks are symbolically encoded (we spontaneously trust the stranger with the Boston Red Sox cap rather than the stranger with the New York Yankees cap) as well as historically embedded and culturally entrenched. In terms of social groups, cultural heritage, and other institutions in the phenomenological sense of *Stiftungen*, trust networks are inscribed into symbolic forms, or symbolic systems, that mediate and, in this sense, enable the coupling of values, discourse, and action.[40] In edging our identity, trust institutes a border of inclusion, edging away the foreigner, who is placed outside the sphere of our trust in an atmosphere of distrust. Trust constitutes bonds as well as boundaries: the stronger our emotional investment and feelings of mutual trust, the stronger the inclusionary affect of trust's assuredness, and, likewise, the stronger the exclusionary repulsion of distrust's assurances. Trust's emotional lining, as bonding and boundary marking, is exemplified by nation-states and religious communities. As Geoffrey Hosking observes, "Nations create both strong solidarities and also rigid boundaries. A major component of national feeling is the sense of the Other, the certainty about who one is *not*, whom one tends to distrust, or certainly trusts less readily."[41]

Trust in the world is woven from social and institutional trusts (along with their respective symbolic forms and historical sedimentations) along with the underpinning of such trust networks in the truthfulness/trustworthiness of others. In its primordial form, this trust is an *openness* (or "general" in the specified sense here) toward others molded on an assuredness that the Other is first neither my friend nor my enemy but a Stranger with whom communication, commerce, and concourse are possible, but not guaranteed. Openness toward the Other is to trust that there is a possible future of encounter with the Stranger. What distinguishes this assuredness is its thinness with regard to the instituted robustness of modal specification, collective differentiation, and symbolic forms, as well as its robustness—yet in a different sense than afforded in modal specification—in the face of innumerable betrayals, deceits, antagonisms, and conflicts induced by the specification of instituted trust. If we were deprived of any general openness toward others, were we to live entirely distrustful of others, we would very much become the Misanthrope in the image of the Underground Man, whose general distrust of others manifests itself in the heady mixture of aggression against others and toxic volatility of his own pride and shame, self-assuredness (egotism) and self-doubt. We cannot live with a complete lack of assuredness with regard to others. Yet we cannot live trusting others *equally and universally*, in which case we would become either the Idiot (Prince Myshkin), who remains socially illiterate to social intrigues and codes, or Candide, whose unperturbed faith in humankind remains innocent yet *blank* in the stare of noncomprehension, despite the patent evils of the world.

As with Candide, unflagging optimism in humankind is bolstered by an unimpeachable trust in the rationality of the world, or trust in the world in its maximized form of rational intelligibility and necessity. Pangloss's metaphysical "best of all possible worlds" accompanies Candide's faith in human beings with its constant reassurance that optimism with regard to others is not misplaced from the vantage point of trust in the world, this best of all possible worlds. Candide wanders across different stagings of human unreason, ever in search of returning to the garden from which he was ejected. These various gardens scattered throughout Candide's journey represent different images of being at home in the world. Ejected into his adventures in the world from the garden of paradise (Baron Thunder-ten-Tronckh's keep), Candide comes across in his worldly wanderings the False Garden of Eldorado, only to end his travels in a more modest garden with the memorable counsel, "Il faut cultiver notre jardin."[42] Trust in the world as structured through social, cultural, and political institutions, as well as the general assuredness of human truthfulness, rests on an ontological sense of being at home in the world, or trust in the world in this more fundamental sense, one that is not constituted through trust networks but disclosed as their very condition. Loss of trust in the world in this more fundamental or primordial sense— when the gods fall silent—unhinges and uncouples social, cultural, and discursive symbolic systems of trust, but likewise, the withering away of such trust in the world can be precipitated by the erosion and collapse of those very same institutions.

Edgings and Couplings of Trust

Gaining the Other's trust and trusting in the Other allows the Other to enter into our lives as an involved and invested participant. The Other accompanies us in our bond of trust. In granting the Other our trust, we give the Other a discretionary power of judgment over our lives, or something (or someone) we care about, in the hold of assuredness, that we can rest assured in the Other's beneficence.[43] The Other becomes our better angel, thus alleviating the burden of our lives in bolstering our own freedom insofar as bonds of trust must be freely given and accepted for our own self-realization. The Other in this manner lines our subjectivity from within; our sense of self becomes edged with the Other. Allowing the Other to stand as my witness, as critic and confidant (as well as, once I pass from the scene of the world, in remembrance), the Other is given an edge over my subjectivity. In moments of personal indecision, ambivalence, or crisis, I look to the Other's better judgment and wise counsel. Bonds of trust give greater leeway for confrontation and critique. We are more apt to be accepting and responsible (in both senses of responding to the Other and holding ourselves responsible) to critique, counsel, and confrontation from those whom we trust than from those whom we do not trust. I allow the Other a wider berth within which to confront me with myself *through the Other* with a directness and truthfulness that I would find either too intrusive (as with my office colleagues) or too obsequious (as with the sycophant), or too suspicious (as with the Confidence Man) with regard to others outside my bond of trust. Indeed, this edging of the self in the Other can be leveraged against me when the Other abuses or manipulates my trust to cause my ruin or gain an advantage at my expense. In allowing the trusted person to participate in our lives and exercise discretionary judgment, we have placed ourselves in their hands—hands that now move against us.

Relations of trust must be nourished and nurtured. Through a mutual edging, or lining, of one another's sense of self, a space and time of trust emerges between us, bonding us to each other in the allowance of the Other's accompaniment from within. This span of trust is held between two extremes: blind devotion or loyalty in which our autonomy and own discretion become entirely dissipated into the Other and paranoid vigilance and corrosive distrust by which the Other's discretionary power of judgment and beneficence has been entirely ejected from having a place in my life. How easily the one we trusted becomes hated when we feel deeply betrayed; how easily we surrender to the Other's trust when we feel we have betrayed our own self-trust. Between these two poles, the nourishment and nurturing of trust require the exercise of "functional virtues," or, in other words, virtues appropriate for the nourishment and nurturing of trust.[44] We are each entrusted as the keepers of our trust. We are each challenged to calibrate and check upon our trust without obtrusive and suspicious monitoring. Such measured monitoring of trust involves a degree of emotional intelligence and cognitive tact. We must feel our way within our trust: adjusting its contours, shaping its substance, and guiding its future.

Trusting relationships operate within a tensor of different vectors: cognitive, affective, and conative. Rather than reduce trust to an emotion, a knowing and judging, or an enduring disposition of goodwill, a bond of trust is formed in the conglomeration of emotions, cognition, and benevolent desire within an atmosphere of assuredness. Trust is often described as "atmospheric," and not without reason; it is descriptively challenging to track the distinctive phenomenological features of trust.[45] Unlike emotions such as anger and love, or attitudes such as indifference or obsequiousness, *to be* trusting or *to be* trusted does not exhibit any *specific* style. This appears to be especially significant for any proposed characterization of trust as a specific kind of emotion.[46] Even love, which is often identified as the emotional register of trust, proves elusive to specify in this context, other than through attributes that could just as well be taken as characteristic of an affective attitude of goodwill toward the Other.[47] And yet the emotional indexes of trusting relationships— intimacy, confidence, peace of mind, love, and so on—are nowhere more clearly manifest as when trust is misplaced or betrayed. The experience of despair, anger, and even hatred with the betrayal of trust attest, as negative images, to the positive emotional registers of trusting relationships. The emotional presentness of trust is nowhere more distinctly manifest as when it becomes lost. This is especially apparent with the transfigura-tion of love into hate: we come to hate the person who betrays us as the reverse image of our intense attachment to that person in love. Much as we can speak, as Stendhal does, of the "crystallization" of love, we can speak of the "crystallization" of hate: the despised Other becomes our entire universe, and even as we seek to expel the despised Other from our lives, her presence nonetheless remains within us to the degree that we remain unable to escape from our own compulsive obsession and consuming passion for the Other. We are at times never so close to the Other as in hatred.

As an emotional attachment, trust rests upon cognitive assuredness in granting discretionary power of judgment to the Other. Assuredness is not merely a felt emotional quality of nearness (the Other as lined within me). This assuredness within me allows, most critically, for an affordance of distance from the trusted Other. As argued by Erik Erikson, the for-mation of basic trust within the mother-child relationship during infant development hinges on the capacity of the child to let go of the immedi-ate presence of the mother in the expectation, or trust, that the absent mother will return. Even when the child cannot call upon the mother directly, trust in the mother's benevolence for the child and, crucially, eventual return allows the child to overcome the anxiety of separation.[48] This trust in the mother's return, for Erikson, underpins all forms of social trust and requires a degree of self-trust in the child's capacity to endure the absence of the trusted mother. The assuredness of trust that develops when a mother (or caregiver) responds to an infant's needs (when prompted, for example, by an infant's cry) forms the basis for psychological attachment and recognition.[49] Critical for the formation of the child's sense of having a place in the world in relation to others, and hence to themselves, is "the enduring belief in the attainability of fervent wishes," or, in other words, *hope,* "in spite of the dark urges and rages that mark the beginning of existence."[50]

More generally, the assuredness of trust allows for a settled confi-dence in *coupling* the Other's motivations, values, and possible courses of action. Trusting is not *merely* based on the cognitive or the affective. Trusting is an assured capacity of coupling the cognitive, the affective, and the conative and, through this operation of coupling, apprehend-ing the Other as *known* to me, as known *in* me, within the arc of my own self-knowledge. This operation of coupling is intrinsic to the knowledge I form of the Other in trusting them. Trust is knowing and being-known. In trusting the Other, I can more ably and assuredly predict their ac-tions, reactions, and responses on the basis of more ably and assuredly coupling their possible motivations, reasons, and values, so as to plot and understand, approve or disapprove their chosen course of action, or lack thereof. The inscrutability of the Other becomes *for me* leavened with the assuredness of my coupling together who they *might be* in any given situation. In trusting the Other, I can rest assured that the Other will most likely behave in such and such a manner, be motivated to doing such and such an action, and to act according to such and such a value. In this assured capacity of coupling together the Other's possible courses of action and reasoning, I identify myself with the *kind* of individual who, as the Other who is not me, is nonetheless like me. I trust that the Other would do as I would do in any given situation or trust that the Other will act in a way with which I could identify and hence endorse. Even when the Other's actions, motivations, and values remain opaque, we are more disposed to give the trusted Other the benefit of our doubt and rule out more incriminating or trust-corrosive motivations, values, and actions. When our trust becomes tested, challenged, or betrayed, the assuredness of our coupling operation (imagining what the Other would do, knowing that the Other would not do this and that, etc.) becomes itself tested, challenged, or, in cases of betrayal, broken.

Much as this coupling operation in trusting the Other gives us assurances in granting discretionary judgment and embedding emotional investment, this knowing of the Other can also be used against me, for in trust I myself become known (and in ways I may not know of myself) to the Other. The Confidence-Man's self-assuredness, charisma, and rhetorical prowess allow him to insinuate himself into my trust-network, or in-group, and through this perspicuous vantage point over who I am—what I value, how I would act, and so forth—he deftly uses the coupling intelligence of trust against me. Addressing us in ways that speak to what we value, a shared past, and our membership community, the Confidence-Man employs a strategy of *mirroring*, and in this mirroring we, the marker, become captivated and held captive by an image of ourselves, or an image of our in-group identity. In this mirror we see likeness and fellow feeling without seeing our own blindness, for it is this very mirroring that makes us blind to the Confidence-Man's dissimulation and manipulation of our trust. We have been duped in having been seen through without seeing through our own blindness.

This betrayal of trust often provokes pronounced incredulity on the side of the betrayed person. That the Other would have betrayed me seems unimaginable and unfathomable. Something profound in me has been broken. I no longer know *who* it is in whom I once trusted. I no longer know *who* I am to have once trusted. This existential plunge of betrayal attests to the existential depth of trust in the formation of self-assuredness. Even when registering and suffering the dissimulation of trust, betrayed persons can nonetheless cling to their trust in the Other to the point of overtrust despite any revealed untrustworthiness. Compromised trust has a way of calling the trust of the betrayed person *more into question* than that of the betrayer, as if the accusation of unfaithfulness to the bond of trust rebounded back onto the person betrayed. Because trust involves the assurance of benefit—achieving a goal, upholding a value, and so on—we often find ourselves still wanting to believe in the Other by virtue of still wanting to believe what our relation of trust promised us. Our wanting to believe becomes all the more intense given the sown seed of doubt that has insinuated itself into us. We become blind to the Other's failing of our trust and turn to accuse ourselves instead, thus allowing ourselves, in the most pathological cases, to enter even more into the spell of the Other's machinations and duplicity.

Overtrust has a way of inducing a critical blindness often coupled with the leveraging of fear. Overtrust obscures its own misplaced excess through the incitement of fear of losing what an empty trust promises but cannot in fact deliver. The fear of losing what trust promises but cannot deliver inflates trust to overtrust. We desperately *want to believe* and allow ourselves too much trust, which, however, we can ill afford. Fearmongering covers over and motivates the misplaced trust of overtrust: in fearing the disaster said to come, we throw ourselves more willingly (and blindly) into the promise of a protection in fact never needed, and once we have given ourselves over to overtrust, we cannot let go for fear of having nowhere or no one else to trust. Demagogues, like the trickster, thrive on trust upon which they themselves stand at the expense of all others—that is, Trumping all others.

The Adversary of Trust

Much as trust critically operates in the interdependent welfare of human existence, trust can just as critically facilitate the exploitation, deceit, and ruin of human existence. Trusting too much can be as hazardous as not trusting enough, or not at all. This slippage of trust from a conduit of welfare to a conduit of ruin exploits the emotional assuredness upon which we live when trust contributes to and fosters our well-being. Trust nourishes for its own well-being an intrinsic insouciance. In emotionally investing ourselves in relations of trust and benefiting from its felt assuredness, we cultivate an insouciance with regard to the Other in whom we trust as well as toward our bond of trust as such. We rest assured in our trusts, trusting in trust itself. We can afford to become more attentive and sympathetic toward the Other—more involved—on the basis of such an insouciance of caring for the Other. Not only does the unreflective condition of trust become further engrained as a matter of course; on the basis of such a habitus of trust routines can in turn be established and run on this basis of settled and unquestioned trust. A habitus of trust reduces the complexity of basal interactions in order to allow us to confront the unfamiliar and unexpected in an atmosphere of assuredness.[51] Founded trusts have our back as we confront the unforeseen. As Onora O'Neil notes, obtrusive monitoring of trust undermines trust.[52] Conversely, complete insouciance within trust (trusting without any monitoring) renders trust more vulnerable to its abuse or withering away. Trust must be nourished and nurtured once established, yet even in the best of cases bonds of trust can become transformed into misplaced trust or broken after a betrayal of trust. Given the latitude of involvement and leeway of permissiveness granted to the Other in their entrustment with discretionary judgment over our cares and concerns, a relationship of trust allows for generosity and benefit as well as for grief and ruin. The entrusted Other edges our subjectivity; our own sense of self is lined with the Other. Framed in this manner, the betrayal of trust is emotionally suffered as an internal wounding that frequently threatens our sense of self to the point of "ego death." In this rupture of assuredness and attachment, we suffer a marked (wounding) incredulity not only with regard to the Other ("How could she have done this to me?") but also with regard to ourselves ("How stupid was I to have trusted her!"). We feel that we could never forgive the Other. Just as much, we feel that we could never forgive ourselves.

There are evidently many ways by which we come to grief and to ruin in relations of trust. The spectrum of misplaced trust ranges from falling prey to the Confidence-Man to instances of trust slipping off track without any apparent or initial awareness or even intention among the trusting persons to the Impostor who suddenly reveals himself to not have been the person we always took him and trusted him to be. Ruptures in the credibility and trustworthiness of others need not always produce clean breaks. Severed bonds of trust can often be jagged, with a residual degree of fragmented or perverse trust remaining even in our own despair at having been deceived or betrayed. Whereas with misplaced trust, as with the Confidence-Man, the Other who abuses our trust feigns trustworthiness, sincerity, and interest in our well-being, in cases of displaced trust, a relationship of trust suffers an internal slippage between trustworthiness and trust. In such instances, trust becomes hollowed out from within. Though I remain trusting, the person has become unbeknownst to me no longer trustworthy. My trust becomes misplaced in having become displaced within our relationship of trust. Whereas the Confidence-Man orchestrates behind our backs the manipulation of our trust for the sake of our grief and ruin, slippages of displaced trust are differently complex, since both persons can at first be caught in trust's dissimulation, even if one party ultimately gains the upper hand as the puppet master of the relationship.

With the Impostor, the situation is once again different.[53] Of all the forms of trust's betrayal, it is significant that the Impostor, one who plays a role that does not properly belong to him but who otherwise acts faithfully and even considerately, wounds profoundly. The unmasking of the Impostor represents an existential catastrophe not only for those persons entrapped in the circuit of betrayed trusts—trust as such seems to be voided. In the spectacular case of Jean-Claude Romand, who convincingly pretended from 1975 to 1993 to be a successful doctor and esteemed local citizen until he murdered his family and his parents when about to be exposed as an impostor, rather than confess to his fraudulence and become unmasked, Romand brutally killed his unsuspecting family, burned his house, and attempted unsuccessfully to commit suicide. That Romand was led to murder his wife, children, and parents, erasing both his origins and his progeny, rather than own up to his fraudulent existence, did not stem from any desperation to keep his "true" or "authentic" identity a secret from the world. Of secrets, Romand had a few and confided his secret love affair with his mistress to one of his friends even while keeping this relationship hidden from his own wife. As Emmanuel Carrère explores in his literary creation *The Adversary* (based, in part, on a letter correspondence with Romand), Romand's "motivation," if the notion even applies here (a questionable assumption examined in Carrère's novel), was not based on either a decision or project to become an Impostor. Romand's secret was that there was no secret to be unlocked, no hidden identity to be unmasked. Romand fell into his role of Impostor as a way of being and fitting in the world. "Romand" literally emerged from nothing to crystallize incrementally into a self-absorbing deception in which others became unknowingly entrapped. As Romand explained to Carrère, "When you get caught in that endless effort not to disappoint people, the first lie leads to another, and then it's your whole life."[54]

In Carrère's telling of this dramatic tale, this betrayal of trust among Romand's friends provoked mourning for the meaningfulness of trust itself. A life once shared in genuine friendship now seemed, for Romand's closest friends, to have been a life exposed as having been stolen under their watch by Romand's deception, as if the lives of those betrayed now became seen in their truth as an *imposed* life in two senses: as a life imposed on the betrayed by the Impostor's deception *and* the life of the Impostor now exposed to have been false. The betrayed no longer recognize their lives as having once been their own. When betrayed by the Other, my own life takes on the character of an imposture that, unbeknownst to me, I had been living all along. The Impostor has passed beyond the threshold of life and death, the real and the unreal. Romand's abortive suicide leaves him within the world of the living, but as the living symbol of the living who are dead, and the dead no longer living, and whether the living *are dead*, masquerading in trust and charity, in community and humanity. "He was somewhere outside life, outside death, where he no longer had a name." That we have a proper name that tracks us through our lives and publicly as well as privately anchors our identity is essentially a matter of trust—that I am the person named—and once that name has been substantially revealed to have been a lie, the name becomes hollow, collapses into the void left behind, and, in this sense, "Romand" *could never find or receive another name.* As Carrère writes, "When they [his friends] spoke of him, late at night, they couldn't manage to call him Jean-Claude anymore. They didn't call him Romand, either. He was somewhere outside life, outside death, where he no longer had a name." That Romand remains within the living as "death made man" ensures that "peace [will] never be restored [and] that the horror [will] never end."[55]

The case of Romand presents an instance in which trust's betrayal is in the service of no material, psychological, or social gain. Although Romand lived from the trusts he inspired and cultivated with his family and friends, he does not cut the figure of the sociopath, so currently *en vogue* in the popular imagination, who ruthlessly pursues (on this common notion) his own self-interest at the expense of all others, expertly honing his charm and inspired trusts into instruments for his own self-advancement in the world. Romand, on the contrary, lacked any ambition. Sustaining a living lie of claiming to work as a doctor in Geneva at the World Health Organization (he and his family resided in a small town near Geneva, in France), Romand would in fact spend many of his days wandering about the mountains of the Jura. When feigning to be away on business trips, Romand would in fact spend his time in a Geneva hotel and return home with gifts to the pleasure of his family from an airport gift shop. Romand's cultivation of trust was in an important sense sincere: his longtime friend Luc "valued [his] reliability and loyalty."[56] The fraudulence of his voided trusts, sincere and yet empty, was not motivated by the pleasure of deception, as it is with the Confidence-Man, who targets his marks out of a perverse kind of pleasure. Instead, Romand's case highlights in extremis the intrigue of how trust invites and, in acute cases, licenses its own abuse, indeed to the extreme that the person whose trust has been turned against them no longer trusts in themselves as to whether or not they are themselves complicit or to blame in the ruin brought upon themselves in trusting the Other. Under such circumstances, trust emerges as an exposure not only to unexpected harms but also to an unexpected vulnerability toward itself, often without our reflective knowing or attentive complicity. We are lulled into unthinking by trust and allow trust to have its way in our allowance of its sway over us, even when turned against us by the Other in whom we trust. Romand's fabrication of his life progressed incrementally, as he was pulled further into deception by an accreditation of trust among his family and friends.

In the aftermath, Romand's friends passed through stages of mourning for their trust in their friend, for trust in the world, and for trust in themselves and each other. This mourning for what had always been taken as self-evidently impossible passed through different stages: disbelief at the unveiled horror of Romand's years of deceit; hope for the best for their former friend and confidant, despite all evidence to the contrary; continued faith in Romand even after he had been criminally prosecuted and found guilty; then acceptance and reconciliation—without any forgiveness—for the "grief of trust betrayed, of life completely corrupted by lies."[57] The "reality principle" of trust became broken *within* Luc's family. As Carrère writes, "Both they and their children had been robbed of childhood, for never again would the little ones nestle in their arms with the trust that is miraculous but normal, at their age, in normal families."[58] In Romand's deceit at being a father, husband, and friend, as well as with the murder of his own children, wife, and parents, any meaningfulness to trust of children for their parents and of parents toward their children seemed impossible and irrevocably stained by the despair of betrayal and blasphemy; not just a betrayal of particular bonds of trust but also a blasphemy against the value of trust as such. Luc and his wife wanted to protect their children from this onset of corruption within their family and searched for how to protect their children not only from the death of their playmates and close family friends but also from the death of trust itself. Their children were stricken with anxiety that their own house might one day be engulfed in flames and, more disturbingly, that "their daddies were doing what Antoine's and Caroline's father had done."[59] What plays out in the scene of mourning in Luc's family is the destitution of the responsibility and care for children; the children now live in fear of their deaths at the hands of their own parents. The parents attempted to reassure these little ones in offering soothing, parental words of love, bolstering the crumbling edges of a trust that had already collapsed from within, for the parents "could tell that their words had lost their former magical power." The magic spell of "trust me, I will protect you" and "everything is all right" is the power of drawing a magic circle of protection and assuredness in the embrace of trust. With the realization that this entrustment of having been born was irreparably devastated for their children, the parents began to mourn for their own deaths as parents.[60]

Romand's revolt against *being-in* the world was absolute: he did not murder only his children but also his own parents, thus betraying the conditions of his own being born, his natality. In the police reconstruction of what had occurred in his parents' house, Romand's father was unsuspectingly shot in the back. Romand's mother, however, appears to have been facing her son when she was killed. Face-to-face with her son, what might she have thought as she beheld her son pointing a rifle at her? As Carrère observes, in the hour of death we need to be released from the world, either through a religious belief in God's assurance and reception or in the trust that those around us, and especially our children, will remember us. In the hour of death, our lives pass before us: "The dying see the movie of their whole lives flashed by, its meaning clear at last."[61] The clarity of this vision is a function of our trust in the remembrance of others, that the life we ever so briefly see flash before our eyes, our own, will remain visible, remembered, by those around us, in whom we trust to live after our lives have been lived. We pass in the trust that we will be remembered and cherished, that even in death our lives remain entrusted to others, that our lives are in the hands of others. It is not only upon trust that we live but also upon trust that we die. We are released from this world and delivered upon a death held in trust by others. We enter the world in trust; we depart from the world in trust. At the funeral for Romand's parents, the priest sought to reassure those gathered there that, in the moment of their deaths, Romand's parents "saw God" and now abide in God. But as his mother stood facing her son, as Carrère observes, "This vision that should have brought the elderly Romands the joy of accomplishment had been the triumph of deception and evil. They should have seen God and in his place they had seen, taking on the features of their beloved son, the one the Bible calls Satan, 'the adversary.'"[62]

After his trial and conviction, Romand discovered in prison the Christian faith and its message of redemption and forgiveness. Romand embraced prayer and speaks of having undergone a "mystical experience" of conversion, contrition, and repentance. As he admitted to Carrère, "I have never been so free; life has never been so beautiful. I am a murderer, I'm seen as the lowest possible thing in society, but that's easier to bear than the twenty years of lies that came before."[63] In prison, he even befriended through letters a woman named Marie-France, who came to believe in him, trust him, and even fell in love with him. She bolsters him in his newfound faith and path upon repentance and forgiveness. There is even a "club" of outside supporters, including a certain Bernard, an "elderly Gaullist," a pious Catholic, and a survivor of Buchenwald during World War II. Bernard speaks of having forged a "real friendship" with Romand and praises the "good" that Romand is doing around him in prison as a model inmate. As he confided to Carrère, "Everything works out and finds its meaning in the end for those who love God."[64] Among this "club," there is also a local schoolteacher, Mme Milo, who, in fact, had been the teacher of Romand's son, Antoine; she asks the children of her class to make drawings for "someone in trouble"—which she sends to Romand in prison. He confesses to Marie-France that "I have decided to assume that suffering for Florence's family, for my friends," and she speaks of the "forgiveness he cannot expect from others because he does not forgive himself."[65] Carrère characterizes Marie-France as a "church hen" who brings a new role to Roland on "a silver platter, the part of the great sinner who expiates his crime by saying the rosary."[66] As he writes, "I found its wooden Catholic jargon truly mysterious. In the logical sense, *undecidable*"—"he is not putting on an act, of that I'm sure, but isn't the liar inside of him putting one over on him? When Christ enters into his heart, when the certainty of being loved in spite of everything makes tears of joy run down his cheeks, isn't it the adversary deceiving him again?"[67]

If Carrère adopts an attitude of refraining from blame or judgment toward the Adversary, it is not only because there remains forever suspended before us the question of whether there ever was a genuine or true person behind Romand's masks; it is also because the accretion of the Impostor's assured *and* assuring identity was necessarily oiled with the lubricant of trust, without which human existence might risk becoming even more nefariously precarious, and yet *less* audacious. He admits in the parting declaration of his own account, "I thought that writing this story could only be either a crime or a prayer." As in the book of Job, the Adversary roams the Earth and puts to the test those in whom trust is entrusted the most, absolutely, so as to render present in its questioning the presentness of trust to be the very ground upon which human life stands and falls on Earth. But this, dear reader, you must already know in having trusted me to take you this far.

Forgiveness and the Human Condition

If we begin with a cursory survey of literary portrayals of forgiveness, narratives of forgiveness exhibit a recognizable pattern of crystallizing in dramatic scenes of encounter between the one who forgives (or refuses to forgive) and the one who stands to be forgiven (or not to be forgiven). Such encounters unfold around an axis of recognition and transformation for those who come to see each other anew in forgiveness: the person who forgives forswears resentment and revenge in accepting the forgiven person's declarations of remorse and responsibility; the forgiven person commits herself to becoming otherwise than who she had been in light of which the forgiving person adopts a change of heart, releasing her from the lien of moral resentment, revenge, and vindictiveness. Whether in the fabric of literary portraits or in the folds of everyday life, forgiveness is a space of encounter, a time of transformation, and a form of recognition. Under the heading of "forgiveness as encounter," let me broadly delineate the contours of this common framing of forgiveness before examining in detail one of its more original statements in Arendt's *The Human Condition.*

Encounters in forgiveness are usually animated by the dynamic of reconciliation and regeneration; yet they can often possess sharpened edges against forgiveness, as when an aggrieved person lords the request for forgiveness over her aggressor, or when feigned forgiveness becomes weaponized into an instrument of revenge (as it is in *Jane Eyre* with Mrs. Reed on her deathbed), or when David Lurie's search for absolution in *Disgrace* further eviscerates his own sense of accountability. However we judge these scenes of forgiveness, however forgiveness becomes enacted or misfires, different conceptions of forgiveness can be seen as varied proposals for the orchestration of forgiveness as an encounter. Conceptions of forgiveness are transposable into staging instructions for the narrative emplotment of forgiveness; theories of forgiveness contain virtual theaters of forgiveness.

Seen in this way, claims regarding the proper conditions of forgiveness, for the person who forgives as well as for the person standing to be forgiven, function as structuring principles for the encounter of forgiveness, its performance. What it means to prescribe and describe such conditions is itself varied, open to debate: conditions of achievement, conditions of warrant, conditions of initiation. In Charles Griswold's account, for example, "paradigmatic forgiveness" between two persons aims at mutual reconciliation on the basis of sympathetic understanding and forswearing of resentment (on the part of the forgiving person) in light of the acceptance of self-responsibility and self-repudiation (on the part of the person beseeching forgiveness). Considered as a virtue, forgiveness occurs "at its best" under reciprocal (though asymmetrical) conditions: forswearing of revenge, mitigation and eventual abdication of resentment, and change of heart for the forgiving person; repudiation of the past self, respect toward the injured person, sincere remorse and shouldering of responsibility for the person standing to be forgiven.[1] According to Griswold's account, "paradigmatic forgiveness" is a "face-to-face" interpersonal relation between an aggrieved person and an offending person in which the offender has inflicted a moral harm against the aggrieved, such that the proper and primary moral response of the aggrieved consists in the retributive attitude of moral resentment, as distinguished from revenge, vindictiveness, and indifference. Setting aside the distinctive merits or particular inadequacies of Griswold's account, this approach to forgiveness exemplifies how debates and disagreements concerning the conditions for forgiveness, or, even more strongly, for requiring forgiving (such that failing to act under such stipulated conditions would become blameworthy), are translatable into debates and disagreements regarding the proper orchestration of forgiveness as a space of encounter, time of transformation, and form of recognition.

Even proponents of unconditional forgiveness (often called unilateral forgiveness), or more nuanced proposals for the volatility of the distinction between conditional and unconditional forgiveness, are beholden to this framing of forgiveness as an encounter in response to antecedent harm, which may become for that reason especially, or all the more, susceptible to theatricality. Margaret Holmgren, for example, argues for "unconditional genuine forgiveness" where the victim "*unilaterally* cultivates *her own attitude* of genuine forgiveness *independent* of the offender's actions and attitudes."[2] This independence of what she calls the "internal preparation of the person who forgives" stands under the imperative of forgiveness, since, by her claim, failing to forgive would amount to the hardening of a victim in a retributive attitude of resentment and thus commit the fault of failing to respect the wrongdoer as a moral person. This emphasis on respecting the wrongdoer as a "sentient and moral agent" impels us to forgive unilaterally; in failing to do so, our abiding resentment would forever fix the person to their wrongdoing and thus fail to recognize in respect, compassion, and benevolence the person as distinct, for her own sake and future flourishing, from her misdeed. In this view, forgiveness is not "an expressed emotion in an interaction but a continuous conviction about the basis of what it means to live as a flawed being."[3]

Even as Derrida's reflections on the aporia of forgiveness might seem at first glance far removed from the approach to forgiveness in Griswold's account (or Holmgren's), Derrida's argument for the undecidable situation of forgiveness, caught between conditional forgiveness and unconditional forgiveness, nonetheless retains the recognizable gestalt of forgiveness as an encounter—to wit, as an undecidable encounter and encounter with the undecidable.[4] As Derrida insists, conditional forgiveness and unconditional forgiveness are "absolutely heterogeneous" and irreconcilable, and yet indissociable; the "purity" of unconditional forgiveness "becomes effective in a series of all kinds of conditions."[5] Derrida's own posture of asking to be forgiven when addressing forgiveness reflects a conscientious responsibility dictated by the aporia of forgiveness itself: speaking about forgiveness must here ask to be forgiven, given the dual risk of succumbing to the theatricality of its own rhetorical performance *or* remaining suspended within a capricious profundity (and often wrongly seen as a "negative theology" of forgiveness), even as this suspense bears the weight of being haunted by what appears impossible— namely, forgiveness, "s'il y en a," as Derrida never fails to remind us.[6]

Much as different theoretical conceptions of forgiveness can be read as implicit prescriptions for the staging of forgiveness, portrayals of forgiveness in literature can be read as implied theories of forgiveness. In both instances, forgiveness is cast as a space of encounter, a time of transformation, and a form of recognition in response to antecedent harm.

Whether among philosophers or writers, whether among the theologically minded or the secular in persuasion (as well as those who challenge the meaningfulness of this distinction), and however we might argue for the proper configuration of forgiveness as concept and orchestration, the common framing notion underlying different theories and theaters of forgiveness as an encounter is additionally beholden to an understanding of forgiveness as a capacity, or "moral power," of transformation and beginning anew in response to antecedent harm. Forgiveness is not only a space of encounter between persons; it is inseparably a time of transformation and transformation of time itself, centered on the promise and significance of renewal. A space of encounter in forgiveness is inscribed within narrative temporality, or, more accurately stated, within the temporality of narrative contestation (in both subjective genitive and objective genitive senses). Such contestation regarding the truthful narrative for the soliciting, warranting, and meaningfulness of forgiveness becomes woven around a determinate past. This contested past is both what is common to us and what separates us from each other. Bound to each other on account of this past, we encounter one another across the divide placed between us by this past. The past binds us to the encounter of forgiveness (what you have done to me or what I have done to you) insofar as we find ourselves confronted with each other and with the question of forgiveness. This damaged past divides us in setting contested narratives against each other: we fail to share and accept the same narrative of events; we wish that the Other and her deed could be expelled from our own life story; we feel ourselves belonging and wanting to belong to a time that is not yours, or yours to own, even as we are each held hostage to this past as well as to each other in terms of the wrongdoing that you committed against me, or that I committed against you. We are forgiven (or not forgiven) for what we have done, yet only because what has been done remains not entirely over and done with, not settled once and for all, must forgiveness happen (or fail to happen) in the present in response to a determinate yet unsettled past. Responsive to antecedent harm, after injury, forgiveness performs in the present. I now forgive you (or refuse to forgive you) for what you once did to me. I now beseech your forgiveness for what I once did to you. Whatever it is that forgiveness seeks or achieves, its redress occurs in the present in view of a future where we might find ourselves reconciled, together once more, or, alternatively, where we might *not* find ourselves together again, having been allowed to take leave of each other in the benediction of peace and safe travels.

As space of encounter and transformation of time as well as time for transformation, forgiveness unfolds around an axis of recognition. In the encounter of forgiveness, I stand recognized before you and you stand recognized before me; each of us does not leave the stage of forgiveness untransformed. Altered self-recognition is equally implied: recognizing myself *as forgiven* or recognizing myself as *forgiving*. Forgiveness turns on conversion, transformation, moral (or spiritual) rebirth, or metanoia. This transformative recognition of persons in forgiveness is predicated on the impossibility of self-forgiveness: I cannot forgive myself for what I did against you.[7] I might struggle to reconcile myself with my poor judgment, character flaws, and miscalculations and, in this sense, forgive myself but remain beholden to your forgiveness for what I did *to you.* Likewise, you cannot forgive yourself on my behalf for wrongdoings done against me. Only the Other, the aggrieved, can forgive me; only I, the aggressor, can stand to be forgiven by the Other. What it *is* that forgiveness accomplishes and signifies can be variously understood (and hence debated) as reconciliation, regeneration, or rebirth. In its most elemental form, as portrayed in the biblical narrative of the prodigal son, forgiveness announces the homecoming of finding one's place among others once again. The wayward person who has departed returns to the fold of friendship, family, community, nation, or humanity.

Forgiveness in *The Human Condition*

This framing of forgiveness as space of encounter, form of recognition, and time of transformation is nowhere more compellingly elaborated in its ontological significance for human existence than in Arendt's *The Human Condition*. As Karen Pagani remarks, Arendt's discussion of forgiveness remains "*the* seminal text in critical literature on forgiveness in contemporary secular ethics" and "exceptional insofar as it has become a touchstone for a wide variety of approaches."[8] Although Arendt does not provide "any detail of how the individual . . . conceives of the process (or even whether the individual conceives of forgiveness as a process at all," as Pagani justly recognizes, what Arendt's compact discussion of forgiveness lacks in development it more than makes up for in suggestiveness.[9] Arendt's discussion of forgiveness is notable for proposing an original conception of forgiveness even as it draws from traditional features of forgiveness, thus placing her account within a conceptual history of forgiveness that she herself traces back to the origin of Christianity with the life of Jesus. This invocation of the origin of forgiveness with Christianity masks, however, Arendt's subtle restitution of the "very ancient symbolism" of *unbinding/binding*. In this manner, her account of forgiveness circumvents an established grammar of forgiveness as gift and grace (as inscribed in the etymologies of the terms "forgive," "pardoner," *Vergeben*) that remains prevalent within a Christian discourse of forgiveness and its more contemporary, philosophical variants.[10] Arendt effectively "unlearns" a Christian conception of forgiveness and, more specifically, a Pauline understanding of interpersonal forgiveness as conditioned by divine forgiveness, in order to think once again, and hence learn once more, the significance and meaning of interpersonal forgiveness for the human condition.[11]

Arendt argues for the fundamental bearing of forgiveness on the human condition in a manner that "had yet to be so forcefully articulated in modern times."[12] Arendt's innovation consists in reformulating the traditional framing of forgiveness as space of encounter, form of recognition, and time of transformation in its ontological significance for human plurality in the life-world. *The Human Condition* does not provide a "theory" of forgiveness but sketches instead "trains of thought" from which a more elaborated account might find inspiration and orientation.[13] Within the sweep of her trains of thought, Arendt inscribes as well as deepens the paradigmatic framing of forgiveness as encounter within an analysis of the human condition. This existential deepening of forgiveness accounts for its *indeterminate* position within the established topological distinction between "the moral" and "the political." Arendt's treatment of forgiveness in *The Human Condition* has often been seen as "baffling," given that forgiveness here "is not of the moral domain as traditionally conceived."[14] In the same vein, Arendtian forgiveness should not be placed within the political domain as traditionally conceived. Arendt's concern is neither politics nor political philosophy but rather "the predicament from which politics must start," yet equally from which moral thinking, as traditionally conceived, must likewise begin anew.[15] This indeterminacy of where to situate the hold of forgiveness on the human condition scrambles any facile assumption of what "ontological" means in Arendt's analysis. At best, Arendt's thinking offers a "prolegomenon" with its "preliminary investigation of human activities that have most bearing upon politics and have been most misunderstood" and, by the same token, that have the most bearing not only upon moral thinking (as conventionally construed) but also upon a renewed thinking of the human condition in its being-in-the-world.[16]

In its most general expression, Arendt understands forgiveness as indispensable for human agency in coexistence with others in the life-world, or, in her terms, plurality. This emphasis on forgiveness attests to plurality's robustness as well as its vulnerability. The life-world, as sustained through human action (and speech), is exposed to ruptures of its own doing, but likewise renewals of its own undertaking. In terms of "openness" in an entwined sense of openness toward the manifestation of the world and openness toward the manifestation of others, Arendt astutely develops an appropriation of the phenomenological concern with the life-world, or "being-in-the-world."[17] In recognizing the existential import of forgiveness for the vitality of plurality in the life-world, forgiveness contributes critically to the disclosure of the world in truth. Arendt follows a central Heideggerian insight that "reality" becomes genuinely disclosed only within the life-world of human plurality. The life-world is the opening "where-in" the world comes into its own self-manifestation and, inseparably, where others, as persons, come into their own self-manifestation for each other. Insofar as forgiveness proves indispensable to the life-world as the vital space of world-manifestation, the world cannot enduringly be held in truth without the possibility of truthful forgiveness. Would the human capacity for forgiveness become irrevocably silenced or indefinitely curtailed, the disclosing locus of the life-world in which the world becomes truthfully manifest would likewise become severely foreclosed. In a world thus fallen under the sway of *ressentiment* and the reign of indifference, as Kierkegaard diagnosed his present age, the leveling of respectful distance and increasing anonymity of individual life governed by abstract principles make for a world where "modesty, repentance and responsibility cannot easily strike root in the ground."[18] Forgiveness proves indispensable not only for the restoration of human plurality but also, insofar as human plurality remains entwined with the openness of the life-world as such, for the renewal of this openness of the world held in truth. In speaking the truth, one bespeaks the world beheld in truth.

In addition to this depth of forgiveness for the life-world, Arendt emphasizes the ontological purchase of forgiveness for human agency and plurality. In Arendt's conception, forgiveness intimately expresses natality, the human capacity for beginning anew. The genuine orientation of human existence toward its beginnings, that we are created and conditioned beings, is not backward-looking but forward-looking, thrust into the future in natality, as the capacity for new beginnings. Along with our exposure to existential rupture, the breakages and crises of human existence, we are endowed in our freedom to originate new beginnings. Within the finite span of birth and death, human existence is storied with multiple beginnings and endings. Within the finite span of human existence, the unfolding of an individual life is structured by the pluralization of temporality, insofar as we can endeavor new beginnings in forgiveness yet conversely remain hostage to the purgatory of an unyielding past that never truly comes to pass. Moreover, within the human condition in its "being-in-the-world," human existence as such is structured by the pluralization of temporality. The intrinsic connection between both these essential forms of temporalization (within an individual life, within the human condition) becomes exemplified in forgiveness, given the way in which *The Human Condition* situates the existential temporalization of forgiveness on the axis of "conversion" or "transformation" (metanoia) within a consideration of the human condition as composed of different forms of temporalization. In forgiveness, the drama of the human condition plays itself out in concentrated form within the drama of an individual human existence in concert and conflict with others.

Within the sweep of her analysis of the human condition, Arendt argues that what renders forgiveness indispensable for human plurality must be situated within the domain of acting in relation to laboring and making. Forgiveness encapsulates the predicament of the human condition and its redemption. If acting is always marked by exposure to unpredictable contingency, where the significance and consequence of acting in the world along with others remain perpetually at risk through its own temporal openness, such a defining vulnerability of action becomes redeemed only through forgiveness in undoing the *bondage* of irreversibility. No contingency (as haunts every human action) should ever pass from the past present to the eternal past that would thus establish an unalterable, timeless ground for the present, and so fashion within time a dimension of necessity other than time's self-defining contingency. Against such fatalism produced by a devolution of natality, forgiveness proclaims the advent of beginning anew through a renewal of time itself. Arendt's thinking in this manner assigns to forgiveness a sacralized power of redemption for the human condition without which there could be neither enduring plurality or love of the world. What is at stake in Arendt's account is nothing less than the redemption of the human condition, albeit without any offer of historical finality to the world or theological salvation from the world.[19]

Being in the World

In *The Human Condition*, Arendt's threefold distinction of laboring, working, and acting characterizes three different forms of temporality in their respective ontological significance—that is, as temporalizations of human existence. Human existence thus conceived is conditioned through a nexus of ontological movements, or ways of being in the world, with each movement (laboring, working, acting) unfolding in tandem with the others, the constellation of which as a whole defines and textures what it is for human life to be. What distinguishes the temporality of acting and the life-world sustained through acting is that human existence breaks with the cyclical temporality of metabolic life, or *animal laborans*, as well as with the rectilinear temporality of making, or homo faber. Whereas *animal laborans* lives immanently within repeating, and hence transient, cycles of biological need and satisfaction in the maintenance of life for the sake of living, the fabrication of a world of things, tools, and institutions, which endure beyond the life span of individuals, inscribes human life, as homo faber, within a chronological order of temporality, or "world-time."

One of the more suggestive ways in which Arendt understands the relation between these ontological movements, between *animal laborans*, homo faber, and *vita activa*, is in terms of the problem of redemption. This concern with redemption runs throughout Arendt's understanding of the human condition, including, most crucially, her account of acting and forgiveness. In Arendt's understanding, redemption expresses two distinct meanings: release from and liberation to. Within each movement of human existence, redemption releases from and liberates to without abolishing or sublimating the respectively redeemed movement of human existence. Already in the movement of labor—laboring to secure the necessary resources for the maintenance of biological existence—human existence confronts the issue of redemption. This need for redemption points beyond the domain of labor to the movement of working, thus implicating the world of work in the field of labor. As Arendt argues, "the redemption of life, which is sustained by labor, is worldliness, which is sustained by fabrication."[20] In this argument, the production of a durable world through work releases—distances—human life from metabolic temporality while simultaneously incorporating it into the world of work. With this separation from biological life, human existence attains a form of life that Arendt broadly calls the social. This distancing from biological life opens a space of visibility (worldliness) essentially determined by the form of visibility of fabricated things while projecting human life onto another axis of orientation toward the world, or, to speak more exactly, of nature transformed into a world of human habitation by means of human artifice. It is only upon this constructed stage of worldliness, as the world of institutions, dwellings, and artifacts, that human existence finds a place of inhabitation and cohabitation. The world of durable institutions— taken widely to span culture, language, and social organizations—allows for a common world between humans in which human beings can appear to and encounter each other. The durable world founds *stability*— the lived space of appearances—against an inhospitable and inhuman movement without any sort of permanence. Through human artifice, the earth becomes a home, a place of dwelling, storytelling, and encounter.

The durable worldliness of homo faber and its dominant instrumental rationality stands itself, however, in need of redemption, given its own predicament of meaninglessness, understood as "the impossibility of finding valid standards in a world determined by the category of means and ends."[21] Techne transforms the relationship of human existence to what is through a transformation of the relation of human existence toward itself as well as toward meaning and value. Although fabricated worldliness redeems the life of *animal laborans* by instituting another (incorporating) order of meaning and habitation for human life, this accomplishment of homo faber suffers from its own unsuccessfulness to safeguard against the relativity of its own worldliness. Any effort of providing any theoretical foundation, or justification, for the instituted meanings of the world of human making by thinking, and hence, in this sense, a theoretical redemption of the world, is likewise judged by Arendt as leading to an impasse, since theoretical thought is itself afflicted by a predicament that thinking engenders but that thinking cannot on its own resolve or redeem. As Arendt argues, the threat of meaninglessness belonging to the worldliness of homo faber, in its pinnacle form as the "devaluation of all values," finds redemption only in acting and speaking (*vita activa*), the latter as fashioning "meaningful stories" that reconfigure the significance of acting from a purely instrumental logic of means and ends.

It is, however, this promise of redemption for worldliness through *vita activa* that the historical primacy of *vita contemplativa* effectively suppressed since the establishment of Western philosophical thought with Plato. In Plato's doctrine of Ideas, Arendt discerns an inaugural image of theoretical thinking that captivated the history of philosophy. The mechanism of this self-fashioning of thought attests to the impasse of *vita contemplativa* for the redemption of worldliness. Arendt's treatment of Plato is much broader in significance than simply offering a critique of Plato per se, since Plato, or, better, Platonism, represents in her view the original model and inspiration for the Idea of political utopia and the entrenched conceit of Western philosophy that human action requires a theoretical foundation. Plato's image of theoretical thinking and its doctrine of Ideas are based on the hypostatization of fabricated things and the inversion of worldliness. Fabricated things are defined by a permanence outlasting the activity of their own making as well as outliving the finite span of individual human existence. This quality of permanence characterizes the substantial form of a thing with its definitiveness of beginning and ending, hence as intrinsically imbued with predictability. The *Idea* of the bed, to which Plato (in Arendt's reading) ascribes true-being, is said to enjoy permanence over and above the impermanence of individual material beds. Thought in terms of the Idea, being is elevated above becoming; eternity as a permanence without beginning and end is foisted above endurance through beginnings and endings. Under the titular guise of the Idea, Plato effectively projects into the sphere of thinking the very form of permanence that characterizes fabricated things of the world while in the same gesture *inverting* the relationship between theoretical thinking and the worldliness of things. Whereas the term *eidos* originally designated the form of things in the world of making ("the look of things"), *eidos* now comes to take a displaced philosophical meaning as designating the Idea of a thing, as the truth of the thing that in itself is not a thing and, indeed, outlasts all things.

Plato's legacy is thus twofold: making usurps acting, which in turn facilitates the establishment of thinking as a foundation for acting, albeit in the image of action fashioned on the model of making. As Arendt notes, "Von der 'vita contemplativa' her gesehen, werden alle Formen nicht-denkender Aktivität essentiell identisch, weil ihnen allen das Um-willen zu eigen scheint."[22] The circle is complete: only an image of think-ing fashioned in the image of making can establish itself as providing a foundation for worldliness. In this metaphysical view, an action without foundation either in an Idea or a telos is unthinkable, but only because thinking has appointed itself as the foundation for acting on the image of making. Arendt's argument drives against this dual Platonic-Aristotelian legacy of metaphysical thought since, in her argument, "in der *praxis* gibt es weder *telos* noch Idee."[23] Without disregarding the weight of thought for determining our actions (indeed, in strident argument against the prevalence of "thoughtlessness" in our world), acting remains, in this sense for Arendt, *anarchic*, without *theoretical foundations*, first principles or eternal laws, and, for that reason, in need of promising and the exercise of critical judgment, as well as, most significantly, the eminently *humane* power of redemption called forgiveness.

Aside from such ontological consequence, it is the political implica-tions of this Platonic doctrine of Ideas that especially concerns Arendt. When transposed into political thinking, as with Plato's *Republic*, the vision of an Ideal polis, which, as a model for political existence, offers a theo-retical framework for the shaping of human plurality, represents an effort to eradicate human vulnerability from the world, and hence the creativity *and* risk of acting. There always remains a discrepancy between how one thinks the world to be, or should be, and how it will become. The value of this discrepancy is essential for judgments about how to act as well as the possibility of forgiveness in the aftermath of injury, harm, and er-rancy.[24] Whether political utopia is understood in Platonic terms, in terms of the City of God, or, in its modern variation, as a historical telos meant to determine the course of history, such an understanding of the rela-tion between worldliness and theoretical thought hinges on a promised unification of the world of actuality with the world of thinking. The re-demption of worldliness is thus conceived as involving a volatile mixture of principled violence and extraterrestrial miracle: the course of human existence must be shaped according to an image or ideal in such a man-ner that requires the necessary reduction of plurality and ever-elusive quest for that apocalyptic instant when the world would become *one* with its envisioned Idea, Telos, or Principle.

In Arendt's argument, however, for each of these movements of human existence—*animal laborans*, homo faber, and *vita contemplativa*—redemption can occur only from *outside* these respective domains, arriving as a non-self-generated "miracle." The predicament of each movement of existence is compounded by this inability to secure redemption through its own means. As Arendt writes, "What in each of these instances saves man—man *qua animal laborans, qua homo faber, qua* thinker—is something altogether different; it comes from outside—not, to be sure, outside of man, but outside each of the respective activities."[25] Ushering or guiding the world toward an Idea or telos does not accomplish genuine redemption but confuses redemption of the world with salvation from the creative volatility of the life-world. An image of redemption that thus becomes seen as arriving only from *outside* the world of human activity, as with laboring, working, and thinking, easily offers up the temptation for an escape from the world or the absolutization of the world in the promise of finality. This shift from *redemption* of the world to *salvation* of the world incites a desire for salvation *from* the world, at the expense, paradoxically, of the world said to be in need of salvation. Such a displacement of redemption by salvation motivates an attitude of *contemptus mundi*: the desire for salvation from the world facilitates the destruction of the world as the destruction of plurality and openness toward the future as inescapable openness. This movement of salvation in view of an outside, or transcendence, or beyond, throws the world off-kilter by decentering the world from the precariousness and creativity of human acting in the situated context of plurality. As Arendt argued in her analysis of totalitarianism, this conflation of salvation for redemption was most acutely manifest with the apocalyptic narrative of salvation coursing through Nazi ideology as a political religion. In this virulent form, Nazism represents an unbridled fanaticism for an idol of salvation armed with a perverse mixture of technological-bureaucratic mania, *völkisch* culture, and cultish mysticism. *Welt-Erlösung* becomes horrifically disfigured into *Welt-Erlöschung*. Sovereignty becomes fictionalized absolutely and thus all the more prodigal in its rampant destruction of worldliness and plurality. Yet even in politically and ethically less-catastrophic forms, this fanaticism for salvation, as the quest for overcoming the worldliness and finite condition of the human, of the humane, arguably drives transhumanism and other concerted efforts to extricate human existence from its earthbound condition, which, as Arendt so eloquently stated, was first heralded with the launch of Sputnik and its symbolization of the cosmic allure to taking leave of the Earth in Promethean shame.

Acting and Narration

The domain of acting enjoys a categorically different status. Unlike laboring, working, and thinking, the predicament of acting finds its redemption through a distinctive power of acting, and through this distinction the predicament of the human condition in its finitude becomes redeemed, not abolished or suppressed. Redemption does not arrive from beyond the domain of acting but emerges immanently within acting itself in order to transcend and transform—to begin anew—human relations forged in the plurality of the life-world. Redemption arises from the potentiality of acting insofar as the domain of acting contains the potentiality for two kinds of acting uniquely capable of redressing the predicaments of irreversibility and unpredictability: forgiving and promising. Whereas promising liberates us from the predicament of the unpredictability of the future, forgiving liberates us from the predicament of the irreversibility of the past. "Without being forgiven," Arendt writes, "released from the consequences of what we have done, our capacity to act would, as it were, be confined to one single deed from which we could never recover."[26] Such a characterization of forgiveness in no way implies the forgetting of the past, the condoning of past wrongdoings, or the exculpation of the wrongdoer from her deed. As an ontological feat, forgiveness transforms, or "retemporalizes," the relationship between who the person is and what she has done, as well as the relation between the person who forgives and the person who stands to be forgiven. This transformation of temporality, as binding persons to their own self-manifestation through acting, as well as binding persons to other persons, becomes effected not only within the ambit of those lives principally affected (the person who forgives, the person who is forgiven). Just as significantly, the life-world as such, as woven from reconfigured vectors of acting and story lines, becomes duly transformed in forgiveness.

Even as forgiveness centers on an interpersonal encounter involving the transformation of the forgiven person and the forgiving person, forgiveness critically reinvigorates the life-world in its openness to self-manifestation, not only with respect to others (the affected parties in forgiveness as well as the community of spectators) but also with respect to the world in its truthfulness. Persons who would remain unforgiving toward each other, engaged in consuming cycles of retribution and revenge, or who would remain stagnant in resentment without end, facilitate the withering away of world-openness. Fragmented and atomized within prideful self-righteousness or stubbornness against seeking forgiveness, the failure of interpersonal reconciliation brings along a failed reconciliation of the life-world with itself. Worlds in which forgiveness becomes increasingly scarce, feigned, or theatrical become increasingly subject to the automatism of violence, endemic tribalism, and the flattening of complexity. Within such an unforgiving world in its loss of the humane, the truthful disclosure of the life-world becomes foreclosed as well as the truthful self-disclosure of our respective standing toward each other, as well as for ourselves.[27]

This imperative of forgiveness for the reinvigoration of the life-world as "stage of appearance" reflects one of the more compelling consequences of Arendt's dismantling of Platonism. Metaphysical thought is founded on the conceit of thinking over acting—namely, that action requires theoretical foundations, and hence that the world in truth depends on a theoretical foundation or justification of truth. This conceit of thinking relates directly to Plato's doctrine of truth as correspondence, or what became canonized in the medieval ages as the doctrine of *veritas* as *adaequatio intellectus et rei.* In Arendt's (Heideggerian) reading, truth is established in Plato as a correspondence between Idea and thing on the basis of an ontological divide between "being" and "appearance" at the expense of obfuscating a more primordial sense of truth as revealing or disclosure. In dismantling this metaphysical separation between "being" and "appearance," or what Arendt identifies as the "two world theory" of canonical metaphysical thought, Arendt's return "to the things themselves" in their respective manners of manifestation (and what she cleverly calls "the value of the surface") inaugurates a thinking of the life-world as a stage of appearance in which "being" and "appearance" are not ontologically divided. As Arendt writes, "In this world which we enter, appearing from a nowhere, and from which we disappear into a nowhere, *Being and Appearing* coincide."[28]

This coincidence of being and appearing does not, however, imply identity. On the contrary, this coincidence of being and appearing implies *plurality* and, in fact, plurality in plural senses as the principle of being *in* appearances. Appearances are always appearances for someone for whom there are appearances. Nothing appears without an attestation of appearance. This implication of attestation for appearances further implies that the someone for whom there are appearances (to whom something appears) must likewise appear. Given our sentient being, we are present *to the world* as much as the world is present *to us.* We are, accordingly, not just "in the world," we are "of the world," and this precisely because we "are subjects and objects—perceiving and being perceived—at the same time."[29] *How* we exist in the world, not only with regard to ourselves but also with regard to others—how we are *here* in the world—conditions how the world becomes disclosed, and thus appears to us—how the world is *there* for us. This does not make human existence the condition for the disclosure of the world. Appearances are there not for the sake of life but, on the contrary, life is here for the sake of there being appearances, including its own. In this respect, sentient life is animated by an urge for self-display: "*Whatever can see wants to be seen, whatever can hear calls out to be heard, whatever can touch presents itself to be touched.*"[30] This "urge for self-display" provides the ground for the *meaningfulness* of different functions of human life, such that, in the framework of *The Human Condition*, the meaningfulness of different movements of human existence (labor, work, contemplation) are grounded in the domain of acting and speaking insofar as the life-world opens the stage of self-appearance, of the world, of others, of ourselves. To be in the world in attestation of other appearances in our own self-display is further inscribed within appearing onto and disappearing from the world. We appear on the stage of the life-world "from a nowhere" and likewise disappear from the stage of the life-world "to a nowhere." We find ourselves in a world always already there as a world preceding us and already always there as a world continuing without us. Appearing to a world that has appeared (to others) and disappearing from a world that will continue to appear (to others) define the "primordial events" that "mark out the time, the time span between birth and death." These various aspects of the sense in which being and appearance coincide define the elemental sense in which we exist in the openness of the life-world. As Arendt notes, "Nobody has succeeded in *living* in a world that does not manifest itself of its own accord."[31]

That appearance implies openness toward other appearances (no appearance without plural appearances) gives space for attestation in the "potential recognition and acknowledgement" of appearance. To recognize appearances for what they are (or, conversely, to be taken in by appearances that seem to be what they are not) is to recognize the *sense* of what appears as not fully determined in its appearance for us. "Reality," that vexing term in philosophy, becomes geared into the many senses of appearances. "Reality" is not divorced from or veiled by appearances, for the sense in which we adhere to "reality" always hangs on how we adhere to appearances. As Arendt writes,

> That appearance always demands spectators and thus implies at least potential recognition and acknowledgement has far-reaching consequences for what we, appearing beings in a world of appearances, understand by reality, our own as well as that of the world. In both cases, our "perceptual faith," as Merleau-Ponty has called it, our certainty that what we perceive has an existence independent of the act of perceiving, depends entirely on the object's also appearing as such to others and being acknowledged by them. Without this tacit acknowledgement by others we would not even be able to put faith in the way we appear to ourselves.[32]

This "perceptual faith" in "reality" is visceral, inscribed within the five senses of attestation (seeing, hearing, touching, smelling, tasting), as well as woven into the intersubjective fabric of the life-world, as referring to the implied attestation of others. Yet this anchoring of "perceptual faith" in "reality" is not merely intersubjectively textured; it depends just as much on what Arendt calls the "context *qua* context," which itself never appears clearly and distinctly within the situated encounters of the world, and yet which, in turn, should not be designated as "Being." Common sense is that pervading sense for the "reality" of appearances that is "guaranteed by its worldly context," or "worldliness as such." This rejection of an embracing and unified sense of "Being" sparkling through the manifold differences of being, or the plurality of appearances, holds on to the meaning of an "ontological difference," while dislocating this original difference from its inscription into the difference between Being and beings. This dislocation of the ontological difference serves, on the one hand, to dismantle Plato's doctrine of truth as correspondence and, on the other, to slip away from any devotion to "the truth of Being." Both Plato and Heidegger (at least, the Heidegger of Arendt's concern) are committed to subsuming meaning to truth and thus, in their own way, to a suppression of an open politics in favor of a regime of truth.[33] But, as Arendt expresses her critical insight, "*The need of reason is not inspired by the quest for truth but by the quest for meaning. And truth and meaning are not the same.* The basic fallacy, taking precedence over all specific metaphysical fallacies, is to interpret meaning on the model of truth."[34] *Platonism* names this inaugural metaphysical fallacy.

Arendt does not thereby abandon "reason" or "thinking," nor the significance of truth for human existence. On the contrary, she proposes a reformulation of their respective stature for human existence. Taking her cue from Kant's distinction between *Verstand* (translated into English by Arendt as "cognition" and "intellect," not as "understanding") and *Vernunft*, whereas the intellect looks for correctness in whether something exists and measures its meaning according to the correspondence of truth, reason ("thinking") does not inquire into whether something exists but as to the meaning for something to be—that is, for how something appears in attestation.[35] As Arendt remarks, "Thinking is equally dangerous to all creeds and, by itself, does not bring forth any new creed." In the domain of acting, as Arendt further comments, "practically, thinking means that each time you are confronted with some difficulty in life you have to make up your mind anew." This renewed quest for meaning is the animating principle of the human condition in its attestation of appearances and self-appearance. It is, however, a principle that can betray itself. As Arendt writes, "The quest for meaning, which relentlessly dissolves and examines anew all accepted doctrines and rules, can at any moment turn against itself, produce a reversal of the old values, and declare these contraries to be 'new values.'"[36] Thinking can revolt against itself to become thoughtlessness much as thinking can revolt against thoughtlessness to renew thinking.

When reformulated in terms of the ascendency of meaning over truth as well as the inseparability of appearance to being and being in appearance, the traditional concern for *truth*, configured as correspondence between *thinking and thing*, becomes reconfigured into a primary concern for the *truthfulness* of appearances. This emphasis on truthfulness forms the core of Arendt's account of thinking as intrinsically a form of conscience through which the thinking and acting subject crystallizes as a person in the element of freedom. For Arendt, "nothing perhaps indicates more strongly that man exists *essentially* in the plural than that his solitude actualizes his merely being conscious of himself . . . into a duality during the thinking activity. It is this *duality* of myself with myself that makes thinking a true activity, in which I am both the one who asks and the one who answers."[37]

This inner dialogue takes the form of self-possession in thinking where thinking is not construed as correspondence or correctness, either in the mode of intuition or logical reasoning. Looking back to Socrates, Arendt argues that thinking, as an inner dialogue, takes the form of striving to be consistent with oneself (*homologein autos heautō*). To think is to be truthful to oneself. The opposite of thinking is self-contradiction and bad faith; that is, a failure or absence of self-attestation (not attesting to one's contradictions or attesting in order not to attest). To have a conscience is to possess oneself in truthful self-attestation; it is to stand before oneself, yet not before the tribunal of guilt, before oneself in giving a truthful account of oneself as informed by the capacity of judgment—namely, to take into one's own consideration the standpoint of others and thus become for oneself a stranger while remaining a friend to oneself. In thinking, self-questioning, and judging, we are at home with ourselves. To be at home with oneself, however, is to contest any absolute self-identification with oneself by welcoming alterity (the viewpoints of others) within oneself. To be at home with oneself—to think—is to be "two in one," as both friend and stranger to myself in truthful self-attestation. As Arendt quotes from *Hippias Minor*, "Even Socrates, so much in love with the marketplace, has to go home, where he will be alone, in solitude, in order to meet the other fellow." It is in this Socratic sense that the voice of conscience, as the *daimon* within us, is neither the commandment of God, nor natural law within the heart, nor *lumen natural*. The *daimon* of thinking speaks without prescribing, instructs without commanding, and inspires without absorbing; it "fills a man full of obstacles." As Arendt observes, "What causes a man to fear it [voice of conscience] is the anticipation of the presence of a witness who awaits him only *if* and when he goes home."

In her brilliant words, "Conscience is the anticipation of the fellow who awaits you if and when you come home."[38]

This precedence of the self-disclosure of appearances, as truthfulness, is defining not only of *how* persons are disclosed to each other within the life-world but also of how the world as such becomes self-disclosed and to whom. The indispensable significance of forgiveness, and hence redemption, for the life-world follows from this reversal of Platonism and, especially, Arendt's argument for the precedence of meaning over truth. Forgiveness becomes ontologically indispensable in terms of its regeneration of the *meaningfulness* of the life-world through the redemption of *self-disclosure* from the predicament of its own obfuscation.

Because acting almost never achieves its intended purpose, according to Arendt, given that acting always operates within entangled webs of human relationships and the discrepancy between our considered ambitions and their unconsidered effects, the exposure of acting to contingent consequence and unexpected significance solicits and situates the generation of narratives such that acting comes to have weight and substance only by virtue of narrative incarnation. As founded on acting, the public sphere of the life-world is a space of narration in which different narratives concerning the consequence and significance of acting become fashioned, recounted, and contested. Acting always finds itself oriented within a space of narrative contestation. Different narratives regarding the how, what, where, and why of acting provide the threads from which the fabric of how we appear to each other becomes woven— that is, told. Arendt's claim, however, is not that we just *are* our stories but rather that the meaningfulness of who we are and what we do comes fully into appearance only in narrative manifestation.[39] Acting finds fulfillment in narratives, not in the sense of finality but as openness to accountability, responsibility, and truthfulness. We are launched into narrative from acting and turn to acting within narratives already under way. The initiation of acting is at the same time an invitation to speak and to be spoken about.

The intentionality of acting therefore not merely aligns itself toward its intended object and effect but also does so in such a manner that the *meaningfulness* of acting—its significance and consequence—comes into play and is displayed through narration. There is no claim to the truth of what we do without a certain meaningful narration of what we did do and who we are in this doing. The movement toward the fulfillment of acting in narration, not in terms of its completion but in terms of its completing incompleteness—that is, its openness to contested meaning—issues from acting in its ontological predicament. What is profoundly human about the appearance of unpredictability and irreversibility in our world is that both predicaments incite us to speech and, more generally, storytelling. Stories give place in our world to contingencies such that we can grant ourselves leeway and orientation toward their inevitability. Acting and speaking each bear witness to the finitude of the human condition, yet each are expressive of the robustness of the human condition insofar as it is only through storytelling that who we are becomes revealed to each other through our acting. As Arendt remarks, "The world is not humane just because it is made by human beings, and it does not become humane just because the human voice sounds in it, but only when it becomes a topic of discourse. However much we are affected by the things of the world, however they may stir and stimulate us, they become human for us only when we can discuss them with our fellows . . . We humanize what is going on in the world and in ourselves only by speaking of it, and in the course of speaking of it we learn to be human."[40]

We are manifest to each other in both word and deed. To act, to be acted upon, to speak, and to be spoken about are different ways in which a person becomes manifest to other persons within the life-world's stage of appearance. Arendt distinguishes between the *subject* of narrative and the *author* of narrative. Although I am the subject of those narratives that reveal *who* I am in the context of my acting, I am not the exclusive author of such narratives. To have a life is to span a stretch of time marked by a beginning and an end, yet this span of time is emphatically a time *for* narration as well as a time *of* narration. In an important sense, our lives have already begun even before we enter the world; we are first born to the world before being born *into* the world, insofar as we have already appeared within the narratives of others, which serve as placeholders and places of welcome for our own living yet to come. We are born to the world as singular beings already lovingly bespoken; we enter plurality in the baptismal act of being-properly-named (an act that we never witness ourselves); our lives have already accrued meaning and value with respect to who (and for whom) we are yet to be. As Arendt remarks, "We are born into this world of plurality where father and mother stand ready for us, ready to receive us and welcome and guide us and prove that we are not strangers."[41] Our lives begin already begun, not in thrownness but in natality, and hence as entrusted to others and in trust with others. We are received into the world in the berth and birth of narration. Likewise, our narrative incarnation does not cease with our passing from the stage of the world; our lives continue after we die in narrated afterlives insofar as stories from our lives continue to be fashioned, recounted, and contested after we have passed away.[42] This span of time called my life is a space of self-manifestation and contestation of who I am through stories told about me in the context of what I do, my acting in the world. I am the subject of my life narrative, yet I am not the author of my life narrative, since the author function is essentially plural. What is specifically human about human life as *bios*, as distinguished from animal life (*zoe*), is this possibility of a narrating and narrated life (*bio-graphie*).[43]

This distinction between subjects and authors of narratives receives Arendt's qualification that who I am in fact never entirely coincides, and hence becomes revealed, with how I appear to others in either word or deed. The engagement with others and appearance to others that properly constitute the humaneness of life are at the same time an "in-between" of distance and discretion. The "who" of the person, her singularity, retains what Arendt calls a "curious intangibility" throughout the narratives of her individuation and individual actions. While we become manifest to others in our words and deeds, *who* we are remains an unfinished question, an open question for a life as yet unfinished, such that who we are can never become completely captured or absorbed by what we say or do. As Arendt expresses this insight, "The revelatory character of action as well as the ability to produce stories and become historical, which together form the very source from which meaningfulness springs into and illuminates human existence."[44] This paradoxical combination of distance toward the life-world of public appearance *and* engagement with others in the life-world is crucial for any sustaining and nurturing of the life-world. The collapse of such proper distance and intangibility of the person (or the "who"), as fostered by the excessive demand to make oneself known and predictable, but equally with the increasing absorption of the political into the social, produces a withering away of the critical distance required for thought and judgment within oneself, as the space within for any willingness and capacity to take into account another person's perspective. Without this distance toward the world reflected within a distance toward oneself, as the "two-in-one" of thinking, the "who" cannot discover and define herself in the partisanship for the world of *amor mundi.*

Forgiveness as Encounter

Arendt recognizes forgiveness, like its counterpart promising, as an indispensable act without which the fabric of human coexistence in the life-world would not be durably renewed—that is, enduringly possible, time and again. Forgiveness exemplifies natality and plurality.[45] I cannot forgive myself on your behalf for what I have done against you. Only you can forgive me for what I have done against you and thus allow me to regain a potentiality for acting and standing as a person that I myself have forfeited in having wronged you. Along with this dimension, forgiveness brings redemption to the human condition, albeit in a form that, as opposed to eschatological salvation, remains itself precarious and in need of renewal. Redemption must become perpetually redeemed given its exposure, on the one hand, to the vulnerability of redemption to unforeseeable trials of the future and, on the other, to the unforgivable.

In drawing on an established idiom of forgiveness as transformation or conversion (metanoia), Arendt understands forgiveness as enabling the recovery of a person from her past wrongdoing, or what she did. As Arendt notes, "das Unrechte, das man getan hat, ist die Last auf den Schultern, etwas, was man trägt, weil man es sich aufgeladen hat."[46] In forgiveness, who you are becomes released from the entrapping burden of what you did. Arendt's account suggests a constitutive role for the attitude of moral resentment on the part of the injured person and, more broadly, the community (or moral spectator). Insofar as wrongdoing provokes indignation, or moral resentment, as well as the demand for retribution and even revenge, the wrongdoer remains bound to her wrongful deed in the condemning eyes of the victim and the community. Our sense of having been wronged by the doings of others motivates us to regard the other's agency as indistinguishable from her wrongdoing: in my resentful eyes, you will remain this person who wronged and harmed me. Ever since the influential sermons of Bishop Butler, moral resentment has been recognized as an essential acknowledgment and registering of moral wrongdoing on the part of the victim and the moral community.[47] While we are resentful for wrongdoings and injury toward ourselves, we are indignant at wrongdoings and injuries to others, and although the line demarcating resentment and indignation is not always stable, in an ideal case when we find ourselves the victim of moral harm, we are both resentful *and* indignant, insofar as we combine, as Adam Smith argues, both "first person" and "third person" judgments. We are resentful for the harm done against our standing as a moral individual, yet we are likewise indignant that a moral value has been violated from the perspective of the moral spectator.[48] This conjunction of first- and third-person judgments proves critical for the sway of the impartial spectator (indignation) over a first-person resentment.[49] The former keeps the latter measured, while the latter directs and anchors the former. As a "reactive attitude" that is neither indifference nor morally culpable revenge (or vindictiveness), moral resentment registers the wrongdoing both emotionally and cognitively (as moral judgment of disapprobation). Resentment holds the wrongdoer accountable and responsible while at the same time placing a demand on their responsibility; in resenting the other, I place a moral lien on the other's standing as a moral agent until that time when self-repudiation and self-responsibility are sincerely and adequately expressed. We cannot forgive what we have not properly resented; forgiveness thus requires the forswearing of resentment. To be sure, the forswearing of resentment is not exhaustive in forgiveness's overcoming; it might also include overcoming other vindictive passions such as anger and sadness.[50]

In forgiveness, the person becomes released from the claim made upon her by past wrongdoings as well as liberated for a revitalized future and renewed potentiality for acting. Forgiveness recovers—and, in this sense, redeems—who the person can (still) *become* from (just) *being* what the person has done. As Arendt explains, "Forgiving does not aim at the destruction but on the contrary at the restoration of the persons involved and of the relationship between them."[51] Such recovery of the person neither covers over nor forgets the past, nor all too conveniently consigns the past to irrelevance. As transformed, the person gains a new lease on her own agency through a power that only the Other, as the person who forgives, can bestow. This recovery of the person from her (past) actions is never possible through the power of one's own agency but granted, as an act of generosity and respect, only by the person who has been wronged. The person who once wronged me becomes reborn in her potentiality for acting and appearance through a forgiveness that gives back to the person, without any lording sense of sovereignty, what the person took away from herself in her wrongdoing against me. In so doing, on the basis of remorse and responsibility on the part of the wrongdoer, as well as self-repudiation of her past self (or that aspect of her self responsible for wrongdoing), the person who forgives must release herself from the grasp of anger, vindictiveness, and revenge. The past remains what it was: irreversible. A past wrongdoing can neither be undone, nor forgotten, nor made as if it had never happened. Yet the person, or the "who," becomes restored to her proper standing as *not* fully coinciding with her action. What becomes recovered is not what you did but who you are as distinct from what you once did.

In an important sense, a past wrongdoing can be said to have attained its constitutive sense of irreversibility only once forgiveness has released its hold on the present and, as significantly, on the future. Irreversibility here afflicts not only the past wrongdoing with regard to the victim; it likewise afflicts the wrongdoer, who, until released and redeemed, cannot get past her own wrongdoing. Only through forgiveness is the past granted passage to the past, as opposed to remaining rigidly fixed in its claim on the present, and hence as a past that remains impossible to overcome in the present. The wrongdoer remains beholden to accountability and responsibility, yet, per Arendt's argument, reconciliation with the wrongdoer releases her wrongdoing from the corrosive impermanence of fixing the person to her past as well as the "automatism" of revenge with its cycles of retributive violence. It is only in terms of forgiveness that a distance between the past and the future can be forged in such a manner as to allow for a genuine remembrance of *and* responsibility for the past. Only when we find ourselves rehabilitated to each other as well as reconciled with ourselves can we truthfully come to terms with the significance and consequence of what *we* have been through. The encounter of forgiveness is therefore never without a pacification of narrative contestation, such that the act of forgiveness requires the *joint* authoring of a truthful narrative of what has been done, to whom, and by whom, which, as with any author function, essentially invokes the attestation of plurality.[52] The act of forgiveness requires narrative fulfillment, or completion, in which the "who" of the person can be revealed; forgiveness requires self-disclosure in acted narratives. What becomes restored is the truthfulness of the world, or the world *in* truth. Forgiveness lays the past (wrongdoing) to rest in giving it a proper, truthful place in narrative (and public) remembrance. Even if wrongdoing should ever have any place, or remain accommodated, in our world (so as to not be condoned), forgiveness forges a place in the world for wrongdoing under the sign of truthfulness and remembrance. That place in which a wrongdoing finds place in the world is no longer the place of its wrongdoing but the place forged together in forgiveness, hence in plurality, through which the life-world can be held in truth once more. Forgiveness is thus not only "place forging" for those who stand toward each other reconciled; it is just as significantly place forging for the wrongdoing itself—the event—in the space of truthful remembrance.[53] This restoration of the world to truth is directed as much toward the past as toward a future. Forgiveness is thus not directed exclusively toward the past, since in asking to be forgiven there emerges an implicit (or explicit) promise to not wrong or harm you in the way I once did wrong or harm you. Forgiveness and promising imply each other as *ecstatic events* structured along the horizons of past, present, and future.

In this temporalizing form, forgiveness is an ontological performative: it reactualizes the potentiality of acting qua potentiality. It is transformative of human existence qua capacity to begin again *as such*. As Arendt notes, the predicament of irreversibility is not just that what is done cannot be undone—namely, what is done remains unfinished (unchangeable yet unfinished) as long as consequences continue to reverberate; it is also that, if bound to irreversibility, our "capacity to act would be confined to a single deed from which we could never recover." Our *capacity* to act falls victim to its own effected single deed. This ontological accomplishment of forgiveness as the repotentialization of potentiality accounts for its *virtuality* as an act. It should not be conflated with its invisibility *as opposed to* its visibility, since, in Arendt's thinking, forgiveness remains a public, that is, self-disclosing, act. Nonetheless, forgiveness retains a virtual character, as expressive of the intangibility of the person at stake (or, in cases where forgiveness is refused or feigned, the person at risk) in its "miraculous" transformation (as both transformation of the person who forgives and transformation of the forgiven person). When regarded as ontologically *more* effective than merely involving reconciliation, rehabilitation, and recognition, the act of forgiveness would seem *to do nothing*. The act of forgiveness would seem curiously intangible to the point that forgiveness might seem to genuinely occur only silently, without any flash of theatricality, even if such silence bespeaks a performative self-disclosing act (for example, Jane Eyre's forgiveness of Rochester).[54] Forgiveness would seem to do nothing in the present since its accomplishment resides at once in the past as well as in the future, as renewing the capacity, or potentiality, of acting as such to the person, or, in other words, the person in her natality. In releasing us from the consequences of what we have done, forgiveness releases the *capacity to act* from its petrification in the amber of wrongdoing. This regeneration of the capacity to act is tantamount to granting again the standing of the person to be forgiven as a person. We forgive *the person* for what she did and for her sake; in so doing, we proclaim the person to be forgiven for what she did, not innocent for what she has done.[55] This repotentialization of the potentiality of becoming other than who I have been—that is, other than the person who committed a wrongdoing against you—speaks to the generosity of the person who forgives me, as giving back to me what I had forfeited from myself, and, in so doing, removing herself, as the one who forgives, from any position of authority over me, other than this granting recuperation of my own agency and standing as a person.

Unlike the durability of fabricated things and worldliness in the form of substantial permanence, the durability of human potentiality for acting does not enjoy any substantial permanence; its *endurance* comes instead from a continual renewal of potentiality through forgiveness. Potentiality must always become repotentialized through itself—that is, through an acting that reactualizes potentiality qua potentiality in the act of actualizing itself as forgiveness. Without forgiving, there would be no enduring potentiality of beginning anew *in* human acting, yet precisely because the potentiality of acting anew must repeatedly become repotentialized there is nothing eternal to the human potentiality for acting, including forgiveness, even though there remains something immortal in the aspiration of such acting. Without erasing or undoing the irreversibility of past actions per se, forgiveness liberates human agency from the *fatalism* of irreversibility, not irreversibility as such. Unlike a Christian conception of forgiveness, where forgiveness, as proposed by the orthodox theologian John Milbank, is conceived as "decreation," forgiveness for Arendt re-creates without ontologically undoing the fact that "it was." For Milbank, God's forgiveness is "miraculous" since it brings being into nothing, thus echoing in reverse the miracle of God's creation (bringing being out of nothing). As he writes, "With equal miraculousness [forgiveness] decreates, and causes what is not merely to be as if it were not, but literally not to be."[56] When Arendt, however, argues that forgiveness responds to the predicament of irreversibility, she does not mean to claim that forgiveness *undoes* the past in this metaphysical sense of "decreation." The past is neither literally or figuratively erased; rather, it is given place and meaning, laid to rest. This redemption of the life-world from fatalism by means of the potentiality of acting itself gives to forgiveness the power of sacralization in placing the redemption of the world within the reach of human acting in the world. Forgiveness does not break into the world from the outside but emerges gracefully and generously from within. In forgiveness, there is redemption without salvation.

This transformation of forgiveness critically assumes that *who* we are has *not* become entirely absorbed or eviscerated by what we have done. Forgiveness presupposes a salvageable form of recognition in which the person who wronged me remains *potentially* and meaningfully distinguishable as a who, as "curiously intangible" *within* her appearance, despite the collapse of her agency into her wrongdoing, as petrified in the amber of her acting. A difference, or "space," between who the person is and what she has done must survive her wrongdoing. Without this space remaining intact, there would be no room for forgiveness. This space between the who and the what, between the person and her act, must be recognizable by *both* the person standing to be forgiven, as a condition for self-repudiation and self-responsibility, and the person offering her forgiveness, as a condition for respect.[57] But likewise, the person who falls victim to wrongdoing must have also survived; a space within the victim between her agency, or "who," and what happened to her must retain a recognizable form for the victim herself. Such recognition (as recognition of the wrongdoer and self-recognition of the victim) presupposed in the encounter of forgiveness, such that both persons still stand as recognizable to each other as persons, hinges on a minimal distance between what she did (the wrongdoer) and who she remains—namely, that the wrongdoer *could have done otherwise*, and might have thought otherwise, or had the circumstances of her acting been otherwise. The person who forgives must still recognize herself as distinct from her desire for vengeance and moral resentment as well as the wrongdoer as distinct from her wrongdoing. Forgiveness reopens a space for the singular intangibility of the Other, or, in other words, for the Other to no longer have to appear as who she appears to have been in terms of what she did against me.

When such distance between the who and the what fails, when such a form of recognition has itself become an ontological victim to wrongdoing, we stand before the inhumanity of evil. Either as the absorption of the person into her wrongdoing or as the evisceration of the person from her wrongdoing, such wrongdoings are emphatically evil in an unforgivable sense. The unforgivable represents a scandal against plurality, in contrast to those trespasses of plurality called wrongdoings, which remain forgivable in principle. In the instance of diabolic evil—knowingly committing evil for the sake of evil (which admittedly Arendt seems to rule out)—the person has become entirely absorbed into her evil deed; it is as if the deed itself received the unfathomable depth, or intangibility, of the who, and yet, paradoxically, of a who who has abdicated her agency entirely to her evil doing. In the second instance, we find the meaning of Arendt's controversial and often misunderstood notion of the "banality of evil." Whereas those who knowingly commit evil are wicked, those who mindlessly enact evil are thoughtless. Wickedness and thoughtlessness share in the complete destruction of any distance within the person, as the "two-in-one" of thinking and judgment, that constitutes the dialogue of thought with oneself. For Arendt, what she identifies as unforgivable "radical evil," even as she misuses this Kantian term, "transcends the realm of human affairs and the potentialities of human power, both of which they radically destroy wherever they make their appearance."[58] Cases in which who the person is has not survived (in the Arendtian sense of "who") their own wrongdoing, as with diabolic evil or the banality of evil, are cases in which there is no possible form of recognition; there no longer remains a person *there to be forgiven.* Evil in this radical form is the place where there no longer stands a subject. The unforgivable would thus represent a catastrophic situation for plurality as such, since this touch of evil consists in the "radical destruction" of "potentialities of human power," including, most imperatively, the power of forgiveness itself. With the potentiality *for* forgiveness destroyed in a world perforated by holes of oblivion, the potentiality for the endurance of the world of plurality becomes directly threatened. Can there remain a meaningful common world in plurality in the aftermath of the radical destruction of the potentiality *to be human,* that is, in a world in which being-human has been renditioned into superfluousness? As

Arendt observes in *The Origins of Totalitarianism,* perpetrators of radical evil in the Nazi regime did not "care if they themselves are *alive or dead,* if they ever *lived* or never were *born.*"[59] A world in which the human, the humane, becomes ever more superfluous, whether in explicit or silent complicity with totalitarian means, or by the pursuit of totalitarian ends by other (including putatively "democratic") means, becomes an anti-world in which forgiveness itself becomes impossible. Such destruction of forgiveness remains, however, topological, circumscribed to spaces within the world, without engulfing the public stage of the world as such, as long as there remains spaces for distance, from which evil can be *thought,* without thereby becoming forgiven. When forgiveness becomes impossible, the love of the world remains, only on the condition that truth can (and must) still be spoken, and, especially, the truth about what is unforgivable. Understanding allows for reconciliation with the world marked by evil, allowing human beings to find peace in the world, even as evil itself remains without redemption.

Forgiveness, Redemption, and Trust

In a marked break with a Christian vision of forgiveness, forgiveness does not centrally involve love, but respect. We forgive essentially not from love for the Other but in respect for the Other as a person, as a "who," as discerned in her potentiality for acting and beginning anew, or, in other words, her *freedom.* In distinguishing respect from love as the axis upon which forgiveness turns, Arendt separates her conception of forgiveness from established Christian notions, for which forgiveness is intimately bound up with the promise of salvation, unbounded charity, and the equality of human beings under the doctrine of original sin, and, moreover, the original dispensation of forgiveness in God. This emphasis on respect, not love, further sharpens the ontological sense in which forgiveness restores that critical element of *distance,* or in-between, within the world without which plurality could not endure and remain potently creative. In contrast to love as "destroying the in-between which relates us to and separates us from others," respect is a form of recognition without "intimacy" and "closeness." As a renewal of the respect for the Other, forgiveness enables a recognition of *nonidentification* with the Other, thus preserving, in retrieving, the other's "curious intangibility" as a person. And yet insofar as respect is bound to self-disclosure, the standing of the Other in respect allows for a bond of "civic friendship" or "friendship without intimacy" with the Other as a person. Love regards the Other independently of what they do and have done, or, in other words, the qualities that give form and substance to their appearance in the world. Love is absolute, unconditional, and, in an Arendtian sense, bound to "unworldliness."[60] This displacement of forgiveness from love to respect does not discount the possible and meaningful significance of love, as either an emotional bond to an individual or benevolent fellow feeling, in the transaction of forgiveness. Arendt's point is rather to recover an original meaning of interpersonal forgiveness. According to a theological model, interpersonal forgiveness is anchored in God's forgiveness: we are to forgive each other because we are forgiven in God. Human forgiveness imitates God's forgiveness, given that we, in our finite condition, as created and dependent beings, "do not have enough being for this kind of forgiveness" in lacking the requisite "ontic weight."[61] Arendt's foreclosure of theological forgiveness recognizes this lack of ontic weight (for, indeed, humans do not have the power to *literally*—that is, ontologically—"decreate" the past) as giving forgiveness its meaning: because it is impossible for the past to be undone, it becomes all the more necessary to be done with the past, as something we must endure and survive in forgiveness, despite its irreversibility.[62]

With an emphasis on respect as the axis of recognition upon which forgiveness turns, Arendt broadens as well as deepens her account of forgiveness in its significance for the restoration and redemption of plurality in the life-world. As based on respect, forgiveness entails, as often recognized, not only the forswearing of vengeful intention and resentment but also a revision of my standing toward the Other, such that my judgment of the Other becomes revised in such a manner that I liberate who the person is from what she did. Forgiveness requires that the forgiving person adopt a position of "due distance" toward the other.[63] This due distance likewise appeals to the standpoint of the moral spectator, as an impersonal perspective capable of taking into account appropriate circumstances in terms of which the standing of the person to be forgiven becomes revised and restored.[64] More to Arendt's point, this distance of respect grants the Other the dignity of being *more* and potentially *other* than what she did. This renewed discernment of the Other as a "who" entails a restored acceptance of her potentiality to begin anew. To allow the Other to be "reborn" in forgiveness is to recognize, grant, and affirm the Other's natality. Forgiving the Other for her sake (and not for what she did) requires due recognition of the other person, as to who she might still become, in a way that a forgiven person is not able to recognize completely about herself and hence grant to herself. In standing to be forgiven, I must proclaim, "Here I am" and disclose myself truthfully in self-responsibility and self-repudiation, yet I am able to disclose myself as *here* only in the eyes of the Other who stands *there* to forgive me. Self-repudiation and self-responsibility on the part of the person standing to be forgiven mirror the respect granted by the forgiven person; the due distance of respect *accepts* once again the unpredictability of the forgiven person even as she promises to be otherwise than how she had been. On the part of the forgiving person, the forswearing of resentment and retribution allows the ontological vulnerability of acting *as such* to be afforded once again in the world not only for the sake of the person's restitution to the world but also for the sake of the life-world's restoration to itself. In respecting the Other, I recognize that the Other might have acted without truly knowing what she was doing, for which she now claims before me her own responsibility. In respecting the Other in her finite human condition, the forgiving person must not remain hard of heart or take up the position of the beautiful soul but must respect the condition of being human that dramatically plays itself out in the acted narratives of each individual human existence. The connection with promising is robust here: in asking for forgiveness, I promise to be other than the person who did what I did, and so promise to become the kind of person who would not have done what I did do. This element of respect and due distance restores a space of equality in which we can appear to each other and act in concert with others as *unequal* with each other. The uniqueness, or "curious intangibility," which the Other had forfeited in her wrongdoing is given back to her again and anew, such that she might once again respectfully stand as *unequal* to her appearance. Forgiveness is the allowance to receive the Other as once more both friend *and* stranger.

Through forgiveness, this restoration of the Other who stands forgiven as friend and stranger allows for the reaffordance of the predicament of the human condition with its characteristic unpredictability of action. This reaccepted unpredictability within the life-world becomes enacted in the unpredictability of forgiveness itself. Arendt speaks of the "miraculous" quality of forgiveness as consisting in its interruption of the automatic reaction of revenge and retribution as well as the hardening of retributive attitudes (i.e., endless moral resentment). As an expression of freedom, as forging a new beginning, the spontaneity of forgiveness is "always startling and occurring under the guise of the miraculous."[65] The supererogatory act of forgiving detaches itself from the conditions of its own provocation and priming. In this sense, forgiveness is not reactive but creatively responsive. As an act of freedom, or, better, an act *in* freedom, forgiveness is not reducible to or captured by its motivation and anticipated aims; it unfolds in the element of freedom and duly renders manifest this elemental human freedom in *transcending* its own determining conditions.

This supererogatory unfolding of forgiveness with its reconfiguring interruption of temporality is not without dramatic effect. While vengeance and resentment tend to paralyze and to petrify the temporality of the life-world, any strong tethering of forgiveness to promising and priming conditions, including the occasion of wrongdoing itself, renders forgiveness automatic and habitual; in both instances, history loses its dramatic character. Forgiveness, by contrast, "appears on the stage as an unexpected development in a story that was tending toward a predictable outcome."[66] As Arendt herself observes,

> Assuming that history is nothing but the miserable story of mankind's eternal ups and downs, the spectacle of sound and fury may perhaps be moving for a while; but the curtain must eventually descend. For in the long run, it becomes a farce. And even if the actors do not tire of it— for they are fools—the spectator does, for any single act will be enough for him if he can reasonably conclude from it that the never-ending play will be of eternal sameness.[67]

The "miraculous" quality of forgiveness does not issue from beyond the remit of forgiveness as human action, yet forgiveness remains intrinsically "unpredictable" and, in this sense, *impossible* until its advent, when, in the opacity of whether it is we who seize upon forgiveness or we who are seized by forgiveness, forgiveness becomes imminently possible *and* urgently actual in situ.[68] This virtual impossibility does not stand outside the capacity to forgive (its potentiality) but attests instead to that curious and insightful paradox inherent to Arendt's account that I can neither promise nor expect that I am to forgive, nor can I promise or expect never to forgive.[69] Whereas forgiveness is the unwinding of the unbindable, promising is the winding of the unbindable. Forgiveness thus stands in an orthogonal relationship to promising. I cannot promise that I will forgive you, but nonetheless I must stand able to forgive, or, as implied in Arendt's thinking, *available* to forgive without ever having promised myself in this manner to you. Were I to promise that I will or should forgive, the act of forgiveness would become beholden to the self-prescribing predictability of promising. On the other hand, were I to promise that I will or should never forgive you, I would remain hostage to the automatism of revenge and the purgatory of a past never laid to rest. Forgiveness "gives a new beginning to the one who is forgiven" and, at the same time, to the one who forgives, "and this is precisely where [a] new beginning seems most impossible."[70] Forgiveness is the anarchy of the impossible, resisting any normalization or institutionalization. As Arendt writes,

> Insofar as morality is more than the sum total of *mores*, of customs and standards of behavior solidified through tradition and valid on the ground of agreements . . . it has, at least politically, no more to support itself than the good will to counter the enormous risks of action by readiness to forgive and to be forgiven, to make promises and to keep them. These moral precepts are the only ones that are not applied to action from outside, from some supposedly higher faculty or from experiences outside action's own reach. They arise, on the contrary, directly out of the will to live together with others in the mode of acting and speaking.[71]

If forgiveness remains unpredictable, I must *trust in myself* that, despite this accepted unexpectedness, I could still stand able to forgive when finding myself in the encounter of forgiveness. *Self-trust* is the unspoken and tacit dimension to this apparent paradox that forgiveness must remain unpredictable even as I must remain in good standing with forgiveness—that is, available, without expecting or promising, to the possibility of forgiveness. For if, on the one hand, the miraculous quality and unpredictability of forgiveness prevent any promising of forgiveness in advance, I must trust in myself that, when called to the encounter of forgiveness, I am available to forgive, not just as a capacity of acting in my possession but also as a possibility to which I am available, and upon which I am able to act.

The "miraculous" advent of forgiveness should not be construed, moreover, as a surreptitious incarnation of violence, given its intrinsic disruption and, hence, anarchic manifestation, including the interruption of promising itself. Every act of forgiveness would have something revolutionary about it, and so, as with revolution, would appear to be imbued with violence. Yet if forgiveness expresses the purest pitch of prodigal human natality, how could forgiveness *be* violence and thus be caught up with "power," which are (for Arendt) "diametrically opposed"?[72] Forgiveness, however, does not circumvent violence through the incarnation of another violence; on the contrary, it circumvents violence by disarming violence of its need in respecting the Other in her need. Even as forgiveness cannot be promised, its marked unpredictability cannot be said to "conspire with the chaotic uncertainty of the future."[73] Instead, forgiveness issues a *benediction* of the restored person in the element of her freedom; the forgiven person's standing—her "curious intangibility"—and natality are granted once more, in the granting of respect. To forgive the Other is to allow and afford once again the "unpredictability" of the Other, even as the Other *must* meaningfully promise to be the kind of person who would not do again what she once did (self-repudiation and self-responsibility).

On the one hand, forgiveness restores through the due distance of respect "self-disclosing action," but, on the other, respect cannot obtain without self-disclosure, and self-disclosure cannot obtain without "self-revelatory action" (namely, the truthful character of her acts of remorse and the like).[74] This circularity between "respect" and "forgiveness"—no respect without forgiveness, no forgiveness without respect—reveals the unspoken and unexamined assumption in Arendt's account of forgiveness in its ontological significance for the life-world. This allowance and affordance of the unpredictability of the Other rests on a form of "perceptual faith," or *trust*, in the Other. In giving ourselves once again to the unpredictability of the Other, licensed, as it were, in the unpredictability of our own forgiveness, we must trust again in the Other as friend and stranger. Even when trust has been broken, in order for the Other to be forgiven, to be recognized as forgivable, I must still recognize the Other as *trustworthy* despite her wrongdoing against me. Despite the "collapse of her agency" into wrongdoing, I must nonetheless still find the Other trustworthy enough to accept as *sincere and truthful* her expression of remorse, declaration of self-repudiation, and shouldering of self-responsibility. In so trusting that the Other remains trustworthy, forgiveness reinstates the Other in trust. Arendt briefly signals—but never examines—this operative function of trust in the following manner: "Only through this constant mutual release from what they do can men remain free-agents, only by constant willingness to change their minds and start again can they be *trusted* with so great a power as that to begin something new."[75]

The rebirth (metanoia) in forgiveness critically hinges on trust: to receive the Other is to receive them in trust but also to entrust ourselves to them once more, as well as to entrust the world to the Other.[76] We allow ourselves and others to become unpredictable once more, and, in this sense, to trust and be trusted once again. Forgiveness grants again the very predicament of acting against which it reacts and redeems. Human frailty is once again accepted in welcoming back into the sphere of public appearance a person who, in her wrongdoing, had trespassed and placed at risk the plurality in which we had once found ourselves and to which we now return together, in civic friendship. There is, in this regard, no final act of redemption in forgiveness since, even as there is deliverance and release, the Other stands before me as the person who might wound me again, and whom I might have to forgive once more, without ever having thereby to forgive myself for having once already forgiven them.[77] As implied by Arendt's own suggestive statement that in forgiveness we make ourselves ready "to receive the new arrivals, newcomers to whom we prove what we no longer quite believe, that they are not strangers after all," to forgive the Other is to entrust myself once again to the Other as well as to trust the Other in order to forgive.[78] It is to place my hope again in the hands of the Other and the world of others—plurality—as if for first time, once more. As Arendt writes, "It is this faith in and hope for the world that found perhaps its most glorious and succinct expression in the few words with which the Gospel announced their 'glad tidings': 'A child has been born unto us.'"[79]

The Unforgivable and Forgiving without Forgiveness

The Sunflower tells the story of Simon Wiesenthal's fateful encounter with a dying young SS soldier during World War II. This SS soldier has been frightfully injured during combat on the Eastern Front. His entire body is wrapped in dressings mottled with yellowed stains of pus and ointment, giving his figure the appearance of a mummified corpse; save for the eyes, nose, and ears, his face is entirely bandaged. He lies alone in a room, known as the death room, awaiting his painful end in a technical high school in Lemberg (today L'viv, Ukraine), which, requisitioned by the occupying Germans, has been turned into a military hospital. Wiesenthal is a Jewish prisoner in the nearby Janowska concentration camp who one day becomes assigned to a work detail with orders to clean the detritus of the hospital under the watchful eyes of auxiliary Ukrainian guards. Before the war, this school building was once where Wiesenthal had studied architecture. If the function of architecture is to build a durable world for human habitation, in this transformed service as a German military hospital it now houses those (German) injured and dying in the midst of the world's destruction and ethical devastation. During a pause from his forced labor, a German nurse quite by chance commands him to follow her. Apprehensive, yet not daring to deny the request of his German oppressors, Wiesenthal follows her through once-familiar hallways and up once-familiar stairwells, which have now become disturbingly unfamiliar as passages in a military hospital in time of war in which he finds himself a victim of Nazi persecution. As he follows the nurse knowing not where or why, he recalls his student days amid the anti-semitism of Polish students and professors. The atmosphere and sporadic violence of prewar anti-semitism have now become, with the Nazi invasion, an unforgiving savage reality. The nurse takes him to one of the uppermost rooms in the building and, without saying a word, bids him enter. He is left alone, without any choice, without felt coercion, to approach in semidarkness the outlined figure of a wounded soldier in bed. It is the young SS soldier. He identifies himself as Karl and asks Wiesenthal to come closer, to hear his story, and, in this telling, the soldier seeks forgiveness for the unspeakable things he has done.

Strange Encounter

This encounter between Wiesenthal (never asked for his name) and Karl (who volunteers only his first name) is set against the horizon of God's retreat from the world. Prior to this encounter, as the unforeseen consequence of his assignment to a work detail outside the confines of the camp, Wiesenthal recounts having once heard about an old woman from the Ghetto who, when asked about the latest news, looked up to heaven and implored God to return. As Wiesenthal recalls, he was not shocked by this proclamation of God's absence; "she had simply stated what I had long felt to be true." As he reflects, "It is impossible to believe anything in a world that has ceased to regard man as man, which repeatedly 'proves' that one is no longer a man."[1] In a world devoid of recognition of human beings among human beings, can one still trust in the meaningfulness of forgiveness? Is forgiveness still to be encountered? On his way to the hospital, Wiesenthal marches past the graves of German soldiers, each freshly adorned with a sunflower. These sunflowers, as he remarks, connect the living with the dead. Each flower stands as a bright symbol of the fidelity of the living toward the dead in mourning. For these soldiers, death is not absolute abandonment, for they rest in peace in the entrustment of remembrance. He wonders whether when he dies—a death he knows to be inevitable—there will be a sunflower for him, as well as for those innumerable other victims of Nazi violence, who must die anonymously "buried in a mass grave," made to be superfluous (as Arendt characterized brute Nazi evil), a thing (*ein Stück*—in the Nazi jargon) to be thrown away.[2]

Wiesenthal finds himself with Karl at his bedside in a "strange encounter" with the unforgivable; it is an encounter suffused with a sense of unreality and the uncanny (*unheimlich*). In German, the term *unheimlich* would seem to be the opposite of *heimlich* and draw its meaning as the contrary or negation of what is at home, domestic, or native. But as Freud remarks, this opposition is only apparent, for "among its different meanings the word *heimlich* exhibits one that is identical with its opposite, *unheimlich*. What is *heimlich* thus comes to be *unheimlich*."[3] What is *unheimlich* issues as the strange within the familiar; the familiar retreats in front of the strange, only to discover itself as strangely familiar. Hence the ambivalence of fascination and disgust, proximity and distance, attraction and repulsion that conglomerate in repetition and doubling: mechanical dolls, doppelgängers, and ghosts. Karl's face is bandaged, covering over his disfigurement and thus making it all the more symbolically poignant. Although his first name is known to Wiesenthal, his face remains unseen. Whereas Wiesenthal's face can be addressed, Karl speaks as a corpselike figure, bespeaking the death of an ethical person who has not survived his own perpetrated acts of evil. Even as his face and body remain covered, a barely audible appeal for forgiveness begins to confess its evil. What proves "unreal" and "uncanny" about this encounter gathers about this speaking corpse, symbolic of the ethically undead, who addresses a living representative of those whom he has wronged—murdered—in evil. Karl is an ethical zombie: despite the visible contours of a human figure, there is nothing of what "it is like to be" Karl in any ethically salient sense that might relate him to Wiesenthal or any other human being not corrupted by the systematic Nazi destruction of ethical selfhood. Karl's standing as an ethical person is dead, even as his body tenuously clings to the bare (and fading) functioning of life. He speaks as the ghost of an ethical being who once lived, who perished through his own committed evil. What remains is a mortal figure devoid of any moral life, thus calling into question the redemption of his human condition upon the scene of forgiveness, its possibilities and limits.

After this "strange encounter," when Wiesenthal returns to the camp later that evening, and long thereafter during his internment until the end of the war and beyond, once the war is over, he remains obsessed by this ghostly encounter and spectral request for forgiveness. In this obsession, there is both an appeal for and an address of forgiveness. During his extended imprisonment in the camp, Wiesenthal repeatedly dreams of this strange meeting with Karl. After the war, he feels compelled to write his story and ask others to address the impossible question of forgiveness that confronted him that fateful day and that continues to agitate within him without rest. Karl appealed for forgiveness not only for his committed evils, for what he has done, but also in order to be released from an ethically unsalvageable life so that he might die in peace, redeemed. This encounter with forgiveness is an encounter with a perpetrator of evils who seeks to have his person released from the unbearable weight of his crimes; and yet such is the gravity of his evils that nothing of the ethical person remains recognizable, and hence can at all become renewed to the living. His committed evils have completely defaced his ethical being, foreclosing any possibility of regenerative rebirth in forgiveness. Even though forgiveness has been foreclosed to life, there becomes traced upon the horizon of an afterlife a fleeting silhouette of forgiveness. In the passage to death, we still stand to be forgiven, or not to be forgiven. In appealing to Wiesenthal, Karl seeks expiation and atonement before a witness to his confessing; his is not the challenge of telling to live but of telling to die, to facilitate a peaceful release from a life in which the ethical person has not survived their own misdeeds. To be forgiven is here to be entrusted to a benevolent remembrance that recognizes the irrevocable ethical death of the person in life while restoring the ethical standing of that person in death. In seeking to be released from his committed evils through forgiveness, Karl yearns to return home to the life-world in the fellow feeling of remembrance. It is Wiesenthal whom he calls as his witness, to stand there at his side as his brother's keeper in the hour of his death, so that he might humanely remain once more among the memory of the living, even as he remains no more. Although it is impossible for him to return to life, ethically or physically, it is possible for him to return ethically to the living, on condition, however, that the living remain not unforgiving to his truthful confrontation with himself and the world in the face of his own death. Death is not the ultimate horizon: when life is barred from receiving a final chance, a second chance at life even when life can be no more, there is still time enough for one last human breath in asking for forgiveness, as the last aspiration for making the passage from the stage of the world to "nowhere" at least breathable—that is, bearable in the hope of forgiveness.

This encounter between Karl and Wiesenthal is charged with an ambivalence that plays itself out both physically and narratively. At his bedside, Wiesenthal maintains a guarded attitude toward any physical contact with Karl. He remains understandably hesitant to take hold of Karl's hand. Likewise, while listening to Karl's confession, Wiesenthal's conscience is frequently interrupted by arresting doubts and hesitations; he is often taken by the urge to stop listening and leave the room. But much as Karl takes Wiesenthal's hand without resistance, his words take hold of Wiesenthal's conscience, even as Wiesenthal constantly remains uneasy as witness and confessor. Although the touch of Karl's hand and penitent words are cause of "physical pain" and moral distress, *something* in Wiesenthal has been obscurely addressed, *touched*. This contact between Karl and Wiesenthal remains volatile throughout. During their encounter, both Karl and Wiesenthal in fact momentarily lose contact with each other and the encounter in which they each find themselves. At a certain moment while listening, Wiesenthal feels that Karl is merely talking to himself and not really addressing him, thus raising the suspicion that Karl's repentance and telling might be nothing more than unilateral self-forgiveness; he needs an imaginary audience, or prop, any given Jew, in order to feel himself atoned for his guilty conscience (hence his lack of interest in knowing Wiesenthal's name?). There is an equally telling moment when it is, by contrast, Wiesenthal who forgets whom he is facing: he hears the buzzing of a bluebottle hovering around Karl's head; he waves it away, a gesture for which Karl duly thanks him.[4] Coming back to himself in his situation, Wiesenthal observes, "And for the first time I realized that I, a defenseless subhuman, had contrived to lighten the lot of an equally defenseless superman, without thinking, simply as a matter of course."[5]

After narrating in detail his participation in a particularly horrific killing of Jews in a village, Karl recounts how he was thereafter haunted by what he had done and seen done. During subsequent combat, he is hit by a Soviet shell burst and grievously wounded at the very moment that a traumatic memory of his earlier killing returned to him.[6] He, too, is hauntingly addressed by what he has done to others, by the unforgivable. This coincidence of his physical wounding and repetition of his ethical wounding symbolizes the destruction of his ethical being, not only for others but also for himself. Once his telling is complete, Karl asks for forgiveness from Wiesenthal, even though he admits that "what I have told you is terrible," that, in other words, he asks for the impossible; he must ask for forgiveness for this impossible asking of forgiveness, without which, however, it would be impossible for him to die in peace. Karl's hands are folded, as if in prayer, waiting. For Wiesenthal, "there seemed to rest a sunflower" between them. Nothing stirs; "at last I made up my mind and without a word I left the room."[7]

By his own account, Wiesenthal accepts the sincerity of Karl's repentance and remorse. Nonetheless, his silence bespeaks a certain refusal to forgive, not a resounding or self-righteous no but more akin to a preferring not to. Even as this answer would seem to settle the question of forgiveness by taking leave of Karl in silence, the question of forgiveness remains unresolved, repositioned within a restless, obsessing silence without end. As Wiesenthal remarks, the critical question that troubled him was not the question posed to him by Karl per se but the surviving disquiet in the wake of his silent departure. To encounter the question of forgiveness in this exacting form is to endure the question of forgiveness beyond, and despite, its apparent answer.

Availability to Forgiveness

Upon his return to the camp, Wiesenthal tells of his strange encounter to two of his companions: Josek, a devout Jew whose faith has not been broken in the camp, and Arthur, a pragmatic nonbeliever. Josek seeks to assuage Wiesenthal of his disquiet by telling him that he was right not to forgive the SS solider. As he explains, "You would have no right to do this in the name of people who had not authorized you to do so." How can one forgive evils of which one is not directly the victim? How can one forgive in the name of others? Even if this argument rationalizes

Wiesenthal's silence, it does not leaven Wiesenthal's disquiet that he was unforgiving toward Karl's dying appeal. Arthur, on the other hand, tells Wiesenthal that it was good that he did not forgive the SS soldier, for if he had, "you would have never forgiven yourself all your life."[8] Arthur observes, somewhat cynically, that the SS solider should have "sent for a priest from his own church," with whom he might have "soon come to an agreement," rather than seeking out Wiesenthal. In a relativist key, Arthur remarks that "every religion has its own ethics, its own answers." One forgives one's own, not strangers. Whatever the merits of these various arguments, these well-meaning and reasonable reactions from his two friends do nothing to alleviate the burden of Wiesenthal's silence. After listening to his two friends, he remains none the wiser. As he remarks, "I thought I was still in the death chamber of the German hospital . . . And suddenly I was assailed by a doubt as to the reality of all this. Had I actually been in the Dean's room that day? It all seemed to me as doubtful and unreal as our whole existence in those days . . . it was too illogical, like the whole of our existence."[9] The next day, Wiesenthal is part of another contingent of prisoners who must return to the hospital. The nurse finds him again, orders him to follow her, and then informs him that the SS soldier died during the night. She offers him the soldier's remaining possessions. Wiesenthal refuses to accept.

Two years later, with his friends Arthur and Josek now dead, Wiesenthal, after a series of displacements to other camps owing to advancing Soviet troops, finds himself at Mauthausen concentration camp. There he befriends a young Polish Catholic novitiate named Bolek, to whom he confides his enduring disquiet after his strange encounter with Karl. Bolek argues, as did Josek, that you can forgive only a wrong that has been done against you, but he recognizes the complication that the victims of Karl's evils are dead. The dead cannot be asked for forgiveness; the living cannot stand in their place. Who dares to speak, let alone forgive, for the drowned? In such instances, the question of forgiveness would seem to weigh with even more necessity, yet remains ever more impossible. Karl's demonstration of repentance, remorse, and seeking of forgiveness might, for some, be understood as addressable only to God, who eternally stands ready to hear the appeals of forgiveness in the name of the dead, of those no longer there to forgive, and where no human being might rightfully stand in their place. But here, in this hour, God is passed over in silence. And even if there were a God, it is *we* who would have to ask forgiveness for having spoiled in such an unredeemable and shameless fashion the order of divine creation and the world entrusted to us. Bolek's reflections remain rooted to the human condition in its finitude. As Bolek remarks, Karl's appeal for forgiveness represents the final request of a dying person in search of expiation and atonement for his crimes. If Karl was genuinely repentant and remorseful in the hour of his death (which Wiesenthal confirms), then, in Bolek's view, "he deserved the mercy of forgiveness."[10] The approach of death compels a truthfulness toward life in knowing that life is soon to be no more; once there is no longer any allowance, ethical or otherwise, for life to deserve another chance or receive a novel future, we feel impelled to a truthful accounting of ourselves before others and ourselves, as a final act of self-disclosure, without which we could not pass from the stage of appearance in peace. To remain unforgiving toward such truthfulness and self-attestation in the hour of death, as with Karl's confession, would seem to refuse any redeeming recognition of human life in its existential singularity. An ethically defaced existence cannot be undone. The defunct ethical person cannot be salvaged from the gravity of her evils, and yet her standing can be restored through a forgiveness that would allow those who are ethically dead in life to rest peacefully in the mourning of others. This passage to death in forgiveness, as forgiven by the living, allows the forgiven to find peace with themselves and the world; this forgiveness renders the passage of death something properly human, giving mortal life its proper due. Forgiveness here is not rebirth or regeneration in living once again but release to death in the generation of an afterlife for the living. Karl fears the death that awaits him on account of fearing the life he had chosen for himself. Without being unable to undo the life he has lived from the things he has done, he nonetheless seeks to be redeemed in remembrance as *not* being equal to the evils that he is unable not to be or overcome in life.

The ambiguity of whether Karl should or should not have been forgiven remains unresolved in Wiesenthal's mind. Arguments speak against forgiveness. Arguments speak in favor of forgiveness. The disquiet of Wiesenthal's silence in the encounter of forgiveness nonetheless endures. Karl's three interlocutors speak to him very much in the vein of Job's three friends, but unlike in the biblical narrative, it is not faith in God but the faith in "forgiveness"—*its availability*—that stands under the ordeal of evil. Wiesenthal is put to the test in his encounter with the affliction of forgiveness, the restlessness of its appeal. And much as the biblical Job, Wiesenthal's well-meaning friends deliver different forms of "theodicy," leaving him none the wiser. As Wiesenthal observes, he could not put the question of forgiveness behind him even though it was answered in his silence. This enduring question of forgiveness survives its own answer, not only Wiesenthal's but any and all answers, even those of future generations. The question of forgiveness remains an open wound.[11] Bolek suggests to Wiesenthal—whose first name, Simon, means in Hebrew "the one who has heard" (Genesis 29:33)—that even though he did not grant

Karl's final request, *having listened at all* to Karl's confession nonetheless allowed him to die in peace.[12] Without displacing or contradicting Wiesenthal's parting silence in response to Karl's appeal for forgiveness, listening to Karl rendered Wiesenthal *available* for the encounter of forgiveness. The dawn of listening inaugurates a space for speech and silence, while remaining itself, in its inception, neither an act of speech nor form of silence; although one listens silently, one never listens in silence, and although one does not speak when listening, listening always speaks to itself in hearing itself (or another). In first giving oneself to the Other without already fore-giving anything, listening does not condescend to the Other. Wiesenthal does not listen from a posture of magnanimity or a position of sovereignty but stands at his bedside, not unforgiving toward the possibility of forgiveness without declaring in advance either yes or no to forgiveness. This openness to the encounter of forgiveness does not become canceled or sublimated (confirmed or denied) once forgiveness has been decided upon; even as Wiesenthal in the end "made up his mind" and departed from the scene of forgiveness in silence, his availability to forgiveness endured—to wit, survived as the impossibility of ever departing from the encounter with Karl in the question of forgiveness. For Bolek, this availability in listening gives peace to Karl's expiration, even as he has not been forgiven. Wiesenthal's narrative bears witness to Karl's death, planting the sunflower of remembrance upon the grave of Karl's own avowal, which now becomes Wiesenthal's telling as well.[13]

Still obsessed with his encounter with Karl, Wiesenthal decides after the war to locate Karl's mother in the ruins of Stuttgart. Wiesenthal happened to remember her name and address, which he had gleaned when he had refused to accept Karl's possessions from the nurse. He is welcomed into Karl's home by his mother. For the first time, Wiesenthal sees Karl's face in a portrait photograph. When asked for what occasioned his visit, Wiesenthal informs her that he once knew her son and came here to convey his greetings. Her grief at his death is visible upon the mother's face as she evokes the memory of her "good son." While recounting to Wiesenthal the narrative of her son's life (how he joined the Hitler Youth, the opposition from his now-deceased father), she asks if he is German. Wiesenthal answers that he is Jewish. Wiesenthal is touched by the mother's grief at the death of her son, as well as her mournful attitude toward the "dreadful things," in her words, that were committed against the Jews. She survives amid the ruins of the world trusting that her son remained innocent. Wiesenthal does not contradict her image, even though he knows the truth, as confessed to him by Karl. Truth must make room for a kindly forgiveness that allows the repentant dead to rest in peace. He takes leave of Karl's mother in silence, thus granting her a "last surviving consolation—faith in the goodness of her son."[14] This silence allows the silence with which he departed the disfigured Karl to stand, even as this silence before his mother's image of her good son grants Karl a homecoming, to rest in peace in his mother's mourning embrace of her good son. Karl is not forgiven, yet Wiesenthal is not unforgiving toward Karl in forgiving his mother's beholding of her dead son in benevolent remembrance. Wiesenthal's silence does not forgive Karl's mother for her naïveté (which would be condescending) nor does he speak the truth of her son in order to dismantle her cherished image (which would be unforgiving vengeance). His forgiving understanding toward Karl's mother expresses his not unforgiving attitude toward Karl's narrative, even as nothing has been forgiven. Wiesenthal returns the redeemed ghost home, as if the photograph on the mantelpiece only now becomes *visible* to the world of the living through the graciousness of Wiesenthal's second—and not a seconded—silence.

"Your problem is not a problem for me"

Wiesenthal concludes his story by addressing his readers with his enduring disquiet on the question of forgiveness: "What would you have done?" This address speaks to the present as well as the future in making of Wiesenthal's strange encounter a question toward which we, as an open community of readers, cannot be indifferent and unconcerned. After the war, Wiesenthal circulated his narrative to individuals with an appeal to respond. In its published form, *The Sunflower* exemplifies how the survival of the question of forgiveness engages a plurality of spectators in the encounter of forgiveness. Once a question of forgiveness becomes opened in the aftermath of injury, answers and responses become positioned *within* the encounter in question but do not thereby close or settle the question, once and for all. There are always ghosts and remainders of forgiveness that return after forgiveness has been pronounced or denounced. The included responses from "fifty-three distinguished men and women" ranges over different views: some endorse Wiesenthal's silence at Karl's appeal with arguments already anticipated in his narrative; others invoke their own spiritual traditions and propose that only God is there to forgive; others confess their own uneasiness with the question thrust upon them.[15]

Within this spectrum, one response stands apart. A Jewish survivor like Wiesenthal himself, Jean Améry begins his remarks by announcing that "you will inevitably be disappointed by my comments."[16] The cause of this disappointment does not stem from any answer contrary to Wiesenthal's silence or any judgment regarding the deserving or undeserving nature of Karl's asking of forgiveness. Instead, as Améry declares, "Your problem is not a problem for me." As he continues, "As I see it, the issue of forgiving or not-forgiving in such a case has only two aspects: a psychological one and a political one." Whereas in the first case, forgiveness is "nothing more than a question of temperament" and hence capricious and therapeutically self-serving, in the second case it proves to be "quite irrelevant." Améry observes that he could accept "the whole question of forgiveness" only in political terms; yet it is precisely as a political issue that forgiveness is deemed irrelevant, making no difference either way.[17] This brusque rejection of the question of forgiveness is not meant to diminish, ignore, or forget what Améry acknowledges as "the problematic base of your story"—namely, the ethical atrocities committed by the Nazis. Nevertheless, as he exclaims, "Politically, I don't want to hear anything of forgiveness!"[18]

There is a tactless and provocative intent to Améry's brusque retort to Wiesenthal's question, even as he stresses that his refusal to grant any standing to the question of forgiveness, not only in this (Wiesenthal's) specific instance but also, as evident from the categorical tone of this declaration, to the question of forgiveness as such (with regard to Nazi crimes), should not be taken as discounting "the problematic basis" of forgiveness. The sharpness of Améry's tone is meant to amplify "the problematic basis" of Wiesenthal's story, for which, however, the question of forgiveness is deemed an unfitting response and measure. Améry's refusal *to hear anything of forgiveness* strikes a chord of existential *ressentiment*, which should not be identified with either a psychological *or* political attitude but, on the contrary, surpasses *both*. As Améry remarks in his essay "Ressentiments," *ressentiments* are "the existential dominant" of individuals like himself, survivors of Nazi violence whose enduring disquiet and discomfort during the years after the war, "in this peaceful, lovely land, inhabited by hardworking, efficient, and modern people," have made it easy for those who live and rest in peace to begrudge his reactive spleen.[19] Admittedly, to remain unforgiving and resentful as a principle of survival, as expressed with his *refoulement* of Wiesenthal's question of forgiveness, of there being any question of forgiveness, could be considered tactless. But, as Améry observes, "It may be that many of us victims have lost the feeling for tact altogether."[20]

The tactlessness of refusing to hear anything of forgiveness, not even *availing* oneself to the address, the appeal, and the approach of the Other in forgiveness—to categorically refuse any encounter with the question of forgiveness—issues from a devastation of any freedom to choose either to forgive or not forgive. This *refoulement* of forgiveness is not the expression of a choice, decision, or attitude but testifies instead to an abjection of human condition, or better: an *inhuman condition* within which forgiveness itself becomes, as either possible or impossible, destitute. This destitution of the availability of forgiveness, let alone its possibility or impossibility, its entertainment as either, issues directly from the condition, in Améry's case (as with so many countless and often nameless others), of having been tortured. As Robert Antelme, another victim of Nazism, asserts, torture irrevocably devastates the sense of belonging to the human species. The human condition has been *touched* in a manner in which it should never be touched, violated in an unforgiving desecration that never ends. For Améry, this human, all-too-human power of abjecting existence from the human condition resides in the power of transforming a human being like himself into an insect (*Wanze*) and a ghost, to the degree that the person who has been tortured remains tortured. What remains of a tortured life is to be neither alive nor dead, but to be undead—not dead, not living—suspended in a disjointed temporality, contorted corporeality, fragmented speech, abject loneliness and a world in which one is fundamentally no longer *at home*. Even the term "loneliness" falls short and fails to express the abjection of neither being in the world, being-in oneself, or being-with others.

Unforgiving

What is it to be unforgiving? Two distinct forms of being unforgiving are often identified: an undue hardening of moral resentment that transforms a justified retributive attitude into its opposite, the "wild beast" of unyielding resentment without end or cause,[21] and a pathological *ressentiment* of revenge and retribution for harms done, whether real or imagined. For the tradition of moral resentment stemming from the writings of Butler and Adam Smith (with contemporary voices in Strawson, Griswold, and others), moral resentment registers moral injury and harm in adopting a retributive attitude toward the offender.[22] Moral resentment opens the horizon for forgiveness such that, in turn, failure to forswear moral resentment in cases where the offender has requested forgiveness under warranting conditions transforms an initially justified moral resentment into an unjustified—in its most extreme and unbending case—pathological *ressentiment*. Resentment is a retributive passion, distinct from though not opposed to anger; it is deliberative, not impulsive. In resenting of an offender's wrongdoing, her character and action are judged blameworthy; resentment is part and parcel of the victim's exercise of her own responsibility. A victim failing to resent an offender would in turn become morally blameworthy. Following Adam Smith, resentment attests on the part of the victim to a respect for the moral norms of her community as well as to her own self-esteem as a moral agent. Resentment combines the third-party perspective of the impartial spectator *and* the first-person perspective of an impacted victim. Resenting an offender performs a double temporalization of her (the offender's) subjectivity in terms of which the victim comes to affect herself. The constitutional relationship between act and self (past wrongdoing and past self) becomes inverted; consequently, a temporal lien is placed on the existence of the offender such that her subjectivity, centered on her present self, becomes barred from temporal renewal—her subjectivity becomes suspended in the amber of her past wrongdoing, thus foreclosing her temporal existence from any genuine future. Within this constitutional schema, the victim's resentment constitutes the offender by *inverting* the relationship between her (constituted) past wrongdoing and her (constituting) past self. This inversion retrospectively suppresses, as it were, the constitutional sovereignty of the offender's self over her own actions by interjecting the sovereignty of the victim's (resentful) agency. Specifically, in resenting the offender for her wrongdoing, her past self comes to be exhausted through her past wrongdoing; her past self is suspended in the amber of her action. The offender's past wrongdoing is worn as a scarlet letter that marks, and so objectifies, her entire self in the eyes of the victim, and as further reflected in the eyes of the moral community. Indeed, the victim may seek to make public her resentment of the offender and reveal to others the corrosion of the offender's self by the acid of her wrongdoing. This is the sense in which a resentful gaze holds the offender's wrongdoing against her; indeed, holds it exhaustively and untiringly *as her.*[23]

An example of this dynamic of resentment can be found in Charlotte Brontë's *Jane Eyre*. The orphan Jane Eyre is resented by her aunt, Mrs. Reed, who begrudgingly promised her dying husband (Jane's uncle) to adopt Jane as a child. However, Mrs. Reed immensely favors her own children and, blindly and repeatedly, unfairly faults Jane for various misdeeds and wrongdoings. On one particular occasion, Jane is wrongly accused of a transgression against Mrs. Reed's spoiled son; Jane is locked up in an attic, pleads forgiveness from her aunt, is refused, and is eventually packed off to a dour boarding school. When the headmaster appears to take away his new charge, Mrs. Reed proclaims to Mr. Brocklehurst in the presence of Jane that she, Jane, is a liar and is not to be trusted—that her subjectivity is irredeemably defined by past wrongdoings. This public scene of constituting the young Jane through the resentful eye of her aunt is repeated at the boarding school when the headmaster announces the same about Jane in front of the students. The point illustrated here is how Mrs. Reed's resentful gaze has suspended Jane's subjectivity in time, damned her to the perpetual repetition of her past wrongdoings. In the character of Mrs. Reed, Brontë crystallizes how resentment exercises a temporal lien on the offender's subjectivity that forecloses, in the eyes of the moral community, the victim, and most important of all, the offender herself, the promise of becoming different and other in the future. Jane Eyre will always be a liar, and, indeed, Jane comes to doubt herself in light of her aunt's self-proliferating resentment.

This lien of past wrongdoings (imaginary or otherwise, as the case may be) placed on the offender in resentment is meant to secure *in retrospect* a respect and recognition that the offender did not offer in the past to the extent that she committed a wrongdoing against the victim. The lien of resentment forecloses time itself for the offender in order to secure an obligation due but not given to the victim in the past. Yet in foreclosing a genuine future in which she could be different from how she has been fossilized in her past, resentment seeks recognition and accountability in the future while at the same time foreclosing that future for the offender by condemning her to a perpetual past. In the eyes of Mrs. Reed, Jane Eyre will always be a liar and fail to respect her. In its most viral form, resentment places a lien on the offender precisely in order to prevent forgiveness; resentment is counterpurposive to its own intention. The point is worth stressing. Resentment places a lien on the offender in order to obtain the respect that the victim should have given. Yet given that the offender *did* commit a wrong, and thus failed in her obligation toward the victim to respect her, the victim now holds the offender in disdain and resentment. Resentment can, in this regard, run itself to infinity—since the lien of resentment is meant to secure recognition that paradoxically could have been given only in the past, it tends to fester without end, running in circles after itself, and chasing its own tail, only to devolve into self-pity. To pity oneself is for one's own resentment to make an end run against itself.

What Brontë perspicuously examines in *Jane Eyre* is how resentment appears to be at cross-purposes with itself: resentment is a demand for respect and recognition that resentment itself bars the offender from offering in damning her to a past abjection. To draw this contradictory and revelatory paradox into fuller clarity: resentment can be seen as oscillating between two opposing poles that divide the resentful self from within, and with contradictory impulses. The challenge of forswearing resentment in the name of forgiveness resides in struggling against the inertia and self-affection of one's own resentment. The retributive character of resentment resides in this affirmation of the victim's alterity as sovereign over the victim's subjectivity at the expense of her own alterity, insofar as the victim has placed a lien on the offender's existence in light of her wrongdoing. The inherent proclivity of resentment consists in ensnaring the victim within her own resentment so as to revictimize the victim from within, and by her own means.

In contrast to moral resentment, *ressentiment* represents an unjustified response from the beginning to *imagined* harms, or a disproportionate and immoderate response to a harm not befitting the animus of *ressentiment*. In its most prodigal expression, *ressentiment* transfigures itself into *rage*.[24] Rage against the world's injustice and injury, whether real or imagined, often takes one of two forms (or both, as with Achilles) as a project of revenge and *ressentiment*: inward contraction and isolation from the world or outward expansion against and devouring of the world.[25] Unlike other, kindred emotions such as anger, rage is an explosive condition *in* which the enraging person finds themself transformed; it is not an emotion that we possess, direct, and master but one that, much like an obsession, consumes and dispossesses us.[26] In *Notes from Underground*, the Underground Man opens his narrative with a confession of his *ressentiment*. Widely considered as the epitome of pathological *ressentiment*, he speaks against the world from underground. As he declares, "There, in its loathsome, stinking underground, our offended, beaten-down, and derided mouse at once immerses itself in cold, venomous, and above all, everlasting spite." This spiteful *ressentiment* takes the form of self-consumption to the point of despair and delirium, in blurring any sense of the real and imaginary. *Ressentiment* festers as a wound—wounded pride, real or imaginary wounds—without end; as an open and incurable wound that sustains itself in its own wounding. It is a vindictive and immoderate passion; forswears the forswearing of resentment in forgiveness, and thus transforms any justifiable moral resentment into unjustifiable pathological *ressentiment*. His wound, or illness, *is* his unbearable *ressentiment* in despairing for himself and despising of others. This condition of purgatorial *ressentiment* becomes directed against the world as envy toward Others (his friends, his servant) and culminates in blasphemy against forgiveness itself.

The encounter between the Underground Man and Liza in his apartment stages in dramatic form a Christian ideal of forgiveness as redemptive sacrifice for the Other. Beginning with their fateful and violent encounter in the brothel, the unfolding narrative of the Underground Man's spurned redemption, despite the self-sacrificing forgiveness extended to him, culminates with Liza's departure from his apartment. Her refusal to accept his five rubles, which she unceremoniously leaves on the table as she takes her leave, symbolizes her refusal to debase the act of forgiveness to a logic of economic exchange and reciprocity. Forgiveness stands beyond any form of debt, obligation, or universal moral imperative. This height of forgiveness shines in the humility of offering forgiveness without affirmation of sovereignty or lording magnanimity.[27] Even as such humility incarnates the grace of forgiveness, it likewise exposes the precariousness of forgiveness. In her humility, Liza does not stand or lord over the Underground Man. Her forgiveness is not predicated on the pronouncement of his guilt. The grace of such a disarming encounter with the Underground Man puts his arrogant pride to shame, yet not in the face of a sovereign gaze standing in judgment. In his shame before Liza's humility, he comes face-to-face with himself in his condition of despair and fault. Feeling shame and powerlessness before his own despair, he becomes ashamed of his own shame. Unable to bear standing, however, he is ashamed before himself in the presence of the Good, and his shame sublimates itself into a rebounding rage against the Good, taking aim with a vengeance. This rebounding of shame into rage allows for his own prideful self-affirmation over Liza's humility in the sharpened form of his resentful refusal of her forgiveness. Envious of the Good that he remains unable to accept, he comes to hate the source of his own shame without recognizing that this source resides within himself. Whereas Liza adopts a posture of humility to disarm the logic of power and exchange from the scene of forgiveness (in renouncing any sovereignty in her forgiveness— i.e., not standing in judgment), the Underground Man can perceive only with squinting eyes this abdication of power as establishing an imbalance of power—namely, between the power of the Other (Liza) who stands in judgment (and claims herself to stand in innocence) and the powerlessness of the one at fault, who stands judged. The *height* of Liza's forgiveness—the glory of her saintly humility—becomes misperceived as the *height of power* over the depth of his despair in fault, which he in turn misconstrues as powerlessness in need of power. In his blindness toward the height of forgiveness, as a scene other than the scene of judgment, sovereignty, and the law, the Underground Man seeks to redress this (perceived) defamation of forgiveness through its refusal. It is not that the Underground Man cannot be forgiven; it is that even when forgiven for the unforgivable, he does not want *to be forgiven*, thus compounding the unforgivable for which he stands. In his attempt to humiliate Liza in her forgiveness, the Underground Man commits the truly unforgivable: blasphemy against forgiveness itself. Unforgivable is not evil on its own but hatred against the forgiveness of evils. The precariousness of forgiveness resides in this exposure to its refusal. Humility must endure the humiliation of this blasphemy and revolt. There is no forgiveness without exposure to the refusal of forgiveness; there is no forgiveness without forgiveness for the refusal of forgiveness itself. When Liza quietly leaves the five rubles on the table, her dignified silence proclaims that her forgiveness will not be undone by the attempted humiliation of his blasphemy (had she accepted the rubles). She endures the purity of forgiveness in the face of the unforgivable—namely, blasphemy against the grace of forgiveness itself.

In Kleist's *Michael Kohlhaas,* we are presented with an "old chronicle" of a horse trader named Michael Kohlhaas, who was honest in his business, an upright citizen in his community, devoted husband, and caring father; "in short, the world would have had to bless his memory had he not gone too far in one virtue"—desire for justice and Goodness in the world.[28] The story is as follows: he takes a group of horses to the market and must cross a number of borders. He enters a territory in which the lord of the keep, a Junker, has changed and the horse trader is now asked to pay for the right of passage, for a passport. In expectation of securing this newly required document at his final destination, Kohlhaas must leave horses behind as security and does so in good faith. He learns at his destination, Dresden, that this required passport—a specious new law in its arbitrary violence—is, in fact, "a lot of bunk." Upon his return to the castle with official attestation of this revocation of any required passport, he discovers that his horses have been used for work in the fields without his permission and are now in the most deplorable of conditions. His trust in the Junker broken, he nonetheless "swallows his anger" despite his outrage. He curbs his resentment and decides to appeal to the justice system of the land and brings this matter to the courts. And he does this not only for himself but also because he feels it is his "obligation to do everything in his power to demand redress for the offense he'd suffered and to insure the future safe passage of his fellow travelers."[29] What has been offended is hospitality toward strangers and a more general sense of trust in fellow human beings.

His assistant, Herse, faithful and trustworthy, was abused at the castle while keeping an eye of Kohlhaas's horses during his absence. At first incredulous that his trusted servant would have abandoned his horses, Kohlhaas extends a charity of interpretation and benevolence toward the inhabitants of the castle and calls into question Herse's story, despite his proven trustworthiness. He extends his interpretive charity to a stranger rather than to his own kin. But then he becomes convinced that indeed his assistant was wronged and injured. The legality of his complaint is clear. Yet through the machinations and influence of the Junker, and despite the clarity of his case and his own network of influence and good standing, his legal grievance goes nowhere. In a moment of despair, no longer feeling at home in his own land given this breach of trust in the function of the law, he decides to take matters into his own hands: he gathers men from his farm and collects weapons. The courtroom, as a space for resentment, is now surpassed, and so he must take his claim for justice not to the world but *against the world.* His desire for justice, left unsatisfied because of the pretense of justice and legality, becomes transformed into rage against the injustice of the world. His wife, Lisbeth, confronts him; she offers to go and appeal personally to the Elector. She returns, however, from her appeal without success and punished for her good intentions; she has been assaulted physically. In bed, she is dying, and as a Lutheran priest is reading from the Bible, she grabs the book from his hands, "as if to say that there was nothing more in it for her," and leafs through it until she points to a verse, turning to her husband, "Forgive your enemies . . . do good to them that hate you." She squeezes his hand and dies. Kohlhaas makes a promise to himself: "'Let God never forgive me if I forgive the Junker!' and kissed her, the tears welling up, pressed her eyes shut, and left the room."[30] He gathers a band of men and begins to lay siege to the castle, embarks on a war in search of the Junker, and brings devastation to the villages. His rage devours the world and expands beyond his own injury: he becomes "an emissary of the Archangel Michael come to punish all those with sword and fire who sided with the Junker in this dispute, and thereby cleanse the world of the sorry state it had fallen into."[31] This uprising becomes so extreme that Martin Luther is called upon to intercede. He urges Kohlhaas to return to social order and appeals to his "heart" and "humanity." As Luther warns him, one is godless in rebellion against God and His world. Luther encourages him to forgive—he would have been better to do this in the eyes of the Redeemer. Luther asks Kohlhaas to forgive as God forgives, to forgive in the name of God. In anger, and clutching Luther's hands, Kohlhaas exclaims that God in fact did not forgive all his enemies and insists that the original injury against him must be righted: his nags must be returned to him, fed, in the healthy condition in which he left them. As he takes his leave, he asks for absolution from Luther. Luther refuses, for it is unforgivable to be unforgiving toward forgiveness.

Beyond Guilt and Atonement

If it is tactless to voice *ressentiments* and remain unforgiving toward hearing anything of forgiveness, it nonetheless speaks an appeal and an address, timely in its untimeliness, that seeks to *touch*, and hence provoke, something essential, indeed, forgotten, in those who would begrudge Améry's reactive spite as pathological, self-pitying, or otherwise immoderate in its unyielding and unapologetic intransigence toward any *availability* to forgiveness. Améry's *ressentiments* are not pathological but principled; his unforgiving passion is neither rage nor revenge but issues from a place beyond "guilt and atonement," beyond the possibility *or* impossibility of forgiveness.[32]

In Améry's expressed *ressentiments*, remaining unforgiving is not identical with deciding not to forgive or standing before the alternatives of the possibility or impossibility of forgiveness. If the refusal to forgive is predicated on the freedom to decide, accept, and allow forgiveness, Améry's *ressentiment* speaks from a condition, to wit, an inhuman condition, behind, as it were, any possible freedom; if Wiesenthal is obsessed by the question of forgiveness, as an open wound, Améry is obsessed by there being no question of forgiveness, not as its impossibility (an impossibility to actualize what could be possible) but as a refusal to *hear* anything of forgiveness. We recognize not just an unforgiving attitude or choice predicated on freedom standing before a set of alternatives but also an unforgiving condition, or predicament, toward the possibility or impossibility of forgiveness, and hence toward any question and encounter of forgiveness. This refusal is, strictly speaking, not a refusal set against the possibility of having chosen otherwise, it is not a response or answer to the question of forgiveness, but a *refoulement* of there being any question of forgiveness. In moving beyond guilt and atonement, forgiveness or nonforgiveness, Améry's *ressentiment* speaks from a place *apart from* any possible encounter in forgiveness—to wit, from an inhuman condition for which forgiveness has become irrevocably annihilated in its promise and potentiality of natality. As both a passion and a principle in unforgiveness, *ressentiment* speaks from a place apart, not in retreat from the world, speaking at the world from an underground or island of *ressentiment*, nor in an aggressive expansion toward the world, devouring the world through an explosive rage.

While Améry's *ressentiment* is both judgment and appeal (and thus shares these elements with moral resentment), it is equally a form of resentment not predicated on the expectation or horizon of forgiveness. It is not, in other words, a failure of appropriately forswearing moral resentment but an active closure of the possibility—the encounter—of forgiveness. Seen from these two contrasting conceptions of moral resentment and *ressentiment*, Améry's *ressentiment* appears unintelligible.[33] In the classic form of the Underground Man, *ressentiment* refuses *to be forgiven*, thus hardening itself in a self-deprecating condition of remaining unforgiving. The unforgiveness of this form of *ressentiment* represents a *blasphemy* against forgiveness. In the case of Michael Kohlhaas, we witness an engulfing rage against the world in pursuit of cataclysmic justice. The unforgiveness of this form of *ressentiment* represents a *defiance* against forgiving. Caught within the self-avowed absurdity of demanding "the irreversible be turned around, that the event be undone," unlike forgiveness, however, the spur of *ressentiment* makes as its urgent issue not to resolve, restore, reconcile, or redeem but to reveal, time and again, the conflict—itself unending—unleashed into the world in the unforgivable.[34] Whereas the Underground Man seeks to destroy the world through his own self-destruction, Kohlhaas seeks to destroy himself through the destruction of the world.[35] Améry's *ressentiment* does not speak from an underground or desolate island, nor does it engulf the world in a maelstrom of revenge and retribution. Améry's *ressentiment* does not wish to be hidden or remote, even as it speaks of its ethical loneliness. It does not shout at the world nor murmur resentfully, nor is it marked by self-righteousness, as with Kohlhaas, or self-deprecation, as with the Underground Man, even as it seeks to provoke us. *Ressentiment* does not speak from wounded pride or inflated moral worth but testifies to an inflicted *inhuman* condition to which it seems forever condemned and from which we ourselves cannot claim immunity, indifference, or exception, even as we would want not to hear of it, or hear from it no more.

4

The Unforgivable and the Inhuman Condition

In W. G. Sebald's *Austerlitz*, the narrator recounts his visit to the Belgian fortress of Breendonk. Constructed before World War I as part of a massive complex of defensive fortifications, only to become redundant upon its completion because of advances in weapons technology and the outward expansion of the city of Antwerp, the fortress came to house the headquarters of the German SS and served as a prison camp during World War II. With the end of the war, the fortress was transformed into the National Memorial Fort Breendonk to receive an inquisitive public (and which, most recently, can now be toured virtually).[1] As the narrator approaches the imposing fortress, he is at pains to discern any recognizable architectural plan or relate "with anything shaped by human civilization, or even with the silent relics of our prehistory and early history."[2] As he nears the entrance, "what I saw now before me was a low built concrete mass, rounded at its outer edges and giving the gruesome impression of something hunched and misshapen: the broad back of a monster, I thought, risen from this Flemish soil like a whale from the deep." The walls and casemates of this Leviathan are "covered in places by open ulcers with raw-crushed stone erupting from them," giving the impression of "a monolithic, monstrous incarnation of ugliness and blind violence." The layout of the fortress resembles the "anatomical blueprint of some alien and crab-like creature." In certain places along its misshaped configuration, it is indistinguishable whether the fortress bears the scars of history—explosions of shells and shrapnel—or those of time's natural undoing—erosion and entropy; or whether nature has itself become unrecognizable much as history has become unidentifiable. In its disfigured contortion, the fortress attests to the collapse of any distinction between nature and history, between natural decline and human destruction, even as Breendonk would seem to have as its original and intended purpose the protection against both.[3]

The narrator enters the fortress and visits a chamber that, during the German occupation, served as a mess hall for SS soldiers. As he looks at the tables, dinnerware, and other artifacts from the German occupation— as if time there became frozen, arrested in everyday objects—he can imagine "the sight of good fathers and dutiful sons" from various parts of Germany "sitting here when they came off duty to play cards or write letters to their loved ones at home."[4] He continues his exploration, penetrating ever deeper into darker corridors and remoter spaces, until he finds himself alone beyond the sight of any visitors. Wandering aimlessly, he makes his way down a narrow hallway leading into a lower passage within a casemate. With every step, he recalls how he felt a foreboding sense of claustrophobia, with "the air getting thinner and the weight above me heavier."[5] He arrives at a chamber, bowled like a pit, with a smooth floor in the middle of which lies a drain. A slender meat hook hangs from the ceiling. Looking at this chamber, he becomes seized by an involuntary childhood memory of the butcher's shop in his hometown, where he would see Benedikt—the local butcher—washing the floor tiles after an honest day's work. A nauseating smell of soap floods his nostrils. This memory image haunts him, as an affect dislocated from its proper context, while he stands in this present context without any affect: the nauseating smell that envelopes him does not issue from the emptiness of the Breendonk chamber, yet it cannot be the context of his childhood that presently affects his nose with the disgusting smell of bloodied soap. It is an ambiguous, visceral image as it suggests both the cleansing of butchered blood with soap and the contamination of soap with spilled blood. The anguish of this returned remembrance, turned inside out, remains distinctly vague, otherwise empty of any prompting content in the present, and hence in this obscured refraction all the more acute in an anguish rooted in the present, here in this dark chamber. At the time of this uncanny flashback from his childhood and the unsettling sense that *something else* haunts and inhabits this memory, a memory not his own, the narrator recalls how he had not yet read Jean Améry's essay on torture and the horror he suffered in this very chamber during the war. The (near) coincidence of the publication date of Améry's essay "Torture" (1966) with the narrator's recounted visit in *Austerlitz* (1967) is not simply fortuitous, for it suggests a culpability for what the narrator could not have participated in directly (he was a boy at the time during the war) or even known. His childhood memory is a screen memory for a memory not his own, a collective haunting, as an echo before a resounding sound; for it is only *after* this visit to Breendonk that he discovers Améry's essay on torture and thus comes to know what he had already "remembered" before, that nauseating smell of what had once occurred in this chamber. It is only because that echo has already been heard, without yet having first been recognized as a sound, that the nauseating smell of his involuntary memory poignantly suggests that collective memory—and time itself—have been traumatized, contaminated.

"Dort geschah es mir"

A tourist visiting Belgium might one day find themselves lost between the urban centers of Brussels and Antwerp in the middle of nowhere and chance upon a historical relic. As Améry begins his essay, "Whoever visits Belgium as a tourist may perhaps chance upon Fort Breendonk, which lies halfway between Brussels and Antwerp."[6] We are not extended any formal or acknowledged invitation to follow these reflections but implicitly assigned the role of an accidental reader—to wit, an accidental tourist. From this initial position, we are led into the subject matter of the essay: torture. Whether we are entirely unsuspecting regarding what we are about to discover or confident in the knowledge of what awaits us, we already in some sense imagine what to expect and hence how to react; if not with any presumed understanding (for how could we?) then at least with considerate sympathy and disposition to listen and hence believe.

Fort Breendonk stands today as a national museum in remembrance of the recent past—a past within the lifetime of most actual tourists (and readers) at the time of Améry's writing in 1966. As virtual tourists, as readers, we are ascribed an attitude of enlightened curiosity toward the past: we want to remember and never forget from the secure vantage point of a world now (apparently) at peace with itself. We are said to approach Fort Breendonk through the sedimentations of history as we spy from afar this low-lying complex beneath an overcast Flemish sky. From a distance, Fort Breendonk gives the impression of a quaint historical site. We look upon it as if beholding a "melancholic engraving" of the war of 1870–71, with associations coming to mind of the battles at Gravelotte and Sedan, the crestfallen Emperor Napoleon III. As we come closer, this image of the expired (*abgelebten*) past cedes to a more familiar image, no longer a *historical* image of the past but an image belonging to the contemporary past. The imagined "copperplate of 1870 is abruptly obscured by gruesome photos (*Greuelphotos*) from the world that David Rousset has called *L'universe concentrationnaire*." We now behold the fortress during World War II as a German prison camp and SS headquarters. As we pass through its portal, we have crossed the threshold of the present. We find ourselves within the Fort Breendonk National Museum, where everything has been preserved as it was on the day of its liberation. We have arrived at a site of memory.[7]

As you explore the buildings, you visit the so-called business rooms, where German soldiers and security personnel once plied their trade and diligently went about their daily affairs. You penetrate deeper into remoter, more solemn places within the fortress and then suddenly find yourself in a windowless room, from which you *know* with an uncanny feeling that cries and whispers could never escape from these walls nor could any witness from outside ever appear in attestation or assistance. Once you have arrived *here*, you have arrived at the place of Améry's essay, from where *it* speaks. You have arrived at a place within the museum beyond the visible hold of its sanctioned remembrance. Beneath the encasement of memory there lies the unimaginable; beyond the place of remembrance, there lies the nonplace of the unforgivable. You have arrived at a place both inside and outside historical consciousness, as well as outside and inside the present. The uneasy stillness of the museum is ambiguous: it cannot remember what has yet to become past but cannot recall what remains present, a past yet to pass away. As with the drain hole in the floor of this desolate chamber, it is both inconspicuous and ingurgitating— you have arrived at the ground zero of ethical annihilation, an abyss into which everything meaningful of the world has drowned. Where are we? Améry tells us: "Dort geschah es mir: die Tortur."[8]

It is significant that Améry does not write, "I was tortured there" or "There I suffered torture," or any comparable sentence where a subject of experience, the I or an ego, stands before us to (pro)claim its own testimony. His clinical statement delineates the specificity of torture and, through the contours of this event, the essence of Nazism, the unforgivable. The subject matter of torture is not introduced through another subject, either victim or agent. There is no subject standing after torture who stands there before us to speak about what happened to him as *his* experience. The statement begins not with a subject (a first-person declaration, a subject of experience) but with the place of an event that befell a subject. It does not begin by assuming a subject of experience who has survived enough to remain able to speak about what happened to him as his to tell, thus allowing us, as well as the teller, to become wiser. The telling of this essay befalls him here as well. Dispossessed of his own proper subjectivity and freedom to appropriate and constitute events as his own experience, the place of torture remains the place where the subject remains no more, yet is still there to remain tortured forevermore and nonetheless speak. As Améry writes, "Torture is the most horrible event a human being can retain within himself."[9] If retaining within means to hold in truth (*in Wahrheit halten*), to remain beholden to the truth of what endures, the truth of torture becomes existentially inscribed within the being tortured of human abjection. The place of torture (and the time of torture) *retain* the tortured; it is a place outside over there as well as inside in here, and so much so that in a subsequent essay Améry proposes that aging—his aging—is torture from within.[10] The horror of torture is already intimated: it is the place where the world has been drained and a subject dispossessed of their freedom, autonomy of self-constitution, and authenticity in their own death. The abject dative of torture *remains* subject no more. Torture becomes its own subject that imposes its sovereignty in unmaking the subject it annihilates and the world it eviscerates. It realizes itself as sovereign through this annihilation of subjects. Hence the stark title of Améry's essay, "Die Tortur." It reigns there absolute, allowing for nothing other.

The circumstances of Améry's arrest in 1943 were ordinary, of neither heroic nor historical significance. A member of a Belgian resistance group that clandestinely distributed antiwar leaflets to German troops (a gesture of resistance, not a veritable action, which Améry himself admits was futile), his activities are one day discovered; he is arrested. The unexpected appearance of Gestapo officers with their iconic leather coats and drawn pistols did not leave him, as Améry recalls, with any doubts regarding the situation into which he suddenly found himself thrust. In the presence of Gestapo officers without possibility of escape, it became all too clear what awaited him. As he recalls, he had already read about the concentration camps in newspapers and knew all too well what happened to prisoners at the hands of the Nazis. Now a prisoner himself, his future seemed certain. As he remarks, "I thought that there could be nothing new to be given in this field." His narrative seemed already scripted: imprisonment, interrogation, torture, and, most certainly, death: "So stand es geschrieben und so würde es verlaufen."[11] Standing before such projected possibilities, he might be able to prepare himself in mustering the courage, conviction, and composure necessary to meet his fate. We are never entirely unprepared when violence irrupts within our lives, for we remain able to take measure of ourselves even in the most dire of situations through our repertoire of available capacities, even if such self-measure does not quiet the dread we might nonetheless feel. Even if arrest and torture were nothing ever suffered in the past, even if he never imagined that he would be caught (who does?) or even considered himself important enough to be arrested, he must now trust in himself and prepare, or, as the case may be, fail in his preparations. He must constitute himself in this situation on the basis of resolute expectations of known vulnerabilities and anticipated death.

This anticipation of suffering, torture, and death is further stressed and thus rendered indispensable to Améry's narrative with his account of how a Gestapo officer commanded him during his arrest to distance himself from a nearby window. The Gestapo was well versed in the "trick of cornered individuals jumping out the window to their death, rather than being captured."[12] Faced with an existential choice, either to accept his anticipated suffering and death or to flee from his situation in taking his life by his own hands, Améry obeys the Gestapo officer's command.

He winks in acknowledgment as he moves away from the window. As Améry writes, he did not possess "the physical disposition of intention to avoid his destiny in such an adventurous manner." This *acceptance* of what he knows awaits him ("I knew what was coming and they could count on my consent") in no manner suggests that his subsequent interrogation and torture are thus "justified." As with every aspect in Améry's essay, this description of his knowing acceptance of what awaited him is not merely autobiographical or psychological detail but also a subtle articulation, and therefore all the more effective advancing, of an argument. Thrown into a situation of imminent harm, suffering, and death, does one remain in freedom? Does freedom always endure, come what may? As Sartre conjectures, "Whatever pressure is brought to bear on the victim [of torture], her abjuration remains *free*: it is a spontaneous production, a response to the situation; it manifests human-reality."[13] As Sartre further imagines, "We are not dispossessed of our freedom even by torture: we give in to it *freely*."[14] Every situation is, in this Sartrean sense, grounded on the *impossibility* of the annihilation of *being* subject to our own freedom, or, in other words, the impossibility of the dispossession of the nothingness of our freedom, that inviolable fracture between me and my situation in the world, through which I can always transcend myself in order to become another day or perish with my freedom still intact in my hands (or at my hands). Freedom is that depth of negation, of saying no to the world, in me through which I can survive myself, come what may. Although the Other is said to be a drain hole into which my projects risk being flushed away, there is no drain in the world in which my freedom could become entirely flushed. Even in torture, for Sartre at least, "human-reality" remains manifest and, most critically, endures so as to salvage itself on another possible project of its own freedom. Fascinated throughout his writings with torture, Sartre depicted it as "a supreme test" for the endurance of being-human.[15]

In Sartre's story "The Wall," this nothingness of freedom becomes manifest in the resolute attitude of self-attestation and the narrative imagination. A prisoner of the Spanish fascist regime, Ibbieta has been condemned to execution. As he awaits his fate the next morning, he experiences an anxious night of self-reckoning and truthfulness toward his inescapable situation. Waiting for his death, he already witnesses his own dying, thus coming to terms with—appropriating, not just accepting— his execution at dawn. Through the night, he experiences an amplification of his physical existence—heightened sensory perception, more intense sense of his embodiment—as well as a detachment from his embodied situation in the world. His lived-body is experienced as already dying and yet contemplated as a spectacle outside himself: he perceives his body as something to which he is bound, an "enormous vermin," but with which he feels no intimacy and identification. He is both facticity *and* transcendence, death and its appropriation as *his* telling and testimony.[16] Ibbieta, in this Sartrean fashion, exhibits the conjunction of suffering his own death while not succumbing to his death, or, as Sartre writes of Roquentin in *Nausea*, "There is a consciousness of suffering, but no one there to suffer." Here we have in an exemplary fashion what Denis Hollier terms "the profound transcendental anesthesia" in Sartre's conception of human existence as developed equally in his theatrical and theoretical works.[17] Torture is the supreme test for how consciousness never coincides with itself. In "deciding" to allow himself to be tortured, a tortured individual can in freedom decide to remain silent under the violent duress of being made to speak, and thus, in his manner, "reaffirm the human" in "breaking the circle of Evil."[18]

In anticipating the fate that awaits him at the hands of his captors, Améry finds himself in a situation in which he is thrown back upon himself in facing the imminent possibility of suffering and death. The various possibilities that we project in any given situation structure how we are concerned with ourselves in our engagements and encounters in the world. As Améry observes, everyday life is "nothing but codified abstraction," by which he understands: our capacities for response, acceptance of risk and trusts, habits and dispositions, and scripted possibilities of our being-in-the-world. We are ahead of ourselves in projecting possibilities, yet behind ourselves, already scripted in advance, and in light of these scripted possibilities—codified abstractions—we make sense of our situation in the world *for and from* ourselves. In drawing attention to this anticipation of suffering and death, Améry's is not claiming that he merely (and perhaps foolishly) possessed a bookish knowledge that nothing "new" awaited him, or that his imagining of what awaited him would soon become cruelly exposed as naive, shattered against the brute reality of the suffering and indignity that would befall him. As Améry wonders, with such knowing acceptance, "does one actually know?" One does and does not know. As he remarks (citing Proust), nothing in fact happens either as we anticipated *or* feared. What happens often exceeds the alternatives of projected possibilities in terms of either "fulfillment" or "disappointment." Even as our encounter with the world might outstrip our anticipations and fears, our confidences and capacities, we still endure through a responsibility for ourselves as the subject of our experiences. Faced with the possibility of our own death, we can stand resolute and thus remain at home within ourselves in owning up to the defining possibility for us to be, our own mortality. Homeless in the world, we might still rest at home with our mortality and freedom. We can become dispossessed of our worldly projects, but never, in this line of thinking, dispossessed of our *Seinskönnen*—our capacity *to be*, or, in Sartre, our freedom "to 'to be'" (*a à être*). In Heidegger's account of my "being-toward-death," what remains "the closest proximity" is my being-toward-death as the innermost possibility of my own impossibility. In Sartre's "The Wall," this unbreachable intimacy within ourselves finds place in the narrative form of telling and testimony, and thus presupposes, as with Ibbieta, the endurance of a voice that can speak of itself from the untouchable place of its own transcendence in freedom.

Standing before himself, face-to-face with the prospects of suffering and death, Améry remains resolute. He *decided* not to escape from his situation in obeying the command of the Gestapo officer, thus accepting the fate thrust upon him.[19] What Améry finds baffling and unexpected during his arrest is that the Gestapo officers did not have "'Gestapo faces' with twisted noses, hypertrophied chins, pockmarks, and knife scars" but "rather faces like anyone." Contrary to his anticipated image of Gestapo officers as well as the foreboding presence of their clothing, weapons, and conduct, these men possessed ordinary faces; it is just such ordinariness that prompted him to obey, and hence, in this sense, strangely *trust*.[20] Entrusted into the hands of these others, the infliction of torture soon transfigures these ordinary faces into "Gestapo faces after all."[21] This transfiguration becomes set into motion as soon as he is brought to a police station for interrogation. For despite protests that he possesses no relevant or significant information, he is roughly and rudely handled, physically assaulted. The first blow is apocalyptic: it brings an end to an impossibility in an obscene flash of revelation. As Améry writes, "The first blow brings home to the prisoner that he is *helpless*, and thus it already contains the seed [*Keim*] of everything that is to come."[22] A drain hole becomes torn within being-in-the-world. What becomes essentially drained from the world is the hold of its meaningfulness: *trust in the world* (*Weltvertrauen*). This drainage of trust with the first blow is instantaneous (collapsing) and engorging (expanding); it marks a rupture within time through which another, disjointed temporality sets into place along the fractured lines of a fundamental loss of trust in the world (*Verlust des Weltvertrauens*).

Loss of Trust in the World

This acute loss of trust in the world is not a function of completeness or intensity but a modal catastrophe in the form of an existential loss of an impossibility—namely, the taken-for-granted impossibility of ever losing trust in the world to such an irrevocable degree. The significance of this loss is not primarily ontological but ethical and has its locus in the violation of incarnation, the embodied materiality of being-in-the-world. This loss of trust in the world entails a rupture in the trust of others as well as self-trust. With the first physical blow, this impossibility of loss becomes a "real possibility." It is instantaneous, there all at once, and temporally engulfing, in a catastrophic contortion of time from which there is no end. The person who *was* tortured *remains* tortured; time becomes wretched, out of joint, much as the tortured body becomes disjointed from itself and the world. This modal catastrophe of trust in the world cannot be adequately described as a transformation from an "impossibility" to a "possibility" or a "possibility" to an "actuality." What was once held inviolable and impossible becomes *certain* as the only possibility under which existence can continue and yet no longer continue. What seemed impossible ever to lose and always taken for granted as unimaginable, this loss of trust in the world cannot be anticipated or expected beforehand. Even when we *think we know* what it would mean to lose trust in the world, to know what it is to be tortured, as with Améry prior to his own torture, as with readers following Améry along in his reflections, we writers who might strive to imagine what occurs in those dark chambers, it is strictly speaking never a possibility that could ever be anticipated *or* imagined. As betrayed with Sartre's own obsession, the imagination of torture is liable to produce fantasies of torture that remain narrow while conflating it with sexuality, heroism, and martyrdom.[23] Every narrative in expectation or knowing will be unexceptional in failing to adequately express the singularity of befalling to the loss of the world in trust.

When trust in the world becomes eviscerated, as with torture, the catastrophe singularly exceeds what could ever be feared, dreaded, or imagined, whether individually or collectively.[24] The horror of torture is not just what is feared of it; it is (contrary to Sartre) the unimaginable surprise that *it* dispossesses the freedom of projecting fears, thus leaving the person gaping, staring with mouth wide open at the drain hole into which the world flushes away along with any sense of being-in oneself. The freedom of transcendental anesthesia becomes transfigured into a purgatory of transcendental abjection. The loss of this impossibility of losing trust in the world becomes the certainty that now structures, in transfiguring, the real in its continued (im)possibility. Resonating in Améry's writings is that life after torture remains hostage to torture, and so becomes an impossible life, one that becomes "lived" despite itself, for and against itself. The world can continue to be possible only as an impossibility—namely, under the dark sun of the impossibility of trust in the world. Rather than stand upon trust, or indeed fall upon trust, a person remains suspended in a sequestered space without atmosphere *or* ground, much as Améry becomes hoisted up on a meat hook hanging from the ceiling, dangling above the drain below. It is not, however, that with this catastrophe of trust we recognize in hindsight that trust in the world had all along been deceptive or fraudulent. We have not been deceived in trusting in the impossibility of loss of trust in the world, yet once it has become lost, what remains is a world everywhere haunted by the incredulity of its loss. The condition of the survivor is not paranoia but *ressentiment,* as the ethical demand for this trust to become possible once more in the midst—the remains—of its impossible loss. With the event of torture, Améry's insight is not the banal recognition that events happen to us mostly as other than we anticipated or feared; nor that the encounter with the real—events that happen to us—often surpasses and disabuses our imagination. The insight is rather that our everyday projection of possibilities, our sense in which our expectations can either be fulfilled or disappointed, rests on the unspoken and self-evident assumed *inviolability* of the impossibility of loss of trust in the world. It is not that the world becomes "destroyed," however. The world *after* the loss of trust in the world remains reliable, instrumental, predictable, indeed pleasant and attractive to the eye, as Améry describes the "miracle" of Germany's rebuilding during the 1950s.[25] Nor does this condition of loss of trust in the world motivate paranoia or extreme distrust with regard to others, as if would-be torturers might be lurking around every corner. Loss of trust in the world hollows out the world from the inside while leaving intact its ethically hollowed-out form. The world *is* the same, and yet, still within this world, the tortured person finds himself abandoned, ejected into a liminal condition of transcendental homelessness and abjection. As Améry remarks, torture is "die verkehrte Welt"—a world turned inside out, upside down. The world becomes *voided* or *ghosted,* annihilated in the sense characterized by Améry as *Vernichtungsvollzug*: the accomplishment of annihilation as an abiding condition—to wit, an inhuman condition.

Loss of trust in the world encompasses trust in others as well as self-trust. Much like trust itself, the fundamental violation of trust through torture is multiplanar. With torture, the drainage of trust from the world becomes accomplished not only through the infliction of physical suffering and harm but also through verbal interrogation and destruction of the human voice. The ordeal of torture dislocates a person's being-in-the-world in terms of her spatial extension in relation to objects in the world as well as her extension into the world beyond the boundaries of her embodiment. In having a voice, a person projects her presentness to others in the world; in moving through space, a person projects her presentness in relation to objects in the world. As a person's body becomes abused, whether with instruments or the bodily force of another human, spatial being-in-the-world contracts upon itself much as the person's being-in-language contracts under the mounting assault of verbal interrogation.

Having a voice is not only an issue of being heard by others. It is also an issue of *hearing* others. Verbal abuse, threats, and insults give the scene of torture its theatricality, and is commonly experienced as being as destructive, and inseparable from, physical torture. The torturer's power over language renders a person mute, encapsulating the person in the lasting violence of a dislocated position within language. Torture silences (*faire taire*).[26] Verbal assault in the service of torturing a person's relation to language does not only "penetrate" their being but also, more insidiously, "devours" their being in dislocating any delimitation between inside and outside, self and other, human and animal.[27]

After his arrest, Améry's first interrogation occurs at a police station, where a Flemish policeman roughly questions him regarding his accomplices, their whereabouts and identities. He is promised that, if he confesses, he will be spared going to Breendonk, where "you know what fate awaits you there." In Améry's mind, the absurdity of his situation is that he in fact possesses no information of value or significance. He harbors no secrets that he could either vocally betray or silently guard. His interrogator remains unconvinced and physically assaults him in order to force the truth, any truth, from his lips. Améry's predicament poignantly exposes the perverse logic of interrogational torture. In such a circumstance, a prisoner becomes caught in a double bind: the prisoner must be assumed to be trustworthy (otherwise nothing reliable could be assumed to be divulged) even as the premise of torture is that the victim cannot be trusted given the presumed necessity of violent coercion to induce speech. A prisoner perpetually remains under the shadow of suspicion that he is always withholding one more secret or speaking to deceive, thus justifying increased violence and humiliation. Interrogational torture subverts the basis of truthful confession and communication, indeed self-expression and self-extension in the world through speaking.

With voluntary acts of confession, we do not merely speak the truth but also enter into truth in speaking and, in this light, appear to others truthfully. The more I confess or speak the truth, the more I appear truthfully to the Other. With interrogational torture, this confessional form of truthful self-manifestation becomes perverted. The infliction of physical pain compels a person to betray his trusts, thus making a person complicit in the loss of trust in the world, trust in others, and trust in himself. Regardless of what information might be divulged and the objectification of power over the helpless condition of the victim in making him speak, the victim's identity becomes flayed in being made to betray those who have entrusted themselves to him.[28] Much as physical abuse contracts the victim's sense of spatiality, interrogation contracts the victim's sense of appearance for others. The more a victim is forced to speak, the more a victim feels herself disappearing from the presentness of others whom she has betrayed, or thought to have betrayed, within her trust networks. This rupture of trust not only extends to entrusted affiliations but also involves the forced repudiation of one's beliefs, commitments, and identities. Through such coerced betrayal of her trusts, the victim enters into falsity with regard to herself. As Elaine Scarry comments, echoing a central insight in Améry's essay, "Torture systematically prevents the prisoner from being the agent of anything and simultaneously pretends that he is the agent of some things . . . In forcing him to confess or, as often happens, to sign an unread confession, the torturers are producing a mime in which the one annihilated shifts to being the agent of his own annihilation . . . his own body as the agent of his agony."[29]

Loss of trust in the world becomes induced through forced confession, contraction of spatial extension, and weaponization of objects into instruments of harm and suffering. Each of these—voice, spatiality, and objects—partakes in the annihilation of trust in the world and its constitutive sense of being *in* the world, held within the hold of trust. Enclosed spaces protect the human body from external harm and extend a humanizing claim on space as an articulated expanse of possible bodily motion, exploration, and standing. We are housed in defined spaces—"rooms" of the world—much as we are housed in our bodies. Being-housed-in-space is intimately connected to being-housed-in-ourselves, our embodiment.[30] Architectural spaces are commonly described as skin, and much as with skin the borders of built space structure our encounters with the world.[31] One can remain within a space as much as one can enter and exit a space to move about the world. The place of torture—a basement, a prison cell, a room—becomes the locus for the drainage of the world, leaving behind the discarded shell of a world and the detritus of its malignant objects. Temporality becomes equally voided as a medium of trust. The evisceration of trust occurs through the insertion of a person into a condition of absolute *unpredictability* regarding the next interrogation session, the duration of each beating, and so forth.[32] This obliteration of structured distances and nearness (in both time and space) becomes acoustically manifest, for as Améry remarks, the abused and beaten prisoner hears only the obscure roar (*Brausen*) of the world's evisceration.[33]

Hilfserwartung

Loss of trust in the world catastrophically entails an existential sense of having been forsaken by others, thus exposing the fundamental condition of human vulnerability toward others, but likewise the fundamental demand placed on others with regard to our defining vulnerability, as keepers of our vulnerability vis-à-vis one another. The absolute helplessness of the victim with regard to others is twofold: in relation to the presence of those others who violate one's existence—those Gestapo faces—and in relation to the absence of those others who remain unavailable and silent in time of need. As Améry argues, *die Hilfserwartung* and *die Hilfsgewißheit* are fundamental to the human condition, as fundamental as the struggle for existence. In so many instances, the former *responds* to the latter, for what is implicit in existence in its struggle to be is vulnerability and exposure to the "struggle of existence" of others. In situations of daily human life (*Lebenslagen*), physical suffering and harm are experienced along with an implicit expectation of assistance. In the human cry of suffering there issues an appeal, address, and approach. To the extent that Améry considers *Hilfserwartung* an existential condition, it is also an assignment or entrustment, that I am entrusted with the solicitude of others. *Hilfserwartung* and *Hilfsgewißheit* are indispensable forms of original trust in terms of which one rests assured in belonging to the human, as participant in the plurality of the human condition. As with the taken-for-granted and, in this sense, "understood" impossibility of loss of trust in the world, *Hilfserwartung* and *Hilfsgewißheit* are "understood" to be impossible to lose catastrophically. This trust in the responsiveness and solicitude of others toward my suffering and vulnerability is neither a deliberate, intended, or projected expectation. An infant need not and cannot *know* or *intend* this demand for assistance. In this unknowing cry of the infant there echoes nonetheless, as issuing before any freedom on the part of the child to decide, an appeal, address, and assignment to others. With the rupture of this trust in others, the sense of belonging to the human becomes ruptured. To belong to the human is to rest assured in the *availability of others* in time of need, and especially, as what catastrophically *fails* in Améry's tortured condition, when this trust in others becomes betrayed by some other. All would seem to bear responsibility for this failure of some other. All are entrusted with remaining available when some other violates this trust in human plurality.

Along with loss of trust in the world, absolute helplessness (*Hilflosigkeit*) breaks into the world as an impossibility that unexpectedly becomes a possibility in certainty. With the expressions *Hilfserwartung* and *Hilfsgewißheit*, the term "expectation" is not meant to suggest a framed expectation, social norm or convention, acquired disposition or habitus but rather a *demand*, and hence the assignment of a responsibility. By the same token, the term *Gewißheit* is not meant to suggest a cognitive certainty, justified belief, or *doxic* attitude. *Gewißheit* here is a primitive assurance or original confidence; the term *Gewißheit* signposts an original faith, or trust, in others as my keeper in time of need. For Améry, the sentiment of belonging to the human, of *being* human along with other human beings, is anchored in this assuredness, or faith, in others as my keeper, in their availability for me in my time of abandonment and destitution at the hands of others. This original trust that others come to my assistance and not abandon me in my suffering becomes expressed in the cry of pain itself as a primitive appeal and address. For Améry, this appeal—or "expectation"—resounds more emphatically even *after* torture, given that the victim retains torture within herself in becoming forever detained, or deported, in torture.[34] As Améry writes in his essay "Ressentiments," it was after the war and so-called liberation that his *ressentiment* took sharpened form in the absence of outrage and presence of bad faith in the postwar European (especially German) collective consciousness. What distinguishes Améry's *ressentiment* is this aftereffect of the event from which it issues. Aimed at the continued absence of the other's availability and conscientiousness after the war, *ressentiment* attests to an abiding deafness of the world. Torture triumphs as the sovereign silencing of speech and destruction of the availability of others. It is not so much that torture silences the victim; more significantly, it silences the witness, in foreclosing the availability of others as the most dramatic aftereffect of torture's violence. Silence perpetuates torture's violence against speaking, even if the victim regains speech; the victim who speaks returns to a language but finds himself within a place where there is no longer anybody available to listen. As Améry states, "Das Erlebnis der Verfolgung war im letzten Grund das einer äussersten *Einsamkeit*."[35] The world does not want to hear anything of torture, for reasons that mirror Améry's own refusal to hear anything of forgiveness: psychologically, it is too capricious; politically, it is too irrelevant. In this sense, existential helplessness carries not only an appeal for "assistance" but also an address to a witness. Cries of suffering appeal to the Other even unto the order of angels to bear witness to my suffering such that I might bear what is unbearable, so that I am not abandoned to my suffering.[36] It is not just a suffering unbearable for me to bear but also a suffering not mine to bear alone.

The condition of *Hilflosigkeit* entails the collapse of any ability to defend oneself and what Améry calls "counter-violence." In finding oneself helpless before the Other who inflicts suffering, the victim is unable to defend herself and resist in self-defense (*Not-Wehr*). The victim can neither fight nor flee. Unable to return violence upon violence, the victim is paralyzed, unable to reconstitute the violated boundaries of her physical being and reintegrate herself into trust in the world. The significance of this collapse of any possible form of counterviolence marks the collapse of any *relatedness* between victim and others.[37] For Améry, this produces a neutralization of any possibility of *jus talionis* and so undermines any possible conflation of Améry's *ressentiment* with revenge or vindictiveness. The acute social death of the tortured victim is registered most dramatically with this existential collapse of any possible relation of *reciprocity*. *Ressentiment* is not only beyond guilt and atonement but also beyond revenge and retribution.[38]

The Skin-Me

Catastrophic loss of trust in the world is localized in the violation of trust that others respect my "physical and metaphysical condition [*Bestand*]."[39] This respect for the incarnation of the self and incorporation of the self in the world along with others is not understood by Améry in terms of respect for the dignity of a rational, autonomous moral agent imbued with rights. It is, rather, understood, emphatically, as carnal regard for the boundaries of the self and, more specifically, for the *skin*, for oneself as one's own skin, that both demarcates the self from others and envelops— holds—the self in itself, held together within its skin. As the incarnation of separation and proximity, skin is imbued with *ethical* significance, and not merely to be taken in an ontological (or phenomenological) sense. Skin is the materialized interface of *presence* and *absence* in the primordial ethical signification of incarnation. My trust in others begins and ends with my skin. Underwriting trust in others—being-with-others—is the demand of the skin, "Do not touch me." Once violated, that addressed demand to others becomes transformed into the appeal for Others to come to my assistance, "to touch me" and contain me, in holding me and making contact with me, from draining away from the world. *Hilfserwartung* is thus not so much an explicit expectation or cognitive attitude as it is a *visceral* form of trust, a trust that others will heed the assignment "Do not touch me" (i.e., do not violate my physical and metaphysical condition [*Bestand*]) and that, if violated, others will not forsake me to my suffering. Violated skin becomes an appeal for the tendering of tenderness and solicitude.

To stand in the proximity of others, when standing in a queue, for example, is to trust that others will not violate my skin. The bodily incarnation of *Hilfserwartung* incorporates the proximity as well as the distance of the Other, as prescribed by the trust that others will not violate the prohibition of touching me as well as trust that others will come to me, in the proximity of being touched, once my skin has been violated. The confidence that the Other will not touch me, in the sense of violating the integrity of my boundary and embodied sense of self, allows the Other, as standing against me, or opposite me (*gegen*), to stand along "with me" (*mit*). To exist *with* Others, such that the Other does not stand against me as my enemy, hinges on this confidence that the Other will not violate the boundary of my skin, that I can feel at one with my skin in the presence of another. The expectation or demand for solicitude is, as with the exemplary instance of the bond of trust between mother and child, the inverse of the helplessness of the victim before an aggressor's violence. This assistance is intimately expressed in the act of touching, holding, and embracing, such that if the physical abuse of torture violates the *untouchability* of the Other's lived-body, through the violation of the boundaries of the self and violation of "self-feeling," assistance from others materializes itself first and foremost through physical contact: holding, caressing, touching, and so on. For Elias Canetti, this inviolability of being touched by others represents an anthropological constant, where the fear of being touched becomes surpassed with the experience of crowds, when individuals surrender themselves to moving and acting with others in close physical contact with each other.[40] That "fear," or, for Améry, implied command, "Thou shall not touch me," becomes overcome in the condition of need for another's assistance. In arriving for another's assistance, the physical act of touching, consoling, and embracing responds to the suffering of others, whereby the Other is no longer abandoned and forsaken, even if the Other's suffering remains their own.[41]

In keeping within an inscribed historical semantic field, skin functions in Améry's characterization along the lines of two complementary significations: skin as the synecdoche for the self and skin as the marker of otherness with regard to the self.[42] As developed within a psychoanalytic framework, Didier Anzieu proposes that various functions of a unified consciousness (in his terminology, the "psychic apparatus") become developed on the basis of the formation of what he calls "the skin-me" or "skin-ego" (*le moi-peau*). The "skin-ego," or, "skin-me," is the projection of the psyche on the surface of the body.[43] The skin-me emerges during the early stages of infancy as a "psychic ego," which is, on the one hand, distinct from the body-ego (physical ego) and yet, on the other, "confused" with it, thus forming a "figurative skin-ego"—namely, the infant representing itself ("me-self") as its skin. As a "two-sided envelope," skin encloses the self in establishing a border, or barrier, between the self and the world while at the same time allowing for the incorporation (eating, etc.) and ex-corporation of objects from the outside. This primitive skin-me provides the operative basis for the developed functions of the ego: sensory perception, representation of the world, and symbolic expression. In this view, the elementary functions of consciousness (the psyche), such as reception, protection, cohesion, and identity, are critically dependent on the skin-me. Along the lines of Donald Winnicott and Wilfred Bion, the formation of the "true self" occurs for Anzieu through the mother's care (or parental care), which structures the child's sense of identity as contained and bordered.[44] Essential to the genesis of one's self-definition, or identity, the formation of the skin-ego is intrinsically connected to the prohibition of touching: to touch this and that object in this way, not to touch these objects, to touch others' bodies in a certain manner (or not at all), and so forth. The prohibition of touching structures and directs the drive for attachment against an unregulated and undifferentiated touching of objects (differentiation in terms of controlling objects, possessing objects, etc.). This prohibition of touching proves indispensable for the differentiation of reality: the difference between the child's body and the bodies of others, between space and objects, between animate subjects and inanimate objects, between friendly and dangerous, and so on. As Anzieu observes, the infant "acquires a power of endogenous control that oscillates between a feeling of confidence in his own activities and a euphoric feeling of unlimited omnipotence." This sense of trust in its own bodily movements ("confidence") underlies and enables the child's sense of itself as an agent acting on the world as well as a sense of itself as an agent in the absence of the world, or, more specifically: the temporary absence of the mother. Without this nascent sense of trust *in and as* one's skin, the absence of objects and others cannot be supported, nor, by the same token, one's own self-presence. Symbolic representation of objects (language) also requires this trust in one's own body, to feel at home in one's skin, to ensure the transfer from a desire for the presence of the object to its evoked presence through nomination, or naming—that is: signification.

Skin is the boundary that shields oneself against the world and hence marks the terms of distance between oneself and the world but also, by the same token, the terms of encounter and proximity with the world and others. As Améry writes, "The boundaries of my body are also the boundaries of myself. My skin surface shields me against the external world. If I am to have trust, I must feel on it only what I *want* to feel."[45] The incarnation of self-trust is a function of confidence in *what* (and how) I want to feel and who I am to be in this confidence, or the self-constitution of *my* body as *lived* from within ("immanently"), as *Erlebnis* in the strict phenomenological sense. In incarnating a stable distinction between myself and what Améry terms the alien world (*die fremde Welt*) through my lived-body, I am *available* to the world as well as for myself, and available precisely in terms of self-trust, trust in others, and trust in the world. There obtains a reciprocal circuit between basic trust, the differentiation of distance, experience of absence as noncatastrophic (in other words: *endured*), and symbolic reference (and manipulation) to the world.[46] Skin *is* trust as the envelope of the self in its relatedness to the world (as contained or being-in), in its relatedness toward others (as being-with), and as related to itself (as being-itself).

When developed along phenomenological lines, skin demarcates the self from the world and others; the integrity of skin sets the world at a distance of regard for the inviolability of my bodily integrity—but also sets the terms for contact and, indeed, intimacy with the world in being touched by the Other, or in caressing the Other. The sentience of skin serves as the medium in which I sense the world as other than myself while simultaneously inserting myself, or positioning myself, with regard to the world and others. In Husserl's analysis of the lived-body (*Leib-Körper*), the animate body is both self-constituted and other-constituted, a *Leib*, or self-animating *lived*-body, as well as *Körper*, a material object.[47] *To be* my lived-body is to feel myself "in" my body and initiate movements of my lived-body while also feeling myself a body for others and in relation to other bodies, seen under the gaze of others and present for the touch of others. Within the lived-body as the self-moving organ of perception (seeing, hearing, etc.), the sentience of touch occupies a privileged place. What distinguishes tactile sensations, for which Husserl reserves the German term *Empfindnisse* (in contrast to the more general term *Empfindung*), is the self-localization of sensing. When I touch an object, I sense my own touching at the place of my touching: at the tip of my finger, on the surface of my palm, and so forth. The primacy of tactile perception is a function of the tactile horizon that establishes a measure of distance—I can go over there to touch those objects, I can move away from those objects, and so on—as well as a function of the self-localization of my own sensing on my lived-body. This "own-body" sensation, or touch, is not only localizable on the surface of the skin but also a felt presentness of oneself as one's skin. The lived-body as both an "absolute here" and a "relative there," as the singular here from which I engage the world and the singular being-there in the world relative to other bodies, is implicitly constituted *as skin*, though Husserl himself never calls attention to the necessarily skinned constitution of the lived-body (and without which, indeed, my body would have no recognizable form, or gestalt, and unity as a system of kinesthetic, or proprioception, and perceptual operations).[48] Skin is itself neither "outside" nor "inside" but the medium of differentiation between "inside" and "outside," intimacy and violation, enveloped into one—that is, oneself. Without this feeling of being-in one's own skin, the lived-body cannot be constituted as both subject and object, nor, critically, *can* the lived-body function as the absolute center of movement, expression, and response to the world. Self-trust and trust in the world are thus not only issues of autonomy: this autonomy is anchored in self-constituted sentience, of feeling how and what I want to feel on my skin. When the existential regard for the skin becomes betrayed, with the violation of the prohibition "Do not touch me," in conjunction with the lack of contact with others, in the absence of any care and solicitude of being touched, there can be, strictly speaking, no incarnation of my freedom in the world, given this rupture of the *incarnate* appeal and assignment of responsibility toward others as viscerally constituted *as my skin.*

Vernichtungsvollzug

Transported to Breendonk for enhanced interrogation, there Améry is hoisted, with arms cuffed behind his back, onto a hook dangling from the ceiling in the very chamber later visited by *Austerlitz*'s narrator. As he is lifted upward, the weight of his body bears down against itself—he hears an unforgettable crack and splintering of his shoulders as his arms become dislocated. As Améry writes, torture brings about an *existentieller Vernichtungsvollzug* (an existential accomplishment, or execution, of annihilation) of human subjectivity through its disjointing of the lived-body into an abject materiality. In Améry's expression, the "metaphysical content," or incarnation, of a human being becomes "realized" into *meat* by means of a complete—that is, *unforgiving*—self-negation. As he writes, "Sein Fleisch realisiert sich total in der Selbst-negation."[49] This existential flaying deconstitutes the lived-body as both a "lived" *and* "material body," thus rendering the tortured victim neither a "subject" nor an "object." Tortured, a person can neither distance herself from her material being nor identify herself with her own material being. The inviolable bond between the lived and the material, of the lived-body as both subject and object, becomes rendered inside out, without, however, the remains of any recognizable sense of belongingness within one's material body *or* lived-body. Implied in Améry's chilling characterization, the self-constitution of the lived-body becomes "deconstituted" or "uncreated," disjoined from its own self-constitution in the "I can" of self-initiated movement and feeling what it wants to feel ("lived") on its skinned body. Disjointed of *Leib* and *Körper*, the victim becomes at once an abject body in the world and an ejected subject from the world: *she is made meat.* Torture does violence against the lived-body that I have at my free disposal as the medium for the exploration of the world and the body that I am, as the presentness of myself with others, the sense in which I can embrace the body of others and be myself embraced by them, placed in the care of their arms, and caressed. As proposed by Tobie Nathan, to be tortured is to be "subjugated to a deliberate enterprise of destruction of the envelope and permanent rupture of relations."[50] It is to "flay," or "skin," the self of its being-in itself, the world, and for others.

The tortured body is not merely a lived-body reduced to an inarticulate and brutal state of materiality, since it is in terms of the material suffering of the body that torture effects its sinister *complicity* with the evil it suffers.[51] A victim cannot repossess her body or claim it once again, hence the sense in which Améry considered aging to be a suffering torture from within. The material body of the victim becomes the instrument with which suffering is inflicted upon herself, thus rendering her complicit despite herself and in her helplessness. This forcible complicity with torture is expressed in the frequent experience of victims feeling *shame*. Torture unmakes the essential capacity of self-constitution in terms of what Husserl calls *Ich kann* and what Heidegger called *Seinskönnen*. This annihilation of the "I can" is to be understood not only in terms of the self-constitution of the lived-body but also, as implied in Améry's argument, with the "I can" of the ethical subject. Through the devastation of the lived-body—the abject dative of the event of torture—the "I can" of any possible stance and response becomes annihilated—that is, irrevocably transformed, undone, and defeated in an existential calamity. Elaborated in explicitly phenomenological terms, which, granted, are not employed by Améry himself in his essay, the disjointing of the lived-body materializes, or better, *dematerializes*, the otherwise inviolable "joints," as it were, of transcendental synthesis. Experienced in the meatification of the lived-body through torture, the victim experiences viscerally a nontheoretical "destruction of the world" (*Weltvernichtung*), but dramatically unlike its theoretical counterpart, such an annihilation of the world hinges on a nonrecuperable disjointedness of transcendental synthesis of the lived-body, in terms of which experience of the world becomes possible. It orchestrates a radical "de-mundanization" of the transcendental subject through an irreparable, transcendentally speaking, loss of the obviousness of the world, our trust in the world. Such an experience of the transcendental disjointed synthesis of the lived-body—the disjointing of the transcendental subject as such—can be seen as implicitly suggested in Améry's contention in his extended reflection on aging that *his* aging is "one long death march," indeed comparable to the "death march" of his wartime deportation such that aging is experienced as "torture from within." In this challenging identification of aging with "torture from within" one can nonetheless espy an enduring (and not endurable) condition of perpetually disjointed transcendental synthesis, or, in other words, the disjointing of the lived-body in its *necessary* process of aging (i.e., passive synthesis of aging), which here is turned against the lived-body as such insofar as aging becomes experienced, transcendentally speaking *for Améry,* as the internalization of the death march. Thus transfigured, the tortured body becomes a zone of indiscernibility even more profound and, in this sense, more moving than any form of sentimental identification or common measure of compassion.[52] In the throes of suffering, there no longer stands *there* a subject who speaks and responds, as patently expressed in the grammatical construction of Améry's haunting formulation "Aber nur in der Tortur wird die Verfleischlichung des Menschen vollständig: Aufheulend vor Schmerz ist der Mensch."[53] In the formulation "Aufheulend vor Schmerz," there stands no subject *who* screams. There is the scream itself in lieu of the subject who once was and once could respond.

Torture turns the lived-body "inside out" in pushing the subject through and beyond the distinction between life and death. It is a "ghosting" of existence or, in other words, an expulsion from life *and* death, while nonetheless remaining neither alive nor dead, and ejection from the world while nonetheless remaining within a form, or semblance, of a world.[54] As Améry argues, torture annihilates or obliterates (*auslöschen*) death's contradiction. One's own death becomes lived (*den eigenen Tod erleben lässt*). To be or not to be no longer holds any purchase as a question. Dispossessed of death, the victim is no longer secure in the hold of a death she could claim and appropriate as her own, or ownmost. The tortured victim is made to survive her own death, and yet it is a death that she carries within herself in "living" in the position of death. If death, as Heidegger argued in *Being and Time,* is the possibility of the impossibility of my own singular existence, death gives nothing "to be actualized," it cannot be lived, and it is this measureless impossibility of my own existence that measures the scope of my own possibilities: in comporting toward my own death in an authentic manner, an authentic responsibility for one's own projected possibilities becoming disclosed. In this view, death is a border that cannot be breached: it is in view of this horizon of finitude that Heidegger can speak of a "freedom toward death" as the possibility of Dasein's ownmost in its emancipation from the anonymity of the "they" (*das Man*). In Améry's implicit rejection of Heidegger, torture realizes the "impossibility" of breaching the horizon of death, not through securing an "afterlife" beyond death but in "pushing through" and hence collapsing the ontological *distinction* between "being alive"— living—and "being dead"—death. As Heidegger himself recognizes, Dasein can be either a lived-body, in its "bodying forth" in the world, *or* a corpse, neither a body (*Leib*) nor a lifeless material thing (*lebloses materielles Ding*) but an "unliving" thing (*Unlebendiges*).[55] In Améry's contestation, the tortured body is neither a "lived-body" nor an "unliving thing," a corpse, but something abjectly other, neither alive, as "bodying forth," nor unliving, as a corpse there for others. This pushing through to the hither side of the contradiction between life and death, that one cannot be both "alive" and "dead," occurs through the realization of "annihilation" as the "meatification" (*Verfleischlichung*) of the victim's subjectivity. Torture drives the subject inside out in expulsing the subject beyond the limit of death into nothingness (*über die Todgrenze hinausgetrieben ins Nichts*).[56] This expulsion into nothingness suspends death; it instantiates the death of death itself. Neither alive nor dead, the tortured individual becomes a "zombie."[57]

Torture allows for neither escape or solicitude, nor, most significantly, the *alternative* of death. Hence the care to which the tortured victim is not allowed to die in undergoing torture. For Améry, his torturers did not bring him to the brink of death; they pushed him beyond the pale of life and death. It is this lack of an alternative of death that marks the breaching of the absolute limit of death. The logic of the beautiful death (*la belle mort*), as argued by Jean-François Lyotard, consists in the positioning of the living in the face of death as an alternative, indeed, as the alternative of *authenticity* in the face of something else: to die rather than to escape, to die rather than to serve, to die rather than to be vanquished.[58] The authenticity of "being-toward-death" is situated within such a logic of alternatives (to die rather than . . .). The expulsion of the tortured subject into nothingness represents, however, a death that is suffered beyond any logic of the alternative, including, most significantly, the alternative of life *or* death. The disfigured death in torture is neither the sublimation of sacrifice (in which case death is destroyed and passed through) nor a beautiful death (in which case life is given for death as its most genuine alternative) but, in Lyotard's characterization of what is named with the signifier "Auschwitz," an annihilation of death. This killing of death is "worse than death" because it does not allow or permit a person *to die*. There is no dying as such but only a death that is lived, or, alternatively, there is only an unending dying without any instance of death proper. The one who "survives" torture does not properly survive and yet is not properly dead either.

Sadism and Sovereignty

In Kafka's "In the Penal Colony," the law's inscription upon the body of a convicted soldier through a mechanical writing apparatus is staged through a contrast between the naked, exposed body of the victim and the tightly wrapped uniformed body of the executioner. Stripped of his clothing and made to lie down on the apparatus, the criminal assumes a position symbolizing "the destruction of the integrity of the surface and with it the emptying of the inside," as the law incisively becomes engraved into a living-body turned into "meat," rendering indecipherable the inscribed punishment as well as unrecognizable the tortured body, flayed of its humanness.[59] Keeping in mind Walter Benjamin's measured judgment that Kafka's world represents "the exact complement of his era which is preparing to do away with the inhabitants of this planet on a considerable scale" ("In the Penal Colony" was written in 1914 and published in 1919) without thereby granting his writings any prophetic historical clairvoyance, along with the historical context of colonial deportation from which this particular story drew its critical impetus, the "remarkable [*eigentümlich*] piece of apparatus" in Kafka's narrative illustrates what is distinctive, or, in this sense, *eigentümlich,* of Améry's own understanding of the *political* function of torture.[60] In recounting his experience of being tortured in Breendonk, Améry's prose undergoes a subtle shift from its use of a first-person pronoun to the impersonal and inclusive pronoun *man.* As he writes, "Man führte mich an das Gerät . . . Dann zog man die Kette mit mir auf" (One hoisted me onto the apparatus . . . Then one hoisted the chain up with me [on it]).[61] This inclusive spread of the German *man* to speak of both the victim and the torturer, as well as, implicitly, the reader of Améry's essay, who here becomes "interpellated in this *man* and the present tense, thus appealed to imagine" this scene of torture, is not to be read, however, as an "ironic slippage implying that each of us might stand in either position" but, rather, expresses the insight that the victim *as well as* the torturer are subjected to the apparatus of torture itself (*das Gerät*).[62] The marked absence of a first-person (and past tense) narrative voice at this critical moment in Améry's essay on torture bespeaks the limits of communicability of his experience as well as, in the same shortness of breath, the inclusion of the wider social and political in the machinations of torture to the point of their utter anonymity.[63] In this switch to the impersonal pronoun, Améry's point is not to erase the existential chasm between victim and torturer through this employment of *das Man.* On the contrary, the gulf between both remains unbridgeable, indeed: irrevocable, and yet, nonetheless, what distinguishes torture is the submission of both the victim and the executioner to the sovereignty of *das Gerät.* As in Kafka's narrative, the writing apparatus (incarnating the spectral presence of the "old commander," who, though dead, remains present in the machine itself) symbolizes the triangular relation of torture in the modern world as situated at the intersection of a victim's body, the social body, and conflation of the legibility of the law for its merciless, and, in this sense, illegible (illegitimate) violence.[64] What Kafka reveals with the image of his infernal machine, its monumental madness, is the absolute sovereignty of the torture apparatus over the torturer as well as the tortured. The lesson of Kafka's narrative (when read as a metaleptic machine of torture) is not just that torture is the inscription of the law pushed to an absurdity (the convicted soldier is punished for failing to salute a captain's door on the hour) on the victim's body, as the execution of condemnation without judgment (the convicted soldier is summarily pronounced "guilty beyond a doubt," without trial or inquiry, and hence not properly convicted), but also that torture itself becomes the law, without judgment and condemnation, without mercy, over both the criminal and the torturer, to the point of becoming a self-consuming absolute. As the officer, who once stood as executor of the law's punishment, now finds himself beneath the apparatus at the end of Kafka's story, the machine began going to pieces; "its silent working was a delusion," and as the condemned officer succumbs to "plain murder," and not "exquisite torture," as he himself had once desired, "no sign of life was visible [on the face of the officer's corpse] of the promised redemption."[65]

As Améry proposes, torture enacts the sovereignty of absolute sadism and, in this sense, can be said to express the essence of Nazism itself. Characterized as inseparable from the existential significance of the victim's suffering, Améry underscores the constitutive political function of torture as state-orchestrated and self-legitimating sadism. The brand of sadism at issue here, however, cannot be understood from "handbooks" of psychoanalysis nor, by the same token, from handbooks of philosophers with their frequently invoked master-slave dialectic and existential struggle of freedom and recognition (as in Sartre's *Being and Nothingness*). What proves distinctive of state-sanctioned torture (in the modern world) is not the performed sadism of one person over another, the torturer's sadism over the victim, but the sadism of torture itself, as the genuine *sovereign,* or *master,* such that the torturer himself becomes a servant of torture, not the master who applies torture as a mere instrument of utility or means of perverse pleasure in standing sovereign over the victim. Améry names those who tortured him "Hitlergefolgsmann" (the one, or the man, who follows Hitler) and calls those who meted out torture under the Nazi regime "Folterknecht" (literally, "the servant of torturer" or "torture's henchman"), while reserving the term "torture" (*die Tortur*) to speak of torture itself (as with the title of his essay, "Die Tortur"). Even if the Nazis systematically deployed and deliberately developed torture for a variety of means, individually and collectively (and not to rule out the perversity of sadists among the ranks of such *Folterknechte*), torturers stand at the service of torture; they are not its veritable masters.

As Améry writes, "Sie bedienten sich der Folter. Inbrünstiger aber noch dienten sie ihr."[66]

For such a conception of torture's sadism, Améry draws from Bataille's and Blanchot's complementary readings of Marquis de Sade to underline the function of torture within the transmogrification of sovereignty. As Bataille argues in *Erotism,* sovereignty (as anatomized in de Sade's writings) constitutes itself through an absolute negation to the point of constituting itself through an absolute form of apathy and indifference. With the sadism of de Sade's protagonists, the negation of others leads to the negation of oneself. As Bataille observes, "In the violence of this progression personal enjoyment ceases to count, the crime is the only thing that counts and whether one is the victim or not no matter." The person who inflicts sadistic acts of violence not only negates their victim but also becomes himself negated, or self-negating, through this unleashing of self-sublimating violence. As Bataille writes, "Theoretically, denial of others should be affirmation of oneself, but it is soon obvious that if it is unlimited and pushed as far as it can go, beyond personal enjoyment, it becomes a quest for inflexible sovereignty."[67] In this absolute form that transcends any master-slave dialectic, sovereignty constituted in sadism is not identifiable as an expression of power, since power must remain flexible and responsive in order to remain robust and adaptable as power, nor does sovereignty emerge from a dialectical struggle of freedom. Nor is absolute sovereignty identical with absolute power, for it inaugurates something excessively different, since this self-absolutizing sovereignty, as constituted through sadism, exceeds any reciprocity between sovereign and subject, master and slave, or any relationship to another. Absolute sovereignty is, in this regard, absolutely fictitious, as it is limited by no obligation, principle, or power.

Thus construed, sadism is the praxis of producing "reality" for a fictitious absolute through the annihilation of any real subject other than its fictitious self. As Blanchot in turn argues, "the center of de Sade's world is the necessity for sovereignty to affirm itself through an enormous scale," such that sovereignty surpasses not only "the plane of human existence" but also the legibility and legitimacy of any distinction between the real and the imaginary.[68] Sovereignty constitutes itself as "god" or absolute subject ("Unique Being") through a transcending power of negation; it does not therefore depend on the objects, or persons, it destroys (as with Hegel's classic master-slave dialectic), since it "does not even suppose their existence beforehand, because when it destroys them it has always previously considered them as nothing."[69] In this form as sadism, *inhuman* sovereignty constitutes itself through absolute negation so as to realize the fiction of "god." In negating other human beings through the intermediary notion of god, in the name of the sovereign, the torturer "becomes God, so that, in his presence, other men become inconsequential" and "sheer nothingness," *ein Stück.* Cast in a "bronze-like transcendence," apathy toward others (toward plurality) reigns supreme, for apathy, as Blanchot observes, "is the spirit of negation applied to the man who has chosen to be sovereign."[70] In this excessiveness of unforgiving apathy, the god of sovereignty becomes self-destructive, crushed, as it were, under its own "bronze-like transcendence." Energized into its own nothingness through the excessiveness of negation, absolute sovereignty, politically *or* theologically, constitutes itself as unforgivable in constitutionally becoming itself absolutely unforgiving. As de Sade writes, "The very conceiving of this so infinitely disgusting phantom is, I confess it, the one wrong I am unable to forgive man."[71]

A kindred insight, albeit less dramatically formulated, is stated in Michel de Certeau's argument that the connection between the practice of torture and political sovereignty consists in the former's fabrication of the "simulacra of credibility," and hence believability, for the latter.[72] What fictitious, or ideological, sovereignty lacks—namely, legitimacy through consensus, or, in Arendtian terms, plurality—becomes compensated through an unforgiving employment of absolute violence, most often (and necessarily) against those who are most exposed and vulnerable, so as to fabricate, through merciless and unbelievable violence, the simulacra of consent. As de Certeau writes, "Torture is the technical procedure by which tyrannical power produces for itself this impalpable first matter which it itself has destroyed and which it is lacking: authority, or, if one prefers, a capacity to motivate belief."[73] In torturing a person to "confess" or repudiate their own beliefs, the fiction of absolute sovereignty creates the illusion of its own believability and "satisfies itself with this simulacra." For de Certeau, this adhesion to the violence of make-believe belongs to the inner logic of utopia or other political aspirations of salvation. In Arendtian terms, the necessity of this absolutization of violence becomes more pronounced and deemed more urgent the less any political system is based on trust, deliberation, and consensus. The destruction of the world beheld in plurality becomes savagely conflated with the world's salvation (see chapter 2). In the absence of credibility, totalitarian regimes are at once absolutely paranoid and absolutely destructive of others, of otherness, and hence plurality as such. The practice of torture is thus not without a constitutive dimension of political theatricality within its dark chambers.[74] Critical to this fantasy of sovereignty, the scene of torture becomes the enactment of the imaginative project of the absolutism of an inhuman state.[75] The scene of torture is the liturgical scene for this enactment of the fictional transcendence of absolute sovereignty.

As the essence of Nazism, its fictional sovereignty required torture and, more pervasively, the annihilation of others in order to realize itself in its destructive fantasy. When seen through the prism of torture, as Améry argues, the absolutization of sovereignty (and not just understood as a "totalitarian" regime) can become realized only through the negation of *Mitmenschen.* In the annihilation of the tortured victim's body, the space of appearances for one another and living with one another (plurality) becomes violated as well. The event of torture is, thus, not limited to an individual suffering body but implicates (as with Améry's subtle shift to the inclusive pronoun *man*) the social body as such: *das Man.* Not just a symbol, or set of beliefs, but also a praxis of torture allowed the followers of Hitler to achieve complete identification with Nazism and, in this sense, complete submission and subjection to its perverse sovereignty and sense of belonging to *das Man.* In this establishment of the fiction of absolute sovereignty, torture becomes the "total inversion of the social world." Those who "follow Hitler" can live in this inverted world only by torturing and destroying others. Only when the torturer has "expanded into the body of his fellow man" can he feel himself *heimisch*—that is, have breakfast and smoke a cigarette in the good conscience of his unforgiving attitude toward those whom he has annihilated. In this absolute form, sovereignty transcends authority or legitimacy. Indeed, whereas a traditional (Christian-inspired) conception of sovereignty was wedded to the power of forgiveness and privilege of mercy (political pardon as well as theological grace)—in this theological conception, sovereignty constitutes itself through an exceptional privilege of forgiveness—the essence of sovereignty exhibited in Nazism consists in an absolute and exacting *unforgiveness* toward, in this perverted sense, a privileged enemy: those whose existence is deemed unforgivable as such. If the Christian God's mercy represents an essential feature of its transcendence, in the sadism of absolute sovereignty, as with Nazism, its unmerciful and unforgiving Godhead becomes fictionalized into its faulty transcendence. As voiced in Améry's uncompromising *ressentiment* (here restated in the transplanted echo of de Sade's words), "The very conceiving of this so infinitely disgusting phantom is, I confess it, the one wrong I am unable to forgive man."

Enacted as the perverse liturgical incarnation of sovereignty, torture does not destroy, it annihilates in the specific sense characterized by Améry's provocative claim that human incarnation, the lived-body of a person, becomes transmogrified into *meat*: "Nur in der Tortur wird die Verfleischlichung des Menschen vollständig."[76] The tortured human lived-body is made into meat (*Fleisch*). Hanging by his arms without any support (or, indeed, the ability for his own body to support itself), torture effects the disincarnation of Christ, as expressed with Améry's innovative use of the archaic German term *Verfleischlichung*. Améry brilliantly employs the word *Verfleischlichung*, a theological term traditionally used to designate the incarnation of Christ, against the grain of its original meaning, contorting its theological meaning against itself. For rather than designating "the becoming flesh of God in Christ," and through this incarnation the advent of redemption for humankind through forgiveness, torture as *Verfleischlichung* bespeaks (in Améry's usage) the disincarnation of spirit from the body, of the human from the world, and, more significantly, forecloses the advent of redemption, and hence any possibility of forgiveness in Christ.[77] In its symbolic significance, the body of Christ stands as a tortured body, whose Crucifixion opens onto the redemption for all those who suffer in kind. Christ suffers for the suffering of humankind in expiation for our sins. In Christian ritual, "the Eucharist is the liturgical realization of Christ's suffering and redemptive body in the bodies of his followers."[78] The Eucharist—partaking in the suffering body of Christ—allows for forgiveness and reconciliation with God and among human beings. As William Cavanaugh remarks, "Where torture is an anti-liturgy for the realization of the state's power on the bodies of others, the Eucharist is the liturgical realization of Christ's suffering and redemptive body in the bodies of his followers."[79] For Améry, torture at the hands of the Nazis undoes any Christology of Forgiveness and, more emphatically, *decreates* the advent of forgiveness from the world with the suffering of Christ. If, as Arendt argued, forgiveness enters into history through the body, or incarnation, of Christ, for Améry, with the political sadism of Nazism, as virulently manifest with torture, forgiveness becomes expelled from history with the same epochal significance, in reverse, as its original transformative revelation to the world. Torture enacts the final deportation of forgiveness from the stage of history. If Christ symbolizes the eternal availability of forgiveness, the reversal of Christ through the *Verfleischlichung* of torture comes to symbolize an apocalyptic *unavailability* of forgiveness for the unforgivable. Nor, by the same logic, can the victim of torture be elevated as a *martyr*, whose suffering could be converted into an affirmation or testimony of transcending value. The suffering of the tortured subject remains marked by the stigmata of the unredeemable. For those, like Améry, whose existence has been "pushed beyond" the contradiction of life and death, there stands no possibility of *resurrection*, nor is the question of forgiveness, and hence the possibility and significance of restoration and reconciliation, at all available. Hence the tactlessness, self-avowed, in which Améry wants to *hear* nothing at all, let alone see anything, of forgiveness for those who, in his striking words, need to be "crucified" on the cross of their unforgivable deeds. Crucifixion becomes voided of its redemptive promise and inverted into the unholy symbol of interminable *ressentiment* in witness to an unforgiving evil.

Despair and Deliverance

Neither alive nor dead, this living-on in the position of a death not properly one's own becomes starkly expressed in Améry's reflections on the imperative of his unforgiving *ressentiment*. To be unforgiving is here not to refuse the request of forgiveness; it is to no longer have a place in the world as a person who could respond to and hence receive such a request. It is to no longer be there to respond to evil in the promise of redemption in attestation for a suffering that stands disjointed from the promise of time itself, as once signified by *hope*, as that secret alliance with a possible future to which the past, despite its destitution, could have recourse in order to overcome its petrified and forsaken condition. If forgiveness, as seen through Arendt's consideration of the human condition, addresses the predicament of the irreversibility of a past wrongdoing, thus presupposing to a significant degree that such a wrongdoing *is no longer present* but irreversibly past (hence the crux of the predicament to which forgiveness responds), what remains of the meaningfulness of forgiveness for a suffering that remains irrevocably present (as opposed to irreversibly past)? What remains, when forgiveness cannot enter into question after injury but remains suspended before an injury without end, that, in its abject condition, forecloses the meaningfulness of any deliverance or release? As Améry writes, "Twenty-two years later, I am still dangling over the ground by dislocated arms."[80] In this suspended condition of being unforgiving to the possibility or impossibility of forgiveness—a condition both suffered and endured despite oneself—there is no stubbornness or covert pride, or moralism, against unbinding oneself from an event of the past but rather an insistence on the impossibility of finding any release from a present suffering that resists becoming past. The promise of time itself has become ruptured, disjointed.

With Améry, *ressentiment* becomes the final vestige of a precarious hope that would seem to have lost faith in its own expression, even as it struggles against the forgetting, willful or otherwise, of the unforgivable suffering that has befallen him. *Ressentiment* takes the form of a remembrance of the present: it presses upon the present the urgency of an awakening to an event that remains present but that has already come to pass. Beneath the encasement of memory there lies the unimaginable; beyond the place of remembrance, there lies the nonplace of the unforgivable.

Every site of memory is thus perforated by a drain hole into which the event has become drowned, unless, recalled to the future through an indictment against the present (against forgetting or forgiving) of *ressentiment*. In this manner, *ressentiment* gives voice to the imperative of giving witness to the *truth* of evil—its corrupting presentness in the world—and *absoluteness* in the absence of any meaningful ethical response of forgiveness and restitution of trust in the world. "Die Welt ist fort, ich muss dich tragen," in Celan's haunting statement, but in the instance of Améry's survivance, the "you" is himself as the solitary voice that must bear itself in bearing, in speaking out, an unbearable truth that does want to be heard.[81] What becomes borne in this lonely voice is the gravity of an outstanding ethical trust in a world bereft of ethical conscience, or *Wahrhaftigkeit*. As Améry remarks, "Meine Ressentiments aber sind da, damit das Verbrechen moralische Realität werde für den Verbrecher, damit er hineingerissen sei in die Wahrheit seine Untat."[82] As an indictment against the broken heart of the world, *ressentiment* seeks to eternalize the truth of its own suffering into an absolute testimony in a world devoid of solicitude for those unseen who are made undone.

Having begun his essay with an oblique glance at his readers, invited despite themselves to follow Améry in his reflections, only to be interpellated midway through their reading, *Torture* concludes on a markedly pessimistic note, no longer clearly addressing any reader. Améry openly admits that his essay will be read without consequence and grants a certain futility in giving voice, as appeal and address, to his unforgiving attitude. *Ressentiment* attests to the event of evil in a kind of prophecy in reverse, not foretelling the future from the past despite the blindness of the present but retelling the past for the present despite an onsetting blindness of the future. Much as with Cassandra, no one wants to hear of Améry's despair, his disjointing voice falling through the cracks, or fracture, between speech and silence. Unlike fellow deportee Robert Antelme (a member of the French Resistance, who was deported to Buchenwald, Gandersheim, and Dachau), who articulated in *The Human Race*, published in 1947, a hopeful form of humanism and ethics of writing in response to his own experience of deportation and dehumanization; despite the efforts and intentions of the SS and other participating groups in the camps to establish, through violence, cruelty, and neglect, a fundamental rupture between themselves and their hapless victims, Antelme proposes that the sense of belonging to the human race, to humanity, although savagely and mercilessly destroyed, remained nonetheless inviolable and indestructible. As Antelme writes, "The executioner [*le bourreau*] can kill a man, but he cannot change him into something else [*ne peut pas le changer en autre chose*]." In his humanist declaration, "Nous restons des hommes, nous ne finirons qu'en hommes." This survival of the humanity of the victim is directly related to the survival of the self in its material, embodied functions and survival of the capacity to tell—to live so as to tell, to tell so as to live. In writing, or speaking, there is not only resistance to evil but also openness toward others in the affirmation of an indivisible unity of being human. Although deported, there is the return, and in this return the affirmation of humanism and belonging to the human. Hope, for Antelme, is this promise of return to a belong-ingness, and hence trust in the human. Améry's writing attests instead to a destitution and deportation without return. In speaking from within the place of torture itself it speaks of an irrevocable breach in any sense of belonging to a common humanity and of a world beholden in com-mon trust.[83] This writing of the disaster does not guard against despair but allows for a deported survival, just enough to whisper to itself that, as Améry writes, "soon we must and will be finished."[84] Much as he does not want to hear anything of forgiveness, he implicitly concedes that no one wants to hear anything about his ethical abandonment. We have read, and yet remain none the wiser. Améry's own writing, it would seem, ends unforgiving toward itself. As W. G. Sebald observes, "Seen in this light, the act of writing [for Améry] becomes both liberation and the annulment of *délivrance,* the moment in which a man who has escaped death must recognize that he is no longer alive."[85]

On October 17, 1978, Jean Améry took his own life. It is the leap from the window not taken when arrested by the Gestapo, and even with this "free death" (*Freitod,* not *Selbstmord*) at the end, it remains a leap that could never be taken.[86] What torture takes away *is* that leap, the possibility—freedom—of that leap, of any leap in self-transcendence. Released from this world by his own hands, he places himself in the hand of the Other's forgiveness, even as he himself could never extend his hand in forgiveness for the unforgivable that befell him. As he wrote to his wife, Maria, "Beloved little heart, my darling, to whom I kneel in guilt as I die—I am on my way to freedom. It is not easy, but it means release. Think of me without resentment, if you can, and without too much tor-menting pain . . . Please, please do not feel angry with me—indeed, I feel now as if I could guess that you will forgive me in the end. A shimmer, a faint presentiment of peace of mind."[87]

"I Wonder Men Dare Trust Themselves with Men": The Forked Significance of Trust

It is when we are nearing our inevitable exit from the world, when aging edges us closer to our ineluctable end, that we become more mindful of our presentness to the world, of who we have been and might still become, despite our imminent disappearance. We seek to take full measure and account more completely for the presentness of those who have accompanied us, those participants in our lives to whom we are about to bid farewell or have, through contingency or necessity, already taken leave of in the past. What we take for granted of others, what others take for granted of ourselves, no summation or summoning would seem to do justice or provide adequate testimony. Of those with whom we have entered into commerce, communication, and concourse, how many have been genuinely encountered, in whose proximity we truly stood and stood truly, so that we enjoyed an assured standing in the world? "All actually effective life is encounter," writes Martin Buber, in drawing a contrast between our experience of others, as determined through diverse kinds of relationships (social, cultural, economic, political), yet removed from any integral participation in our lives, and our encounter with others, as partaking in and accompanying who we are.[1] To encounter the Other is to stand in the actually effective presence of the Other as Thou in a singular presentness neither exclusively mine nor yours but as the "between" (*Zwischen*), or between-us, of participation, where we are proximately with another, for each other as well as for ourselves. Trust edges, or lines, our subjectivity from within, couched in an atmosphere of belonging and assuredness in the world, come what may. In trusting one another, we participate in each other's lives, effectively and affectively shaping *who* we are through engaged and invested openness toward each other (see chapter 1). When cast in the mold of Buber's conception of the human in-between (*Zwischenmenschliche*), when we trust others in the paradigmatic form of standing in their meaningful presence, we do not "have"—that is, possess—trust as a proprietary relation toward the Other, as an accidental or incidental property of our being. We *are* our trusts, as bonded to the lives of others, and of those others, as bound to partaking in our own. We are mutually beholden in trust as "where-in" we encounter one another, as *here* for each other, as *there* for ourselves. Without such participation in the lives of others, and likewise the participation of others in our lives, we could not truly participate in the world nor take part in the world's configured destiny.[2] As we approach our end, we seek assurances for our presentness to the world, for how we will be remembered, honored, and mourned by those whom we have not merely experienced, or "related-to," but also, in the sense just evoked, effectively and affectively encountered face-to-face. We care as much for how we will be remembered by the living in our death as we care for how we will remember the living unto our death, beheld once more as we take our leave. We bid farewell in the incandescence of that flickering image of our beloved ones and friends with a final glimpse of their assured presence as we pass quietly into a night without end.

The shape of final hours is often determined by the rendering present of the presentness of others: words become spoken that had never been dared before, a chance offers itself for final amends, secrets are confided and confessed, gratitude is expressed, or a joy has been rekindled in the warmth of distant memories. The hour of death presents itself as the occasion to know the *meaningfulness* of who we are in the grasp of what others have been for us and what we have been—and might still be—for others. This summation and summoning of the presentness of others facilitates our passage: we want to go into the night *in peace*. We want to rest assured that we remain in the hands of others, in their care, entrusted to their living memories, but, likewise, that we still trust others unto death, as the passage that makes death bearable, indeed, breathable, even if it be our last.

Yet it is as we approach our end that we become vulnerable as never before to the betrayal of the presentness of trust and assuredness of trustworthiness that we so pressingly seek to summon for ourselves. Aging exposes us to the vulnerability of abandonment as the converse of the original helplessness in which we are born to the world. Aging courses against the grain of our self-constitution, projects, and aspirations, exposing us to others, as those in whose care we have befallen, and to whom we become, if not outrightly entrusted, at least implicitly delivered. This exposure of aging is at times not without our own complicity, as we are easily tempted to take stock and measure of the presentness of others with a wanton directness that risks the very assurances we urgently seek to secure. We want to reassure ourselves as to their real presence as sustained throughout our lives in putting to the test the loves received, the generosities extended, and the trusts invested. Those whom we have trusted as well as those who have given us their trust, all those in whose lives we have participated in trust, such trusts rest on an assured commitment and unspoiled assumption of trustworthiness (in others as well as in ourselves) that must sustainably remain unquestioned, however weathered and battered the history of such trusts may be. In wanting to summon and make present the presentness of others, we become exposed to the possibilities of ingratitude or flattery. Ingratitude: we find the declarations of others to be less than what we had ourselves expected (even as we called for its expression), thus feeling ourselves less honored in the trusts given and received, and so cheated of gaining from others an image of our own conceited self-measure. Flattery: the declarations of others are greater than our proper merit and due, thus inflating our pride and vanity and hence blinding us to the obsequiousness and disingenuousness of mock words and rote gestures. In the demand to know the truth of our trusts there emerges acutely the paradox of trust's presentness: it vanishes in the exact measure to which we seek to take complete stock and full measure of its presence. The presentness of the world beheld in trust is, in this regard, complex as well as elusive. It is complex given the imbrications of trust: in the world, in others, and in oneself. It is elusive given that the fundamentals of trust easily become distorted with the effort to render it emphatically present. Standing in trust, we often seek to stand *before* our trusting relations, with no accounts left outstanding, at the risk of its own compromise.[3] As with Shakespeare's poignant narrative of *King Lear*, the temptation to know the truth of our trusts renders us vulnerable to their betrayal, not only by the hands of others but also, more tragically, by our own.

King Lear and the Forked Significance of Trust

Recall that the aging Lear, having reigned over the peace and welfare of his kingdom, decided to entrust what he cares for, for what has been held in his trust, to the hands of others, to his three daughters. In deciding to divest himself of his kingdom, he delivers himself over to those who have trusted him as father and king, those whose lives he has begotten. This divestment of his kingdom and kingship does not only perform a "depoliticization" of his self through the abdication of his power, sovereignty, and identity as king. It is inseparably a "defathering," as it were, of his self through a release from the world of cares and concerns, but just as much, in this release from himself as king and father, from the prescribed duties and roles that bind him to himself. Faced with the sharpened possibility of mortality, Lear entrusts his kingdom and himself to those whom he already holds in trust, his daughters, in order to facilitate his passage from the world, so that he might "shake all cares and business from our age, / Conferring them on younger strengths while we / Unburdened crawl toward death" (I.1.37–39). Lear seeks to spend his final days in Cordelia's "kind nursery," thus allowing him to go calmly into the night in her keep, crawling trustingly to the grave.[4] Once disarmed and disrobed of his identity as king and father, Lear's mortality would become not just accepted but also duly appropriated, as sustained within a fundamental trust in the world, trusting that the world he leaves behind remains ordered and meaningful in the hands of others. We want to die in the caring hands of others, beheld in the trust of those whom we have begotten, trusting in their keep and remembrance, as the only expressed act of gratitude we seek for the unspoken generosity we have extended to them in trust. We want to be led away from the stage of the world much as we first entered it, as children of the grave, borne by the Other toward our own death as a child of our sometime children.

As observed by Coleridge, "It is not without due significance" that the division of Lear's kingdom was determined "in all its particulars, previously to the trial of professions, as the relative rewards of which the daughters were to be made to consider their several portions."[5] Entering the convocation of his daughters and betrothal of his youngest, Cordelia, with a readied map of his partitioned lands at his side, Lear had already forethought and decided the terms of his distribution and divestment. As audience members (or readers), we already know by way of gossip whispered beforehand between Gloucester and Kent that, contrary to earlier estimations, it no longer appears "which of the dukes [the two husbands of his married daughters] he values most," thus suggesting a certain penchant for Cordelia (as apparently likewise known to her two suitors, the Duke of Burgundy and the King of France). Contrary to the lawful regime of royal inheritance, the youngest child, Cordelia, is set to inherit a disproportionate share. Lear enters the play already having betrayed his office as king with this patent inversion of the right of inheritance. If, in this respect, Lear arrives in arbitrary breach of the trust of his office, its modal specification, he will just as immediately violate his fatherly bonds of trust toward his children. For Lear abruptly demands that each of his daughters publicly declare their love for him, thus causing the mimetic rivalry between two of his daughters, Goneril and Regan, and their shared ingratitude toward him, to become grossly manifest through their obsequious flattery and fawning, while Cordelia keeps her silence and love, both wise and foolish, against such blasphemy and betrayal. "What shall

Cordelia speak? Love, and be silent." Incensed at her insolence, Lear becomes enraged and banishes his once-beloved, now-cursed, Cordelia: "Here I disclaim all my paternal care, / Propinquity and property of blood / And as a stranger to my heart and me . . . As thou my sometime daughter" (I.1.114–116, 121). In disowning and disavowing his "sometime daughter," Lear commits the unforgivable. Expelled from any standing as a "thou," and cast off to a suitor in a marriage with neither blessing nor dowry, Lear *exterminates* her existence, driving her out beyond the boundaries of his (former) kingdom to far-off France as well as unbegetting his own begotten daughter: "Better thou / Hadst not been born than not to have pleased me better" (I.1.236).[6] Unable to master the infinite distance of Cordelia's singular love, its absolute *inequality* to any measure or exchange, through his demand for her to speak, and hence the exercise of his sovereignty in language (the power to force the Other to speak), Lear attempts to master her infinite distance through murder: to speak *or* to kill, and to *kill* in order to master what no power can possess, *the word of the Other*.[7] The better third of the kingdom, which had been earmarked for Cordelia ("A third more opulent than your sisters") becomes divided among her two sisters (and their husbands), who now each inherit half of Lear's kingdom. When his loyal servant, Kent, intervenes to caution Lear against his "hideous rashness" and "folly," in witness of what is plain for all to see—his injustice toward his daughter—Lear turns against Kent's speaking of truth to power and exterminates him in turn by exiling him from his kingdom, commanded never to return under penalty of death.

As often remarked upon, there is something capricious and foolish in Lear's demand that his daughters publicly declare their love for him ostensibly in exchange for a division of lands already determined as to their distribution.[8] Though lacking forethought or reasoned motivation, there is nonetheless something *sincere* in the rashness of this demand; much as Cordelia's own refusal to heed her father's command, even if streaked with her own defiant pride, is sincere in its silence.[9] Had Cordelia accepted the rules of the game, she would not have been able to forgive herself for her betrayal of the unspoken bond of trust and love, or, in Kierkegaard's emphatic view, its "bottomless mystery," which must be preserved from any "talkativeness" and "pandering" at the behest of selfish, idle, or scheming curiosity.[10] Despite the thoughtlessness of Lear's demand for declarations of love, his impulsiveness cannot be entirely ascribed to a condition of senility (as repeatedly held against him by Goneril and Regan), incipient madness (as insinuated by Kent's futile protest), or the puerility of power (as pointedly noted by the Fool), nor, as Stanley Cavell ingeniously proposes, to avoid in shame the utterance and hence acknowledgment of love.[11] Nor, as Coleridge avers, is Lear's trial of love but "a silly trick suddenly and most unexpectedly baffled and disappointed."[12] What is distinctively grotesque about this fall of the House of Lear is its *comedic* occasioning with Lear's own fumbling of the ritual of power's display and transfer, to be sure, with unforeseen catastrophic consequence. As G. Wilson Knight observes, it is "childish, foolish—but very human."[13] Launched with such "absence of tragic purpose," what unfolds before our eyes is the "tragic purification of the essentially untragic" as the essence of the tragic itself.[14]

This unfolding of the tragic purification of the untragic comprises different ways of world unmaking. If, as Knight writes, "*King Lear* gives one the impression of life's abundance magnificently compressed in one play," such that its "philosophical vision" encompasses "mankind's relation to the universe as its theme," its narrative framing is the rupture of trust in its multiplanar dimensions: trust in the world, trust in others, trust in oneself. Shakespeare's mapping explores the dissolution of the ties that bind human beings to each other, to the world, and to themselves.[15] The double plot of King Lear in relation to his daughters and the Earl of Gloucester in relation to his sons develops across a fractious landscape of trust's undoing: *betrayal* (Lear's betrayal of Cordelia's love; Edmund's betrayal of his father and half brother); *deceit* (Regan's and Goneril's mutual sisterly deceits; Edmund's deceit of this father); and *abandonment* (Lear's banishment of Cordelia; Edgar's exile as Poor Tom; Lear's abandonment to the tempest on the heath; Gloucester's blind wanderings to the brink of suicide). These betrayals, deceits, and abandonments cut across social and familial relations, provoke internal political division and external invasion, and underpin the rebellion of daughters and sons against their fathers—all of which becomes situated within the tempest of a fundamental metaphysical loss of trust in the world, as voiced in a Beckettian pitch of despair with the abjection of Poor Tom, his blinded and tortured father, and the madness of Lear ejected beyond the pale of a world in dissolution. Each represents a figure of transcendental homelessness.[16] In this manner, the central paradox at play in *King Lear* is the many senses in which trust functions as that upon which we stand in the world as well as that upon which we fall from the world. Institutions of trust, trusting relationships, and assured worldviews are essential for buffering humankind from its own "naked helplessness" in shaping a world of human plurality, communication, and significance. Upon trust human life stands. And yet it is just as much upon trust—its betrayals, deceptions, and abandonments—that human life comes to ruin. Expelled from the bonds of trust in the turning of trust against itself, human existence reverts to an *inhuman condition*—unsheltered in a world devoid of trust; to wit, a tempest devoid of a world—as but a "poor, bare, forked animal" (III.4.105–6).[17] Shorn of trust, humankind becomes transfigured into the motley band of a mad, errant king, a poor philosopher, a concerned fool, and a banished servant, all scattered upon an indifferent heath. In the words of Apemantus in *Timon of Athens*: "I wonder men dare trust themselves with men" (I.2.42).

Yet the originality of Shakespeare's vision in *King Lear* does not gravitate just around this exploration of trust in its forked significance for humankind as fostering well-being and facilitating its ruin. Its originality consists foremost in the sagacity that such ways of world unmaking, as the undoing of trust, are shadowed by an enduring *availability* of those who have been betrayed, deceived, or abandoned. *King Lear* is fundamentally a narrative of trusts undone and availabilities suffered. Shakespeare explores not only the fundamental ways in which the human condition is woven (and unwoven) from original bonds of trust but also how such bonds and breakages of trust are originally shadowed by counterpart forms of availability: how those who have been betrayed might remain available to those who have betrayed them and so remain committed to their bond of trust despite the abandonment of the person once trusted. Once bitten, perhaps twice shy, but still available nonetheless. Essential to the bond of trust, as the mettle of its integrity and endurance, is this steadfastness of the betrayed individual, as variously represented by Cordelia, Kent, and the Fool. Each in their own singular way remains available to Lear in the *travaille* of trust: the availability of forgiveness (Cordelia), the availability of fidelity (Kent), and the availability of candor (Fool).[18] If we are to speak of redemption in *King Lear*, it can be only in terms of the suffering of an *original availability* of others for others that the world in its ruin and dismay can still be said to have its promised end, no more nor less.

Trust as I-Thou Relationship

"Childish, foolish—but very human" is first the knotted complexity of Lear's intractable demand. A primal anxiety cascades through this demand's concatenations, the source of which is originally found in Lear's desire of "crawling unburdened to the grave." His attitude toward death, as wanting release from the world and assurance of his standing to the world, hangs critically on the vested hospitality for his own mortality from his own daughter, Cordelia, into whose "kind nursery" Lear seeks to rest. To unburden oneself of oneself, not as the avoidance of death or love but as their appropriation, is conditioned upon standing in the proximity of the Other, in the hour of death as much as during the hours of life. To stand in the presence of the Other as Thou (to enter into her "kind nursery") facilitates the passage toward death ("crawling unburdened"). And yet even as Lear evokes a prodigal need for proximity with the Other in the face of death, his uncouth demand, as the rough summoning of the presentness of his daughters' love, is ambivalently fraught with that "strange, yet by no means unnatural, mixture . . . of the intense desire to be intensely beloved, selfish, and yet characteristic of the selfishness of a loving and kindly nature; the craving after a sympathy with a prodigal disinterestedness, contradicted by its own ostentation, and the mode and nature of its claims."[19] Such cascading contradistinctions, as noted by Coleridge, on which the drama of Lear is founded, "are all prepared for, and will to the retrospect be found implied, in the first four or five lines of the play." Against Coleridge's assessment, such a trial is not "a silly trick" but an anxious test of the mettle of trust in the vein of Job (in Lear's universe, however, charged with a profundity *as if* issued from the gods, though ordained by no God), its endurance and suffering, from which nothing less than the meaningfulness and redemption of trust in others, in the world, and in oneself—the truth of trust as such—is at stake.

In its most manifest form, Lear's demand for the public declaration of love from his daughters enacts dramatically a conflict between Law and Love. Law and Love are not reducible to particular emotions or a single type of relationship but are forms of experience "from within which we can view the entire social and political world."[20] Much as with the dimensions of trust implied in each, Law and Love cannot be defined but only explored in their respective configurations as ways of making the world. Each expresses an ordering of the world as well as a standing of the self within the world, in relation to oneself as well as toward others. Within this frame of conflict, Lear seeks to reconcile his identity as conferred by power and sovereignty with his identity as granted by love and fatherhood, and, in so doing, unite power and love through a penultimate acting out of power *in* love and love *in* power. In dividing his kingdom to Cordelia's favor, Lear violates the prescribed trust in his sovereignty to ensure the progeniture of law, power, and sovereignty. Does Lear orchestrate a public trial of his daughters' love for the self-serving purpose of vindicating his own injustice—namely, his division of the kingdom according to the conceit of love?

In effect, Lear short-circuits the trust that the sovereign will act in conformity with his office—that is, as the rightful dispenser of justice—with an appeal to the equity of Love beyond the Law. Yet Lear's injustice in the name of Love commits in turn an injustice against Love with its implicit demand for the symbolic exchange of love for power and, in the first instance, not only with the command that love speak and serve at the behest of power but also with the lording demand *to be loved*, and thus, to be served in love. Lear betrays the trust of his daughter in him as father that the bond of love will not be inscribed within an economy of exchange, that love remain *unconditional* and never to be demanded. As Cordelia answers her father-king, "I love your majesty / According to my bond, no more nor less" (I.1.105–6)—that is, as prescribing its own proper measure, and hence as not commensurate to any measure or relation other than its own singular absoluteness. The majesty of Love stands beyond the measure of any Majesty, including the winged measure of majestic words, as apparent in the shrill contrast between Cordelia's silence and the superlatives of love in the talkative declarations of her two sisters. Even as Goneril professes, "Sir, I do love you more than words can wield the matter" (I.1.53–54), such candied words only serve to wield the venomous power of love's *appearance.* The mimetic rivalry between Regan and Goneril exposes the falsity of their respective, and dueling, flatteries of love. In the nothing of Cordelia's silence, everything is said while remaining silent, that love is absolutely nothing other than itself, no more nor less, and hence that nothing of love should be sullied within an economy of exchange or gift giving for power, symbolic or otherwise.

To demand from the Other a declaration of love, for the Other to be commanded to speak the truth of their love, is to betray any sustaining trust in the Other's love. It is above all to undermine the bespoken dialogue of love. Where Kierkegaard speaks of the "unseemly, impious, and culpable wish of curiosity" that taints the silent goodness of love, it is just as unseemly to require those whom we trust in love, or trust in other paradigmatic ways, to speak the truth of their trust in demanding from them a declaration of trust's presentness, and so frontally testing, indeed, calling into question, for the sake of trust's assurance, their trustworthiness.[21] Does the demand for a person whom one ostensibly trusts to prove their trust not sharply reveal the lack of one's trust? Neither to be dissimulated from plain view (as when feigned, as with the impostor or the Confidence-Man, as with Edmund, or, to wit, as Lear painfully discovers with Goneril and Regan) nor to be rendered demandingly present and accounted for, the presentness of trust can sustain itself only when taken for granted and hence, in this regard, "understood" as self-evident, without, however, anything of the other's presence being taken for granted; that is, without honoring our trusting relationship. Even as we must monitor and calibrate our trusts, there resides a constitutive sense of assuredness, belongingness, and proximity that resists and defies head-on and headstrong clarification, formulation, or explication. The temptation to know the truth of our trusts, whether by proof or display, renders us vulnerable to their betrayal by this very demand to know, by inciting the revelation of the absence of trustworthiness on the part of those whom we had all along trusted or, as with Cordelia, who is resented by Lear as insolent and ungrateful for her steadfastness in refusing to participate in its—*their*—betrayal. In contrast to her sisters, Cordelia remains truthful, and hence trustworthy. When tested to demonstrate her trustworthiness, Cordelia remains steadfast, even as she refuses to prove it. The mettle of her trust passes the test even as she fails it in the eyes of Lear.

Revealingly, Lear's violence against Cordelia's perceived insolence and ingratitude manifests itself as rage, not anger. Unlike anger, rage is all-consuming and categorically imperative, totalizing as well as existential in its judgment. Although aimed at a target and incited through some cause or circumstance, rage exceeds its mark as well as itself, devouring alongside the target of its ire the enraged person himself. Rage is other-devouring and self-devouring; one loses oneself as well as the Other against whom one is enraged. By his own feeble reckoning, Lear becomes transfigured into a "dragon" in reaction to the "monster of ingratitude" he resents in his daughters; if Lear has become in his rage a monster ("dragon"), his daughter (Goneril) has become a deformed monstrosity: "How sharper than a serpent's tooth it is to have a thankless child" (I.4.282). When giving of ourselves in trust, through our cares, concerns, and charity, there operates an implicit trust in the gratitude of others. We trust that others recognize and receive our trust with gratitude in the unspoken assumption that gratitude can neither be demanded nor lorded over others. This unspoken acceptance of gratitude's silence mitigates against usurping trust for our own sovereign self-interest or self-proclamation. On the other hand, the "monster of ingratitude" against which Lear rails in cursing in extremis Goneril and Regan registers an existential betrayal of one's trusts, when the Other reveals themselves as (having been) prideful, sovereign, and untrustworthy all along. In the Fool's wise observation with regard to Lear's trust of his lupine daughters: "He's mad that trusts in the tameness of a wolf" (III.6.16). But such madness can equally be a function of compromising self-regard or self-importance as trusting; disproportionately reacting to perceived ingratitude can betray a heightened expectation for the expression of the Other's gratitude, and hence a certain esteem and pride on the part of the person who gives of themselves in trust, for which gratitude becomes demanded. We would not trust without distinctive self-regard for benefits accrued and benefits dispensed from our trust, and yet our trusts must remain animated toward the distinctive beneficence of others. With respect to Cordelia, Lear's rage rumbles with undertones of another sense of betrayal inasmuch as his *perception* of her ingratitude gives vent to his own panic with regard to his anxiety before death. Anxiety toward death, when not vested in the kind nursery of the Other, rebounds into rage against the dying of the light. Directed against Cordelia, Lear fails to recognize the silence of her love as honoring *their* bond of love, hence as honoring the trust that transpires, or should transpire, between them in love. Lear's indignation at Cordelia's perceived insolence inverts her integrity into ingratitude while blinding him to the flattery of his other daughters. Anger benefits from an acuity of vision that one often finds flailing in rage. Lear succumbs to his own rage in suffering from his own blindness.

The sincerity of Lear's demand marks a separation between the self who seeks to crawl unburdened toward the grave and its divested roles— its care and business—in the world. In seeking to rest in the kind nursery of the Other, standing in the presence of the Thou, Lear longs for release from the world through separation of his self from himself, from his personae, or masks, for the world. In the contrasting and conflicting cases of Lear and Cordelia, sincerity enacts the slippage of the self from its social, psychological, and political roles. Lear and Cordelia are each in their own manner sincere, Lear in his imperious demand and Cordelia in her majestic silence. Sincerity here is not configured along Sartrean lines as the assumed coincidence of the self with its roles ("the champion of sincerity") in the bad faith of good faith but, on the contrary, as the performed slipping of the self from its personae, or its sliding out of character.[22] In this slippage, the self becomes desubstantialized of its roles and its symbolically inscribed forms of individuality. Identity becomes lost to the world in favor of recovering the self in its singular being. The "madness" of Lear is but the torsion of this twisting of the self away from itself. In his foolish sincerity, Lear betrays his anxiety before death; it becomes revealed—that is, acted out—with his impossible demand in a manner that betrays his roles as father and king. In this twofold sense, as revealing and releasing, Lear (unconsciously and without deliberation— that is, sincerely) seeks to release himself from his roles, or personae, as prescribed and determined by institutions and codified relations with others. Without the betrayal of the self's prescribed roles, and hence the modal specification of the prescribed trusts of its office, the self cannot be released from itself, and so be itself.

In a parallel manner, "even the wise Cordelia miscalculates her power to absorb the violent emotions in her father which she has provoked; it is not so much raw aggression that leads to tragedy, but the loss of control that results from a simple refusal on the part of a 'character' to conform to a 'role.' Hence, the youngest and fairest daughter of the king refuses to be the daughter of a king, but insists upon speaking as a woman who is Cordelia, and no other."[23] Much as Lear miscalculates the sense and consequence of his demand, given its impulsiveness without forethought or forbearance, Cordelia miscalculates the unhinged reaction of her father. Does Lear count on Cordelia's forgiveness in situ for his unjust demand in the hope that she would play along, in which case she would not be able to forgive herself and, in turn, would need to be forgiven by Lear for not truthfully responding to his injustice in the silence of trust? However this question stands, as Joyce Carol Oates comments, "In this woman's insistence upon moral intelligence not determined by her social role we have rebellion, the first and most surprising of all. The others are for gain, for power, for exciting, new, lustful alliances, but Cordelia's is without any ostensible purpose: she declares herself unwilling to lie, she declares *herself* as self."[24] In this slippage between her role as "Cordelia" and *herself*, she acts, much as Antigone, otherwise than as prescribed, expected, and demanded, thus slipping out from under her *prescribed trusts* into an indeterminate and creative zone of *self-prescribing* trust within which, to draw upon Oates's characterization, there is "a hint of the Void: formless horror." This "formless void" is the nothing in which trust itself takes hold, as that upon which human life and the worlds of its cohabitation take stand, but just as much *into* which human life falls when trust folds in on itself.

Cordelia's singularity unburdens herself of itself through the interruption of her prescribed individuality as an "It," as determined by the cares and concerns of what Buber designates the "It-world" (*Es-Welt*). In keeping silence, she declares herself a Thou standing against Lear's demand for *its* declaration of love. Lear can hear only, or wants to hear only, what *one* would, or should, declare about their love for a father, as with Regan's parroting of Goneril's fawning words of daughterly devotion.[25] Cordelia's silence bespeaks a presentness that cannot be inscribed within determinations of the "It-world," in relation to which her sincere presence can appear, or count, only as the nothing of silence, rather than the silence of nothing. As Buber writes, "What, then, does one experience of the Thou? Nothing at all. For one does not experience it."[26] To stand in the presence of the Other as Thou, in contrast to relating to the Other as an experience, where the Other stands before me as an identifiable "It" (rather than I standing *within* the presence of the Thou), is to be open to the real and effective (*wirkliche*) presence of the Other as "unique," "singular," and "whole." Presentness is grace in exquisite silence. Standing in the meaningful presence of the Other as Thou, the Other participates in my existence, much as I stand in, and so participate in, the life of the Other. Within such a standing for one-another in participation and trust, the Other's presentness is not reducible to qualities or attributes that are "present to hand" (*vorhanden*). The presence of the Other exceeds her qualities and attributes, the ways in which she "stands before me," in finding myself *in* her presence, as "where-in" I encounter her and the world as "existing" (*vorhanden*). This "where-in" in which I encounter others and the world is what Buber terms the original "there-between" (*Dazwischen*) of human facticity, the "in-betweenness" of I-Thou, in its world-disclosing and self-disclosing relief. Rather than speak, as does Heidegger, of the existential originality of Dasein in its being-in-the-world, we should speak, as does Buber, of the existential originality of *Dazwischen* in its being-in-the-world. In the beginning, there is the word, or bond of trust: the "foundational word" (*Grundwort*) of I-Thou in its self-disclosing, other-disclosing, and world-disclosing promise.

In a fateful twist, Lear's demand for love can be seen as the anxious subterfuge for a release of his self from himself insofar as he seeks to slip away from his cares and business—that is, his roles in the world— and thus crawl unburdened, denuded of the weight of the world and the weight of the self as an individual, toward his promised end. This desired release from the world is sought as an absolute separation of the self from its personae as king *and* father. The aged Lear seeks to retire from his roles and identity, as prescribing his standing to the world, in order to become reconciled with his mortality, and hence with himself, as definitive of his standing in the world. Inscribed within Buber's frame of reference, the "It-world" is structured, as an essentially ordered world (*geordnete Welt*), by the prescribed trusts of our roles and offices (the modal specification of trust), institutions, reliability, predictability, and familiarity. It is a world of "density and duration" with bounded and bordered territories, classification of identities, and set-piece relationships. Only in such an ordered, bounded, and symbolically instituted world do we have substance and traction. As Buber writes, "Without it [the ordered world] you cannot remain alive; its reliability preserves you; but if you were to die into it, then you would be buried in nothingness."[27] To die into the world ("aber stürbest du in sie hinein") is to die "fallen" into a world; one would become buried, or recede into the ephemeral fleetingness of the world, despite its manifest order of things. It is only when one becomes released from this ordering of the world, not, however, into another world or afterlife but into the vested hospitality of the Other's kind nursery *within this world*, standing in their presence, that death no longer afflicts us as falling into nothing. The promise of the Other, when encountered in their real and effective presence, is the promise of redemption in the acceptance and appropriation of our standing in this world as death-bound creatures. Though we cannot live without, outside, or beyond the ordered world, were we to die solely "in it," without any standing within the relation of I-Thou, we would be "buried in nothingness." In seeking to "crawl unburdened to the grave," Lear in his anxiety turns on this foreboding possibility of dying in the world without the redemptive promise of dying in the kind nursery of the Other.

The world, in this regard, is twice folded: we both stand in the presence of the world with regard to others and stand in the presence of others with regard to the world. The nexus of relations that forms our standing toward the world as "It" (including relations prescribed toward others through the "It-world") does not "guarantee" our sense of being bonded to the world—our trust in the world—for such trust requires an existential participation in the lives of others. The world as ordered, reliable, and familiar, as the world in which we experience and relate to others, ourselves, and the world, stands there, next to your skin ("sie steht je da, deiner Haut anliegend"), and yet without any standing *within* the proximity of the Other as Thou, the world remains primarily "alien both outside and inside of you." As Buber remarks, "You perceive it [the world] and take it for your 'truth'; it permits itself to be taken by you, but it does not give itself to you." We come to "understandings" (*verständigen*) about the world in relation to others without ever meaningfully encountering others. Without such encounters, in which we stand in the presence of others, nothing of our worldly (*welthaft*) associations and relationships guarantees any "bondedness," or "trust," with the world. Only the proximity of the Other as Thou "vouches for, or authenticates, your connection to the world" (*verbürgt dir deine Verbundenheit mit der Welt*). We are reconciled with ourselves in the world of our orderings, meanings, and relationships only when our standing in the world becomes redeemed through the participation and proximity of Others in our lives as well as our participation and proximity in the lives of Others. As Buber writes, "Only through participation in the being of an existing being [the Other as Thou] does the meaningfulness [*Sinn*] in the very ground of one's own being open up."[28] Lear's panic *at* his anxiety before death turns, however, on the impossible pursuit of seeking release from the world of roles, identities, and institutions—the "It-world"—through an absolute separation in the promise of the kind nursery of Cordelia's presentness. In seeking to "open the meaningfulness in the very ground of one's being" as the passage that would make death bearable, Lear seeks to unbind himself from the twofold forked condition of the human. The essential "twofoldness" of the human condition, however, that we are caught between relations of I-It and in-between encounters of I-Thou, cannot be entirely overcome, neither through mystical absorption in the Other or complete escape into the It-world. As Buber writes, "This, however, is the sublime melancholy of our fate that every Thou must become an It in our world."[29] Our fate becomes a grotesque tragedy when we succumb by our own hand to wanting to escape or evade our sublime melancholy at the price of our own undoing.

In Lear's all-too-human foolishness, there resides an element of sincerity, and hence, in this respect, a truthful attestation to the originality of trust in its essential shaping as a *dialogical* I-Thou relation. The rupture between Lear and Cordelia in the conflict between Law and Love, in the panicked anxiety of "*shaking* all cares and business from our age" (emphasis added) in search of Cordelia's "kind nursery," evinces a breakage in their dialogue of trust. Expressed in Buber's thinking, the *Dazwischen* of the dialogical I-Thou relation, or better, openness ("encounter" in Buber's terms), is existentially original; it characterizes the facticity of human life. This dimension of "in-betweenness" is ontologically prior to the distinction between "subject" and "object"—intentionality—as well as more primordial than Dasein with its purported self-appropriating "authenticity" in being-toward-death. Trust, in this sense of an existential in-betweenness, is ontologically primitive, or "original," in its dialogical and temporal disclosure of myself, others, and the world. As Buber understands, there is no fundamental ontology, or existential analytic, more fundamental than "dialogical life," and hence no foundation for any fundamental ontology, or existential analytic, that is not grounded in the dialogical life of trust, which, as dramatically portrayed in *King Lear*, is that upon which humans stand *and* fall.[30]

The Dialogue of Trust

Trust among individuals is a trust given as well as received. The trust that we give as well as receive is a trust that must be honored. We honor not only the trusted individual but also our relationship of trust as such and, in this relationship of trust, ourselves. To be trusting as well as to be trusted is to become entrusted with the bond of trust itself. When we give our trust to the Other, we give of ourselves freely in placing ourselves or something (or someone) that we care for in the hands of the Other. In honoring our bond of trust, we accept responsibility for a trust received and given, already assigned. The assuredness of trust's bonding, in coming to know the Other and feeling attached to the Other, invested in the Other's well-being and settled that the Other is committed to our own, is never a static affair or inert condition. Our confidence in trust is always shifting, at times more or less pronounced, yet always there. Relationships of trust must be nourished and nurtured so that the assuredness of trust becomes related to a self-monitoring of the relationship itself. The exercise of functional virtues (those virtues appropriate to the nourishing and nurturing of trust) as well as the monitoring of trust presupposes that the intrinsic *value* of trusting is recognized and upheld—lived—by the mutually trusting individuals. It is not only that the individuals in trust must respectively honor their trusts toward each other: the relationship of trust itself must be honored by each entrusted member. I am as much your keeper as we are together the guardians of our trust.

In its paradigmatic form, trusting, as Annette Baier argues, is neither a form of promising nor a contract, implied or otherwise; neither is it willful or purposive. As with trust between children and parents, which Baier identifies (along with child psychologists such as Erikson) as the "seed" for all trusting relationships, we find ourselves trusting without any calculating or cautious deliberation, or as the consequence of instrumental reasoning. To be trusting and trusted is not, in this respect, contrary to freedom of choice, deliberation, and reflection; it is, on the contrary, their indispensable condition. The initiative for trusting is neither distinctly localizable or identifiable in me *or* in the Other but crystallizes between us, when finding myself already trusting, "thrown," as it were, while projecting myself toward a trusting of the Other. Adapting here Buber's felicitous word creations, persons become trusting through and for each other as "I effectively and affectively trusting You" *and* "You effectively and affectively trusting I" (*Ich-wirkende-Du* and *Du-wirkende-Ich*).[31] Hence, the difficulty of reconstructing the genealogy of our trust—who first trusted whom? how and when? why?—as well as anticipating the sustaining of such trust.

As Baier insightfully proposes, trust involves a special kind of vulnerability.[32] As distinct from reliability (when I rely on the proper functioning of equipment or services rendered by others) and familiarity (when routines or the presence of others are habitual for me), what distinguishes the relationship of trust is its specific form of vulnerability, and along with this risk an original form of availability toward the person in whom we trust. Trusts are betrayed, whereas things can only disappoint or fail us. When the hammer fails to function properly, I am disappointed and frustrated but not betrayed by the hammer. Frustration at the hammer's noncompliance to my projects might indeed motivate anger, violence, or revenge. The experience of limitation imposed upon my projects by the materiality of things, as when a doorknob does not turn my way or a hammer fails me, can provoke a senseless expression of counterviolence and aggression against the world: I curse the hammer and throw it against the wall. And yet even with such revenge against inanimate things of the world, it is not because I feel betrayed by them, for, in such cases, my vulnerability to the world of things is a function of anticipated failures and limitations. My reliance on the hammer does not edge, or line, my sense of self from within; when it fails, I do not resent the hammer for failing *me*. With relations of promising or contracts, harms are anticipated and calculated (one promises not to do this, or in promising to do this the harm of not fulfilling my promise is implicitly understood). In contrast to reliability and promising, trust is characterized by a vulnerability to *unanticipated* harms through the discretionary power given to the Other as my keeper (or as keeper over something or someone I myself care for), in the confidence, however, that such empowerment—that is, trust—will not be turned against me.[33] Bonds of trust are constitutive of the self in ways that reliability and familiarity—with things and routines; with other persons—are not. This vulnerability to unanticipated harm in trusting is not merely a function of any limitation of prudential foresight or knowledge. It is constitutive in its paradigmatic form that I cannot anticipate betrayal, or frame the *possibility* of betrayal, for if I did anticipate the betrayal of the trust I give, if, in other words, I gave you my trust on the basis of an expectation of possible harm, I would not be trusting you with any confidence. My trust, in such instances, would be predicated on distrust or only extended—not given—with caution and reservation, not unreservedly and trustingly. Although there is inherent risk in trusting others, we do not stand facing the person *in whom* we trust as dangerous. We do not stand in the precariousness of risk when standing in the Other's trusted presence; we do not *feel* vulnerable in trusting but, on the contrary, feel ourselves confident in our trusts and assured by our trust. We do not merely trust the Other. We trust *in* the Other and so rest assured, or confident, in our trust, standing in the Other's presence as we stand exposed to the risk of trusting. But even as this taken-for-granted impossibility of betrayal sustains trust, if and when betrayal befalls me (or other forms of harm), there often lingers a marked incredulity with regard to having at all trusted the Other (How could I have ever trusted her?) as well as with regard to the violated impossibility of betrayal I had once so assuredly trusted (How is this betrayal of my trust at all possible?).[34]

When we give ourselves to the Other in trust, we entrust ourselves to the Other. In Baier's felicitous formulation, we entrust something we care for (our children, our car, something we value, secrets, etc.)—something already in our trust—or ourselves (our well-being and welfare) in assigning the Other the exercise of discretionary powers.[35] We allow the Other to participate in our lives for the sake of our own beneficence and thus grant them a hand as well as a say in our own self-determination and well-being. Trusting thus requires an acceptance and avowal of interdependency as well as the displacement, or, better, the distribution, of our own autonomy. Trust implies self-recognition and self-attestation of our finite self-sufficiency, that we cannot care for ourselves and the things we value *on our own*, and thus that others are needed to become invested in our well-being and participate in our lives.

To value myself as entrusted, to value the Other in trust, and to value our relationship of trust require that I value my autonomy as well as the autonomy of the Other. The Other lives within me insofar as I am bound to the Other and accompanied by the Other. I value the Other in a determinate kind of relationship (friendship, marriage, etc.) but also value myself as entrusted to the Other in this relationship *as well as* value the relationship in which I find myself with the Other. I must value (honor) the Other's trust; I must value (honor) this election to trust, myself as entrusted; and I must value the relationship of trust to which I am entrusted and which has been entrusted to us. This valuing of being-with-the-Other hinges critically on what Husserl calls self-valuing (*Selbstwertung* or *Selbstwertung des Subjekts*).[36] It is only because I value myself as a subject of freedom (for Husserl, meaning purposive, reflective, responsive, sense bestowing) that values have significance and traction in my life and thus that I must nourish and nurture a relation to myself, as self-valuing, in relations of value with Others. Self-valuing must be exercised in attesting to oneself, esteeming oneself, trusting oneself, and honoring oneself in honoring one's trusts. Self-valuing depends in turn on being recognized by others as a valuing and self-valuing person as well as valuing others as self-valuing persons. We feel honored in being trusted by the Other. We must honor the trust placed in our hands by the Other, and this honoring is anchored in a sentiment of being recognized and valued, elected, of wanting to be truthful and trustworthy for ourselves as well as for the Other. We do not want to let the other person down nor ourselves. We want to live up to our trusts and entrustments in such a manner that we are at once self-regarding and self-valuing as well as self-giving and other-valuing. What shores up against an undue sliding along either pole of regard toward pathological slavishness or obsequious, in giving ourselves *over* to the Other, or toward pathological monopolization and weaponization of trust in the unbridled pursuit of our self-regard, is honoring and valuing the relationship of trust itself in its open promise for each other.

Trusting requires that I value the *autonomy of the relationship of trust itself* through which, or in which, we are bound to each other in the mutual realization of our respective freedom. We must each serve as the Other's keeper while at the same time each serving as keepers of our trusting relationship. Since it remains critical for the vitality of trust to remain *open* toward the future of our respective and reciprocal development in interdependent freedom, relationships of trust can be understood not merely as a sustained dialogue (in word and deed) in an atmosphere of trust (we confide to each other, judge each other critically, do things for and with each other, etc.) but also as a sustaining dialogue *about* trust itself, where the meaningfulness of our bond of trust becomes itself a constitutive component of our dialogues in trust. In whatever it is that transpires between us, in action and speech, there is a continuous and sustaining dialogue about *how* we are to trust each other, measure, adjust, and expand trust's limits, and, when betrayed, how to respond in trust to its breakages, ruptures, and aftermaths. Such a dialogue of trust need not, and most often is not, explicit or emphatic but remains spoken between the lines, shaping from within the in-betweenness of trusting itself in its self-understanding.

Exploring and configuring the *possibilities of trust* are, thus, accordingly entrusted to the relationship of trust itself. Although a measure of how we trust becomes prescribed by the modal specification of our relationship, cultural practice, and symbolic forms (we trust the doctor in ways prescribed by the profession), there is intrinsically no concept or set of rules that prescribes exhaustively the ways in which trust must navigate the course of living with the Other. Trust always entails a creative self-prescribing element and initiative concerning its own self-sustaining meaningfulness and possibilization of itself, as it were. Trust must trust in its own capacity to educate itself on how best to nourish and nurture itself, even when trust is mediated by its modal specification, cultural heritage, and symbolic forms. There is no trust without experimentation at trust. In trusting one another, we must trust in the possibilities of trust's consideration and allowance, which are not clearly and distinctly prescribed or ordained ahead of time. These possibilities of trust delineate potentialities of our being and depend on sustaining an openness to who we are to become together in trust. Trust empowers potentialities of being along the lines of trust's multiplanar dimensions: being in the world, being with and for others, being oneself. *Seinskönnen* is not without *Vertrauenkönnen*.

In this regard, trust is an exemplary dialogical relationship in Mikhail Bakhtin's sense: a dialogue in which the meaningfulness of the dialogue itself becomes a critical and constitutive component of the dialogue. The dialogical relationship of trust is, in this sense, structured according to three positions: the first, the second, and the third (me, the Other, and the self-understanding of the relationship itself, its meaningfulness, *between us*).[37] The dialogical form of trust is therefore not dyadic but triadic.[38] With trust in its paradigmatic form as mutual trust between persons, the position of the third is to remain *unclaimed* and *unoccupied* by either person in the bond of trust. This autonomy of the relation of trust does not imply that none of the entrusted persons cannot speak for and from the position of the third but that each speaks in turn on behalf of the third without claiming to speak exclusively for the third—that is, the self-understanding of our trust. We are each keepers of our trust without any one of us becoming the lord of our trust. Each of us can speak for our trusting relationship, speaking on its behalf, while also speaking for ourselves and for each other. We might leverage this position of the third when we encourage a friend to act in a certain way "for the sake of our friendship" or when we confront a spouse with an unpleasant truth "for the good of our marriage." Within a dialogical relationship, this position of the third is an "extralocation" that must remain open toward the future, *as* the future that becomes us. This extralocation is the "where-in" of the trusting relationship's meaningfulness where we can encounter each other, bound to each other, as entrusted to one other. The meaningfulness of trust is to be guarded against succumbing to being instrumentalized, monopolized, or manipulated for the gain of one person at the expense of the other. The openness of the position of the third allows for an equalization and mitigation of encroaching power relations within trust. When trust becomes the conduit to my ruin, when I am deceived in trust, this position of the third becomes claimed by the individual who deceives me; he plays at trust all the while understanding what this relation is about, which I myself do not see, believing that this place of the third remains between us, neither mine nor his, but open. When trust turns against me, the position of the third has been seized from within, thus producing a split vision within the relationship of trust.[39] The Confidence-Man or Abuser of Trust runs a certain narrative of our trust while I run a different narrative; both narratives fail to touch each other and communicate. The dialogue has been severed (much as with Cordelia and Lear in the opening of the play). When I realize in hindsight that my trust was geared against me, my established perception and narrative of our trust becomes voided from the inside: I was playing a part in a game that I did not perceive and understand, and trust blinded me to while capturing me within its game. The wounding of betrayal runs deep and catches us from behind, from where we thought our backs were covered.

6

"No Cause, No Cause": Breakages of Trust and the Availability of Forgiveness

In Shakespeare's mapping of trusts undone, as unmaking of the world, the self, and relations to others, the intrinsic vulnerability of trusting to unanticipated harms is traveled alongside the counterpart availability for others despite their deceit, betrayal, and abandonment. Essential in belonging to others in giving ourselves over to their trust is a commitment to stand by the Other in whom we trust, come what may. When the Other betrays our trust, our commitment to the Other need not necessarily devolve into pathological overtrust or provoke a crisis in our own self-trust when coming to doubt ourselves, rather than coming to terms with the Other who has betrayed us. As represented by Cordelia, Kent, Edgar, and the Fool in different ways, trust entails an availability, however precarious and fragile, for those in whom we trust. In honoring ourselves as trusted and trusting, we are entrusted with remaining available for the Other when the Other fails or abuses her granted discretionary power, or otherwise betrays the trust invested in her. The mettle of our trust becomes galvanized in the endurance of our committed availability for the Other. This connection between trust and availability, theatrically explored in *King Lear*, can be philosophically developed by turning to Gabriel Marcel's reflections on *disponibilité*—a term for which there exists no single English equivalent. Possible candidates such as "availability," "disposition," "readiness," "reachable," and "on call" gravitate around the phenomenon richly encompassed by Marcel's term *disponibilité*. This challenge of translation is not merely an issue of finding a suitable English term; the underlying challenge is philosophical in translating a hitherto unrecognized dimension of trust into a thematic conception. As Marcel remarks, his reflections on *disponibilité* circumscribe "a group of problems for which [philosophers] have rarely considered looking for a solution."[1] Given the absence of any direct historical precedence or established pedigree, Marcel styles his exploration of *disponibilité* as a *défrichage*, meaning both "clearing," as in clearing the ground in agriculture, and "groundwork," as in laying the groundwork for construction. Hence, as he adds, the "circuitous and perhaps *perplexing*" character of his reflections on *disponibilité*. As with so many other fertile conceptual creations, Marcel's reflections on *disponibilité* have fallen by the wayside; *disponibilité* has been relegated to that remote island of forgotten thought where fertile conceptions so often seem to vanish without a trace.[2]

Much to the spirit of Marcel's exploratory practice of philosophical thinking, *disponibilité* is not a finished or settled concept but a probing constellation of reflections that address from different angles a central question. In moving through, and thus connecting, the different points of bearing within the conceptual constellation of *disponibilité*, its animating question emerges: what does it mean to belong to the Other?[3] In what sense do we participate in the lives of others through trust (and, likewise, in what sense do others participate in our lives)? Whereas the expression "you belong to me," Marcel notes, signals a demanding and possessive posture toward the Other (as with Lear's command for Cordelia to proclaim her love for him), the expression "I belong to you" voices the assuredness of availability for the Other (as with Cordelia's spoken validation of her bond to her father). Speaking at cross-purposes to each other, Lear proclaims to Cordelia, "You belong to me," while she responds to Lear, "I belong to you."[4] In saying that "I belong to you," I attest to my availability for you in the various senses suggested by Marcel's term *disponibilité*: to be there for you, to stand by you, to be "on call" and "reachable." In trusting you, I do not just give myself to you in placing something I care for, or myself, in your hands. In thus belonging to you, I am equally giving of myself to you in *making* myself available *for you* in the charge of my trust. In this entwined sense of "belonging to you" and "availability for you," trusting relationships can be characterized as a relation of what Marcel calls "substitution"—namely, that I freely substitute the Other's freedom for my own, not, however, that I divest myself of my freedom but that I freely grant the Other a discretionary power of judgment *into* (and not *over*) my autonomy (to hark back to Baier's felicitous formulation) in the confidence that the Other will not turn my own empowerment of them in my life against me. "Substitution" in this sense designates the fundamental way in which I participate in the life of the Other (and likewise, how the Other participates in mine). I appoint the Other to be my keeper in this election of trust and come to stand in the presence of the Other in whom I trust. In the rupture of dialogue that occurs between Lear and Cordelia, whereas Lear seeks to secure the appointment of a successor through his demand for a declaration of love, Cordelia affirms with dignity and grace the standing of their relationship, not in terms of standing *under* Lear in submission but in standing alongside in "substitution"—that is, in participation and belonging. The rupture of their dialogical bond of trust turns on the confused misunderstanding of its unspoken and underwritten word: *substitution*. More profoundly and profusely, each character in *King Lear* can in their own manner be seen as "wrong about the word"—the words, both spoken and unspoken, that bind them to the world as well as to each other.[5]

I cannot sustainably trust the Other with caring for myself, or something or someone I value and care for, without faith, belief, or confidence (these terms understood here interchangeably as is often the case in everyday speech) in the Other into whose hands I have thus placed myself. In granting you such discretionary power and elected participation in my life, I take on a responsibility for this trust in remaining available for you, if and when you betray or fail me in your discretionary power and presence for me. Even though it is I who invest you with trust in the confidence that you will not turn this trust against me, I thereby become responsible *for you* in being available, if and when you turn away from me. This passage from "to you" (giving you my trust) to "for you" (remaining available for you) is substitution in the dual sense of electing you as my keeper as well as appointing myself as your keeper. We are mutually the keepers of *our* trust (see chapter 5). To belong to the Other in whom I trust is decidedly not to become the Other's servant, possession, or otherwise rendered at their disposal. Remaining available for you does not abrogate, mitigate, or supplant your own responsibility toward me in trust, nor, conversely, does it grant to me a paternalistic and lording attitude over you. It is, on the contrary, to place oneself in the care of the Other while availing oneself to the Other, as the gift of oneself in receiving (but not in exchange for) the gift of the Other's trust. As Marcel writes, "The proper function of the subject is to emerge from itself and realize itself primarily in the gift of oneself and in the various forms of creativity."[6] We are called upon to be creatively self-fashioning in an exemplary manner when called upon to remain available for others.

An empowering faith in the Other's election underwrites the sustainability and meaningfulness of trust—its endurance. As Marcel writes, "To believe in someone is to put one's trust in him, i.e., 'I am sure you will not let me down, that you will instead fulfill my expectations, that you will realize them.' . . . One can only trust a 'thou,' of being invoked, of becoming something I can fall back on."[7] Faith in the Other, however, is not a passive stance or inert attitude, for it requires a nourishing draw of creativity regarding the ways in which I am able to remain available in times when the Other fails, betrays, or abandons me, when my faith in the Other—in their trustworthiness, in their judgment, and so forth—is put to the test. This intrinsic connection within trusting relations between belonging to the Other and availability for the Other brings into relief the "metatrust" in the Other's trust and trustworthiness as a function of our faith in the Other as well as our commitment to our relationship of trust itself, given its dialogical constitution.

This constitutive dimension of faith in the trusted Other places temporality at its center in a self-configuring way. As Niklas Luhmann stresses, "The theme of trust involves a problematic relationship to time," such that "a theory of trust presupposes a theory of time."[8] The assuredness of trust in its coupling of cognitive, conative, and affective linkages (see chapter 1) shapes the temporality of one's relation to the Other. In providing assuredness and assurances toward the future, trust does not supersede or suppress the openness of time, but nor, as Luhmann himself proposes, does trust exclusively function as a means for the reduction of complexity with regard to the future.[9] When predominantly determined through institutional forms of modal specification (i.e., trusting the pilot of an airplane), trust significantly reduces social *and* psychological complexity in contracting the indeterminacy of the future in its manifold possibilities into the determinacy of a present from which the future can be grasped, anticipated, or mastered in advance. The indeterminate complexity of the future becomes contracted through trust in order to provide orientation and bearing for our future-directed actions in the present, much as the past becomes contracted through habit in order to allow for action in the present to be geared into the world from the past.[10] Trust and habit each conspire to render the future *and* the past "ready at hand," as it were. Yet trust in its paradigmatic form, as indispensable for participating in the lives of others, just as significantly sustains itself through the *futural affordance* of complexity. In trusting and being trusted, the messiness both inside and outside becomes more navigable as we negotiate together the waterways of our intersecting and cojointed lives. As an assured coupling mechanism of the cognitive, the affective, and the conative capacities of the Other, trust breeds its own indigenous intelligence, or dialogical self-understanding, in terms of which I do not merely anticipate the actions, reactions, and projects of my friend (for example). As significantly, I am able to perspicuously discern and live through the complexity of my friend's character, motivations, and reasoning, or, as the case may be, lack thereof. The modus vivendi of a trusting relationship consists in the affordance of complexity in both senses of the term: I can afford complexity, bear its costs and make due for its allowance; I know how to navigate and negotiate complexity through its affordances. In both these senses of affordance, I am open (embrace and invite) to the complexity of the Other and thus good-naturedly participate in her (entangled and invested) complexity, standing within its presence, rather than outside or against it.

In trusting relationships, each person acquires a "knowing how" and affordance of each other's complexity, and hence the complexity of being in *this* relationship *together*, that otherwise remains ungraspable and unintelligible—that is, unlived from the outside. Trusting affords a degree of granularity in our perception, judgment, and knowledge of the Other that otherwise remains critically lacking with regard to those whom we mistrust or merely reply upon. By contrast, overtrust and pathological forms of trusting can foster a blindness or fixity of perception; the Other becomes less seen for who she truly is in her complexity. By the same token, mistrust tends to flatten our perception of others, making us less accepting and acknowledging of the complexity of their lives. Conversely, certain forms of distrust can sharpen our perception and assessment of the Other's complexity, thus allowing for the development of an acutely strategic intelligence against them. Generally speaking, however, in trusting the Other, I avail myself to the challenge of trust in the affordance of interpersonal complexity: to remain patient in exploring, configuring, and negotiating the complexities, confrontations, and conflicts *within* our bond of trust. This affordance of complexity essentially entails belonging to and participating in the dialogue of trust, which, in turn, requires an acquired and exercised fluency (and hence the talent for a certain tact with those in whom we trust) not only in emotional, or affective, terms but also in cognitive terms. Those in whom we trust are those lives in which we generously allow ourselves, without any sense of magnanimity or subservience (groveling, etc.), to get involved and stay involved through thick and thin. We are committed to navigating the complexity of the Other, allowing the Other to take us wherever our trusting relationship might lead, or fall, trusting them as both friend *and* stranger.

Creative Fidelity

Given this self-availing faith in the Other in whom we trust, *disponibilité* is no mere acceptance of belonging to the Other (accepting that I am not self-sufficient or tolerating the Other's complexity) nor a resigned or begrudging acknowledgment of the Other's finitude. To be "available," "reachable," and "on call" for the Other—to be there for the Other—is to engagingly stand in affordance of the Other's singular being in its infinitely complex finitude, becoming, as it were, a rallying partisan to their own cause into whose hands I have placed myself. To render oneself available for the Other does not make a claim on the Other or demand of the Other to make themselves available for us in return. There is no duty or obligation imposed on the Other, but the "awaiting of a gift or favor from the other being but only on the grounds of his freedom," much as our own faith in the Other, as availability for the Other, stems from neither duty or obligation but from generosity and goodwill. There is thus no implied imposition of trust on the Other, given that the Other must freely and generously receive and honor trust for trust to be constituted between us. To give our trust to the Other and so place ourselves in the presence of the Other issues an invocation to the Other (not a demand) to receive ourselves in trust; in this summons, we ourselves are called upon to consecrate our faith in the Other in giving them our trust. Whereas the person who remains unavailable for the Other, from pride or assumed self-sufficiency, in distrust or indifference, stands apart and absent, a trusting person wants to be present for the Other in whom they trust, trusting that the Other likewise stands present for them. In the refusal to become present in the lives of others, the prideful individual becomes blind to, or seeks to avoid or discount, the complex singularity of the Other, and looks upon others only through images, prejudices, and generalizations, or not at all. In its most pathological form, as with the Underground Man in his rejection of being forgiven, the resentful misanthrope remains fundamentally unavailable not just for others but also, as tellingly, for themselves (see chapter 3). Whereas a reduction of complexity goes hand in hand with an increased quotient of typecasting and abstraction, paradigmatic trust in its affordance of complexity allows for a more sagacious and nuanced understanding of and involvement with the Other's singular being. In this affordance of complexity, we allow for a constitutive *gap* between our knowledge of the Other and their unfolding lives. In this sense, we stand in the presence of the Other as friend *and* stranger, where the "and" measures the leeway of flexibility and fluidity that we willingly afford for the sake of trusting—that is, being with each other in standing there for one another.

As portrayed in Marcel's theatrical works, *disponibilité* constitutes a configured openness to time through the Other.[11] We stand in trust such that our availability becomes directed toward the future in the self-sustaining acceptance and affirmation of the Other's complex finitude while remaining anchored in the past in the sustained accrual, or density, of trusting one another. The temporal horizon of being-in-the-world becomes inscribed within a horizon of temporality between-us in trusting one another. Availability for the Other, much as belonging to the Other, is not circumscribed to the present but perpetually inaugurates an openness toward the future that mutually becomes us. If future embracing trust intrinsically entails vulnerability to unanticipated harms, it thereby essentially entails vulnerability to the unanticipated Other, given that I cannot anticipate and determine the ways in which the Other, in whom I trust, might nonetheless become other than my trusted Other. To trust the Other is to entrust oneself to an unimaginable *otherness of the Other*, to the point, as with the spectacular case of Jean-Claude Romand (see chapter 1), that the Other who fundamentally betrays me now appears as the Adversary in voiding the meaningfulness of trusting as such. When the Other in whom I trust egregiously fails my trust, putting the mettle of our relationship to the test, I am bitterly (and often catastrophically) caught by surprise. I never expected the trusted person to be "that one person in the world," as we commonly say, who would or could betray my confidence in them. In such instances, the Other does not just become a stranger, since trust affords an openness to the Other as friend and stranger. When the Other betrays my trust in a manner that calls into question my faith in the Other, the stranger whom I could afford becomes the adversary, or unaffordable stranger, who stands outside or against any bond of openness. No longer friend *and* stranger, the treasonous Other becomes revealed as beyond the pale of trust, testing the possibility of remaining available for them.

Remaining available for the Other operates both "inside" and "outside" the bond of trust: outside, insofar that when the Other has ruptured our bond of trust, I am beholden to remaining available, even as I might fail to do so or decide to abandon the Other in turn; inside, insofar as remaining there for the Other even when the Other is no longer here for me attests to the intrinsic relation between trust and availability, the reach of trust beyond its own betrayal. In trusting, I stand before an unanticipated possibility of the Other—to wit, an *impossibility* of the Other (impossible, that is, from within my faith in the Other) that becomes all too real with her grievous betrayal. In giving discretionary power of judgment to the Other in the confidence that it will not be used against me, I have placed myself alongside the Other in making myself available for those occasions when the Other would fail in her honoring of my trust or betray this election of trusting. This is not to condone naively or foolishly in advance come what may; it is to *commit to*—and not simply acknowledge or tolerate—the Other's infinitely (and changing) complex finitude with an openness toward a future in which I would have to encounter the Other as being otherwise than the Other in whom I (had) trusted and nonetheless persevere in availing myself for the Other who has now become an unaffordable stranger, indeed, more than a stranger but an adversary foreign to my trust and yet threateningly, strangely, couched within it. In hindsight, it appears *weird* that I had ever trusted the Other, who has now betrayed me; the familiarity of trusting has been unmasked as disturbingly unsettling from within. Likewise, with regard to myself: I cannot anticipate the singular person I would have or need to become in order to remain available for the Other, if and when the Other betrays or fails me. In the exposure to the unanticipated possibility of the otherness of the Other—their unimaginable betrayal of me—there resides the unanticipated possibility of the otherness of myself in having to become other than the person I thought or imagined I could ever be.

How is one to remain available for the Other whom one no longer recognizes as trusted and trustworthy when, in other words, there no longer stands the "who" in whom I trusted, before whom I could still stand? How do I remain available for the Other when I myself am no longer here for the Other, when, in other words, I can no longer stand before the Other and say, "Here I am"? Stated in these terms, *disponibilité* critically invokes what Marcel calls (in echo of Bergson's *élan vital* in its ethical form of openness) *fidélité créatrice*.[12] Given that relationships of trust are vitally evolving and discovering themselves dialogically through the thicket of ever-new possibilities, engagements, and situations in which we find ourselves together in the world, what is asked of me in remaining available for the Other is openness toward creative and imaginative ways of *becoming* available, or staying available without necessarily remaining who I am, or better, who I *was*. In trust, that "I belong to you" is not a unilateral arrangement of placing myself in your hands, for in belonging to you I must have faith in you as my caretaker, and within such faith, commit myself to remaining available for you. This "remaining" or "enduring" is quintessentially a becoming-other and other-becoming. As exemplified in *King Lear*, creatively remaining available for the Other, when the Other deceives, betrays, or abandons me, admits of different forms, as with Cordelia, Kent, the Fool, each of whom remains there for Lear; likewise Edgar with respect to his father, the Earl of Gloucester. The fiction acted out by Edgar for his blinded father upon the cliffs of Dover or the playacting of the disguised Kent as Caius who faithfully remains in Lear's service are no mere illusions, artifices of the imaginary, or make-believe but expressions of the productive creativity of self-fashioning without which availability for the Other (Edgar leading his father to the cliff's precipice; Kent returning to Lear's service) cannot persevere and prevail.

In its various manifestations, creatively remaining available for the Other gravitates around what Marcel calls the "essentially mysterious act" of keeping faith in the Other. Faith in the Other becomes prodigal "when it defies absence," when, in other words, you are no longer there for me, having broken my trust, or otherwise become absent from me.[13] Enduring the Other's failure involves rallying to the Other through an "inner gathering of oneself" (or self-rallying) for the sake of the Other. In its most extreme manifestations, as with Cordelia, it requires that one survives one's own figurative death, or symbolic "extermination," in having been ejected from the bond of trust through its treason. The survival of availability in the death of trust constitutes the veritable mystery of its generosity. What is required of me in remaining available for you is my own creative self-transformation into the singular person I would have to become so as to not abandon you when you nevertheless have forsaken me. Creative faithfulness, essential for renewing the vitality of trusting relationships, is not reducible to a virtuous disposition, habit, or training, or prescribed by norms or duties. Much as trust itself does not spring from a rational norm, obligation, or habit (even though trust can become habitual, virtuous, and norm enhancing), faith in the Other involves creative self-becoming in terms of which I am called upon to become other than who I have been, indeed other than who I *can* be, or thought myself *I* could be. Neither a pregiven possibility of my being (as habit or disposition) nor an actual given to my being (a prescribed duty or obligation), creative faithfulness operates as a virtual "I can" that can become actualized only in the grasp of its own supererogatory self-possibilization. The "I can" of creative fidelity remains always in suspense until the seized moment of the becoming that I can. *Seinskönnen*, reinscribed as *Vetrauenkönnen*, critically operates through the "I can" of creative fidelity. If availability is a function of giving oneself to the Other, even when the Other no longer receives or gives of herself (in no longer honoring the bond of trust), the creative dimension implicit in remaining available makes of honoring trust a question of creatively *self-prescribing* how to remain available beyond (and at times against) the modal prescriptions of the trusting (or *prescribed* trust) relationship itself. This self-possibilization, in which the self who can give itself this possibility must itself become possible for itself as "I can," exceeds any knowledge, accounting, or certainty I might possess about myself, my capacities, and motivations. The "I can" of *creative* fidelity exceeds what I can be or do. In thus transcending what I can be or do, and hence who I am in terms of what I can, the "I can" that becomes me in creative fidelity self-prescribes who I thought I could not or never be to whom I can become, thus inscribing into my own self-transcendence an "impossibility" ("Oh, how I could never be the person who forgives you") that nonetheless becomes me. Self-possibilization thus hangs (or falters) on *fidelité à moi-même,* or "creative faithfulness in myself/creative faith in myself." I can only trust in myself (trust that "I can") that when called upon not to abandon you in a situation of crisis within the dialogue of our trust, that I am able to creatively and virtually become other than myself for your sake as well as for mine, indeed for the sake of our bond of trust and standing in the world. This trust in myself that I can delineates a halo of hope around my *improbable* self—the constitutive eccentricity of myself—in specifying a meeting point between the possible and the improbable where I could encounter myself in the future as the future I would find improbable, indeed impossible, only from the present, let alone in light of my past.[14] An obscure me becomes me in the self-seizing upsurge that I can.

The Mystery of Creative Faithfulness

In Marcel's characterization, the "mystery of creative fidelity" bespeaks the "mystery of commitment" to the Other. To have faith in the Other in whom one trusts is not based on any particular conviction or attitude toward the Other but on the acceptance of the Other's trustworthiness and the intrinsic goodness of trusting itself. Whereas a conviction, opinion, or image that I *have* of the Other refers to them without necessarily involving any binding of myself to the Other, to *keep faith* in the Other is not based on a species of belief, opinion, or conviction that I *have* but institutes a faith that I *am*, which underwrites the modus vivendi of sustaining trust in the Other and retaining faith in myself.[15] In this respect, Marcel characterizes the commitment to the Other as the benevolent offering (or "gift") of an "infinite credit." This extension of credit, or charity, is not to be understood in an economic sense, or in terms of an accounting or calculation that would leave no account outstanding or otherwise risk one thought too many. The Other can bank on me in the sense that my goodwill and availability manifest themselves actively in the creative fidelity that perpetually must become me. As Marcel writes, "Actually, the credit I extend is, in a way, myself. I lend myself to X."[16] Credit here is my belief (or faith) in the Other itself, that I am there for the Other. In its original meaning, *credo* (I believe), in the sense of "I have faith," calls to mind "I set my heart to" (from *cor, cordis*), taken here in the sense of "I devote myself to the cause of the Other" in rendering myself available for them.[17] Crucially, however, "setting my heart to the Other" does not extend any license for making myself *disposable* or otherwise pathologically self-sacrificing for the Other, nor pledge an unimpeachable and unilateral fealty that would enforce itself, blindly and mechanically, without any creative uptake on my part (as is so often the case with political and tribal loyalties). Nevertheless, there obtains an intrinsic risk in keeping faith in the Other. In belonging to the Other in trust, we not only stand exposed to the vulnerability of unanticipated harms and the other of the Other but also stand vulnerable toward the pathologization of our own availability for the Other, or its prodigal abuse and rank manipulation by the Other. Enduring faith in the Other exposes itself to exploitation and can often facilitate and prompt deplorable forms of overtrust or slavish allegiance, but not for what Josiah Royce insightfully calls "loyalty to loyalty."[18] As Baier puts it in reformulating Royce's insight, "bad forms [of deplorable trust] tend to be temporary since self-undermining, while forms that are self-strengthening and that tend to produce meta-trust, trust in trust-involving relationships and forms of cooperation," or what Marcel designates as faith in the Other, "are the ones that we have good reason to welcome from a moral point of view."[19] For Marcel, trust is a supreme good (Baier speaks of it as a "supreme virtue") founded on infinite charity toward the Other or, in other words, the "mysterious act" of creative faithfulness. The courage required to keep faith in the Other attests to the intrinsic goodness of trusting and, in this sense, can be considered as involving a "transcendental courage" in attestation to the transcendence of the Good. In contrast to Paul Tillich's "courage to be," courage in this enactment of creative fidelity attests to the Good in the affirmation of the supreme *goodness* of being-with Others, of participation, as constitutive of creation itself, or "created being," as against all odds, and hence, in this sense, as over and above being.[20]

The supreme good in keeping faith in the Other whom I trust is nonetheless just as supremely vulnerable to abuse and exploitation. At times indistinguishable from graciousness or foolishness, we are bewildered in standing by the Other who has betrayed our trust as we nonetheless hold on to our faith in the Other and, indeed, in the value of trust itself, despite evidence to the contrary, when our trust has become hopeless, or so it often seems, put to the test. In holding on to our faith in the Other we just as much hold on to the goodness of trust itself and likewise the goodness of keeping faith in *another*, and not just *this* Other—hence the abysmal depth to which our faith in human beings as such can plummet when *this* Other has betrayed me. As with the case of Jean-Claude Romand, the violation of trust in its most intimate form is experienced as nothing less than a violation in the goodness of being itself (see chapter 1). Keeping faith in the Other is at times mysteriously indistinguishable from stupidity, much as it can mysteriously play itself out as saintly grace. How often have we judged others to be foolish in holding on to their faith in the Other that the Other clearly no longer merits or reciprocates; by the same token, how often have we admired others who hold on to their faith in the Other when everyone else, including ourselves, have abandoned the Other, judging any faith in their trustworthiness to be at most a forlorn hope, at worst categorically hopeless. Under the best of circumstances, the exercise of creative faithfulness requires the exercise of critical intelligence, fertile imagination, and discerning judgment for the sake of the Other's regard as well as my own self-regard, but just as much for the sake of the "in-betweenness" of our relationship itself. And yet because I cannot *be* myself in advance (there will always be a gap between who I know myself to be and who I would have to be), I must commit myself to keeping faith in the Other neither in the despair of unknowing nor in the optimism of thinking to know myself better but in the hope of my own self-unknowing, hoping in myself—the self yet to come and the "I can" yet to be what I can—so that I might become inspired to create myself anew as the person who could remain available, come what may. Unlike the countless forms of unavailability that stem from pride, indifference, ethical myopia, self-absorption, cowardice, or failure of the imagination (the catalog of which is potentially unending), the day in which I fundamentally lose faith in the Other, or, indeed, in the human condition as such, is the day I become fundamentally *un-available*, beyond guilt and atonement, but equally beyond revenge and retribution. Thus, whereas Marcel equates unavailability (*indisponibilité*) with the root cause of pride and selfishness, there lurks a more radical form of *indisponibilité* (to be sure, unimaginable for Marcel, given that there is always a subject who remains available: God) beyond pride and prejudice, when the afflicted person would have been pushed through the contradiction of life and death so to lose *any* availability for others, as manifest in its most extreme form with the categorical unavailability for forgiveness *tout court*.

Although navigating the course of a trusting relationship often calls it into question and tests our commitment to the Other, an underwriting faith in the Other, without which trusting could not sustain itself, retains an irrevocable character that resists succumbing *irredeemably* to questioning or, by the same token, that never stands in need of demonstrative proof or fully redeemable evidence. To have faith in the Other is to grant that my faith will not be put into question, either by my own doing or the doings of the Other; it is to live in the confidence that my investment of the Other with discretionary power ("substitution") will not be turned fundamentally against me. In its modus vivendi, faith in the Other operates through patience and postponement: patience with the Other's missteps, miscues, and miscommunications within the dialogue of our trust along with the postponement of any final reckoning or accounting of my faith in the Other. This does not preclude occasions in which special assurances, reaffirming glances and embraces, and other gestures of validation and calibration would have to find place and significance in the ongoing dialogue of trust. Any dialogue in trust (in word and deed) is at the same time a dialogue of trust itself ("about" its self-understanding). Yet, as Baier insightfully observes, "if to trust is to be willing to delay the accounting, then, when trust is successfully sustained, some accounts are bound to be outstanding. And as for sustainable accounts of trust, we may have to wait equally indefinitely before we get them."[21] As exemplified with Lear, however, the need to *know* the truth of trust in the demand for a final reckoning or definitive accounting can become maddeningly pressing as we approach our end, or whenever we find ourselves in a situation of an encroaching ending marked with absoluteness. In Lear's panic at his anxiety before death, patience and postponement become inverted into rash impatience and imperious demanding.

Given that wanting to know the truth of our trusts without leaving any outstanding account risks the flourishing of trust, we are sustained in our outstanding faith in the Other not in knowing its truth but with living in its *hope*. In hope, we live in the truth of our trust without thereby knowing it. Faith in the Other draw its sustenance from hope. As Marcel writes, "Hope affirms that reality will ultimately prove worthy of an infinite credit, the complete engagement and availability of myself . . . The only way in which an unbounded commitment on the part of the subject is conceivable is if it draws strength from something more than itself, from an appeal to something greater, something transcendent—and this appeal is hope . . . Hope consists in asserting that there is at the heart of being, beyond all givens, beyond all inventories and all calculations, a mysterious principle which is in connivance with me."[22] In Marcel's conception, in opening an "infinite credit" for the Other in keeping faith in the Other, such faith in another human being testifies to faith in God, as the mysterious principle of hope and source of supreme goodness, that, in trusting others, abides in me. Faith, Marcel believes, is "the opening of a credit, and it is a belief in God that is entailed in my belief in you."[23] There is no absolute commitment to the Other without commitment to the Other of the Other—God. In Marcel's words, "One might say that conditional pledges are only possible in a world from which God is absent. Unconditionality is the true sign of God's presence."[24] We stand available for the Other, on this theological assumption, only because God always and already stands available for us; we belong to the Other in trust because God already belongs in trust to us. In these adduced senses, we are said to participate in the "mystery of creation" in the mystery of belonging to the Other and rendering ourselves available for the Other, thus perpetually enacting between ourselves the original covenant between ourselves and God.

Cordelia's Forgiveness

Setting aside additional considerations of Marcel's handling of forgiveness in his theatrical works as well as his response to Nazi atrocities during World War II, these reflections on availability and creative fidelity, deployed here within the broader consideration of trust advanced in the preceding pages, allows for a recasting of forgiveness beyond its established framing as "forgiveness as encounter."[25] In broaching a "new set of problems," the conceptual constellation of *disponibilité*, as explored above *through* (and not necessarily in accordance with) Marcel's *défrichage*, can be harnessed to motivate and delineate more emphatically a distinction between "availability to forgiveness" and "encounter in forgiveness" and, in this regard, consolidate a view of "original availability" as espied in earlier chapters (chapters 2 and 3, and negatively, as unavailability, in chapter 4). In exploring the intrinsic bond between trust and availability within a mapping of how trust accounts for ways of world making and unmaking (the forked significance of trust for the human condition), Shakespeare casts Cordelia's forgiveness of Lear through an implied distinction between "availability to forgiveness" and "encounter in forgiveness." In order to think theoretically what Shakespeare portrays theatrically, the originality of Cordelia's forgiveness can be more sharply discerned through an instructive contrast with an exemplary *misinterpretation* of this celebrated scene of forgiveness, one that fails to recognize this operative distinction at work in Cordelia's forgiveness. Understanding the originality of Cordelia's forgiveness in this way provokes a displacement of *disponibilité* (availability) and creative fidelity from their theological moorings (i.e., with Marcel's reflections). *Disponibilité* thus becomes molded in the figure of Cordelia as the anarchic availability of forgiveness that is not predicated or dependent on divine presence, nor any other comparative kind of principle, source, or ground. Expressed differently, the self-sourcing availability of Cordelia's creative fidelity is anarchic in the sense of "without principle" or "determinate ground," unpredictable and uncontrollable, and yet original and "from the beginning." Whereas in Marcel's elaboration, what "guarantees" creative fidelity is an "infinite credit of charity" toward the Other graced by the mysterious presence of God in connivance through me, in Cordelia's setting of her heart for her father, this mysterious impetus becomes revealed as the anarchy of forgiveness, its original availability without promise, and hence without guarantee, even as it stands primed "to hope till Hope creates / From its own wreck the thing it contemplates."[26]

In Jean-Luc Marion's reading of *King Lear*, we find an interpretation of Cordelia's forgiveness that, on the one hand, fails to recognize the *anarchic* distinction between "availability" and "encounter" while, on the other, reflects on its own terms Marcel's construal of availability as "guaranteed" by divine grace.[27] In this skewed perspective, the originality of Cordelia's forgiveness becomes misappropriated into a theological narrative of redemption; as significantly, the originality of forgiveness as availability becomes distorted through the *misrecognition* of Cordelia's anarchic setting of her heart.

For Marion, the opening scene of *King Lear* turns on the idolatrous demand of exchanging power for love. In divesting himself of his sovereignty and wealth, Lear with his request that Cordelia declare her love for him, and, in this sense, make of her love a gift, illicitly inscribes love into an economy of exchange, or the economy of the gift.[28] Lear seeks to give away his power and possessions on condition that Cordelia's love and gratitude become visible; he demands the rendering present of the presentness of her love such that through this visibility (or "phenomenalization"), the gift of love can be received in exchange for something: recognition, power, and possession. Lear's egregious demand does not represent an affront against justice but against the "invisibility" of the gift with this command for the visibility of the gift as the condition for its reception, and hence inscription within a circuit of exchange, reciprocity, and correlation. As noted by Cordelia herself, because her two sisters have already given their love, or part of their love, to their respective husbands, Lear's demand strikes *them* as an injustice, whereas, in her case, it is not an injustice committed against her but Lear's idolatry of love, which, in Marion's thinking, invokes forgiveness, rather than justice.[29] Crucial for Marion's way of thinking is his rejection of any conception of forgiveness as the annulment of debt or restoration of justice; such notions remain hostage to a logic of exchange, thus compromising the distinct logic of the gift. Beyond justice or injustice, forgiveness attests to the surplus of the gift of love and thus remains predicated to the original gift of love as "invisible" and "incommensurable," or, in other words, as beyond Law and Reason.

When Cordelia is called upon to render her love manifest, she withholds any such declaration and guards her unconditional love from blasphemy and betrayal. "Unhappy that I am, I cannot heave / My heart into my mouth. I love your majesty / According to my bond, no more nor less" (I.1.90–92). When urged to make a present of her love in speech, Cordelia responds with nothing, and hence appears to give nothing—that is, to not give anything at all. The unconditionality of her love is nothing that allows itself to become inscribed within an economy of exchange.[30] In his rage at Cordelia's perceived insolence in this offering nothing of her love to him, Lear fails to recognize the constitutive "nothingness" of love (its "negative certainty")—namely, in Marion's thinking, the impossibility of inscribing love within any form of reciprocal relation, measure, or conditionality, and hence any form of "phenomenality." In one respect, Cordelia's gift of love is not received by Lear, given his demand to receive the gift under the condition of an exchange for power, possession, and symbolic recognition. In another respect, Cordelia's gift of love has rendered itself certain in the "nothingness" of her response. For in saying nothing, she neither refuses to give her love for something nor accepts her love to be given (or taken) away. The nothingness of her response stands beyond the measure of yes *or* no. In this withdrawal from the principle of measure and exchange, the presentness of her love stands clear (though not for Lear). Cordelia's withholding of love's gift retains the gift of love from idolatry or univocity, thus more assuredly giving Lear the gift of her love in not having received anything for it.

According to Marion's reading, Cordelia's unconditional gift of love can become manifest only in forgiveness. In receiving Cordelia's forgiveness, generously and freely given, her gift of love becomes *received* as a gift in its redoubling as the gift of forgiveness. As Marion writes, "Forgiveness [*le pardon*] does not correct a deficit of justice in the exchange, but a deficit of visibility of the first gift [*un premier don*]. Forgiveness thus labors for the phenomenality of the gift."[31] If forgiveness thus renders visible the original gift, it follows that forgiveness can appear only *after* injury or an affront toward *un premier don.* Forgiveness "regives" but is itself not originally (or first) given or originally (or firstly) giving. As Marion states, "No forgiveness can take place except on the basis of a prior gift."[32] Forgiveness "regives" the gift of love to the Other ("le pardon redone le don"), and, in this giving once more, the original gift becomes *manifestly given*, not repeated again as if either having been lost, or withdrawn, or not truly or exhaustively given at first but seconded in its redundancy as beyond the measure of usefulness, exchange, or justice. In this sense, as regiving superfluity, forgiveness does not render the original gift of love present as a phenomenon but only as a "negative certainty." As with Harriet Bulstrode's forgiveness in *Middlemarch*, it is through forgiveness that her unconditional love becomes received by her husband in silent benediction. "Her promise of faithfulness was silent," and in this nothingness of her silence (or "negative certitude," in Marion's terminology), what becomes all the more passionately manifest is her original love for him and accepting staunchness of her availability, or faithfulness. It is not only in the grace of forgiveness that the original gift of love becomes revealed to its beneficiary; in this negative certainty, the person who gives stands herself revealed to the beneficiary as having never abandoned the

Other in her gift of love. Only when Lear becomes forgiven by Cordelia does he come to see the presentness of her love as having been given from the beginning. He comes to see *her* as for who she is, as bespeaks her name. Whereas Goneril and Regan, whose relationship with Lear is defined entirely by power and economy under the rule of justice, cannot be forgiven by Lear nor would they ever stand to forgive their father, it is only with Cordelia that the promised end of love becomes achieved with its consecrated revelation in forgiveness.[33]

As Marion further examines in turning to the biblical parable of the prodigal son, the father with his forgiveness of his profligate son does not offer a new robe, sandals, and rings—a feast of riches—at his return to either restore what his son has given away nor to restore symbolically, in exchange, what his son owes him. Instead, in the father's declaration "For this here is my son, he was dead and is alive again; he was lost and is now found" (Luke 15:24), the son stands resurrected in the consecration of forgiveness. Forgiveness, in this consummate form, does not just "regive" in redundancy the original gift. In this regiving, the forgiven person becomes returned to the gift, gifted once more with the gift of life: risen again in the gift. In forgiveness, the absent father becomes present to the absent son (now returned) in reestablishing the movement of givenness, emancipated from any corrosive logic of exchange; the father appears to the son "for the first time as father-giver, and makes the son appear himself for the first time as son-recipient."[34] In proclaiming, "This is my son," the father likewise reveals himself as being-there for this son; this passage from father to son, from son to father, through the "redounding of the gift" in forgiveness takes on "nothing less than a trinitarian status." This marked emphasis on the biblical father's forgiveness of the son allows Marion to illustrate how divine forgiveness is the original form of forgiveness in which forgiveness between human beings operates. God is the source of *all gifts,* and hence all faults are committed against God. Given the original forgiveness of God, it becomes possible for humans to forgive each other in giving each other their due. As Marion advocates, "In fact, forgiveness reaches into the misery of the everyday as regularly and as powerfully as within the Trinity." We thus stand before the alternative: we are either the wayward son who returns in forgiveness to the Father or the resentful son who can understand the gift only as "possession" and thus fail to accept the gift of the gift, or "paternity." In the parable of the prodigal son, "each of us can decide what the son will or would respond, since each of us *is* this son."[35]

Substantial differences notwithstanding, philosophical as well as theological, between Marion's thinking and Marcel's, this reading of Cordelia's forgiveness nonetheless accords with Marcel's construal of *dis-*

ponibilité as guaranteed by the "mysterious grace" of divine presence. Unconditional love, as infinite credit and faithfulness in the Other, represents an original charity, or "first gift," which, when we enter into the encounter of forgiveness, becomes "manifest" or "revealed" and, in Marion's sense, "regiven" in a supererogatory act of forgiveness. We forgive in excess of love, and to love is to give excessively, given excessively once more in forgiving, when the Other betrays me. What guarantees the "regiving" of love in forgiveness is the infinite charity of love, its original gift, anchored in the source of "all gifts," God.[36] Strictly speaking, forgiveness does not give *again*, but regives more, and in this surplus the original surplus of the gift of love becomes revealed and manifestly received as a "negative certainty." As Marion states, "Le pardon suppose le don, parce qu'il consiste en sa redondance."[37] Even if this original gift takes the form of infinite charity, and hence "availability" (*disponibilité*), forgiveness itself is not original; the original gift of love is not itself already forgiving, but giving, even as it stands originally not unforgiving ("unavailable") toward forgiveness.

In Marcel's understanding, the "infinite credit," or charity, extended to the Other (my faith in the Other that becomes me) is underwritten (or "guaranteed") by the infinite and unconditional charity of God's love. In drawing upon myself creatively to rally around the Other, the grace of divine presence mysteriously operates in connivance through me.[38] The Other's betrayal of my faith presents in this manner a temptation to lose faith in the Other, and in this tempting of my creative and creaturely fidelity there occurs an existential temptation to lose faith in faith itself, given that "a belief in God . . . is entailed in my belief in you."[39] Because an "infinite credit" has been extended to me in God, I am to extend an infinite credit to you. In this view, Marcel considers that even in circumstances of the most egregious betrayal by the Other, it nonetheless remains *my failure* rather than the failure of the Other that becomes expressed when I abandon the Other in becoming unavailable for them. Only I can betray my creative fidelity toward the Other, even as it is the Other who betrays me. The many ways in which the Other fails me are always, in this account, reflective of my own failings, or self-failure, to creatively revitalize myself in order to keep faith in the Other. Given our finite condition, however, absolute *disponibilité* remains as impossible for humans, or saintly, as unconditional fidelity. Yet given that my infinite credit, as an impossible infinite credit nonetheless given to the Other, is underwritten by God's presence, when I am either unable (when facing the unforgivable) or fail (when I make myself unavailable) to forgive, it is always unto God to forgive. The resilience of faith is woven in the hope that the Father always stands available to forgive. Even when the dialogue of trust between us, as humans, becomes broken, there always remains the implied superaddressee, God, who stands available to forgive, thus ensuring that a ruptured dialogue among human beings in trust would not amount to a dialogue of trust in vain. There will always remain a "who" in whom we can have faith, in hope of forgiveness to come. In this regard, although I cannot forgive myself for *my* failing to keep faith in the Other, when I become unavailable for the Other, I nonetheless stand to be forgiven and thus remain in the good standing of hope, given God's original forgiveness of the fallible condition of humankind. As well, I can forgive myself for not being able to forgive what is impossible to forgive—the unforgivable—in the unassailable hope that God can forgive. As with Marcel's response to Nazi atrocities, when it is impossible for us to forgive, it remains for God to forgive.[40] Likewise for Marion, "God alone can remit sins, no matter what sin, because he alone satisfies the conditions of forgiveness: every fault against any man proves to be a fault as well against God." Indeed, "God alone can forgive absolutely with a forgiveness that is impossible for us."[41] Because God is goodness itself, where goodness *is* the gift, God can in his empowered goodness forgive everything and absolutely. As Marion writes, "The power of God, which can accomplish everything, even forgiving, consists therefore only in its goodness."[42] God can forgive the unforgivable, given the excessiveness of his supreme goodness; it is a goodness that can afford everything and anything and, in an essential sense, *already has* in allowing in advance forgiveness without limit, yet without anything of God's goodness *to be* taken for granted. God appears as merciful to the extent of his transcendence in a forgiveness already given and yet still sought for. The *human* impossibility of forgiveness testifies negatively to the impossibility of any limitation to God's forgiveness. In the certainty for us that some things are impossible to forgive resides the certainty of God's forgiveness of the unforgivable; conversely, in the human possibility of forgiveness lies the negative certainty that God guarantees all forgiveness since only God can forgive the unforgivable.[43] The "I can" of God can never be held in suspended animation, even as it remains for us in suspense; there is, in this sense, strictly speaking, no "I can" of God but the always "it is given" as the question of God (God's "negative certainty") that survives and outstrips the impossibility of God as *being* given, known, or otherwise positively, and hence possessively, manifest as a phenomenon. Availability, in this regard, becomes collapsed into the already "it was given" of the "first gift," which, once given in its excessiveness, always remains there to be regiven in its redundancy, and *has been*, thus making forgiveness superfluous, or, what amounts to the same, redundant of a love already first given *à l'outrance*.

"Thou art the thing itself"

Aside from its place within the expanse of Marion's thinking, this interpretation of forgiveness can be placed within an extended tradition that
reads *King Lear* as achieving its promised end with the transcendence of
Cordelia's forgiveness and redemption of her father. As A. C. Bradley
writes, "Should we not be at least as near the truth if we called this poem
The Redemption of King Lear, and declared that the business of 'the gods'
with him was neither to torment him, nor to teach him a 'noble anger,'
but to lead him to attain through apparently hopeless failure the very end
and aim of life?"[44] Stated more directly, Marion's reading proposes, on its
own terms, to be sure, a Christian rendition of Cordelia's forgiveness. It
does not, however, propose an "optimistic" assessment of *King Lear* but
suggests a *hopeful* assessment with its argument for the redemption of Lear
in Cordelia's forgiveness and implication of divine givenness enacted in
connivance through her forgiveness.[45] Marion's Christian reading (and
its variations) stands in sharp contrast to an equally well-developed (and
historically more recent—after World War II) tradition of so-called ex-
istentialist interpretations of *King Lear* that advocate instead a stressed
non-Christian (or anti-Christian) vision of the absurd and helpless plight
of humankind without redemptive promise or restorative hope.[46]

Setting aside the extensive literature on both sides of this interpretative divide, it is worth recalling that the hermeneutical character of
Shakespeare's masterpiece is not defined only by its multivocal composition; it resides just as much with the voicing of conflicting interpretations
regarding its own meaning within the playing out of its double narrative.
Stated in Bakhtinian terms, the polyphonic composition of *King Lear* orchestrates an *open* dialogue about the meaning of the play itself.[47] These
voices taken together do not form a polyphonic chorus but a nonharmo-
nizing polyphonic ensemble. The Fool's apparently deranged telling—
"Then comes the time, who lives to see't / That going shall be used with
feet. This prophecy Merlin shall make, for I live before his time" (III.293–
96)—incisively envisions the "great confusion" of the world's undoing
and upending in a revelation that speaks from a place neither entirely
inside nor completely outside the play's staging. As C. K. Chesterton remarks, the Fool's prophetic vision "is one of the Shakespearian shocks
or blows that take the breath away" with its self-instantiating accentua-
tion of a time out of joint. Edgar's declaration that "the worst is not /
So long as we can say 'This is the worst'" already issues a rejoinder to
Camus's twentieth-century declaration that "a literature of despair is a
contradiction in terms."[48] Edgar's statement does gesture in the direction
of aesthetic redemption in artful and considerate speaking of the worst

but marks the threshold beyond which the poetic word becomes extinguished and denied, leaving us with the unredeemable and unspeakable worst.[49] Edmund mocks his father's consultation of astrology when he divines that the "late eclipses in the sun and moon portend no good to us," tragically without grasping how true this dire predication will be for him (he cannot see what is essential when he has eyes and comes to see what is essential only once his eyes have been savagely torn from him). Edmund's cutting statement—"This is the excellent foppery of the world, that when we are sick in fortune, often the surfeits of our own behavior, we make guilty of our disasters of the sun, the moon and the stars" (I.1.118–21)—arguably applies when we would regard the restoration or redemption of the world as the work of divine providence and so praise the stars; is this not but more "excellent foppery"? To this point, it is revealing that when Edgar makes himself known to his treasonous half brother, he unwittingly renders himself a prime example of such excellent foppery that remains instinctually objectionable to Edmund: "My name is Edgar and thy father's son / The gods are just and of our pleasant vices / Make instruments to plague us: / The dark and vicious place where thee he got / Cost him his eyes" (V.3.167–71). The grim irony is that Edgar's unfaltering faith in the justness of the gods is proclaimed here *before* Cordelia's death while also ascribing to his father's hideous torture a providential reasoning that remains blind to the cause of "the worst"—his father's torture—as solely the work of human, all-too-human hands. Edgar's own blindness turns on his inability (or unwillingness) to give the name "the human" to everything that assails and does violence to the human. His own gullibility at the words of his (half) brother's guile is further reflected in his credulousness of the just gods. Edmund, in his Cainesque coldness, lives instinctually by the implicit recognition that when "everything ceases to be true, 'anthropomorphism' would be truth's ultimate echo."[50] Cordelia's death is cast as a matter of pure contingency given the "bad timing" that arguably allows Edmund's orders to be carried out because of the protracted discussion between Albany and Edgar.[51] Is it still possible to have faith in the just gods *after* Cordelia's gratuitous death as well as when *facing* the Earl of Gloucester's torture at the hands of men?

However these different ways of addressing the question of redemption in *King Lear* are to be further assessed, it is arguably the case that whatever dimension of "the gods" is present in the world of *King Lear*, it is not incontrovertibly Christian, and this has direct bearing on grasping the originality of Cordelia's forgiveness.[52] It is revealing that, as Marion himself notes, Cordelia's forgiveness presents an "inverse paradigm" of the biblical narrative of the prodigal son: it is not the father who forgives the wayward son but the daughter who forgives the wayward father.[53] While making note of this inversion, Marion nonetheless affirms the paradigmatic privilege of the prodigal son narrative, thus placing Cordelia's forgiveness back under the reign of the father's forgiveness of the son. Theologically speaking, the father's forgiveness of the son underwrites any dialogue of forgiveness as such: "Each one of us *is* this son," as Marion writes (emphasis in original). And yet the fine revolution of Shakespeare's conception of forgiveness in *King Lear* resides squarely with this *inversion* taken at its word that situates Cordelia's forgiveness in a space of conception—the theatrical space of the play itself—beyond a theological *or* secular framing of its significance.[54] However notable it is that Cordelia's comparatively sparse lines in the play are richly textured with terms drawn from the discourse of *prisca theologia* ("grace," "benediction," "restoration," "holy water," "thy reverence"), her *argumentum ex silentio* consists in the radicalism of a forgiveness of the father by the daughter without any basis in the forgiveness of the father for the son.[55] If we take the purchase of Lear as father *and* king without any symbolic restriction or ontological conceit, in seeking to "crawl unburdened to the grave" in Cordelia's "kind nursery," *King Lear* sets the stage for a narrative of the father searching to unburden himself of his position as father (paternity) and king (sovereign) by way of seeking a resting place in the kind nursery of human forgiveness without any antecedent guarantee of the father. The father desires to find release from himself in entrusting the world to the age of humankind with, on the one hand, the catastrophic consequence of the undoing of the world through the internecine warfare and mimetic rivalry of sister against sister, son against father, son against son and, on the other, a counterpart redemption through Cordelia's forgiveness, into whose hands alone the father can exit the stage of the world, the stage of history, as well as any staging of himself.[56] It is not the figure of Christ, who interrupts the mimetic rivalry of human beings, but Cordelia's dechristening of forgiveness, as the daughter who forgives in *her name*, rather than the father-become-son who forgives in the name of the father to become the forgiveness of all sons.[57] In Cordelia's forgiveness of the father, the daughter becomes herself a mother to the father who in turn has become a child. Forgiveness here originally turns on the forgiveness of the sometime child of the sometime parent.[58] In this sense, if Cordelia's forgiveness of Lear offers a striking example of natality, in another sense her forgiveness significantly *restores* Lear to the world while not unambiguously *reconciling* the world with itself, given that Lear follows his daughter to the grave or, more exactly stated, accompanies her into the grave. The redemptive significance of Cordelia's forgiveness does not issue any manifest reconciliation but consists in a *release* from a world that has fundamentally become broken in the rupture of our only bond to the world, to each other, and to ourselves: *trust*. As G. K. Chesterton remarks, "treason, or what is felt as treason, does break the heart of the world; and it has seldom been so nearly broken as here [in *King Lear*]."[59]

This breaking of the heart of the world through treason (in the threefold dimensions of trust in others, trust in oneself, and trust in the world) sets the stage for Cordelia's setting of her heart to her father in forgiveness. Deceived, betrayed, and abandoned, abject Lear finds himself wandering upon the welter and waste of the heath with the Fool and Kent (disguised as Caius) in tow. The tempest and the heath are chronotopically symbolic: "for many miles about there is scarce a bush"; the heath represents a nonplace outside any mapping of possessions, power, and social relations, whereas the tempest represents a time out of joint in great confusion.[60] The heath is the nonplace without any horizon of meaning in which these outcast figures stand afflicted and destitute. Wandering upon the heath, Lear's motley crew finds itself expelled into transcendental homelessness, where hierarchies of power and social roles have become entirely evacuated as well as any inner composition, or self-reliance, on personality, or the robustness of the self.[61] The heathen Lear has been dispossessed and decreated ontologically, rendered naked and exposed. When the lendings and trappings of the person have been discarded and violated, there oneself stands unaccommodated within a void of trust as but a helpless forked animal.[62]

And yet the heart of the world is here *nearly* broken. As G. K. Chesterton insightfully remarks, "Regarding the storm that rages round him as a universal rending and uprooting of everything, something that will pluck out the roots of all things, even the darkest and foulest roots of the heart of man deceitful above all things and desperately wicked, he affirms in the face of the most appalling self-knowledge, clear and blasting as the lightning, that his sufferings must still be greater than his sins. It is possibly the most tremendous thing a man ever said; whether or not any man had the right to say it. It would be hard to beat it even in the Book of Job."[63] Lear's "insane impartiality" is twofold: first, with regard to himself in an abject condition of suffering greater than his sin and, second, with regard to others in an awakening to human frailty. The savagery of Lear's transcendental homelessness lays open what nonetheless endures: the touching proximity of the Other in *their* destitution. In the unbinding of Lear from the world, others, and himself, there becomes revealed what originally binds us: our availability for the Other. The human, to adapt here Blanchot's incisive formulation, is "the indestructible that can be destroyed."[64]

An "uprooting of everything" ejects Lear from the hold of the trust in the world as well as any trust in himself or in others.

> Lear. [To Kent] Thou think'st 'tis much that this contentious storm
> Invades us to the skin: so 'tis to thee;
> But where the greater malady is fix'd,
> The lesser is scarce felt . . . When the mind's free
> The body's delicate; this tempest in my mind
> Doth from my senses take all feeling else
> Save what beats there—filial ingratitude! (III.4.6–9, 11–14)

Within this expulsion into homelessness and loss of self (his madness), the beating of filial ingratitude (lodged at the broken heart of the world) invokes a suffering greater than Lear's own sin, and hence, in this visceral awakening, that he has sinned, that those against whom he has sinned have cause *not* to forgive him. This suffering is not merely that he has suffered from the monstrous ingratitude of his two daughters; it is also that he suffers "bound / Upon a wheel of fire, that mine own tears / Do scald like moulten lead" (IV.7.47–48). More searing than just guilt or remorse, the wheel of fire upon which Lear hangs is his own insufferable raging existence: that he has committed the unforgivable, that, in other words, he *is* unforgivable. To suffer being unforgivable is "greater" than one's sin in the sense that it transcends the possibility of forgiveness for one's sins; *to be* unforgivable is *to suffer being* unforgivable, for others to have no cause, no cause to forgive. In contrast to the Underground Man, who, from shame at his own shame, refuses *to be forgiven*, Lear's despair consists in accepting that he is *not to be forgiven*. It is to be oneself unavailable, or dead, to the possibility *or* impossibility of forgiveness, given that this abjection of *being unforgivable* is not the consequence of, and hence dependent upon, *having not been forgiven* by others. To be unforgiven is to have not been forgiven by others; to be unforgivable is to be unforgivable for others, before any encounter with the possibility or impossibility of *being forgiven* (or, likewise, being unforgiven). It is, in other words, to be unforgivable before anyone has arrived upon the scene of forgiveness. In thus being unforgivable, the revenge and resentment of others become themselves short-circuited in advance, given that this suffering of "being unforgivable" will always be greater than any suffering inflicted through revenge and resentment, or being unforgiven—that is, as not being forgiven by others.

In this insane awakening to his own unforgivable existence, there is lodged another awakening (or "insane partiality") in the suffering for the Other. Expulsed into the barren heath, Lear is engulfed in a tempest that enacts the voiding of the world, its "de-creation," through the betrayal of trust in its multiplanar dimensions; and yet within this deported condition of absolute destitution, there is the mysterious upsurge of the indestructible: the Other in the figure of Poor Tom, or, in other words, "alterity that holds in the name of the neutral."[65] As the generic name for he who no longer possesses a proper name and recognizable standing in the world, "Poor Tom" names the absolute poverty of the Other's presence beyond, or otherwise, any mediation of the world. In the welter and waste, there is suddenly the encounter by marvelous chance with the Other, Poor Tom, who suddenly appears at Lear's side: *but who is he?* In his destitution, as stranger and orphan, Poor Tom, as with Lear and his band, is afflicted with expulsion from the world at the treasonous hands of others. It is here, in the nonplace and the dead time of the heath, that the Neutral surges forth as but the poor, bare Other. Revealingly, when Lear meets Poor Tom, he immediately *speaks* and *names* the human: "Is man no more than this? Consider him well. Thou ow'st the worm no silk, the beast no hide, the sheep no wool, the cat no perfume. Ha! here's three on's are sophisticated; thou art the thing itself; unaccommodated man is no more but such a poor, bare, forked animal as thou art. Off, off, you lendings! Come; unbutton here. [Tearing off his clothes]" (III.4.105–12). Reduced to "nothing" in destitution and set outside relations of power and the "I" (the roles of the self), there nonetheless remains speech, not the speech of the sovereign I but the speaking of the Neutral.[66] In tearing off his clothes, Lear makes himself available for Tom in extending to him comfort and shelter, when he himself has none, or barely any. Fallen into the void of trust, standing unaccommodated in the breach of trust as "no more but such a poor, bare, forked animal as thou art," there still endures the "thing itself," the touching availability of the other for the Other in their destitution. Lear's awakening to the plight of the Other is the final act of shedding the lending of his self. Dispossessed as father and king, bereft of any sovereignty or authority, Lear discovers on the hither side of his own suffering the outrage of the Other's vulnerability in the assignation of himself as the Other's keeper. In both instances, the suffering of his own unforgivable being (his own destitution) and the suffering of the Other's destitution (Poor Tom) form an exposure underneath Lear's skin, a nakedness of the human more naked than with the mere shedding of one's clothes. The damnation of Lear to his madness, his being unforgivable, occurs along with its denouement in the encounter with Poor Tom. In naming Poor Tom "his philosopher," this gesture is not made in jest but consecrates "the philosopher" as issuing a provocation to bear an original availability, and hence responsibility, for the Other that gets under one's skin. "The philosopher"—Poor Tom—calls upon responsibility in its nakedness, for the Other, beyond and outside any recognition or reverence for "what is," for *who* the Other is, as determined by relations of power, cultural significance, or social persona.[67] In Lear's "insane impartiality," there speaks an awareness that it is *not* the universe nor the gods who mete out suffering to human beings but that it is of the human condition in its forked significance. It is *this* stupor that forms Lear's lucidity: his "insane impartiality" that Trust is both the God of humankind and the Adversary who roams the Earth in temptation of human beings.

"You are a spirit, I know; where did you die?"

With Cordelia's return to England at the head of a French army in search of her father, Cordelia comes upon an unconscious Lear at the same time that she encounters Kent.[68] Still disguised as Cauis, Cordelia nonetheless recognizes him immediately and duly acknowledges his goodness in having not abandoned her father: "O thou good Kent, how shall I live and work, / To match thy goodness? My life will be too short, / And every measure fail me" (IV.7.1–3). Although "exterminated" and exiled under penalty of death by Lear, Kent promptly returned to his service in donning the mask of Caius so as to remain at his master's side. What characterizes the goodness of Kent's availability is not, as with Cordelia, the availability of forgiveness but the availability of loyalty, in which forgiveness, strictly speaking, finds no place. Kent does not forgive Lear, nor would there be any need to forgive (or not to forgive in begrudging and resenting). Whereas the Fool represents the availability of candor, or speaking the truth to power, Kent represents the availability of loyalty toward the sovereign, which, given the bond of fealty, cannot, paradoxically, be afforded with the plain speaking of truth; it is the Fool who can speak truthfully yet not plainly to Lear, while Kent's plain speaking of truth is received by Lear as insolent and disloyal. Given the differential in power relations between them, Kent is not his master's keeper but his trustworthy steward.[69] In his own manner, Kent manifests creative fidelity is putting on the disguise of Cauis to remain in Lear's service, yet it is significant that his *unbroken* loyalty precludes any encounter in forgiveness, and hence remains without any availability to forgiveness. Forgiveness becomes redundant in regiving the original oath of loyalty or, in other words, in perpetually fulfilling an infinite extension of credit to the person to whom one has pledged oneself. In their relationship of trust, the difference of power remains unchanged, despite the circumstance of its breakage. Kent remains Lear's vassal in a manner that Cordelia does not remain Lear's subservient child. This redundancy of forgiveness in the availability of fealty is further accented with the self-effacing character of Kent's goodness. As Kent insists somewhat cryptically to Cordelia, "Yet to be known shortens my made intent / My boon I make it that you know me not / Till time and I think meet" (IV.7.9–11), thus allowing for an encounter in forgiveness to center around the revived recognition of Cordelia and Lear, with Kent remaining unrecognized by Lear (though not by Cordelia) in witness of a forgiveness beyond his ken and kind.

In contrast to Kent's goodness, the goodness of Cordelia's availability defines itself through forgiveness, as availability to forgiveness. As with Kent, Cordelia must creatively fashion herself into an unexpected self—to wit, from the vantage point of the opening of the play, into an "impossible" or "improbable" character, in her sovereign return at the head of an invading army from France. In honoring his bond of loyalty, Kent's transformation into Caius is, arguably, expected, given the prescriptions of fealty. Kent affirms again his fealty to Lear in its redundancy by remaining in character when adopting the persona of Caius. Cordelia's *offstage* transformation is more remarkably dramatic in altering her narrative trajectory from an expected and precharted course. Her husband, the king of France, is conspicuously absent upon her return to the stage of the world. Where one might expect *him* to lead an invading army, we find instead Cordelia alone as sovereign *and* daughter, thus navigating the roles of power and love that Lear himself had so tragically fumbled. Kent *plays* at being Cauis in order to remain in his master's service, whereas Cordelia *is* arisen anew through her own creative self-transformation from the grave of her extermination and banishment in exile, so as to remain her Majesty's keeper. Cordelia's self-transformation in creative fidelity is never witnessed onstage but occurs offstage, from the grave.

In these contrasting forms of availability, fealty and forgiveness, Cordelia and Kent together find that Lear is "asleep," symbolically dead to the world, to others, and to himself, both literally and figuratively offstage. In appealing to the heavens, "O you kind gods! / Cure this great breach in his abused nature," Cordelia speaks of Lear as "this child-changed father." As *child*-changed, he has been cast into this condition by his own children with the abuses suffered at their hands. The "great breach in his abused nature," his rage at the mistreatment and destitution caused by his children, must now be cured, yet not by the kind gods but in the setting of Cordelia's heart to her child-*changed* father. Much as with a child, her father is entrusted into her care and responsibility.

Lear enters, still unconscious, now dressed in fresh garments; the prodigal father has returned to the kind nursery of his daughter. As a doctor begins to revive Lear, Cordelia addresses her father in absentia and restores him from his transcendental homelessness.

> O my dear father! Restoration hang
> Thy medicine on my lips; and let this kiss
> Repair those violent harms that my two sisters
> Have in thy reverence made! (IV.7.26–28)

Kent's spontaneous remark, "Kind and dear princess!" acknowledges *her* goodness as matching, if not exceeding, his own, even as Lear remains asleep to Cordelia's restorative kiss for the sufferings that have befallen him. With this kiss of blessing and baptism, Lear begins to regain consciousness; he is arisen from the grave in the dual senses of restored to the living from his metaphysical abandonment and destitution *as well as* restored from his rage at the world and "filial ingratitude," sparked at first with his rage at Cordelia and his unforgivable banishment of her.

> Cordelia. How does my royal lord? How fares your majesty?
> Lear. You do me wrong to take me out o' the grave:
> Thou art a soul in bliss; but I am bound
> Upon a wheel of fire, that mine own tears
> Do scald like moulten lead. (IV.7.45–48)

Significantly, Lear still does not recognize Cordelia as she stands before him a soul in bliss:

> Cordelia. Sir, do you know me?
> Lear. You are a spirit, I know: when did you die? (IV.7.48–49)

Implicitly sensing that the spirit before him is itself returned from the grave, much as he finds himself risen from his own, Cordelia stands available for Lear without her availability, and indeed Cordelia "herself," becoming recognized and received by Lear. There is as yet no *encounter* between Lear and Cordelia, nor any act of forgiveness or beseeching of forgiveness, and, in this sense, no encounter in forgiveness. In Cordelia's approach, in the setting of her heart to Lear, she does not stand *revealed* to Lear, though she stands available. Lear's statement is, in fact, revealingly ambiguous: he beholds Cordelia's spectral presence from beyond the grave—"when did you die?"—as he himself stands risen from the grave by the restorative kiss of this spirit. In the pronouncement, "You are a spirit, I know: when did you die?" Lear is doubly startled in addressing both the return of himself from the grave *and* the return of Cordelia from her own, both of his own doing. Whereas Lear fell "below" the world to an outside beyond the world, Cordelia had been exterminated, rendered to an outside *offstage*, not below the world (i.e., the heath represented onstage). When Cordelia returns to the stage of the world, Lear is himself offstage, "asleep" and "unconscious," waiting for her restoration of his own availability to the stage of encounters in the world.

> King Lear. Where have I been? Where am I? Fair daylight?
> I am mightily abused. I should e'en die with pity,
> To see another thus. I know not what to say.
> I will not swear these are my hands: let's see;
> I feel this pin prick. Would I were assured
> Of my condition!

As he regains a sense of himself as here (as oneself) in the world, Cordelia kneels to her father and asks *him*, "O, look upon me, sir, / And hold your hands in benediction o'er me!" but as he himself proceeds to kneel before her, she stays his all-too-humbling descending, "No, sir, you must not kneel." In this restoration of their mutual standing for each other, there is no affirmation of sovereignty or condescension on Cordelia's part but, on the contrary, an appeal for his benediction, while, in the same gesture, the steadying of his standing before her as her Majesty. Kneeling before Lear, Cordelia has neutralized her sovereignty and power; she does not demand of Lear that he ask for forgiveness, as does Regan when she, presumptively and insultingly, suggests to Lear that he should seek forgiveness from Goneril. Cordelia returns as sovereign, as queen, leading her army and, as daughter, in search of her father. When she revives Lear, he is strictly speaking no longer king or father since he has been dispossessed of his lands, ejected by his daughters, and, most critically, divested *himself* of his fatherhood toward Cordelia in cursing that he had ever begotten her. In addressing Lear as Majesty, Cordelia is thus not recognizing Lear *politically* as king, for he is no longer, but addressing the Majesty of the Other, his transcendence, to which he has now become restored. This is not to forgive but to become available for Lear: it does not forecast forgiveness in this forbearance of his being unforgivable.

Still incognizant of where and who he is ("I fear I am not in my perfect mind") and yet impartially aware of himself as "very foolish" and humbled, Lear comes to see Cordelia as his restored child in the instant he comes to see himself restored.[70] In recognizing himself as "here," he recognizes her as there for him; likewise, in restoring Lear to the living,

Cordelia becomes herself revealed: "And so I am, I am." Cordelia now appears to Lear as he could have and should have seen her before he entered into the madness of his rage at her perceived insolence. Unbound from the wheel of his own suffering, Lear is resurrected from the grave of being unforgivable; for he was dead and is alive again, he was lost and is now found. Unlike the prodigal-son narrative, Cordelia's resurrection of Lear does not occur in the enactment of forgiveness but transpires *before* any forgiveness can be given, beseeched, or refused, as its precondition—namely, that *both* Lear's unforgivable existence, his ethical death, or ghosting, *and* Cordelia's "exterminated" existence have each become, and for each other, yet only through the restorative setting of Cordelia's heart, "resurrected." Here I am, there you stand, each from the grave of the unforgivable. Resurrection does not transpire through forgiveness but in virtue of a forbearing availability that opens the possibility of forgiveness—an encounter in forgiveness—without yet having forgiven anything in advance. Resurrected, Lear is no longer unforgivable, even as he is yet to be forgiven *or* not to be forgiven. He stands astride, as it were, that liminal space between being unforgivable and being forgiven. Hence, the obscure awareness on Lear's part that the betrayal of his onetime child remains unforgivable in granting Cordelia that she should be unforgiving toward him and thus refuse to forgive him. Lear knows that he has not yet been forgiven, even as he knows himself returned from the grave of being unforgivable, for he offers that "he will drink the poison" and proclaims that she does not love him. Restored to the living through Cordelia's kiss, the passage toward an encounter in forgiveness, and hence to being forgiven, is not yet entirely secured or guaranteed. Cordelia still stands before a choice to forgive or not to forgive; it is a choice that Lear puts to her in acknowledging that she has just cause not to forgive him for the unforgivable, for the egregious wrongs he committed against her.

> King Lear. Be your tears wet? yes, 'faith. I pray, weep not:
> If you have poison for me, I will drink it.
> I know you do not love me; for your sisters
> Have, as I do remember, done me wrong:
> You have some cause, they have not.
> Cordelia. No cause, no cause
>
> . . . .
>
> Cordelia. Will't please your highness walk?
> King Lear. You must bear with me:
> Pray you now, forget and forgive: I am old and foolish. [IV.7.70–75,
>   84–86]

Without saying, "I forgive you," forgiveness is proffered—tended in tenderness—in these softly spoken words and assistance *to walk*. Forgiven, "child-changed Lear" becomes set upright in the world. In this act of walking in the company of his onetime child, Lear asks and accepts being forgiven.

The Setting of the Heart for Forgiveness

In Cordelia's "no cause, no cause," we witness the anarchy of forgiveness as it "lies beautifully and generously" in the double figure of availability and encounter.[71] Without cause to be unforgiving, yet by the same token without cause for forgiveness, the supererogatory character of Cordelia's forgiveness is predicated on her graceful restoration of Lear to the living from the grave of the unforgivable. Cordelia becomes herself available, and through this availability they stand there together to face each other in the encounter of forgiveness, to ask for forgiveness, to forgive, and to be forgiven. Cordelia's remaining available for her father is not predicated, however, on a constancy of self-presence or self-reliance (as with good Kent's fealty), for what characterizes creative fidelity in this anarchic sense is the constitutive absence of any rule, necessity, or principle for the improbable meeting of the impossible with the possible. In becoming other than oneself in creative fidelity, one *cannot* anticipate and hence project as *one's own* possibility who one must become in the future—in that unimaginable future when one finds oneself betrayed by the Other. In committing oneself to the Other, it is not that one promises the Other that, come what may, one will remain available, for, strictly speaking, one can never know what it is that one is promising of oneself to the Other, since one cannot anticipate (and hence prepare for) who one would have to become in order to remain available to the Other when the Other becomes unavailable to oneself. In other words: I cannot promise "who" I am to become as well as to "to whom" I am to promise myself. The temporality of availability, in its openness toward the future, is thus configured differently from the ordered temporality of promising, in which I project a determinate present into the future so as to safeguard against its indeterminacy and unpredictability. By the same token, availability cannot be universalized into a duty or obligation, since *my* availability to the Other responds to the singularity of the Other held in trust; there is no duty or obligation to trust *you*—that is, to belong to the Other— and hence to remain available to you. Much as trust is characterized by a vulnerability to unexpected harm, availability is likewise not based on any anticipated betrayal but, as significantly, not based on an anticipation of myself, that I can know myself to be the singular kind of person who would and could remain available. The exposure toward vulnerability in trust is not directed only toward others; it is just as significantly directed toward myself, such that, in this fashion, I am vulnerable toward myself and so must remain available to myself in trusting that I am able to create myself anew in response to the novel conditions and situations in which I find myself abandoned by the Other without thereby abandoning her and, in a certain respect, thereby losing faith in myself.

As exemplified with Cordelia's setting of her heart, availability as fashioned in creative faithfulness would at first glance seem to be configured along the same temporal lines as Arendt considered promising to be. In both cases, the question turns on how we are able to bind ourselves to others as well as to ourselves for a future that remains in principle unpredictable and unknown. We are unknown to ourselves with respect to the future that becomes us from others (or because of others—namely, a future instigated through the words and deeds of others) as well as cast into a field of acting with others of indeterminate future complexity. Arendt's image of promising as establishing "islands of security" in the tempest of temporal becoming is revealing of how promising responds to the predicament of unpredictability. Promising guards against the openness of the future from a commitment in the present made to determine in advance the future in its own image. As an "island of security" within temporal becoming, the future becomes determined in advance on the basis of a past present: the performative act of promising constitutes the inversion of the present's passing away. Rather than a present that becomes past, promising for the future makes its own performative present projected into a future to which I am already bound from the present. Promising binds the future to the present. To be sure, I may in the future not accept my own promise, and hence refuse to be the person I promised to be or do what I had once promised to do. In failing to abide by my promise and honor my self-imposed obligation toward others, I would have deviated from my own prescribed—that is, promised—self. It is in failing to uphold my promises that I become other than myself— namely, other than how I once promised myself to the Other to be, or to do. Promising is the remedy against the predicament of unpredictability, including, for Arendt, the human, all-too-human inability to knowingly anticipate the consequences of human action in the world (as entwined in plurality), in determining myself in advance—that is, already committing myself to a predictable course of action.

Unlike promising, availability (in terms of creative fidelity) is not a manner of making oneself predictable in advance; it does not "secure an island of security" within the unpredictability, and hence risk, of the future. Likewise, availability cannot be a speech act, as with promising; as with trust, we enter into trust without having to declare our trust in a baptismal act of speech.[72] Whereas in promising I bind the unknown future *to the known present*, in creatively remaining available for the Other, I bind the known present *to the unknown future*. Not knowing (in predicting or determining) who I will have to become, what I might have to do, and who the Other might become for me in the company of trust, I am nonetheless originally committed, from the beginning, to finding myself still there for the Other, even when the Other is no longer here for me. I must already avail myself to the possibility of accompanying, and hence encountering, the Other in the future, however strange and unsettling it proves to be, without ever being entirely prepared or able beforehand, in knowing or acting, how it is, or would be, to live up to the demands placed upon me when called upon *not* to abandon the Other who has forsaken me. In drawing on creative faithfulness, availability for the Other endures on the condition that I am *able* to become other than myself, even though, paradoxically, I am *unable* to know, adequately prepare for, or decide ahead of time whether, in any given future situation, I would still be able to stand by the Other. In the most challenging of times, creatively remaining faithful to the Other requires breaking my own projected self-determination—for example, in breaking a promise I had made to myself, or to others, that I would never in all the world stand by you, or that I would for all the world abandon you "for sure," should you ever betray me. Recalcitrant to any type of promise or pledge, availability would thus seem more akin to forgiveness, for, as Arendt stresses, forgiveness cannot take the form of a promise, given its "miraculous" (i.e., supererogatory) quality in *breaking* any chain of determination (see chapter 2). Yet unlike forgiveness, availability in creative faithfulness does not redress the predicament of irreversibility in *unbinding the present from the past* (releasing the Other from the lien of her past wrongdoing). Instead, availability in creative faithfulness addresses the predicament of *unbinding the future from the present*, of how to become other than myself when faced with the otherness of the Other, and, indeed, as with Cordelia, of how to "raise oneself from the dead" and reappear from the grave of the unforgivable, in her case, having been "unbegotten" by her own father. *You are a spirit, I know; when did you die?*

What is implied in Arendt's account of forgiveness is the enduring availability—not to be conflated with any promise, duty, or expectation— of coming to the encounter of forgiveness, or, in other words, of returning to the stage of the world (and hence, in Arendtian terms, the stage of appearances) from having been exiled offstage. As the precondition for any encounter in forgiveness, availability addresses the predicament of the unpredictability of the Other in whom I trust in my exposure to the otherness of the Other, that in her strangeness to come, I would remain reachable for the possibility and significance of forgiveness by which I *could* still welcome and receive once again the fallen Other into my trust. This original availability is not to already forgive in advance in extending a blank check for any transgression to come, thus making superfluous the encounter in forgiveness where the question of forgiveness, to forgive or not to forgive, would hang in the balance, with equal weight given to the possibility of forgiving or not forgiving. Nothing forgiven in advance; nothing is made that Cordelia must or should forgive Lear, and yet in this nothing, Cordelia remains available in loving Lear according to her bond. As with Cordelia's restorative kiss, availability to forgiveness does not yet forgive but resurrects the unforgivable one, raising them, as it were, to the standing of a person *who could be forgiven or not forgiven*, allowing them, as well as myself, to enter into the encounter of forgiveness. Though I cannot promise in advance either to forgive or not to forgive, I stand *available* to forgiveness to the extent that I am ready "to receive the new arrivals, newcomers to whom we prove what we no longer quite believe, that they are not strangers after all."[73] I must fore-give of myself without my having to forgive anything of the Other in advance nor with having already given myself away to forgiveness in any bound or predictable manner. Availability to forgiveness would not already *be* forgiveness but would likewise not *be* unforgiving and, in this original sense, already "be" forgiving without forgiving anything in advance, or always having to be forgiving, come what may.

If nothing can save us from that time of great confusion, at least we do not go into the night of the world without the unaccommodated availability to transcend our condition and circumstances, however poor and bare we might be in absolving the fallen Other from the broken world in the kind nursery of one's own forgiveness. Unaccommodated as I am toward the self yet to become me, I am to make myself available to you, and in so doing I have already committed myself down the path of forgiveness. Even if we never arrive (and we never fully arrive nor arrive fully) at forgiveness, I am always walking along this path with you. In belonging to the Other in trust, we are from the beginning already, and, in this sense, "originally," on the path toward—available for—forgiveness; even if we never arrive, or fall short, or stop midway in refusing, or become unavailable in tripping by the wayside, *nous sommes embarqués*.

The Death of the Other as Murder

"The death of the Other is always in a way a murder."[1] This is a striking statement that in its pith epitomizes the poignancy of Levinas's ethical thinking in an "Age of Extremes" (to borrow E. P. Thompson's expression), where killing has attained a historically unsurpassed facility, efficiency, and thoughtlessness. The death of the Other is always in a way a murder. "In death I am exposed to absolute violence, to murder in the night."[2] Given the sheer intensity of violent deaths occurring daily, not to mention the vastness of natural deaths for a human population soon to crest eight billion, what kind of statement is this? Is there not something meaningless, even irresponsible, in such a statement, or, worse, something trivially sentimental? Although this statement does not occur frequently in Levinas's writings, it recurs as something of a mantra, haunting his thinking. At first blush, bereft of adequate contextualization and appropriate texturing this statement might and most probably *should* seem absurd to us and is want to provoke our immediate aversion. It is a statement that every fiber of our being would reject, or at least judge to be hopelessly hyperbolic, needlessly "over the top," *de trop*. As a statement that seems to call us out, we might justly bristle at the pointed implication that if the death of the Other is always in a way a murder then someone among us—maybe even me?—always stands in a way complicit or, more forcefully, culpable for such a death. In our puzzlement, such a statement speaks to us by virtue of our rejection of what we think is said, even as it remains unclear what it is saying and how, despite its manifest obscurity, it refuses to let us go.

Unable to articulate ourselves clearly, we are nonetheless bespoken. Our immediate reaction toward such a statement tacitly reprises Cain's response: "Am I my brother's keeper?" Unlike Cain, we have presumably not killed anyone, let alone any of our siblings. As with Cain, the incredulous tone in our own response reveals a certain unease. As Levinas observes in commenting on this biblical passage, Cain's response is no mere instance of insolence. There is something sincere about Cain's question. As Levinas writes, "Human biological fraternity—considered with sober, Cainesque coldness—is not a sufficient reason for me to be responsible for a separate being; sober, Cainesque coldness consists in thinking of responsibility on the basis of freedom or according to contract."[3] As with biological or social ties, any form of ontological kinship in an appeal to a common condition of humanity, dignity, or vulnerability does not prove robust enough to ensure the *original* significance of our responsibility for others, but not because any appeal to an answer, duty, or principle to the question of the Other could in turn become questioned, challenged, or abandoned. What seems natural and spontaneous, and in this sense sincere and taken for granted, is that we can begin only with ourselves, from ourselves, in asking what the Other is *to me*. That the Other at all comes to mind as a question, of whether I am or should be the Other's keeper, assumes an original separateness between myself and the Other; it assumes that I am originally I much as the Other is the Other, originally not me. On this presumption, ethics hangs on responding from and for myself to the question of the Other. Indeed, what is more intuitive than that I am first for myself, originally anchored in my own freedom and consideration, from which I can *then* ask myself (or then be asked), "What is the Other to me?" For the Other *not to be* an original question, in terms of which my response would frame the terms of our possible encounter, would imply on the contrary that concern and responsibility for the Other would be *unquestionable*, and hence not an issue for me to decide, accept, or determine in any original way. Yet given *my* responsibility for the Other, whom else could I begin with if not with myself? In encountering the Other, from whom else could I begin other than myself? "Why does the Other concern me? What is Hecuba to me? Am I my brother's keeper?" Under such variant formulations, if we begin with ourselves, it remains incomprehensible how the Other could at all *originally* concern me, for any such concern for the Other would, as based on my own original freedom, be, as echoed in Hamlet, either a staged fiction or playacting: "A fiction . . . a dream of passion," the actor's "tears in his eyes, distraction in's aspect, / A broken voice, and his whole function suiting / With forms to his conceit" (II.2.515–16).[4] The question "What is the Other to me?" begins already at a distance from the Other, with the conceit of my own freedom as original, which, in searching for an answer, would seek to bridge a distance from, and hence to arrive at, the position of the Other, as a sufficient reason for bearing a responsibility for the Other.

As with any adroit detective, God asks an apparently straightforward question: "Where is your brother?" In his begrudging retort, Cain betrays himself by answering otherwise in refusing any implication of responsibility for his brother's keep. Without its being said, Cain responds by declaring, "Don't accuse me of irresponsibility" in a tone of bad faith attesting to his own shame before the violation of an unspoken and unavoidable responsibility. Masked by his shame behind this defiant and prideful—wounded—question, another scene in this juxtaposition of question and answer plays itself out. For if, in one scene, the question "Am I my brother's keeper?" makes the entrustment of the Other, their proximity, primarily a question of my freedom, then, in another scene, what becomes betrayed in the defensive presumption of this question—that the Other's proximity is at all a question for me—is an original responsibility residing prior to whether or not the Other is any of my concern. Is the proximity of the Other measured by my response to an original question asked of me, "What is the Other to me?" or, on the contrary, do I myself become measured—given place and standing in the world—through an original responsibility for the Other without question? Is the fundamental relation to the Other a question *asked to me* awaiting my answer, or do I find myself already *in question*, the Other as calling me (out) into question, before any question of the Other can be posed to me? Am I responsible for the Other *because* I am originally free to be myself, or I am free to be myself *because* I am originally responsible for the Other? Ethics is the name for this other scene, the scene of an indeclinable responsibility without alibi for the Other that is always assumed too late, even as we always proclaim our innocence too early. We are latecomers to an original responsibility already entrusted into our hands.

Cain unwittingly attests to, without explicitly avowing, a responsibility for his brother that he obscurely senses to be singularly his own. That Cain did not simply *kill* his brother but *murdered* him bespeaks of an assignment of his brother into his keep, the binding of which conditions the meaningfulness of his relationship to his next of kin as well as to God. Whether Cain explicitly knew or did not know, whether he deliberately accepted or declined, he already finds himself bound to a responsibility for his brother *before* coming to see himself and becoming himself—that is, positioning himself in relation to and encountering his brother within the ambit of his own freedom, decision, and consideration. The ambiguity of this "before" (a "before" that is only recognized too late, after its betrayal) is doubled, however, for what incites Cain to murder his brother is *shame* in the face of his brother. There is a notable degree of arbitrariness in God's favoring the offering of Abel's (fat portion of the season's first calf) rather than Cain's (the fruits of the field).[5] As with Lear, God seems unfair in his preference for Abraham's younger son (Abel) over the elder (Cain), thus contravening the just order of inheritance and seniority in this manifestation of divine partiality.[6] Although the firstborn, Cain feels slighted by God's preference, becoming sullen and jealous of his younger sibling. It is, however, not merely jealousy but also shame that proves critical for his incitement to murder; it is not guilt for having offered an inadequate sacrifice to God (having made a poor or regrettable decision) but shame at having not been recognized as *firstborn* and as at least equal to if not superior to his younger brother. Whereas guilt presupposes a freedom of choice and thus is related to action (I am guilty for what I have done), shame relates to one's existence as such; one reddens with shame, not with guilt. "When Cain," it is said, "saw that the Lord did not accept his sacrifice, he became furious and his face fell" (Genesis 4:5). In thus losing face, angered shame is less manageable and more damning of one's existence, or sense of self, than guilt.[7] We stand exposed in shame, not only before the face of the Other but also before ourselves in the loss of our own. In this loss of face before his brother, Cain fails to see "the incomprehensible inequality of the divine favor" as marking the Other's—his brother's—transcendence.[8] In shame at his own shame, Cain becomes incited to murder by the very face in whose presence he stands ashamed, even as he misses seeing the face of the Other in its present signification.

Our own uneasiness in the face of the statement "the death of the Other is always in a way a murder" belies an obscure sense that we, too, stand as the Other's keeper in a manner more fundamental than our own freedom, and hence that we cannot absolve ourselves of the *significance* to which the Other's death is in a way murder. Less of a proposition (or statement) than a provocation, the refrain that the death of the Other is in a way a murder is a signature Levinasian saying. It resonates as a provocation that we spontaneously resist accepting. If we did accept it immediately, without first having reacted in rejection and protest—that is, without having become *provoked*—our said acceptance would amount to nothing more than pretense, since to accept without having been affected in a manner that calls our own responsiveness into question is, in truth, to receive on our own prescribed terms. Rather than "receive" or "reject" this provocation, it agitates within us through an affective unease and elusive scruple. The nerve of its accusation touches on something obscurely unsettling within our own skin. It is a saying meant to incite a virile resistance on our part, since we would knowingly appeal to our own innocence: how could the death of the Other be murder if, with deaths that have not been inflicted through violent action, "natural deaths," I have done nothing and thus cannot stand accused of complicity in any way in the death of the Other?

Upon further consideration, one might be inclined to lend some plausibility to this provocation by thinking that Levinas is rehabilitating in his own way a notion of natural evil—namely, that natural death is intrinsically a harm. As argued by Thomas Nagel, for example, natural death is to be considered a harm since it deprives us of an intrinsic good—namely, the possibility of continued life, or continued possibility of existing, that essentially defines what it is to be human.[9] Yet Levinas deliberatively seizes on the term "murder," thus implying that death is an evil of a different, more aggressive kind than the deprivation of life's own possibility to "to be." "Murder" suggests a violence inflicted by another and hence a certain complicity in the death of the Other. And yet, as signaled with the unspecified qualification "in a way," Levinas does not intend "murder" as a death inflicted *upon* the Other, whether premeditated or negligently accidental. Every death is not *criminally* a murder, yet every death is *ethically* a murder. With this proposition that the death of the Other is always in a way a murder, Levinas means to ethically countermand (without evidently denying) what we normally and naturally consider most natural about death, that death is natural, or the brute ontological fact that we are finite, that we pass away from "having-been" to "no-longer-being," full stop.

If the death of the Other is always in a way a murder, *who* is the murderer, when clearly not me? How, in the nakedness of my being, without having done anything against anyone, could I already find myself with *your* blood on my hands? Outrageous here is that we stand accused, we the innocent. Even if we were believers of a certain faith, of a faith believing in original sin, and thus acknowledge that no person enters the world in innocence, we would still refuse this provocation, since our lack of innocence bespeaks an inherited guilt that befalls us equally, assigned to me no more than you, thus not uniquely or above all assigned to me. If the death of the Other is always in a way a murder, would not our own implication, that none of us begins in innocence, bespeak a responsibility without precedence or choice, and hence a condition of finding ourselves within an original posture of forgiveness as the condition for any possible encounter with the Other, as already entrusted to our hands, even as their murder is somehow already at our hands?

A Discourse of Exasperation

We might consider that such a statement, even as a provocation, cannot possibly be true and thus cannot (and maybe should not) even be taken seriously as an ethical claim. What kind of claim is advanced here? In what sense could any ethics grant itself, let alone afford, such provocation? Even once we have allowed ourselves, always guardedly, to be led into the intricate weave of Levinas's writings in which this saying recurs, we might still at the end of the day remain unconvinced and uncomprehending, protesting even more vigorously, perhaps too much, that such provocation could amount to nothing more than metaphorical flourish or rhetorical flair. Such a tactical reading would license us to dismiss this saying while maintaining our own good conscience and respectability, morally as well as hermeneutically. Such a defensive posture of reading assumes, however, that Levinas's writings are composed foremost of claims, judgments, and principles in the form of apophantic statements—that is, statements *about* something, the sense of which can be exclusively and exhaustively evaluated as either true or false. When sized up as an apophantic claim, the statement "the death of the Other is always in a way a murder" can arguably be judged only as false, either in empirical terms (I have never actually murdered anybody) or in ontological terms (in what meaningful sense is the death of Other *as such* "murder"?).[10] And yet it is constitutive of this saying that it, strictly speaking, can neither be true *nor* false. We face an apparent statement that exceeds the tribunal of reason, natural reasonableness, or worldly common sense. We are confronted by a provocation reaching beyond truth and falsity and, in this specific sense, an *impossible* statement—a statement that could never possibly be true given that it draws its intrinsic meaningfulness from a center of gravity beyond the measure of what could or could not *be* possible. And yet it still speaks to us, affects us, like a pebble lodged in the shoe of our confident steps, in saying something even more forcefully the less what it says can be mastered, decided, and judged as either true or false. As Levinas signals to be decisive for his own ethical discourse, "apophansis does not exhaust what there is in saying."[11] This is not to say that Levinas abandons the importance of argument, the cogency of description, or the value of truthfulness in his writings. It is to say that the import of argument, description, and truthfulness becomes beholden to a higher instance, otherwise than being, where it is not transcendence tailored to the "truth of being," first principles, or universal moral law but toward the Good that here provides the lodestar of significance.

Without rejecting the rigors of philosophical discourse, Levinas's ethical discourse becomes put to the test within the scene of another form rigor, even more demanding than the rigor of reason since it proves to be more strident, testing the mettle of thinking itself. As Levinas states, his ambition is to "open a philosophical discourse" in forging anew what it means to speak of ethics in the aftermath of ethical devastation.[12] Expressed in Levinas's vocabulary, the challenge becomes to think the significance of the ethical beyond and otherwise than ontological thinking, for which "sense" (*sens*) remains beholden to the so-called fundamental question of the sense of *being*. Is speaking (*le dire*) exclusively and exhaustively at the behest and service of the many senses of being and the sense of being as such? Is the basic form of any sensible saying to state something that could either be true or false? Levinas's ethical discourse is not primarily cast in the mold of normative or ontological thinking (what Levinas calls the language of logos), nor does his discourse jettison entirely a thinking shaped by ontological categories of the understanding and grammars of speaking. Levinas's discourse shuckles in syncopated rhythms between these two registers of discourse, with each register attesting to a different scene of thinking. In one register, there speaks an ontological thinking armed with its language of logos, stamped with a set of proper names (or historical signifiers: Hegel, Husserl, etc.), inscribed with philosophemes, and forged from technical vocabulary. Within this deployed register of discourse, there occurs another scene of thinking as marked by a register of words: assignment, accusation, persecution, hostage, responsibility, trauma, substitution, and so forth. These distinctive Levinasian terms do not form, strictly speaking, a technical vocabulary, nor construct a "theory" *or* "praxis" of ethics, without thereby lessening or mitigating the exigency of thinking in these stated terms. It would be wrong, moreover, to construe this juxtaposition of two registers of discourse and scenes of thinking in dialectical terms, or, as Levinas himself warns, as one register laid out over, or in contrast with, the other. We should not understand this juxtaposition of the ontological and the ethical in either a chronological (before-and-after) or a spatial (side-by-side) sense, and if we fail to grasp the sense of this juxtaposition in terms other than two-dimensional (binary, contradictory, before and after, side by side), it is because we have allowed the materiality of the printed page and the linearity of one-dimensional thinking (*one* assumed form of thought) to impose surreptitiously its own logic of misreading, one that is decidedly not in the vein of Levinas's style of ethical thinking. There is an obsessive quality to Levinas's prose, wavelike, as Derrida observes, much as a traversing tremor of interpellation.[13] The sayings of ethical discourse "interrupt" ontological discourse; by the same token, without ontological discourse, the disruptive force of ethical interpellation could be neither effectively nor affectively emplaced. In Levinas's way of speaking, what *is* said (*le Dit*) must necessarily convey as well as betray "the saying" (*le Dire*). *Le Dire* must be said and thus entangled, contorted, and arrested in being said and must in turn become unsaid, even as what is thus unsaid does not promise the original saying from becoming more accurately or faithfully said. There is no ethical speaking without betrayal, no ethical thought without indiscretion, and thus, implicitly, no opening of philosophical discourse, in the manner endured through Levinas's discourse, without a trust that must be betrayed in order to constitute the entrustment of which it speaks. This especially has bearing on (my own) speaking about Levinas's thinking. One benefits from its fecundity *poorly* when not betraying it.

What characterizes Levinas's ethical discourse is not only the effective and affective force of its interpellation within ontological thinking, from which, however, ethics can never entirely divorce itself completely. Ethics dislocates the ontological without becoming displaced from the ontological.[14] Notable for this originality of the ethical is the perspicuous absence of the expected and established philosophical terminology such as "possibility," "ground," "actuality," "certainty," "principles," "rules," "values," "person," and so on—foundational terms of ontology and much of any ethical theory in its wake. The *strangeness* of Levinas's thinking is essentially profiled in this abandonment of established vernaculars of the ethical. With jarring terms such as "obsession," "hostage," and "trauma," a "central insight of Levinas' ethics," the incomparable Rudi Visker observes, "is that everything in ethics turns on affects which cannot be described without that description falling short."[15] Such ethical discourse provokes affects in terms of which its meaningfulness becomes said; and yet such descriptions, turns of phrase, and styles of argumentation fall short of what it means to say, such that what is thus said must in turn become "unsaid," time and again, so as to resonate in the medium of its saying. Levinas's "hyperbolic" forms of expression ("trauma," "hostage," etc.) are pointed sayings of emphasis and exasperation. As Levinas remarks, "Emphasis signifies at the same time a figure of rhetoric, an excess of expression, a manner of overstating oneself, and a manner of showing oneself. The word is very good, like the word 'hyperbole': there are hyperboles whereby notions are transmitted. To describe this mutation is also to do phenomenology. Exasperation as a method of philosophy!"[16] Crystallized in the provocation that "the death of the Other is always in a way a murder," we stand exasperated before Levinas's ethical thinking, barred, so it would seem, from any approach by our own registered frustration and irritation and yet nonetheless called forth—exposed—in accusation and assignation. "Am *I* the Other's keeper?"

Deaths of Children in *The Brothers Karamazov*

An approach to the provocation "the death of the Other is always in a way a murder" can be ventured with the fundamental unacceptability of death—its scandal—as acutely experienced with the death of children.

This scandal proves central to Dostoevsky's *The Brothers Karamazov* in its obsession with the death of children. Structured around the death of father figures—more pointedly, the death of the father at the hands of his sons—*The Brothers Karamazov* is equally concerned with the forgetting and remembrance of sons. As with *King Lear*, the basic drama of Dostoevsky's narrative turns on the division of the father's possessions among his children—in this instance, three sons—but unlike Lear, who seeks to disburden himself of his sovereignty and power, the father here seeks to selfishly retain and conspicuously waste his wealth at the expense of those whom he has begotten.[17] We are introduced to the three sons of Fyodor Karamazov (Dmitri, Ivan, and Alyosha) with accounts of their successive abandonment by their wayward father. Dominated by a lust for life and sensual pursuits, Fyodor Karamazov forgets each of his sons in turn. Each son is born to the world in the rupture of any original entrustment: each is born an orphan.[18] If, in this manner, *The Brothers Karamazov* begins with the forgetting of sons, it concludes with mourning the death of the young boy Ilyusha and Alyosha's encouragement of a group of children to forge a new community in his remembrance. Standing in front of Ilyusha's favorite stone, underneath which he had wished to be buried, Alyosha is seized by a shudder in his soul as he recalls how little Ilyusha suffered for his father's humiliation. As he addresses the band of children gathered in mourning, Alyosha declares, "Let us agree here, by Ilyusha's stone, that we will never forget—first, Ilyusha, and second, one another."[19] In mourning and remembrance—for the dead, for the living, toward the future—Alyosha declares once again, more emphatically, "let us never forget one another," effectively exhorting remembrance of the fact that we are each other's brothers, the keepers of each other's memories and hearts "for eternity."

This passage from forgetting to remembrance traces across the pages of *The Brothers Karamazov* the arc of Alyosha's transformative awakening to his elected vocation through his expiation for the death of little Ilyusha and steadfastly remaining his brothers' keeper, even as his brothers abandon him and, in the case of Ivan, betray him. Within Dostoevsky's poetics, there are multiple narrative axes and voices structuring *The Brothers Karamazov*'s dramatic unfolding, but arguably its principal axis turns on the conflict between Ivan and Alyosha.[20] Born of the same mother (unlike Dmitri and their half brother Smerdyakov), the confrontation between Ivan and Alyosha suggests the conflict of evil and goodness as ambiguously sourced from the same womb and seed.[21] At the center of their confrontation stands Ivan's Rebellion. In calling upon the suffering of children in its repudiation of faith and reason, Ivan's Rebellion is, in turn, situated narratively between the deaths of two children. The first occurs at the beginning of *The Brothers Karamazov*, when a grieving mother—a local peasant woman—approaches the Elder Zosima seeking consolation for her "little son" who died a few months shy of age three. She exclaims how her "soul is wasted," how she looks at his "clothes, his little shirt or his little boots, and starts howling," and how it is just as if he were still standing there in front of her. As she laments, "If only I could just have one more look at him, if I could see him one more time, I wouldn't even go up to him, I wouldn't speak, I'd hide in the corner, only to see him for one little minute, to hear him the way he used to play in the backyard and come in and shout in his little voice: *Mama, where are you?*[22] This longing to see her son "for one little minute" responds to the immemorial appeal of her son; in this appeal, there is assignment as well as accusation, as if the appeal—"Mama, where are you?"—resonated even more poignantly with his death. The acuity of death's weeping is not only that we, the survivors, now stand alone but also that the dead would seem to stand abandoned to their death, when bereft of the assurance of *our* responding to their appeal. In "Mama, where are you?" there issues the assignment of a responsibility without which the dead could not endure their own passing, but also an accusation of our necessary failing to bear this responsibility to the end. In longing for her son to be present once more, the mother's grief bespeaks a conscientiousness for her son, as his keeper, to respond to the accusation "Why have you forsaken me to my death?" Do we mourn as much for the loneliness of the dead as for our own loneliness, however absurd and hyperbolic such talk of the "loneliness of the dead" might possibly sound? Can the dead even be said to *feel* and hence *be* lonely? And yet even though absurdly said, it affects us nonetheless in saying something, for we would be unfeeling and condescendingly intellectual to rebuff this grief-stricken wanting to assure *ourselves* that the dead are not abandoned to their loneliness beyond the grave.[23] In wanting to "hide in the corner," the mother seeks to insinuate her presence, and hence participate, in her son's death. Exposed in this mother's grief, the "who"—the subjectivity of the subject—marks the place and the time where and when the whisper "Here I am" responds to the eternally echoed appeal "Where are you?" In the mother's grief, there is the ambiguity of a departure without return, of the deceased son, but also the scandal that the death of the Other—her son—cannot be accepted or welcomed, even as her son is not to be abandoned or forsaken to his own death. As poignantly portrayed with the grieving mother, the death of the Other is the scandal of *my* responsibility for the inconsolable and unacceptable: death, unforgiving.

Wisely, it would seem, the Elder Zosima does not seek to console this grieving mother. As he tells her, "And do not be comforted, you should not be comforted, do not be comforted, but weep." This insistence on "do not be comforted, but weep" bespeaks the unacceptability of the death of the Other, that we cannot bear grief without the assurance, or faith, attested to in weeping. Tears of grief look upward, not downward, for as the Elder Zosima reassures her, her child now resides eternal in the Glory of God: "Each time you weep, do not fail to remember that your little son is one of God's angels, and that he looks upon you from there and sees you, and rejoices in your tears and points them out to the Lord God." In mourning there is remembrance, not only of the deceased but also, in this theological vision, of God, to whom the deceased becomes entrusted. The Elder Zosima's call for remembrance is itself an echo of the biblical narrative of "Rachel of old . . . weeping for her children," who "will not be comforted because they are not." We are to be reminded of Job's children and tacitly admonished not to lose faith in God, who himself must weep for the dead. As with the final scene in Krzysztof Kieślowski's *Dekalog: One*, when we weep for the death of the Other (in the film, the young boy Paweł), God also weeps, as candle wax falls onto the icon of Mother Mary's face, pushed over by the distraught and unaccepting father, Krzysztof, streaking tears upon God's commandant *I am the Lord your God; you shall have no other gods before me.* The graven image of Mother Mary's face receives the stigmata of burning tears, much as Krzysztof, the father, receives a baptism of faith in his grief at his son's death, upon his forehead with a frozen tear of holy water. Oddly, however, as the inconsolable mother wryly observes, Zosima's redemptive theodicy utters "word for word" the repeated reprimands of her husband, who succumbed to excessive drinking in unbearable grief: "Foolish woman," he would say, "why do you cry so? Our little son is surely with the Lord God now, singing with the angels." In the simple heart of the grieving mother, a question mark becomes obliquely inserted into the heart of faith with this insinuation that the divine wisdom of the Elder Zosima remains word for word indistinguishable from the earthly condition of her husband's all-too-human inebriation. Within *The Brothers Karamazov*, the stage is set for faith's undoing in God and trust in the world, hinging on the scandal of death, as focalized with the death of children.

The second scene of the death of children occurs in Ivan's Rebellion. Ivan's Rebellion takes the form of a suggestive recasting of the book of Job with its appeal to the gratuitous and unforgivable suffering of children.[24] Significantly, it is to be the despair of Reason, or any theodicy in which evil would be said redeemed, justified, or bestowed with salutary or providential meaning. More directly, Ivan's Rebellion is meant to expose the absurdity of Kant's moral theology since, according to Ivan's reasoning, the conflict between the justified hope in a future convergence of happiness and virtue and the unjustified suffering of children in the present reveals the "diabolical" character of reason. As Ivan addresses Alyosha, "Imagine that you are creating a fabric of human destiny with the object of making men happy in the end . . . but that it was essential and inevitable to torture to death only one tiny creature . . . and to found that edifice on its unavenged tears: would you consent to be the architect on those conditions? Tell me, and tell me the truth!" Sharpened against natural theology as well as critical philosophy, Ivan's Rebellion weaponizes the unforgivable against any form of redemption through Faith or Reason. Having destroyed the foundations of theology through a critique of pure Reason, Reason now itself stands on trial. In the figure of Ivan Karamazov, Dostoevsky incarnates the destructive force and self-destruction of Reason: outwardly, Reason's destruction of any basis for rational (or natural) theology; inwardly, Reason's "diabolic" acceptance of gratuitous suffering for the sake of harmony in the long run and thereby its own self-destruction.[25] In Ivan's statement, "Besides, too high a price is asked for harmony; it's beyond our means to pay so much to enter on it. And so I hasten to give back my entrance ticket, and if I am an honest man I am bound to give it back as soon as possible."

Ivan launches his Rebellion with the admission that he finds the biblical injunction "love thy neighbor" to be incomprehensible. Quite the opposite, he reasons, it is precisely one's neighbor that one cannot love. Love is either commanded by duty, executed as "self-imposed penance," or never truly performed. As Ivan remarks, "Christ's love for people is in its kind a miracle impossible on earth." As soon as a person shows his face, love vanishes, hence one can love one's neighbor only "abstractly, and even occasionally from a distance, but hardly ever up close."[26] To drive this point home, Ivan evokes the story of John the Merciful ("some saint") giving alms and compassion to a hungry, freezing stranger: John laid down "with him in bed, embraced him, and began breathing in his mouth."[27] An exception is made for children, however, whom Ivan professes can be "loved up close, even dirty and homely." With this remark, Ivan comes to dwell on the suffering of children, but as Alyosha comments to him, "You have a strange look as you speak, as if you were in some kind of madness."[28] Alyosha feels himself standing in the presence of the intrinsic mysteriousness of evil in his own brother. Indeed, a prurient fascination with suffering is unmistakable in Ivan's rampant catalog of evils that he parades before Alyosha's eyes: stories of atrocity, cruelty, and violence. Ivan stylizes himself as a "collector of certain little facts" that he keeps together in a "nice collection." As he informs his brother, he relishes gleaning stories of suffering from newspapers and ancient chronicles. Ivan's catalog of evils is essentially pornographic—his atrocity exhibition is unfeelingly populated with endless positions and varieties of maiming, killing, and torture. At one point, when recounting a story of Turks shooting babies in the head, Ivan sardonically remarks, "Artistic, isn't it?"

Ivan's intellectualism protects him against being affected by suffering, even as he is touched by evil. He remains indifferent to the suffering of Others, even as he suffers from *images* of evil he so meticulously catalogs. He does not partake in the deaths he has so scrupulously collected with Cainesque coldness. The *proximity* of the Other remains for Ivan incomprehensible, although his insufferable despair for the gratuitous murder of children wounds him deeply, intimately; or so it would seem. Ivan's chilling statement "I know for certain that there are floggers who get more excited with every stroke, to the point of sensuality, literal sensuality, more and more, progressively, with each new stroke" doubles as a self-characterization of his own morbid curiosity. The "delight" in the torturing of children emphasized in Ivan's narratives becomes performed in Ivan's own telling of these stories. While Edgar in *King Lear* pronounces "the worst is not / So long as we can say 'This is the worst'" (IV.1.32–33), Ivan's loquaciousness of evil evinces a contamination of language brought about by insistently saying and showing "the worst," evil in its manifest savagery. Evil in this manner propagates itself through its own saying, finding renewed form and seduction in its speaking. As with Elizabeth Costello in J. M. Coetzee's story, one is "not sure whether writers who venture into the darker territories of the soul always return unscathed."[29] Clearly, Ivan takes pleasure in inflicting his atrocity exhibition on Alyosha and, in this manner, tortures not merely a child standing speechless there before him in flesh and blood but also his own younger brother. What is my brother to me? Aware that his atrocity exhibition torments Alyosha, there is something sadistic in his showing him these pictures, in their telling, but at the same time something masochistic, given Ivan's delight at his own suffering and torture of his brother. Ivan's insufferable presence is his own existence as expressed in the dual form of intellectualization and pornography: distance from the real presence of evil (standing before his own eyes with the abuse of his own brother) and (self)-absorption in the intimacy of its fascination. Ivan relates to suffering as spectacle: the death of others can be seen only from afar. He is the collector of dead souls and master spectator of distant suffering.

The atrocity exhibition orchestrated by Ivan is suffocating; pictures of atrocities follow one after the other, each more excessively cruel than the next, leaving little space for breath. Much as Alyosha is cornered to stay in the tavern as Ivan's hostage with the lure of fish soup, tea, and cherry preserve, Ivan's catalog of evils is charged with a purpose toward which it mercilessly drives: the cornering of any availability for forgiveness against itself. Suddenly, Ivan remarks, "One more picture, just one more, for curiosity" and proceeds to recount an especially lurid story of a general who orders his hunting dogs to tear apart a child who has injured one of his dog's paws with a thrown stone. The general's cruelty is gratuitous and senseless; it propels Ivan toward the climax of his atrocity exhibition. Confronting his brother, "Well . . . what to do with him? Shoot him? Shoot him for our moral satisfaction? Speak, Alyoshka!" Ivan presses, demands, and coerces Alyosha to speak—to confess—his unfaith. When his younger brother blurts out, "Shoot him!" ("looking up at his brother with a twisted smile"), Ivan experiences a moment of rapture: "Bravo!" he exclaims, "see what a little devil is sitting in your heart, Alyoshka Karamazov!"[30] Had Alyosha responded that the general should be forgiven, it would have sounded either insincere or mechanical, playing to Ivan's advantage, or seemed obscene and verging on a blasphemy of its own. The impasse of forgiveness here is that any gesture toward forgiveness in this suffocating space of atrocity would appear empty or false. Forgiveness has been effectively cornered by the unforgivable, made complicit in the unforgivable, not as the forgiveness of the unforgivable but as the redoubling of the unforgivable, so as provoke the supreme blasphemy against forgiveness, its self-renunciation. In the suffocating drive of Ivan's atrocity exhibition, the temporal horizon of forgiveness has been foreclosed entirely in the absolute demand for forgiveness *now*, in the presence of evil, as the presence of evil. It is as if the availability to forgiveness had become itself tortured in being made complicit—coerced—in its own treason. Thus strangulated, there remains no leeway for the *approach* of forgiveness given that its availability has been cornered against itself in a darkness in which there is no room for light, not even a sliver of slanting light. Responsibility for the Other—to stand as my brother's keeper—has been inverted by Ivan into an unforgiving irresponsibility and abandonment of the Other. This cornering of forgiveness mirrors an opposite sense of cornering, when the demand to seek forgiveness becomes lorded over the offender and wielded against him as an expression of the victim's power. In both instances, we witness the same transformation of forgiveness into a transactional power of *sovereignty* that obscures and perverts the humility and majesty of an original availability to forgiveness, not as the waiting for forgiveness in the aftermath of injury but of that waiting *before* any encounter with the possibility or impossibility of forgiveness.

The third scene of a child's death occurs at the end of *The Brothers Karamazov* with the death of little Ilyusha. These three portraits of a child's death (the grieving mother, Ivan's Rebellion, little Ilyusha) portray three visages of death. The first death of a child depicts a "natural" conception of death and the response of natural theology; the second death of a child at the general's pleasure in Ivan's Rebellion portrays a violent conception of death. If the first represents the natural evil of death, the second represents the moral evil of murder. The death of little Ilyusha is more complex as it embodies neither a natural evil *or* a moral evil. In contrast to the death of the peasant mother's child, little Ilyusha's death is connected to Dmitri's (Alyosha's brother) insults toward and mistreatments of his father: Dmitri's action (his humiliation of the father, who served as a proxy for Fyodor, Dmitri's father) occasioned the boy's death. In a poignant sense, the boy dies for his father, as Alyosha suddenly remembers, with a shudder traversing his soul, during his Speech at the Stone. In contrast to the deaths grimly portrayed in Ivan's prurient catalog, little Ilyusha succumbs to fever and thus, in this sense, dies "naturally." This running together of two implicated circumstances for his death—death as the consequence of Dmitri's action against his father and death as the consequence of his natural illness—undercuts both in revealing a significance of death beyond the entrenched distinction between natural evil (death caused by no hands) and moral evil (death caused by hands).[31] Little Ilyusha is not put to death as with the child in Ivan's story of the general; nor does little Ilyusha pass away naturally, as with the boy of the peasant mother. His death is rather *put to us.* This ambiguity surrounding little Ilyusha's death expresses the significance of the death of the Other as in a way a murder. It expresses the scandal of death as primarily an ethical, not ontological, event, as acutely focalized in the death of children.

Although it was Dmitri's aggression and insult against the boy's father that provided the proximate cause for the boy's demise, it is Alyosha who feels himself complicit in his death. Ilyusha's unprovoked attack (with his throwing of stones) against Alyosha, whom he recognizes as Dmitri's brother upon their first accidental meeting, bespeaks an accusation that Alyosha receives as an assignment of responsibility. Affected by the boy's suffering for his father and the injustice committed against him by his brother (Dmitri), Alyosha comes to bear a responsibility for Ilyusha's death (although biologically and socially—that is, ontologically—not his brother). As Alyosha partakes in his death, Ilyusha's memory is entrusted to Alyosha's mourning and the community of children, as a community bound in remembrance, as consecrated with his Speech at the Stone.[32] With this closing act of *The Brothers Karamazov*, Alyosha incarnates the words inspired in him by his teacher, the Elder Zosima, to which he aspired in his spiritual transfiguration: "Every one of us is guilty before everyone for everyone, and I more than others." In the arc of Dostoevsky's narrative, the confrontation between Ivan and Alyosha encapsulates and enacts a conflict between two fundamental sayings: "Am I my brother's keeper?" as voiced by Ivan, and "Every one of us is guilty before everyone for everyone, and I more than others," as voiced by Alyosha.[33] Embodied in the figure of Alyosha, the statement that "the death of the Other is always in a way a murder" *is* to say that "Every one of us is guilty before everyone for everyone, and I more than others." To stand as the Other's keeper is to bear *singularly* oneself the responsibility for the Other's death as in a way murder.

In fact, the saying "every one of us is guilty before everyone for everyone, and I more than others" is significantly not originally Alyosha's, even as these spirited words become original to him. Reaching beyond the novel itself in its distinct echo of the Bible, the source of this foundational saying remains "immemorial," without a specifiable origin within the memory of the novel, even as it recurs, like a refrain, in different voices in *The Brothers Karamazov* as a resounding echo *before* any first pronouncement could be discernible from an individual speaker and origin. Alyosha receives this saying in entrustment and communion from the teachings of the Elder Zosima, who, in turn, received these words of inspiration and aspiration from his older brother, Markel, as he lay dying at the young age of seventeen. In speaking these eternally resounding words to Alyosha in remembrance of his dead brother, the Elder Zosima sees in Alyosha's face an image of his own deceased brother.[34] In Alyosha's face, the Elder Zosima does not just see an image of his brother but also more directly *hears* the saying "every one of us is guilty before everyone for everyone, and I more than others" in its immemorial signification of transcendence. The face speaks this citation; the face *is* in its original expression, or saying, *a citation*, as Jill Robbins explains, "that is, it is characterized not by phenomenality but by the structure of the mark, with the constitutive absence that it implies."[35] In the communication and communion of this citation, the Elder Zosima's assignment of responsibility to Alyosha is inspiring as well as aspirational. This citation *summons* Alyosha to appear face-to-face with its bespoken inspiration. This summons ("every one of us is guilty before everyone for everyone, and I more than others") inspires Alyosha with the breath of life—his promised end—in instilling an aspiration toward the incarnation of this Word in deed (what the Elder Zosima taught as "active love"). The emphasis "I more than others" does not imply that Alyosha is quantitatively or qualitatively (i.e., comparatively and, hence, relatively) *more* "guilty" than others but addresses Alyosha's singular *election*. In causing jealousy among other monks, this election of responsibility illustrates how "moral perfection" can be a "double-edged weapon, which may lead a person not to humility and ultimate self-control but, on the contrary, to the most satanic pride."[36] In his own perverted manner, Ivan also considers himself elected to suffer more than others before everyone for everyone. It is but a small step that separates "satanic pride" from "saintly humility," Ivan from Alyosha, within the anarchic upsurge of an original responsibility for the Other.

In the *Brothers Karamazov*, the recurrence of the citation, without discernible origin within the novel and running through its inspired characters like a shudder of interpellation, "every one of us is guilty before everyone for everyone, and I more than others" can rightly be considered its discursive stigmata that in turn mark the transcendence of the Other, their face, in an absolute responsibility for which each of us, and I more than others, is elected. As with the tremor passing through Alyosha's Speech at the Stone, the stigmata of responsibility would mark a thinking that incorporates into its ethical aspiration the provocation, as assignment and accusation, that the death of the Other is always in a way a murder. As with Alyosha's summoning, this saying has signification only as a citation that summons before its spoken word another speech that would in turn bear this stigmata within itself and so would, in citing once again what inspired it to speak, incite in turn yet another incarnation of its marked signification. It is not that the "meaning" of this saying is "infinite" or "inexhaustible" but rather that its signification summons without end, not as the summoning of the same or as the same summoning but as an ever-recurring summoning that always transcends any given context in which it finds itself cited, or said. Appropriately, therefore, as marked by the stigmata of this citation, the saying "every one of us is guilty before everyone for everyone, and I more than others" recurs as a "talismanic quotation" throughout Levinas's writings.[37] It is a saying that, as Levinas himself remarks, he "always cites," and in terms of which he repeatedly characterizes his ethical thinking, such that, arguably, the provocation of Levinas's thinking can be read inter alia as inscribed within this singular saying, as thinking through its significance with rigorous consequence.[38] In answer to the question "What led you to philosophy?" Levinas cites Russian novels and, specifically, Dostoevsky's.[39] Exemplified in the figure of Alyosha, as Levinas writes, "The proximity of a neighbor is my responsibility for him; to approach is to be one's brother's keeper; to be one's brother's keeper is to be his hostage . . . it is a responsibility such that my position as a subject in its *as for me* is already my substitution or expiation for others."[40] As Levinas emphatically states with regard to this central thought, "I didn't discover that, Dostoevsky did. It is his great truth: 'We are all guilty in everything in respect to all others, and I more than all the others.' This last 'I more than all the others' is the important thing here, even if that means in a certain sense to be an idiot."[41]

Recurring through Levinas's writings like a tremor, and, in turn, as the "shudder" in Alyosha's heart in the Speech at the Stone, the upsurge of this saying echoes Abraham's intercession on behalf of Sodom (Genesis 18:23), where, in declaring his responsibility for the Other, he proclaims in the same breath, "I am myself but ashes and dust." As Levinas comments on this biblical passage, "Abraham is frightened by the death of others, and he takes responsibility to intercede. It is *then* that he says, 'I am, myself, ashes and dust.'"[42] This responsibility of oneself for another (*autrui*) is "the responsibility of a mortal being for a mortal being" in attestation that each one of us is a *created* being—a being not of our own self-begetting—and thus originally beholden to another.

The Trauma of the Good and the Anarchy of Forgiveness

It is a truism that we are not self-created beings, that each of us has been singularly brought into the world by others, that we did not beget ourselves. Once begotten, we are entrusted into the keep of others as the precondition for the development of who we are, have been, and might become. Neither just thrown into the world nor simply condemned to our own freedom, we are received in the hold of someone else's responsibility, of those who have reared us into the world in stewardship, care, and vigilance. Telling is that this original entrustment to others remains beyond the reach of our remembrance and ambit of our volition. Who can recall those first years of becoming? Who decided to have been born? And yet even as our beginnings remain immemorial and beyond us, such obscured beginnings continually remand us. We live beholden to our begotten past, neither forgotten nor remembered. From this oblivion that I was had, I emerged, whether begrudgingly or precociously, into what is said to be my own claimed and proclaimed autonomy, identity, and world. We do not begin ourselves but begin already begun, sprung from an origin not of our own begetting and yet still of our own keeping.

It would seem self-evident that the original sense of what it is to have been begotten is *to be* rather than not, and thus that to be created possesses the primary sense of born into being. There was a time when I was not. There will be a time when I shall no longer be. Ashes to ashes, dust to dust. We might appropriate Husserl's notion of the natural attitude and inflect within the present compass of reflection this apparent obviousness that to be created is naturally to be understood—it goes without saying—in terms of the distinction between "being" and "nothingness," that, in other words, the *significance* of *being* created appears to be exhaustively and exclusively determined by the *sense* of what it is to be, of what, in being, we are born into. We naturally assume an ontological understanding of the significance of our begotten existence. What it means to have been begotten, is to be, or to "to be." How such an ontological significance of our begotten condition is to be further specified can be variously determined and debated: biologically, anthropologically, theologically, psychoanalytically, metaphysically. To be or not to be, that would seem to be the question, to which, in some form or another, all other questions remain committed and invested.

This ontological framing of what it means to be as a created being, where what distinctively characterizes our existence—the sense of our being—is the salience of having been created, and thus the promise of becoming, is in turn inseparable from the truism that "to be" is originally to have been begotten by some others: parents, God, or Nature. In this regard, to be oneself has ab initio the basal form of "one from another." I am because I am begotten by some others. To become one for myself as well as to be one for others is thus predicated on having first become from some others. From this apparently self-evident assumption, various ethical and religious consequences have historically followed. The significance of such "beholdenness" to others, if we might grant such an ungainly term, has been commonly characterized in terms of debt and gratitude, of giving and receiving. According to this notion, our sense of being is marked by an incurred debt (and in some views guilt) toward deities, God, parents, community, or ancestors. We must give thanks for a life received. My existence is a gift. In an adjoining view, that I am "one from another" is to be spelled out primarily in terms of trust, guardianship, and responsibility. For such an approach, our lives are originally shaped by a paradigmatic foundation of trust (parental trust, trust in God, etc.), without which we would not be able to mature and become ourselves trusting of others as well as become trustworthy for others. Before I can become responsible for others, some others had first to be responsible for me; even their failure or neglect bespeaks of such a needed original responsibility. In a further view, our creaturely feeling is understood either in terms of an absolute sense of dependence on God or as standing before the awe and majesty of a *mysterium tremendum*. In yet another view, our begotten condition is to be understood in terms of the vulnerability and dependence of our finite condition with an emphasis on our embodied incarnation.[1]

Inspired by the talismanic citation "every one of us is guilty before everyone for everyone, and I more than others," what marks the uniqueness of Levinas's ethical thinking is its challenge of this natural assumption that to be created is as to its *original* significance to be understood in terms of the sense of being. The significance of creation, that we are begotten and begetting beings, is, however, not exhaustively and exclusively determinable as an ontological event. As Levinas writes, "Philosophers have always wished to think of creation in ontological terms."[2] The significance of what it is to be created must become reinscribed, in his proposal, into an order of significance otherwise than what it means to be. Yet what would it mean to think of our created condition as otherwise than in ontological terms, as not exhaustively expressed and exclusively captured by the sense, however determined, of what it is, or should be, or can be, "to be"? Frequently cast in shorthand (and all too unthinkingly uttered) formulas such as "the transcendence of the Good beyond being" or "the primacy of the ethical over the ontological," what characterizes our begotten condition, our distinctive creatureliness, is that its significance exceeds the sense of being, or "to be or not to be." In being created, we partake in an adventure whose significance cannot be reduced to the sense of being and nonbeing in which we necessarily, as created beings, find ourselves enthralled. In this transcendence, the begotten subject stands beholden to another order of significance: Goodness otherwise than, or beyond, being. In being, we are beholden to another significance, other than the sense of just being for the sake of being, not as an alternative but as its disruptive realignment. It refers to an order of significance that, when viewed from the many senses of being, is anarchical, without principle, origin, or reason in being or of being. To be begotten is not exhaustively to be subjected to being but to be captivated by the Good and exalted to Goodness from the exclusive hold of what it is to be; through this expulsive subjection, the goodness of creation becomes sanctified. What distinguishes the human being from other created beings is this subjection to an exalted origin beyond and otherwise than its origin in being. In this subjection to the Good, the subjectivity of the subject, as Levinas expresses it, "confers meaning on being itself, and welcomes its gravity."[3] It is not the God but the only begotten ethical subject who declares the goodness of creation in the act of giving bread to someone other in the intrinsic goodness of giving up what of creation is said or claimed to be "mine," or "yours," or "ours." As Levinas writes, "To give, to-be-for-the-other, despite oneself, but in interrupting the for-oneself, is to take the bread out of one's own mouth, to nourish the hunger of the Other with one's own fasting."[4] What is this bit of earth to me, if not to be for someone other, for you? Who are you, if not to be there for someone other, for me? The world comes to have gravity only through this subjection to the Good; otherwise, the world is merely a play at being in which the question "What is Hecuba to me?" remains forever wanting.

We are naturally born into the world, yet in this begotten condition we stand beholden to others in the responsibility of the Good and its investiture within being-in-the-world. In a disruptive sense, to be begotten in being (i.e., that I am) finds itself exposed to the Good otherwise than being, and in this exposure I stand in the world beholden to the Good beyond being. The sense of what it is to be thus becomes outstripped by the significance of the Good, as obtaining concretely with the intrinsic goodness of an irreducible and irrecusable responsibility for others through which we become ourselves begotten and begetting in an ethically primordial sense, where what it is to be becomes redeemed and, in this sense, meaningful. Must we first be in order to do good, or must we first bear ourselves unto Goodness in order to redeem—to render meaningful or significant—what it is to be? At the center of Levinas's revamping of ethical thinking is the restoration of the creaturely significance of our existence, that we are ethical creatures above all: *if you intend good, bear-it-aloft.*

Levinas's inversion of the relation between the Good and Being, marked by the formula "the transcendence of the Good beyond and otherwise than being," should not be understood, however, as the inversion of two questions—namely, the ascendency of the question of the significance of the Good over and above the question of the sense of being. In this inversion, the sense of what it means to question and respond becomes itself inverted through its reinscription into a movement of thinking that does not find itself first launched or motivated (through desire, curiosity, or interest) by a question in search of an answer (i.e., what is the Good?) but that always sees itself already answerable to the Good without question (i.e., how am I *to be* Good given that I am originally beholden to the Good?). There is, in this regard, an inherent mysteriousness to the Good, as befitting the intrinsic goodness of its original beholdenness. This mysterious connivance of the Good becomes manifest in the disarming force of being affected by others in their uniqueness, as their majesty and their destitution, in ways that we cannot easily fathom, even as such ways become us, as with Lear's insane impartiality of remorse for his unforgivable existence and tearing off his clothes for Poor Tom, or the shudder piercing Alyosha's heart with the death of little Ilyusha, or the "no cause, no cause" of Cordelia's forgiveness of her wayward, unforgivable father.[5]

From this inversion of the relation between the Good and Being, where the assumed priority of questioning becomes in turn inverted in favor of an unquestionable responsibility without alibi, there follows a second inversion. Within an ontological register of significance, as a begotten being I am originally from some other. I am ab initio entrusted to others (parents, community, etc.). Hence the indispensability of trust, from birth to grave, upon which human flourishing stands or falls, given our interdependent existence with one another. Only on this precondition of being "one from the Other" can I become "one for the Other" as well as "one for oneself." From the beginning, our existence participates in the lives of others; there would be no participation in being without the creation and creativity of trust. Creation itself becomes held in trust in this participation of being-in-the-world. To be "one for the

Other" is thus not original but achieved or accomplished on the basis of my freedom (or as a constraint on my freedom) as one for myself—that is, as for oneself. Whereas we naturally understand the sense in which we are at the beginning entrusted to the responsibility of others and defined as to our own accountability as being for oneself, it would appear less intuitive, less "natural," to venture that we are entrusted with a responsibility *for the Other* in an original way, "from the beginning," in an irreducible and irrecusable manner, that, in other words, our freedom (to be for oneself—oneself as myself) is already bound to an original responsibility for the Other, indeed for all others, which I did not chose, nor could have at first refused, or even, despite my own pretensions, originally evaded. In Levinas's challenging thought, crystallized in the refrain "the death of the Other is always in a way a murder," the restitution of our begotten condition to the ethical—that ethics revolves around the significance of our creatureliness—hinges on this capital inversion of "from the Other" to "for the Other" through the displacement of an "original freedom" by an "original responsibility." As Levinas remarks, "It [original responsibility] is more ontological than ontology; more *sublime* than ontology. It is from there that a certain equivocation comes—whereby ethics seems laid on top of ontology, whereas it is before ontology. It is thus a transcendentalism that begins with ethics."[6]

In this original binding of responsibility, trust is not given to the Other from my freedom, nor do I receive trust from the Other in my freedom, but rather I am already entrusted with a responsibility for the Other and thus am already bound to be oneself available for the Other as their keeper, I more than anyone else. Rather than begin with a conception of oneself—the subjectivity of the subject—as "freedom," "autonomy," "will," or *conatus essendi,* from which the relation to the Other becomes addressed and approached, framed by the question posed to one's own freedom, interest, and commitment, "am I the Other's keeper?" Levinas proposes to conceive of oneself as beginning, or emerging, in a responsibility for the Other prior to any commitment, reception, or acceptance in freedom. The significance of this "before" or "priority"—namely, that responsibility for the Other precedes and renders possible one's standing in the world as oneself, and thus casts the shadow of Goodness across any and all possible encounters with others—is not easily fathomed. Crucially, the significance of this proclaimed "priority" or "antecedence" of responsibility for the Other over our own freedom (that I am for the Other "before" being for oneself) should not be understood in *ontological terms* according to a temporality of "before" and "after," where the sense of what is "before" must follow in the wake of the primacy, or firstness, of the present, of presentness; namely, that something must first be present in order to become past, or, by the same logic of thinking, that the origin (or what is original) is characterized essentially by the principle of presence. From the vantage point of "after," an origin, when thought in principled terms as presence, becomes thereby construed as either "lost" or "forgotten," or remotely present within an obscuring other form of presence, or confidently projected as the future of any genuine becoming.

In speaking of an "immemorial" responsibility for the Other as an "attachment that has already been made, as something irreversibly past, prior to all memory and all recall" in an "irrecuperable time," this anterior pastness—a pastness that was never itself present in order to become past—defines the condition of oneself as a creature who is already born an orphan of Goodness. We are said to be an "orphan by birth," insofar as we begin in being as separated from the upsurge of responsibility for others; we begin naturally from others with ourselves, our interests, desires, and questions, much as the child in Peter Handke's "Lied vom Kindsein":

> Als das Kind Kind war,
> war es die Zeit der folgenden Fragen:
> Warum bin ich ich und warum nicht du?
> Warum bin ich hier und warum nicht dort?
> Wann begann die Zeit und wo endet der Raum?
> Ist das Leben unter der Sonne nicht bloß ein Traum?
> Ist was ich sehe und höre und rieche
> nicht bloß der Schein einer Welt vor der Welt?
> Gibt es tatsächlich das Böse und Leute,
> die wirklich die Bösen sind?
> Wie kann es sein, daß ich, der ich bin,
> bevor ich wurde, nicht war,
> und daß einmal ich, der ich bin,
> nicht mehr der ich bin, sein werde?[7]

As a child born to the world enthralled in the wonder of questioning who I am and what it means "to be," for there to be a world in which I find myself here, I remain, in this questioning of my own being, unaware of myself as a child of a different kind—namely, that oneself as a creature cannot form, or beget itself, as oneself but finds itself already beholden to a responsibility for the Other, to which one is already irrecusably bound, yet bound in such a manner that we must be seized afterward, again and again, by this responsibility in grasping ourselves as having been elected.

> Als das Kind Kind war,
> wußte es nicht, daß es Kind war,
> alles war ihm beseelt,
> und alle Seelen waren eins.[8]

In stipulating this other beginning, and other way of beginning, with an original entrustment of responsibility and investiture in Goodness, there resides no nostalgia for a recuperation of or return to one's origins *from the Other*, as with the need for fatherlands or other promised lands of salvation. On the contrary, the "immemorial" binding of oneself in a covenant of responsibility recurs afterward, in the wake of one's separation, as the upsurge of responsibility *for the Other* in terms of which the self becomes displaced from its own self-conceited and self-regarding freedom. As with Alyosha in *The Brothers Karamazov*, the orphan of Goodness remains orphaned, despite the uptake of its elected responsibility for others, placing the Other first, before oneself, as oneself for the Other. If "immemorial responsibility" for the Other is said to be "before," and hence, in this sense, to be considered original, it stands, in another sense, before us as the future that already awaits us in a movement (and, for Levinas, a movement of the Infinite to come) that deepens how trust proves indispensable for the meaningfulness of what it is to be.[9]

This original availability for the Other, when conceived along Levinasian lines as responsibility, cannot be considered as a function of trust given and received in freedom but must be seen as inscribed within a more original significance as an original entrustment of the Other to one's own keep, to the point of getting under one's skin, and elected investiture of Goodness into the drama of one's being, to the point of rupturing, or interrupting, the attachment to being, including, most preciously, our own. Expressed in Levinas's conception of temporality as "diachrony," the investiture of Goodness, as bound up with an original entrustment of responsibility, is not an "origin" in the traditional sense of "cause" or "principle," nor an "effect" or "consequence." It is, strictly speaking, anarchic in the sense marked by Levinas's particular employment of the term "trauma" with which to indicate the "afterwardness," or *Nachträglichkeit,* of its upsurge. Original responsibility can be said to be before only if the significance of this "before" is grasped afterward, when revealed as having been before it is received; it is only when received or lost "afterward" that the "before" of responsibility becomes us; it is only after one has been seized into Goodness that one is revealed to have been already elected "before." Thought in terms of the "two times" of trauma, as the "shock" dislocated from its "affect" (a before dislocated from its after) and as the "affect" dislocated from its "shock" (as the after dislocated from its before), the "affect" of responsibility produces a sense of myself as dislocated from the "shock" of its original entrustment, while, in turn, the "shock" of responsibility recurs only as the "afteraffect" that reveals itself to have been "before."[10] Dislocating the "affect" that considered itself separate, and hence before, the recurring scruple of responsibility, its haunting, throws oneself off-kilter from oneself, opening myself to oneself for the Other. The trauma of the Good *heals* the wounds of separation in leaving behind its scars: the stigmata of the Good. In this sense, the mysteriousness of the Good is that no one wants to be Good beforehand, only afterward, once one has been taken up into the Good and disrupted from one's own self-inclination and self-interest. Only when punctured by the shudder of an original responsibility for the Other does the Good become revealed as that mute transcendence that speaks only in echoes and that, in this sense, has already spoken to us, much as the talismanic citation that recurs in Dostoevsky's *The Brothers Karamazov* as well as in Levinas's writings, from an "immemorial" source without origin—anarchic. Is not the mysteriousness of the Good found in the sublimity that the Good abides, even if no one *wants* to be Good or wants to be "good" only on their own conceited and comforting terms? Or, rather, the desire for the Good is not based upon our freedom and volition but dispensed to us in becoming seized into the Good from our own wanting to be, against our intrinsic *conatus essendi*. As Levinas remarks, the rupture of consciousness with its own vested self-interestedness in its exposure to the investiture of the Good is not a "repression into the unconscious, but a sobering up or an awakening, jolting the dogmatic slumber which sleeps at the bottom of every consciousness resting on its object." In this "trauma of awakening," nothing is repressed; on the contrary, what becomes revealed, even as it remains unbearable, too tightly insinuating itself under one's skin, is the surprise of being someone created, not, however, in the sense that I have been created *from someone other* but that I am created *for someone other*. As Levinas writes, "This trauma which cannot be assumed, inflicted by the Infinite on presence, or this affecting of presence by the Infinite—this affectivity—takes shape as a subjection to the neighbor," or, in other words, substitution.[11]

The fundamental significance of trust for the forked creatures who we are becomes in this manner reinscribed—deepened—within an original entrustment of others to oneself upon which human concourse, communication, and commerce stand or fall. As with the spectacular case of Jean-Claude Romand, his revolt against *being-in* the world was absolute: he did not murder only his children but also his own parents, thus betraying the fundamental significance of responsibility for others without which trust in the world, trust in others, as well as trust in oneself, as having a standing in the world, would be forlorn (see chapter 1). Expressive of a comparable insight into the anchoring of trust in an original entrustment of responsibility, the trajectory from presumptuous freedom to original responsibility, as the movement of downfall and elevation, structures the dramatic plotlines of *King Lear* and *The Brothers Karamazov* (see chapters 6 and 7). In *King Lear*, redemption occurs in the revelation of oneself as creature, as oneself beholden to an irrecusable responsibility for the Other (Lear's giving of his clothes to Poor Tom) and as begotten in the kind nursery of the Other's availability for oneself (Cordelia's forgiveness). In *The Brothers Karamazov*, Alyosha's Speech at the Stone founds (called into being from the Good) a new ecclesiastical community of children—the future—in mourning and responsibility for the death of little Ilyusha. As Alyosha declares in his Speech at the Stone, "Ah, children, ah, dear friends, do not be afraid of life! How good life is when you do something good and rightful!"[12]

Such berthing of trust in its fundamental significance for the human condition in the hold of original responsibility does not lessen the significance of "paradigmatic trust" as given, received, and honored between individuals. To give my trust to the Other, in giving the Other a power of discretionary judgment for something I care for, or for myself, presupposes an original openness toward the Other berthed within an entrusted responsibility for them. Underpinning from above, as it were, any encounter with the Other in the transaction of trust, as given and received in reciprocal freedom, there stands an openness beholden in responsibility for others. This openness of responsibility for others, within which trust itself becomes situated, does not issue from me toward the Other but, in an inverse motion, issues from the Other through, or in me, insofar as to proclaim *here I am* is to find oneself already standing there as bound to the Other in a covenant of responsibility. As Levinas remarks, "through trust [*confiance*] in him who speaks, we promise to obey the very origin of trust prior to all examination. Nothing is less paradoxical, except the very origin of trust prior to all examination," and thus, in this sense, the origin of trust in an entrustment to the one who commands us to responsibility.[13] It is not that we come to trust others from and for ourselves "because" others are already entrusted to us; rather, even when we enter into trust from ourselves to the Other, in giving them our trust, and in this giving, offering ourselves in trust, when trust becomes fundamentally betrayed, we find ourselves expelled from trust in an inverse movement of how we first entered it: we are expelled in despair for a more fundamentally ruptured entrustment of responsibility for others. As exemplified in extremis with Romand's close friend Luc, what plays out in the scene of mourning in Luc's family at the horror of Romand's revealed imposture is the destitution of the meaningfulness—its possibility and significance—of responsibility for their own children. Luc's children live in fear for their deaths at the hands of their parents. Luc and this wife attempted to reassure their little ones by offering soothing, parental words of love, bolstering the crumbling edges of a betrayed responsibility (but not through their own doing) that had already collapsed from within; the parents "could tell that their words had lost their former magical power." The magic spell of "trust me, I will protect you" and "everything is all right" is the power of drawing an enchanted circle of assuredness in the hold of trust where what hangs in the balance is the entrustment of responsibility for others. With the realization that this entrustment in being born was irreparably devastated for their children, the parents began to mourn for their own deaths as parents—that is, as originally bound to a responsibility for others. The end of the world is here when there no longer stands any meaningfulness to being either a parent *or* a child.

Given this berthing of trust within an original responsibility, we do not begin with the mistrust of others nor with faith in others but as already answerable to and available for others, not as a function of *my* trust *in you* but in terms of *your* entrustment *to me* without alibi and yet, by the same token, without guarantee, and therefore all the more potent in promise as well as risk. This entrustment of responsibility, as openness for any encounter with others, is not inscribed within a grammar of the gift, or givenness, but, in Levinas's carefully articulated thinking, initialized through a seminal discourse of binding and unbinding. Such an original entrustment of the Other, that I am the Other's keeper, is not given to me, and hence cannot be said to be received, but forms a *binding* that, at the same time, *unbinds me* from being too tightly wrapped, or involved, in myself, with my own being. The natural attitude in which we find ourselves in the world is predicated by an unspoken forgetting that I am a created being, a creature in the sense not only that I am not self-created but also that in not being self-creating I am beholden to others in my responsibility for them. Forgotten is not oneself but oneself for the Other. To be a created being is thus to be separated in this specific sense of forgetting that the Other, as my responsibility, belongs to the significance of oneself as a created, or begotten, being. To forget that I am not a self-created being is not to forget those others *from which I came into being* but to forget that I am *for others*—any and all others, those with whom I have nothing in common or shared origins in being: family, nation, and so on. In this forgetting of oneself for others, what Levinas calls "the atheism of the self" and "orphaned by birth," I remain bound to myself in my own pride, self-regard, and conceit of being: the Other is always given to me in the blasphemy of the question "Am I the Other's keeper?"

To become seized in the upsurge of responsibility for others, touched by a proximity that relentlessly calls me into question without offering any access to the Other, I am given back to myself through the Other in accepting myself as not-self-created, as not my own proper origin, and hence as beholden to an irrecusable responsibility for others. In this regard, in coming to the Other away from myself, in standing here for the Other, I am always too late, given that the "before" of responsibility is revealed only "afterward" as having been before, without ever having been given as a present that, in this sense, I passed through; the Other is always, in this sense, missed, as the originally missed encounter that opens the possibility of any and all encounters. Arriving too late on the scene of encounter, I arrive already entrusted with a responsibility that haunts me. And yet in the encounter with the Other who calls into question my own forgetting of responsibility, the Other always arrives too early, since I can receive the Other only after having already been singled out and bound to the Other in responsibility. In afterward receiving the "beforehand" of responsibility, I am already separated from the Other, oblivious to my original beholdenness to the Other.[14] And yet in this welcoming of the Other, I do not return to a past but am ejected forward to the future of oneself for the Other before oneself for myself. At the core of immemorial responsibility there resides a prophetic dimension; to be answerable to the Other is to entrust oneself to the future and engage oneself in standing available ("here I am") until the end for all and every encounter, come what may.[15] This asymmetrical noncoincidence of the "oneself as too late" and "the Other as too early" forms the distinctive temporality of recurrence and diachrony (not to be conflated with the dialogical temporality of standing in the presence of the Thou, as with Buber), thus foreclosing the possibility of a definitive encircling of myself around myself or, likewise, a complete encompassing of oneself by the Other. Much, if indeed not all, of our encounters with others can be said to play themselves out within this recurrence of "too early" and "too late," in that "dead time" that passes between us, when, in the discomfort of an unbearable silence, we cannot stand to be alone with the Other with nothing to say, do, or think. In the awkwardness of waiting with nothing to say to each other, this dead time between us becomes usurped by a mutual impatience for a synchronous time of meeting that would spell the arrival of a stabilizing and domesticating recognition between us but that always remains haunted by the awkwardness of our original missed encounter that we nonetheless seek forgettingly to master.

One's own freedom (including the freedom of freedom to survive itself: the freedom to speak) is intrinsically valuable only because one is already entrusted with an original responsibility for others that one did not and could not have procured or given to oneself. Underlying the freedom of giving, honoring, and receiving trust ("substitution" in the senses explored in chapter 6) stands the original entrustment of responsibility for the Other, or "substitution" in the sense articulated in Levinas's ethical thought and pronounced with its talismanic citation. As with Améry's revelation of the irrecusable and primordial assignment of responsibility for oneself to others in his suffering and abandonment, one cannot *be* (or "exist") in any existentially significant (i.e., meaningful) sense without the intact significance of being entrusted to the solicitude of others. This "expectation" of solicitude, and hence responsibility, is synonymous with an original entrustment; or rather, it is always to be expected of others because we are already entrusted to others, that others shall not abandon us during our time of need nor forsake us to our death. Responsibility for the Other's death does not turn on the wish that death shall not claim the Other but, as poignantly manifest in Améry's existential abandonment, that the Other shall not die abandoned in their own death, without a sunflower of mourning and remembrance. Loss of trust in the world and betrayal of entrustment leave but the imprint of a voice that speaks, not in order to survive but as a beseeching voice in the desert for those have not survived, speaking from a nonplace beyond the distinction between the living and the dead. This echo of address and assignment incessantly and urgently testifies to what has not survived, and yet to what has not been allowed to perish: the assignment and accusation of responsibility as with its shrill and tactless expression in Améry's *ressentiments*. Even while stridently *unforgiving* toward the significance and possibility of forgiveness itself, Améry's *ressentiments* stand perhaps as the most searing statement of the "indestructible" of the human—infinite responsibility for the Other—for which, however, there is no limit of destruction.[16] Yet unlike Antelme's vouching for the "indestructible" sentiment of *belonging to the human,* and hence a common identification passing through an unbroken humanity with executioners and torturers, Améry's voicing of the "indestructible" does not attest to any "belongingness" but, on the contrary, insists on the strangeness of the destitute and deported one, who, through the indestructible assignment and accusation of responsibility echoed in *ressentiment,* interrupts and disrupts any complacency with being (see chapter 4). Améry's catastrophic loss of trust in the world, in its threefold planar forms (trust in the world, trust in others, trust in oneself), attests to an original entrustment of oneself as the responsibility of others, which, though "indestructible," admits no limit to its destruction. What breaks the heart of the world is this rupture of responsibility, its existential treason, over and over again, in desecration of the indestructible. When we, the living, ask indignantly in response to Améry's tactless *ressentiment*, "Am I the Other's keeper?" or, in the same vein, react in annoyance at the provocation "the death of the Other is always in a way a murder," do we not partake in the blasphemy of the question "What is Hecuba to me?" as our own armored self-conceit? Do we not feign incomprehensibility as the only recourse to save ourselves from the unbearable proximity of the Other, that I am responsible for others, I more than all others? Yet as Levinas writes, "This privilege of the Other ceases being incomprehensible once we admit that the primary fact of existence is neither *in itself,* nor the *for itself,* but the '*for the other*'; in other words, human existence is creature."[17]

Too Audacious, Too Premature

"Substitution" designates the way in which Levinas reconceives the "subjectivity of the subject" as "a creature," as beholden to an original covenant of responsibility for someone other (*l'autrui*). As Levinas writes, "Substitution for another lies at the heart of subjectivity, an undoing of the nucleus of the transcendental subject, the transcendence of the goodness, the nobility of a pure supporting, an ipseity of pure election."[18] The provocation "the death of the Other is always in a way a murder" as well as the talismanic citation "every one of us is guilty before everyone for everyone, and I more than others," functioning as two sides of an original responsibility, as portrayed in Dostoevsky's novel, becomes thought in Levinas's philosophical discourse under the heading of substitution. If one attends to the style of Levinas's writing—not just to what is said but also the manner in which it speaks, or "says"—its idiosyncratic composition is immediately striking, as previously signaled with Levinas's statement "the death of the Other is always in a way a murder." As with other signature Levinasian conceptions, "substitution" is not a concept in any strict sense, nor does its significance unfold on the page in any intuitive manner or according to mysterious ways.[19] As Levinas cautions, his ethical thinking runs against the grain of commonplace intuitions and entrenched concepts. "Substitution" nonetheless remains a philosophical conception, forged with its own rigor and suggestiveness, even if it cannot be identified as a conceptual unity of particulars, a synthesis of concept and intuition, a generalized notion abstracted from empirical instances, or a dialectically generated unity of opposites.[20] The conception of substitution is not a static concept, nor synthetic or dialectical in movement, but becomes configured through different figurations. Unlike Husserl's eidetic method, by which phenomenological concepts are generated through a series of exemplary phenomena, the conception of substitution is not generated through a self-regulating and self-calibrating stepwise variation that progresses from particulars to universal, from individual instances to an eidetic form, or from accidental attributes to necessary features. Rather than a movement of variation, the configuration of substitution resembles a "wavelike" recurrence, not to be mistaken, however, for the "ebb and flow" of an unspooling temporal stream. In characterizing his thinking as an "itinerary" and an "adventure," Levinas notes that "the different concepts" emerging in his "attempt to say [*dire*] transcendence" are echoed in each other and hence "do not lend themselves to linear exposition."[21] The flatness of the page as well as the sequential arrangement of what is said necessarily betrays the generative movement of saying in its intrinsic configuration. Levinas's discourse is neither primarily oral nor entirely written, without thereby becoming any less robustly an original form of discourse. The *ductus* of Levinas's writing arrests its flattening into a merely written text much as the timbre of its voice retains a marked character of strangeness as a liminal form of speaking; the more crisply it sounds other than human, the more profoundly it humanly resonates. Each "concept"—or better, figuration—projects its "shadows and reflections" onto the others, thus forming something of a crystallization effect, running out from a single term in multiple directions at once, with each direction resonating, or echoing, in the others.

What is stylistically distinctive of Levinas's thinking is the way in which the configuration of substitution crystallizes through a series of cascading figurations: obsession *is* persecution, persecution *is* hostage, hostage *is* trauma, and so forth. This cascading movement through different figurations of substitution does not progress by way of variation toward an identity but crystallizes through the recurrence of statements where each figuration ("obsession," "persecution," "expulsion," "hostage," etc.) opens onto another imbricated and complicating figure of substitution. Despite the linear arrangement imposed by the printed page and the grammatical subject-predicate form of sentences, the iteration of the statement "substitution *is*. . . ," as various profiles extending outward in centrifugal motion, and not inward in centripetal motion (as with Husserl's eidetic variation), is not composed according to the logic of "is" but is reminiscent of Franz Rosenzweig's logic of "and." As Rosenzweig writes, "If an is-sentence is to be worthy of its utterance, then it must always introduce something new after the 'is' which was not there before."[22] As what is said, the configuration of substitution passes through a series of "is-sentences," but as to what it says, each recurring figuration reveals something new ("and") that, strictly speaking, could neither be anticipated beforehand nor recollected afterward from what had already been said. It is as if with every added figuration ("persecution," "hostage," etc.) something entered into the scene of thinking from a tangential angle of intersection that could not be anticipated or derived along the hitherto elapsed course of substitution's crystallization.

In Levinas's exposition, the configuration of substitution unfurls through a series of figurations (persecution, expulsion, hostage, transfer, etc.) until the saying of its pronounced word "expiation." With the advent of the statement "substitution is expiation," one arrives at a horizon not entirely inscribed, and hence anticipated, within the sedimentation of proceeding figurations, and yet not entirely emplaced beyond it. In the opening argument of *Otherwise Than Being*, Levinas offers an initial statement regarding the significance of substitution. As he writes, "Here [with substitution] the identity of the subject comes from the impossibility of escaping responsibility, from the taking charge of the Other." Substitution is immediately ruled out as "transubstantiation" or transformation into another identity—"a new avatar"—at the expense of a discarded identity. Nor should one consider substitution as a kind of empathy or compassion, both of which are, in fact, underwritten by substitution.[23] Neither fusion with the Other nor identification with the Other nor absorption into the Other, substitution retains separation from the Other even as it insists on the proximity of the Other. With such cautionary signage in place, Levinas asks, "Have we to give a name to this relationship of signification [substitution] grasped as subjectivity? Must we pronounce the word expiation, and conceive the subjectivity of the subject, the otherwise than being, as an expiation? That would perhaps be bold and premature."[24] The original French is more intriguing in its precision: "Faut-il aller jusqu'à donner un nom à cette relation de la signification saisie comme subjectivité? Faut-il prononcer le mot expiation et penser la subjectivité du sujet, l'autrement qu'être comme expiation?"[25] Must one, or can one, even give a name to the "otherwise than being" of the subjectivity of the subject? Is it necessary to pronounce the word "expiation" and thus think the subjectivity of the subject, as otherwise than being, as expiation? Would this pronouncement of "expiation" represent the baptismal act of naming the subjectivity of the subject? Would going to this extreme ("faut-il aller jusqu'à donner") of giving a name to this signification—to substitution as designating the subjectivity of the subject—not constitute an exasperation of sense, or its betrayal, of any sensible speaking (much as with the provocation "the death of the Other is always in a way a murder")? Once more, we find ourselves on the cusp of an impossible statement, or saying, as the unmistakable stigmata of Levinas's thinking.

And yet once arrived at the main discussion of "substitution" in the exposition of *Otherwise Than Being*, finding ourselves at the acknowledged inseminating thought of Levinas's masterful philosophical work, it is exactly and exactingly this word that *fully* comes to mind, and needs to come to mind, in the naming of substitution as subjectivity:[26] "We have to speak here of expiation as uniting identity and alterity. The ego is not an entity 'capable' of expiating for the others; it is this original expiation." And, "In expiation, the responsibility for the others, the relationship with the non-ego, precedes any relationship of the ego with itself." And, "There is substitution for another, expiation for another." And, "Expiation coincides in the last analysis with the extraordinary and diachronic reversal of the same into the other, in inspiration and the psyche." And, "Subjectivity is from the first substitution offered in place of another, but before the distinction between freedom and non-freedom . . . It is the null-place in which inspiration by the other is also expiation for the other, the psyche by which consciousness itself would come to signify."[27] Whereas in the opening of *Otherwise Than Being* Levinas hesitates (or dares) to pronounce the word "expiation" in the closing stretches of his configuration of "substitution," the word has finally been spoken in baptizing the subjectivity of the subject as an "original expiation." It is as if the entire discourse of *Otherwise Than Being* between these two moments spanned one performative act of speaking, always too premature, and yet in the same breath, always too audacious, with the word "expiation" hanging on the tip of its speaking in tongues. Along the way, an itinerary and adventure of thinking has been pursued from an initially cautious "faut-il prononcer?"—neither definitive anticipation nor distinct refusal—to an emphatic "*il faut* parler ici d'expiation."[28] *One must* speak here of expiation. Initially signaled as going too far in assigning the name "expiation" to the subjectivity of the subject, one finds oneself at an exasperated moment of arrival, still too audacious and yet still too premature, as if something essential has been missed, even as it has passed us by and, in this sense, already occurred without anything seemingly having happened (as expressed with Levinas's favored locution *se passe*). Where have we arrived? What has transpired between the lines?

Nothing less than whether one must think the "subjectivity of the subject" in the configuration of substitution as beholden to *forgiveness* in an original sense, before any question of one's freedom, and hence before anything that one could have done, or failed not to have done. Must we think of "expiation" as the baptismal name of the subjectivity of the subject as the anarchy of a forgiveness inscribed within an immemorial responsibility for the Other? Would this not veer too far, or, conversely, venture not far enough, in thinking through, even beyond and otherwise, at the risk of betrayal, what Levinas has in mind with his own emphatic pronouncement of the word "expiation" as naming the subjectivity of the subject? To speak of forgiveness at the heart of substitution would admittedly represent an invocation and inscription of forgiveness that would remain unrecognizable and illegible, indeed perhaps even illegitimate and nonsensical according to established grammars of forgiveness. Nor would such an original forgiveness seem to be identifiable or claimable as a "new" principle of forgiveness with which to discard and replace "old" principles. This anarchy of forgiveness, as "expiation," would not proclaim an original principle of forgiveness (as duty, demand, imperative, charity, etc.) or propose a form of forgiveness for what I have done or might do. Not a forgiveness for anything done with respect to an irreversible past but a forgiveness *that I am*, as marking the stigmata of *here I am*, without which, pursuant of Levinas's thinking, the significance of what it is to be a creature, beholden to an original responsibility for the Other, could not be thought to its necessary extreme: the transcendence of the Good. As Levinas writes, "Man is not to be conceived in function of being and non-being, taken as ultimate references. Humanity, subjectivity—the excluded middle, excluded from everywhere, null-site—signify breakup of this alternative, the one-in-the-place-of-another, substitution, signification . . . subjectivity, locus and null-site of this breakup . . . It is a substitution for another, one in the place of another, *expiation*."[29] Would expiation, when thought as forgiveness inscribed within an original entrustment of responsibility for the Other, mark the navel of my freedom, as the improbable convergence point for the provocation "the death of the Other is always in a way a murder" and the talismanic citation "every one of us is guilty before everyone for everyone, and I more than others"? An original forgiveness not inscribable within any dialectic *or* dialogue of question and answer but that, in a more original significance, heralds the anarchy of all beginnings, as the condition for any dialogue in trust and encounter in forgiveness with the Other. The issue would therefore not be do I begin already in asking for forgiveness but do I already find myself answerable to the Other in forgiveness, not in *asking* for forgiveness but an interminable passage toward "to forgive or not to forgive," not after injury but before any possible encounter between us under the question of forgiveness in the aftermath of what has transpired between us? How, in other words, can one make sense of a forgiveness that does not emerge in answer to a question or begin as a question in search of a response and thus cannot be said to be "possible" or "impossible," never haunted by its own question mark but that, on the contrary, in a more originary sense, haunts us from the beginning to the point of an unbearable and intolerable obsession?

Myself as Oneself for the Other

In what sense could there be an "expiation," thought here as "original forgiveness," before any question and hence encounter in forgiveness? In what sense can we speak of an original responsibility before one's own freedom and, in this sense, an unquestionable responsibility, even as it provides us with no answer or response to the question "Am I the Other's keeper?" but reveals instead the betrayal of our entrustment as the conceit of this very question? What would it signify to begin not with the question of the Other, with any questionable attitude regarding whether the Other concerns me, or how the Other is "given" to me, however one might deem such a question to be motivated, essential, or fundamental? What would it mean, last, with making a start from the provocation "the death of the Other is always in a way a murder" as an assignment of responsibility for the Other, but in this election as already standing accused, as exemplified with Alyosha in *The Brothers Karamazov*? To thus begin with an unquestionable responsibility for the Other, as an original entrustment, not with regard to any particular Other (as with paradigmatic trust, when I trust this Other in particular), nor with a more fundamental question of trust in others as such, as my faith or confidence in human beings, or humanity, as such, but to begin with an unquestionable responsibility for others, not as generalized or universal Other but as the someone other in their singularity, as the responsibility for the Other that befalls me, to which I am singularly elected, that must always struggle to find its way in concrete and daily encounters with others? In this entrusted proximity of the Other to me, in me, no "access" or "givenness" is granted for the Other, but, on the contrary, there is an incessant questioning of myself that does not bend back upon oneself, returning to one's ownmost, but, in an inverse motion, verses oneself outward toward the Other, outside over there, in responsibility pushed to infinity and, in this sense, versed within an impossible relation that I, more than anyone else, must nonetheless bear.

Before pursuing further how Levinas conceives the creaturely significance of human existence as "expiation," thought here as "original forgiveness," with all the incurred risks of betraying Levinas's own pronouncements, it does well to insist on the distinction drawn by Levinas between *moi* (me) and *soi* (or *soi-même*) (oneself), and thus grasp the thrust of what Levinas is after when speaking of "the subjectivity of the subject" as substitution. In proposing to reconfigure *who* is the subject (or, alternatively, who is oneself?) in terms of substitution, Levinas signals the decisive significance of Heidegger's distinction in *Being and Time* between *Ich* ("I," or ego) and *Dasein*, or, in other words, Heidegger's ontological displacement of any privileged determination of the subject in terms of "consciousness," "the soul," "mind," or other historically entrenched designations (and hence forms of thinking) of *who* is the subject, of whom it can be said (and can always say to itself) that "to be" is always "to be a question for oneself." In this dislocation of "who" is the subject from its metaphysical conceptions based on a "substance" or "reified" ontological understanding, Heidegger speaks of *Selbstheit* ("oneselfness" or "selfhood") to designate not *what* Dasein is but how it exists, one's own way of being, as to be understood existentially in an adverbial sense (the "how" of one's own being oneself is the horizon upon which Dasein exists in the world as being-in-the-world). As Levinas remarks, his own conception of substitution, hinged on the distinction between *moi* and *soi* (or *soi-même*), is meant to recover the "subjectivity of the subject" from beneath consciousness; that is, is meant to argue that "consciousness—knowing of oneself by oneself—does not exhaust the notion of subjectivity."[30] In this recovering of who is the subject from any *primary* ontological determination, substitution provides an "ethical reprisal of the Heideggerian notion of *Jemeinigkeit*." As Levinas writes, "Heidegger does not say that Dasein is *Jemeinigkeit*, because it is an *Ich*; on the contrary, he goes toward the *Ich* from *Jemeinigkeit*, toward the I from the 'superlative' or the emphasis of this subjection, from his being-delivered-over-to-being."[31] Recall that although Dasein is "taken in" by the world, much as Lear is captivated by the roles and personas that determine his relationships to others and standing in the world as "king" and "father," who Dasein is, the singularity of Dasein's oneness, or "mineness" (*Jemeinigkeit*), does not coincide with the draping and clothing of its identities, or "ego-determinations." As Levinas explains, *Jemeinigkeit* designates that Dasein *has to be oneself* (oneself having to be and only be oneself, not another)—namely, that Dasein cannot not be singularly itself as marked by its being-toward-death, which, placed beyond any substitution or exchange, remains Dasein's ownmost possibility of being. The nonsubstitution of Dasein's being-toward-death inscribes the unavoidability and irrecusability of having to "to be" oneself.

Obscured through its worldly determinations as an I, Dasein loses, or forgets, itself in becoming "taken in" by the world, duped, as it were, by the world as to what it considers to be closest to it—the ready to hand of things in the world. Trust in the world (*Weltvertrauen*), as the trusted familiarity of being-in-the-world, obscures Dasein's *Jemeinigkeit*. What is closest to Dasein is what is nearest to itself, its *Jemeinigkeit* and being-toward-death, which, when lived from the world, becomes what is most distant and removed from itself. Dasein, in its *Jemeinigkeit*, is "delivered unto being" (*Ausgeliefertheit*) and in this sense subjected to itself, and this subjection to itself is marked by the *impossibility*, as Levinas comments, of "my declining that this adventure is properly mine, that it is as *eigen* [own] that the *Sein* [being] is *Ereignis* [event]."[32] The stigmata of Dasein's "deliverance unto being," or "exposure to being," is the question mark that perpetually haunts Dasein's ownmost being insofar as Dasein is that being for whom the question "What is the sense of being?" defines its own proper sense of being. The event of Dasein's own being is thus the locus for the event of the question of the sense of being itself, its placeholder and care keeper. Dasein *is* always in question, even when unbeknownst to itself, "to be or not to be." Dasein exists as "fallen" into the world when it fails to grasp its own sense of being as a question for itself, as the question "Who is Dasein?" Hence the methodological covenant between the question "Who is Dasein?" and the question of the sense of being: in order to retrieve the question of the sense of being from its metaphysical oblivion, the question "Who is Dasein?" must itself become retrieved from Dasein's own self-forgetting. By implication, caught within this self-invoking and self-disclosing movement—or better, conversion—of questioning, as being in question for oneself, there occurs a recuperation of oneself from myself as well as from others, such that the Other can be a question only for me: "What is Hecuba to me?" on the basis of the question that I must always be for myself.

The inversion of the relation between Being and the Good hinges on the inversion of Dasein into "substitution" and, in this disruption, dislocating the privilege of questioning as both the fundamental measure of "sense" and the locus for the sense of transcendence. The assumed primacy of the double question "What is Hecuba to me?" and "Who I am to me?" each echoed in the other, has traction only if one grants that the subjectivity of the subject is irrecusably and originally delivered unto being—to its ownmost being (in a dual sense, its ownmost concern is for being; it concerns itself with its ownmost, its own being)—such that, on this presumption, care for the world as well as care for others (*Sorge*, including what Heidegger calls *Fürsorge*) is predicated upon this impossibility of "my declining that this adventure is properly mine, that it is as *eigen* [own] that the *Sein* [being] is *Ereignis* [event]."[33] In Heidegger, one can only truly pronounce the words *here I am* to oneself where, conjointly, to care for oneself is to care for one's own death: care of soul hinges on care for one's own death. The freedom of Dasein's to "to be" is marked by always being in question for itself, in terms of which, the question of the sense of being as such, becomes entrusted. In challenging, however, this Heideggerian presumption (as Levinas remarks in an aside: "These are the most profound things in Heidegger"), the situation becomes inverted: the subjectivity of the subject is understood as that being whose significance is originally defined by the entrustment of the Other to oneself, of oneself as unquestionably responsible for the Other, as the transcendence of the Good otherwise than Being, in terms of which one can have oneself a place and standing in the world. As Levinas remarks, Heidegger's "care [*Sorge*] took the form of the cumbersomeness of existence." Enthralled and entrapped with being-in-the-world, "to escape the 'there is' one must not be posed but deposed; to make an act of deposition, in the sense one speaks of deposed kings."[34] Undercutting the logos of question and response, the "who" of the subject finds itself expelled from the game of being and nonbeing into the "nonplace" and "dead time" of finding oneself beholden to the Other, as with deported Lear's tearing off his clothes and insane revelation when facing Poor Tom upon the heath, or Cordelia's anarchic setting of her heart for her unforgivable father, "no cause, no cause."

The Enigma of the Face

The "assignation of me by another, a responsibility with regard to men we do not even know" is the proximity of someone other (*l'autrui*) in obsession.[35] This obsession is not yet a question, "Who are you?" asked of the Other or the question asked of me, "Am I the Other's keeper?" nor an expression of interest for or empathy toward the Other. Obsession marks the manner in which the Other is at once "under my skin," too close within myself, and yet infinitely removed from me, a stranger who eludes my possession and knowing. *Thou art the thing itself. Unaccommodated man is no more but such a poor, bare, forked animal as thou art.* Obsession is likewise not an attitude or comportment toward the Other that has been initiated by oneself (as desire, wonder, or curiosity), but, on the contrary, the Other obsesses me as already too close within me and, in this sense, as unbearable, without any transparent cause or reason, as not presented to me in a manner that affords any mastery or discretion. In obsession, one is affected by "I know not whom," dispossessed of myself in an interpolation that does not leave one in peace, bespeaking one's own responsibility for the Other as unquestionable, without thereby offering any certainty, knowledge, or guarantee. In obsession, the Other does not let me be. To say that the Other obsesses me as my responsibility is not to claim that I *know* how to answer or respond, nor that I am empowered in this finding myself entrusted with responsibility. Obsessed, I cannot *not* be affected, even though I am none the wiser in knowing how to respond, and, indeed, why I have been chosen. Obsession leaves one speechless with a nagging scruple in which a command comes to be heard. As Levinas writes, "In proximity is heard [*s'entend*] a command come as though from an immemorial past, which was never present, began in no freedom. This way of the neighbor is the face."[36]

In entrusting me with a responsibility for the Other, the face "says" or "commands" in placing a claim on me before I am given any choice in the matter, before my own freedom can take a stance, formulate its own self-interest, and choose any proper course of action. Before (in the specific transcendental sense examined above) the possibility of *encounter* with others in the concourse of communication and commerce, before, in other words, *appearing* to one another in the life-world of plurality, responsibility for the Other has already prevailed itself upon me. In this irrecusable assignment, my own freedom becomes available in the bond of the Other's entrustment to me. Contrary to our ingrained assumption (as well as philosophical habit) of equating the "face" with a form of appearance, or manifestation, the face, in this Levinasian sense, is not describable in terms commonly associated with how others appear to us in face-to-face encounters. The face is not given, seen, or recognized but heard, and yet heard without any clear orientation toward whence, and why, it speaks *to me*. In this regard, the face, as command, is not a phenomenon, a representation, or saturated iconic givenness but, on the contrary, resists and fractures any effort at *Sinngebung* (in the phenomenological sense of constitution by way of intentionality). The face does not look at me in a manner in which I might see myself as looked upon.

Against the proximity of the Other, the self seeks to immunize and protect itself in finding the Other *fascinating* and thus in displacing the Other into the frontality of an encounter. In contrast to finding oneself obsessed with a responsibility for the Other, finding the Other fascinating— differences: celebrated, extolled, championed; such are the manifold ways of distraction—betrays a certain luxury and self-satisfaction with oneself. I am fascinated with the Other such that the Other stops haunting and pursuing me. Within our society of spectacle, fascination keeps the Other at bay in fetishizing its otherness. Much as with Ivan Karamazov's suffering at a distance, our attention, recognition, and interests become consumed by fascination; and yet no demand is ever truly placed on us. Our everyday encounter with others is, in this regard, determined largely by fascination (or aversion, its own form of fascination). We are routinely not obsessed by others but stand before them enchanted and curious, when not indifferent. Obsession is, likewise, not to be conflated with "care" or "concern," which, in so many regards, is not *radical enough* when measured by the incessant and implacable responsibility urged upon us by the face of the Other. And yet the domesticity of the life-world is ensured by our "face-to-face" encounters with others as structured through the frontality of the gaze. We recognize the face of others; we are recognized by others. Rather than allowing ourselves to be caught by obsession, we direct ourselves at others in fascination. We would rather be seen by the other's gaze, and so come to see ourselves in reciprocity with others, as beheld in their gaze, than endure a command for which we are given no choice and that, in a Levinasian sense, cannot be recognized or seen, understood, and hence rationalized and negotiated. Fascination always runs ahead of itself in seeking to grasp the subject of its fascination: the face of the Other becomes single-mindedly absorbed into a theme of fascination, or, when flipped into aversion, the face of the other becomes held at bay, rendered anonymous or erased. As exemplified in voyeurism, fascination is always wanting to see more (or, conversely, not wanting to see at all) of the theme of the gaze while retaining one's proper distance and reserve. The source of our fascination is a theme of representation as well as the lure of someone lurking behind appearances, whom we could spy on or catch off guard. Behind the face, the what of appearance, there is the promise of the who, and hence the measure of a reassurance. By contrast, the face, in the sense of which Levinas speaks, is neither a "plastic form" of manifestation—the visible—or what hides or resides beyond manifestation—the invisible. It is rather the trace of the Infinite, of the investiture of Goodness to no end, yet a trace that resists by its own allowance any convertibility into any possessive revelation or finality. Nothing is there to be revealed, only here to be commanded. If ethics thus begins with the epiphany of the face, it is that we begin not in wonder or fascination—neither wonder at the revelation of the whole in the part or fascination regarding the part that encapsulates the whole. We begin, or rather we have already begun, from an obsession that "traverses consciousness countercurrentwise" and "is inscribed in consciousness as something foreign, a disequilibrium, a delirium," against which stands our fascination with others, in terms of their "identity" and "difference," as determined by the masks and roles ("the comic mask" of proper names and pronouns) we reciprocally take on for each other, our reciprocal ways of appearing, so as to better keep the Other at bay, away from getting too close under our skin.[37]

This obsession of the Other, their proximity, is not pathological, for it is not geared into a repetition that promises a return or coming back to something lost. It does not turn us back to what is missing but turns us inside out in recalling our creaturely condition as beholden to the Other in the covenant of responsibility. Obsession, in this manner, exposes "the borrowed names of our masks," our all-too-convenient and self-serving pseudonyms, which guard against the Other's claiming against us a proximity that has already proclaimed us.[38] Obsession becomes pathological when it makes itself into a theme of our own mastery and insists, against all odds, that we must possess what obsesses us or dispossess ourselves fully—surrender ourselves entirely, slavishly—to our obsession. The Other obsesses me, the Other is obsessed with me, in the sense that, in a further figuration, obsession is a "persecution." I become other than myself through obsession, traversed by a tremor that I neither possess nor that possesses me. The obsession of the Other runs through me as a breathless recurrence that dispossess me of myself so as to inspire me to become otherwise than myself, to be myself otherwise than being (just for myself), to stand as oneself for the Other. This assignment of the Other in my keep is an expulsion, yet an expulsion that allows one to stand oneself as irreplaceable in responsibility for Other. There is no entrustment without expulsion—I am bound to the Other and must bind myself through this bond, and thus unbind myself from myself.

In the command of the face that assigns to me a responsibility, an accusation is spoken against me in the same breath. Obsession is a "persecution" as a haunting that pursues me in calling me "into question prior to questioning, responsibility over and beyond the logos of response."[39] In this twofold figuration as "obsession-persecution," the *enigma* of responsibility becomes palpably manifest as "assignment" and "accusation." The assignment of responsibility is at the same time an *accusative*. The subjectivity of the subject is to be thought, as Levinas stresses, not in *nominative, dative*, or *genitive* forms but in an accusative form, not only in a grammatical sense (the subject *is subjected* in the sense of the object of an action—i.e., the assignment of responsibility without question) but also in the sense of an accusation. One comes into one's own being accusatorially. As assigned and accused, put into place and pursued, I am hostage to the Other's implacable besieging and beseeching of my freedom. In being called into question, the entrusted assignment of responsibility accuses me in the sense of exposing my "unjustified existence," that, in other words, to be struck by an awakening to my own created being, that I am not self-created, is to recognize my own being, despite my self-conceit, as *unjustified* and, in this sense, to be without any redeeming significance that could on its own accord rise above the game of being: ashes to ashes, dust to dust. What we naturally take for granted, as the unspoken presumption of our claimed and proclaimed freedom, is that our existence is "justified" or "redeemable" by its own grace or gravity, either through the efforts of our own self-making or through an arrangement of the world to our exclusive liking, made in our own self-serving image. And yet, in a fundamental way, we are our own "useless passion," adrift upon the raft of being with no rhyme and reason. As Levinas wryly remarks, "No doubt nothing is more comical than the concern that a being has for an existence it could not save from its own destruction."[40] We are not condemned, however, to being without the hope of redemption. Yet unlike for Sartre, we cannot secure the terms for our own significance through the transcendence of our freedom "in choosing for all humanity in choosing for oneself." It is not that I am condemned to be free and thus as thrown into the world, responsible for everything that *I* do, but rather I am condemned to be responsible for the Other, and hence as beholden to others in the world, I more than others.

Responsibility *à l'outrance* renders the death of the Other what resides closest within me, closer than my own being-toward-death, or, as Heidegger thought, one's own freedom toward/for death (*Freiheit zum Tode*). Contrary to Heidegger, my ownmost possibility (*eigenste Möglichkeit*) is not my own death (being-toward-death) but the *impossibility* of the Other's death at my hands as entrusted to me in the prohibition that commands me through the face of the Other. As Levinas writes, "The face is not in front of me [*en face de moi*], but above me; it is the other before death, looking through and exposing death," and who so exposed "asks me not to let him die alone, as if to do so were to become an accomplice in his death. Thus, the face says to me: Thou shall not kill."[41] The commandment *Thou Shall Not Kill* is inscribed in the epiphany of the face of the Other. The primacy accorded to this commandment from the Decalogue in its assigned and accusing responsibility, in which I am originally bound to the Other, is not chosen arbitrarily. Whereas the first commandment, *I am the Lord your God; you shall have no others before me*, announces the uniqueness of God (*Einzigkeit*, not *Einheit*, as Hermann Cohen stressed), the first commandment of the second tablet, *Thou shall not kill*, "exposes ethical meaning as the ultimate intelligibility of the human, and even of the cosmic."[42]

The accusation that accompanies the assignment of responsibility, in the commandment "Thou shall not kill," is not exhausted, in its exasperation of one's being, by calling into question one's "unjustified" existence. Awakening to one's created condition, as beholden to others from the beginning, one stands accused. This accusation bespeaks an incitement *to murder* in the temptation to deface the Other, which, strikingly enigmatic, speaks from the face itself. In standing accused, it is not just that one's own being is called out as "unjustified." Moreover, I stand accused in the shadow of a temptation that has already affected me. In commanding, "Thou shall not kill," the face of the Other is exposed and vulnerable to violence in the night. And yet this entrusting of the Other to me in their vulnerability bespeaks in the same breath a temptation to murder. The face of the Other *itself* incites me to its defacement, to murder. As Levinas writes, "The face is exposed, menaced, as if inviting us to an act of violence. At the same time, the face is what forbids us to kill."[43] Tempting as well as forbidding, the Other gets under my skin in this double sense, each sense contrariwise to the other, in placing me in front of the alternative, "to speak or to kill," where, in each instance, answerability for the Other as well as violence against the Other abides in me more than me.[44] This antinomy of the face as prohibition and temptation, as assignment and accusation, marks the mysterious navel of responsibility in the enigma of the Good. As Levinas writes, "This temptation to murder and this impossibility of murder constitutes the very vision of the face."[45] In the original binding of responsibility, there is already an original betrayal and blasphemy (not against the "sacred" but against the holy), the incitement to arms and the promise of peace. As Levinas writes, "the face of the Other in its precariousness and defenselessness, is for me at once the temptation to kill and the call to peace, the 'You Shall Not Kill.'"[46] The obsession of the Other in me would thus be in one bifurcated stroke, not simply anarchy but the anarchy of our confounded beginnings.

Original Forgiveness

Much as I am bound to the Other in the assignment of a responsibility without question, I stand accused without foundation and, in this distinctive sense, am already unforgiven without having done anything unforgivable. Standing thus assigned and accused, one is expelled from being for the sake of being into being toward Goodness. In Levinas's manner of speaking, the subject becomes dispossessed of itself in finding oneself detached from myself (my masks or persona); the ego is "stripped of its pride," "deposed of its sovereignty" and "dominating imperialism" in this awakening of oneself for the Other. Expressed in this suggestive manner, "the irremissible guilt with regard to the neighbor is like a Nessus tunic under my skin would be."[47] In this Levinasian context, "guilt" does not designate "sin," "failure of duty," or another comparable sense of having *done* something untoward to the Other. One is not guilty for having committed some specific offense or violation, as with the biblical narrative of the original sin, nor does guilt imply here indebtedness or discharging of an incurred debt, or a sentiment of absolute dependency.[48] In the original assignment of responsibility, I stand already accused, yet not for anything that I have done or failed to do but for that I am; not for *who* I am nor for *what* I did (or did not do) but for the unjustifiable existence that oneself is. In this regard, responsibility for the Other is impossible to avoid *as well as* impossible to formulate a response to and, in this sense, impossible to assume completely, since I am not put into question in the sense of *asked* to justify myself or to become righteous on my own. Accused, I am put into question in being exposed as "too tight in my skin" without alibi or recourse to an answer or otherwise self-justifying response. In calling one's existence into question, responsibility for the Other is impossible to bear, not, however, in terms of a modal impossibility, set opposite to a possibility, or as an impossibility defined negatively as the impossibility of realization. Along the same lines, we do not face the Kantian insistence that "ought" must imply "can" nor an "ought" for which we paradoxically cannot but nonetheless must. The commandment of the Other is not a universal duty but a singular calling that elects *me*, I, more than others (even as all others are likewise called out and inspired in their respective singular being). Assigned and accused, the responsibility for the Other is impossible to bear, not in the sense that I cannot but as an endured "I can no longer" of a patience without end for a meeting point of the impossible with the possible (as with Cordelia's creative fidelity; see chapter 6). As a constitutive impossibility, because I cannot formulate a response and am left speechless, *I am free* to creatively become answerable in looking to the Other as *my teacher*, as the teacher who educates me in designating to me those ontological categories of being in terms of which I can give to the Other bread from my mouth and salt of the earth. Speaking, in this issuing from the commandment of the face of the Other (such that every act of speaking is subtended by the prohibition *Thou shall not kill* in order to open the space of listening and responding), is also a teaching, where the exteriority of instruction does not offend one's freedom but, on the contrary, accomplishes it.[49] The Other teaches me how to care and concern myself for the world, how to attend to it and make the world into an object of knowledge and inquiry as well as a space of concourse and commerce. "Care" for the world follows the contours drawn upon the world from the Other's teaching, not from my own being for oneself. Entrusted in the responsibility for the Other is the world itself in which we are to be for each other. Insofar as assignment and accusation turn on the dispossession of sovereignty, any presumed or claimed sovereignty over the world must likewise become deposed, thus elevating the earth under the aegis of the Good in its entrustment to us without its thereby becoming our possession and just at our disposal. The earth only *matters* and possesses gravity, not because it matters *for us* but because it matters *to us* in the entrustment of the Other to our responsibility.

Hence the insistence with which Levinas speaks of *incarnation* as not merely a biological or ontological concept but also an ethical one, as that which makes "giving possible" and thus "makes one *other* without alienating."[50] As with Améry's characterization of skin as incarnating the prohibition "Do not touch me" and the demand "Do not abandon me to my sufferings," sensibility, our incarnate being, is originally *ethically* imbued in significance. "In one's skin," as Levinas proposes, is thus "not a metaphor for the in-itself," nor primarily the barrier that demarcates and distances me from others or the self-embracing envelope of being-in oneself (as with the idiomatic French expression *se sentir bien dans sa peau* and Anzieu's notion of *le moi-peau*). As Levinas writes, "In responsibility as one assigned or elected from the outside, assigned as irreplaceable, the subject is accused in its skin, too tight for its skin."[51] In Levinas's usage, "in one's skin" refers to the interruption of the Other's command within me, an obsession that never lets me be, that has already found itself "inside me," having already gotten under my skin.[52] In this figurative sense, the Other does not get under my skin from the "outside" in penetrating or lacerating the borders of my body. As the scruple that incessantly speaks to me (that little pebble lodged within my confident steps or that annoying itch that, the more I scratch in the hopes of quick dispatch, the more it itches), the Other has already insinuated herself into me from the beginning, such that, in this figurative way of speaking, my skin can function only as the marker of distance toward others (and hence setting the terms and borders for the encounter with others) on the precondition that my begotten incarnation is already *beholden* to the Other "in one's skin." Sensibility *is* proximity of the Other. In finding myself already beholden to the Other in an entrusted responsibility, my being is already "edged" or "lined" from within, not as a function of trust given and received in freedom (see chapter 1) but, more primordially, as a function of already finding myself entrusted with the Other into my keep, in one's skin. The "ultimate secret" of the incarnation of the subject is this anarchical beholdenness to others over and above our begotten condition from others as well as our own being for oneself.

Throughout these figurations, a palpable current of salvific violence animates the configuration of substitution, although this current of violence that leaves me breathless is at the same time an inspiration, or what Levinas calls the *pneuma* of the soul, allowing me to become exalted from the constriction of my own being (the "too tightness of my skin") in aspiration toward the Other. The Other "denucleates me," "persecutes me," and "pursues me." As hostage of the Other, I am exposed to the "trauma" of an awakening of oneself as for the Other that "cuts the thread of consciousness which should have welcomed it in its presence."[53] The enigma of the face, as prohibition and temptation, in its neither-nor configuration, wears the markings of a double face. This enigma of the face gives its imageless vision a lenticular quality, winking, as it were, in temptation in the smiling of its prohibition. In what is arguably the nerve of Levinas's provocative thinking, already encapsulated and, indeed, portended in the statement "the death of the Other is always in a way a murder," the *absoluteness* of the Other's assignment *and* accusation makes of their face the focal point of "hatred" and "malice" against me, as rumbling in the undertones of such expressions as "persecution," "hostage," and "trauma." As Levinas writes, "The face of the neighbor in its persecuting *hatred* can by this very malice obsess as something pitiful."[54] In the "trauma of persecution"—the trauma of the Good in the epiphany of the face—one suffers in "outrage." This outrage consists in the impossibility, or unbearability, of the Other's insufferable commandment. Given that the assignment of responsibility for the Other is not a question of whether I can accept *or* refuse what is already entrusted to me (even as I am awoken to this immemorial responsibility only afterward, already too late), I am commanded to comport myself toward what is *in principle* impossible and unbearable for me to accept given the voided terms of my own consent and freedom. This "in principle" impossibility— the impossibility of choosing responsibility—expresses the salient sense in which responsibility is "anarchic" and "anachronistic" and yet, ahead of its time, as the future that, in recurrence, is prophetically to become me. This "prophetic future" issuing from within an immemorial responsibility does not grant any lucidity of foresight or prophetic assurance, come what may. Instead, one must trust in the Other's commandment in its entrustment without my freedom to decide and accept without thereby receiving or claiming any discretionary power of sovereignty over the Other, indeed, over myself. This prophetic trust, or *hope*, neither trusting in the Other per se (for the Other remains "unknown" to me, beyond the mastery or possession of a knowledge) nor able to trust in myself, attests to the fact that it is without reason or justification as to *why* I must bear this responsibility for the Other, given that it short-circuits any "representation," "thematization," or "mastery." I am not "empowered" to a certain privilege of sovereignty (as with paradigmatic trust; see chapter 5). I am likewise none the wiser in the upsurge of awakening to my responsibility for the Other. In this unknowing that becomes me, the Other pursues me without mercy in the pitiless tonality of an *unforgiving* responsibility—a responsibility that is irrecusable, unavoidable, and impossible to bear. Faced with this pitiless tonality of the Other's command, Thou shall not kill, to which I am bound without having any say in the matter (any word of protest would already be one word too much), and compounded by my singular election—why me?—I am provoked to "outrage" and "indignation," *exasperated,* not only in terms of the suspicion that I have been singled out unjustly but also, precisely, because this assignment has already accused me *before* I have been able to do or not to do anything about it. Before I could be guilty *or* innocent, I stand accused, and in the indignation of *being unforgiven* before having done anything unbecoming—unforgivable—by a responsibility imposed upon me without mercy—unforgiving—the face of the other becomes for me the source of malice and hatred, this face that persecutes me and keeps me awake at night, not letting me be.

One's being affected—touched—beneath the opposition of "innocence" and "guilt," and before the possibility of any action or response, crystallizes as *shame* for one's own existence. In being called into question without the possibility of any recourse or alibi, I am put to the test in the shame of my unjustified existence. I stand ashamed, not for anything that I have done but for that I am. As Levinas writes, this openness to the Other "is accomplished in shame where freedom at the same time is *discovered* in the consciousness of shame and is *concealed* in the shame itself. Shame does not have the structure of consciousness and clarity. It is oriented in the inverse direction; its subject is exterior to me . . . where the Other presents himself as interlocutor, as him over whom I *cannot* have power, whom I cannot kill, condition this shame, where, qua I, I am not innocent spontaneity but usurper and murderer."[55] More stridently, as Levinas writes, in being placed into question, I am not asked, "Who am I?" nor "Who are you?" but, "Do I not kill by being?"[56] The question is not "to be or not to be." It is "to murder or not to murder." *That* is the question to which all other questions return. In this ethical shame that I must not be the murderer of the Other, I am accused without alibi. In this existential awakening, I do not fear for my own death at the hands of the Other (as with the struggle of recognition in Hegel) nor stand anxious for my own being-toward-death (as with the turn toward authenticity in Heidegger). Rather, I fear for the death of the Other at my own hands knowing that we all have dirty hands. In Levinas's words, "I think that in responsibility for the Other, one is, in the final analysis, responsible for the death of the Other . . . the fear for the death of the other is certainly at the basis of the responsibility for him."[57] This responsibility for the Other takes its pointed form in the provocation: the death of the Other is always in a way a murder.

Besieged by the Other's proximity, my own freedom becomes vested to me in responsibility for the Other and investment of the Good, thus rupturing my own self-attachment and conceited freedom in exposing myself to one's own unjustified and arbitrary being. In this shame, there is the upsurge, or interruption, of a transcendence within my own immanence that strips me of my own self-measure. Standing over and against me within a nonhierarchical height, the Other's commandment becomes "accomplished as shame, where freedom discovers itself murderous in its very exercise." As Levinas writes, "morality begins when freedom, instead of being justified by itself, feels itself to be arbitrary and violent."[58] In this shame of oneself, I am called into question, yet not in terms of a consciousness of guilt or consciousness of failure.[59] Consciousness of failure, as when I am ashamed for failing the Other, represents a form of self-criticism and experienced limitation of what I can do, and hence refers to an ability or power of mine that fails me. Exposed in shame, the assignment of responsibility does not impute any guilt (even though Levinas does use this term, as does Dostoevsky), for guilt on a conventional understanding presupposes the violation of a moral norm, or transgression of a value: I am guilty for something that I have done, which I should have not done. Whereas guilt refers to the violation of a moral norm or other form of moral transgression, shame, in the sense proposed by Levinas, does not transpire as a failure of the self nor by dint of an incongruity between oneself and another's expectation. Shame, in this regard, is not inscribed within a hierarchy of gazes. In the case of guilt as well as consciousness of failure, one adopts a self-regarding critical attitude of judgment that *requires*, but does not interrupt, the spontaneity of one's freedom. With shame, by contrast, freedom becomes dispossessed and disabused of its own begotten inborn conceit: to be self-creating—that is, self-justifying—in its being. Unlike guilt and failure, shame in this sense does not attest either to an action or limitation of freedom (an action for which I am guilty or a failure to have achieved something) but attests instead to a nonspecific exposure, the sheer exposure of my existence as such. In the sheerness of this exposure, there is openness toward the Other in welcoming the Other by way of their commandment Thou shall not kill. Unlike in Sartre's analysis of the Gaze, where the Gaze of the Other thwarts the freedom of my self-transcendence, standing ashamed before myself in the proximity of the Other *opens* me to possibilities that are impossible for me but that are nonetheless entrusted to me. The precariousness and preciousness of the Other, their vulnerability and glory, hinge on this entrustment to me of impossibilities for me as the inverse movement of trust given and received, where, on the contrary, the Other gives to me possibilities that I could not have procured for myself. In the entrustment of the Other to me, an impossibility is placed into my own hands. This impossibility of murder, in the prohibition of the Other's face, allows for a world of possibilities not my own but of the Other's to enter into my keep, as possibilities that do not stem from and, indeed, run athwart my own possibility to be but that are all the more to be my ownmost in being oneself for the Other. As Levinas writes, "To be *for* a time that would be without me, *for* a time after my time, over and above the famous 'being for death,' is not an ordinary thought extrapolating my own duration; it is the passage to the time of the Other."[60] To be so entrusted is to be entrusted with the death of the Other, as responsibility for the impossibility of their murder, inscribed in the commandment Thou shall not kill. In the shame of my own murderous existence and unjustified virility of my freedom, the drama of the outrage suffered (Levinas speaks of the "outrage undergone") as hostage of the Other is not just to be endured but also to be transformed, or, in Levinas's idiom, "transferred." This "transference" or "transformation" accomplishes the salient meaning of "substitution." Without "transfer" from outrage to responsibility there would be no drama to substitution, and hence no substitution at all.

There is markedly something "demented" in the assignment and accusation of responsibility without consent or recourse. This "delirium" and "madness" consist in having been assigned and entrusted *without* any regard for what I can do, for what is possible or impossible for me. Adding insult to injury, in this assignment, one is in the same breath accused, not for anything in particular but for that I am. The madness of forgiveness is not *whether* one could or could not forgive the unforgivable; it is rather that we already stand "unforgiven" in the merciless responsibility for the Other entrusted into our keep before any *question* of forgiveness. As Levinas writes, "This exigency with regard to oneself in the form of an accusation preceding the fault, borne against oneself despite one's innocence . . . The accusation that weighs on the self as a self is an exigency without consideration for oneself."[61] The face of the Other and the epiphany of the Good are in this *unforgiving* responsibility without mercy and understanding for who I am and what I can or cannot do. Paradoxically, nothing of who I am is reflected in this assignment, and yet it is I, in my singularity, I more than anyone else, who stand elected. The profundity of election turns on this running together of "anonymity" and "singularity," as if the Good, in the epiphany of the Face, targeted me in particular without its being anything in particular about me, without, in other words, its being fundamentally about who I am, for it is fundamentally about that I am.[62]

As Levinas writes in a critical moment in the configuration of substitution worth quoting in full,

> It [assignment and accusation] is the passivity of a trauma, but one that prevents its own representation, a deafening trauma, cutting the thread of consciousness which *should have welcomed* it in its present, the passivity of being persecuted. This passivity deserves the epithet of *complete or absolute only if the persecuted one is liable to answer* for the persecutor. The face of the neighbor in its persecuting hatred can by this very malice obsess as something pitiful. This equivocation or enigma only the persecuted one who does not evade it, but is without any references, any recourse or help (that is its uniqueness or its identity as unique!) is able to endure. To undergo from the other is an absolute patience *only if by this from-the-other is already for-the-other.* This transfer, other than interested, 'otherwise than essence,' *is subjectivity itself.*[63]

Implied in this characterization of the drama of substitution is a *trial* of the subject, who must not only endure the entrustment of the Other to one's keep but also "undergo" this trial of the self ("transfer"), where what hangs in the balance is subjectivity itself as "otherwise than essence." As suggested by Levinas, the affection of shame is itself *not sufficient, or robust enough*, to "have welcomed" the Other. Shame must undergo a "transfer" from "from the Other" (*put to* shame in the exposure to the Other) into "one-for-Other" (responsibility for the Other's death *put to us*), as with the conversion of Alyosha's shame before little Ilyusha (who accuses and assigns him with the throwing of rocks) into responsibility for his death. It is only if the persecuted one "is liable to answer" for the persecuting Other that the *absoluteness* of assignment and accusation can have been said to be achieved (and keeping in mind, as an aside, that the distinction between "passivity" and "activity" has been surpassed, despite the unavoidable usage of active and passive voices grammatically). It is in this sense that, as Levinas insists, the subject must "expiate" or "atone" for the Other's pitiless tone and merciless persecution—the Other must be forgiven for their unforgiving assignment and accusation. The absoluteness of the command is not just imposed; the Other must be forgiven by me for their unforgiving commandment in order to consecrate the absoluteness of their command. Without this drama of original expiation, not, Levinas makes a point to note, as an "action" or "capacity" of the subject but as the subject in the movement, or temporality, of recurrence, the Other would not be welcomed nor could one declare "here I am" (oneself would not be expelled from myself). Of importance, Levinas never speaks in this considered context of "sacrifice," as a "giving" or surrendering of oneself to the Other.[64] This "transfer" or "passage" is not to be understood according to a logic of the gift or exchange (not as the passage from one thing, or condition, to another thing, or condition). Levinas repeatedly speaks instead of expiation. As he writes, "In the trauma of persecution, it is to pass from the outrage undergone to the responsibility for the persecutor, and, in this sense, from suffering to *expiation for the other*."[65] In being forgiving in substitution toward the Other for their persecution, I am beseeching forgiveness for my accusation, my unjustified existence, despite myself, and without any ostensible doing on my part, and in this breath of expiation I am atoning for the unforgiving and persecuting commandment to which I am subject, hostage.

The face does not speak "absolutely" and "completely" without this expiation, or, original forgiveness, for its unforgiving entrustment. The epiphany of the face is already inscribed within an original scene of forgiveness. This original forgiveness does not "give more" in redundancy of an original gift (see chapter 6). It is itself the condition for the "gift" or, more strictly speaking, the welcoming and hearing of the commandment of the face, Thou shall not kill, and its investiture of the Good: "This passivity [of assignment and accusation] deserves the epithet of complete or absolute *only if* the persecuted one is liable to answer for the persecuted" (emphasis added). In the same vein of consideration, what transpires or "passes" in this passage from "from the Other" to "for the Other"—"to tend the check to the smiter and be filled with shame"—is said to complete the assignment, yet given that this transfer cannot be understood as an "action," and hence can never be considered as completed (as an action), or as past perfect, it is never over and done with, once and for all. The trial of the subject in substitution recurs in the Infinite. Original forgiveness is not an "action" or "act" of the subject but the subjectivity of the subject in its inspiration toward the Other—its openness—and investiture of the Good in being in the world. As Levinas writes, "Substitution is not an act . . . the exception that cannot be fitted into the grammatical categories of noun and verb." Expiation, forgiveness, here is not a "power" or "act" of the subject; "it [the subject] is this original expiation."[66]

The "completeness" or "absoluteness" of the Other's command is, in this specific sense, itself "conditioned" by one's original forgiveness. The assignment of responsibility is "unconditional." Expressed in Levinas's way of speaking, "immemorial" and "anarchic," original forgiveness for the Other, on the condition of which the Other's persecution becomes "welcomed" and, in this specific sense, "commanded" in the form of hospitality. This "condition" of hospitality must preserve the unconditionality of the commandment, and, in this regard, the commandment cannot be said to be "conditioned" by original forgiveness. As both unconditioned and conditioned, the commandment of the Other must command itself to be commanded not in order to give to oneself any command or mastery over the Other but, inversely, to abdicate one's own sovereignty—a sovereignty not thereby *given* to the Other, as with paradigmatic trust, but a sovereignty relinquished in lieu of an openness without a sovereign and yet nonetheless under the aegis of Goodness and height of the Other. Recalling Levinas's talismanic quotation from *The Brothers Karamazov*, it is revealing that Markel's pronouncement of this prophetic statement addresses the issue of how "subordination" can be cast in such a manner as to disable its own relation, or imposition, of command and thus short-circuit, in the performative act of commanding, any dialectical conflict of master and slave, without losing its constitutive unconditionality.[67] When commanded by the Other without mercy, nothing becomes risked by way of an ethical "masochism" on the side of commanded self or an ethical "sadism" on the side of the commanding Other. As with Markel in *The Brothers Karamazov*, the force of command becomes inverted into a hospitality toward its own self-canceling in commanding "to command" of those who are to be commanded. In Markel's words, "Since it is impossible to do without masters and servants in the world, let me also be a servant to my servants, just as they are to me. And I'll tell you also, mother dear—we are all guilty toward others and I am the guiltiest of all." Markel's pronouncement is immediately judged as "madness" by his mother ("It's your illness that makes you talk like this, my dear"). It is not only the "delirium" of responsibility for the Other but also the madness of undercutting one's sovereignty in the act of commanding so as to allow the command to command without the threat or specter of sovereignty, thus releasing it from the hold of any principle of authority to speak from the height of its own powerless glory. In the command, there is the command to be commanded in turn, not as countermanding the command but as allowing for a hospitality for the command in which any lording of the Other would become abrogated but, by the same token, any mastery of conditions counterimposed by the one commanded. Reciprocity as well as hierarchy, the two schemas for the confluence and conflict of power, become neutralized in the commandment of responsibility. As Markel recognizes, it is impossible to do without masters and servants; there must be a command. Because there must be masters and servants, let me be a servant to my servants; let me depose myself of my own sovereignty of commanding in commanding to be commanded so as to command without remaining a master over those commanded, and yet still speak from the height of a commandment that stands absolute toward those who are commanded ("servants").

Within this original drama of substitution, subjectivity stands on trial in an original scene of forgiveness, not for anything that the Other has *done* against me nor does the Other ask for forgiveness for their unforgiving assignment and accusation. Forgiveness here is neither asked for nor a reactive responsive to an antecedent inquiry or harm. The passage from outrage to forgiveness remains without cause. Neither asked for by the Other nor enacted on the basis of a power or capacity, original forgiveness transpires in the "no cause, no cause" on both ends, as it were; neither a cause from the Other nor a cause from myself, original forgiveness can be said to be "supererogatory" in this distinctively transcendental way, given that I am without recourse and cannot engage my own freedom since I stand "before" freedom *can be* at all invested in responsibility. This apparent circularity between "from the Other" and "for the Other," persecution and expiation (forgiveness), encapsulates the temporality of recurrence. On the one hand, persecution is "before," or "the condition," for openness toward the Other but, on the other hand, "from the Other" must *already* be "for the Other"; that is, there must *already be* expiation, or forgiveness, for the Other's pitiless persecution ("To undergo from the other is an absolute patience *only if by this* from-the-other is *already* for-the-other").[68] Forgiveness cannot be said, in this context of consideration, to be "after" assignment and accusation; it is already "before." And yet assignment and accusation are "prior to all reflection, prior to every positing," like "an echo of a sound that would precede the resonance of this sound."

Original forgiveness for the Other cannot therefore be said to ever be "complete" or "accomplished," even as it is said to always "complete" the assignment of responsibility. It is not as if "in the beginning" there was original forgiveness, substitution, as an original openness ("welcome") to the Other. Original forgiveness is always never enough, even as "nothing" is at all "given" or "done." Forgiveness here is not something that I do but my "becoming," understood in terms of recurrence. There is never any end to forgiveness of the Other for their merciless persecution, and yet, by the same token, forgiveness is already anachronistic, too late. The subject as "original forgiveness" is thus in turn never enough for the Other, and it is this "never enough" (I have never forgiven enough the Other for their immoderate and delirious entrustment of responsibility to me) that inspires me to one more breath, itself never enough, nor the last, to be for the Other one degree more, *à l'outrance*. We are never forgiving enough, not for anything done by the Other nor for who they are but for their unforgiving commandment. Equally, we are too late in forgiving, inspiring us to forgive even more in welcoming the entrustment of the Other into my own, so that I aspire to become "one degree of responsibility more." This "original forgiveness" that I am, my standing in the drama of substitution, bespeaks the talismanic citation that echoes throughout this drama of substitution: "To be oneself, the condition of being a hostage, is always to have one degree of responsibility more, the responsibility for the responsibility of the other." Only on the basis of this drama of original forgiveness is any encounter in the forgiveness of others for what they have done against me and, likewise, their forgiving of me for what I have done against them possible—that is, situated and significant. As Levinas writes, "It is through the condition of being hostage [i.e., expiation or original forgiveness] that there can be in the world pity, compassion, forgiveness [*pardon*], and proximity—even the little that there is, even the simple 'after you, sir.'"[69] What could be this perpetual (perpetually lacking as well as perpetually too much) standing in original forgiveness that I am, which becomes me (as recurrence), as the condition for encounters with the question of forgiveness? *Patience,* as neither action nor attitude, as the berth of welcome in incessantly enduring and thus bearing the impossible entrustment of responsibility for the Other. Hence in daily life, even within the grand spectrum of human affairs, a relatively insignificant occurrence, how unforgivable nonetheless I find another's claim on my time, of how they always steal my time and never let me just be in having time to myself, *my time,* the time of my own life that I presumptively consider to be first and foremost mine for the giving or withholding, oblivious to the fact that the time of my life becomes meaningfully present for me, not from myself but from and for the Other.

Rage against the Good

Within this drama of substitution, there lurks a complicating intrigue. The enigma of assignment and accusation must be endured in an original forgiveness without thereby resolving or dissolving the constitutive enigma of entrusted responsibility. What proves unbearable, as impossible to recuse oneself from and yet without any recourse (through any pregiven power or prescribed capability) for responding, is enduring the enigma of the face in its double face as prohibition and temptation. Barring any final resolution, the prohibition and temptation of the face, as forbidding and inciting murder, do not allow for salvation or "some kind of magical redemption" in the form of a dialectical reconciliation that would leave behind no scars, nor in a synthetic unification that would decide and, in this sense, pacify once and for all the enigma of the face as both a smile and a wink. How to resist, in this incessant test of oneself in the drama of substitution, taking the face of the Other as *two-faced* rather than as a double face? How would it be possible *not to* transfer, and thus inhibit or short-circuit, from "from-the-other" to "for-the-other" in substitution and hence not welcome the Other in my shame, neither tending my check to the smiter nor passing from outrage to responsibility but becoming instead oneself enraged against the ethical, against the Good itself?

Original forgiveness in substitution is without cause. Neither asked for by the Other nor "possible" from myself in the sense stipulated by Levinas, as neither an "action" of one's freedom (for, indeed, freedom presupposes openness toward and welcome of the Other) nor a "power" or "capability" of oneself (or "moral power"). One is without recourse to oneself, and yet, nonetheless, one must endure in passing from outrage to forgiveness. It is in this sense that we should speak of the subject as "barred" or "split" from itself, not as inertial impediment but as the animating intrigue of its passage to the Other in substitution. Without this split within the subject, the subject would also be barred from any passage to original forgiveness, and hence any welcoming of the Other as oneself responsible for the Other in substitution. Forked, the barred subject stands at the precipice of responsibility for the Other as well as rage against the Other.

This intrigue lurking within this drama of substitution is that "refusing" to pass from outrage to responsibility cannot be understood as a "failure" (I can only fail at something that I could do) nor be understood as a demurring "response" to one's assignment and accusation, since, strictly speaking, the commandment of the Other cannot *not be heard*, and hence could be "rejected" or "refused" only on the basis of already having been bound to it, and hence never truly rejected or refused. I cannot decline responsibility much as I cannot answer for it either. Whether I respond or fail to respond is secondary to the assignment and accusation of a responsibility to which I am already hostage. We thus arrive at the heart of the enigma of the face of the Other as prohibition and temptation in its tacit reformulation of the problem of good and evil, as inscribed here within the forked anarchy of all beginnings. Of equal significance to the inversion of the relation between Being and the Good, Levinas's thinking, albeit in this regard less pronounced and commented upon, reconceives the relation between Good and evil through its dislocation of the ethical from any ontological conception of its possibility and significance. In speaking of the Good (as well as the Other) as "otherwise than and beyond being," Levinas does not thereby espouse or endorse a notion of the Good (or the Other) as "nonbeing," for such a negative theology (or negative philosophy) of the Good as well as the Other (but also, significantly, of God) would only mark the surreptitious return of ontological thinking. The Good is neither perfected being or "nothingness" beyond Being, much as evil can no longer be thought as the privation of being nor "nonexistent." In thinking the significance of the Good otherwise than and beyond being, the significance of evil in its relation to the Good becomes with equal provocation thought anew.[70]

As marked by the expressions of "trauma," "anarchy," and "immemorial," responsibility for the Other cannot be refused or repealed. In the face of such irrecusable responsibility, there is no possibility of distance or slipping away. Any evasion or separation always remains beholden to the Good; there is, in this sense, no exteriority to the Good even as the Good abides "outside" being. Leaving us speechless and without breath, we are given no leeway for any response, yes or no, in the unforgiving bearing of the Good upon us in the epiphany of the face. Is the face of the Other, as conditioned by our welcoming forgiveness, an invitation *or*, in its pitiless tonality, a command? Is it a command that is an invitation—that is, one hears it only if one accepts it? Is it an invitation that is a command—one accepts it only because one cannot *not* hear it? Is this a call that cannot be heard or a call that cannot not be heard?[71] Either way, it would seem that the enigma of the Good places one on the horns of a dilemma. One alternative is that evil is "contemporaneous" with the Good, if "deafness" to the commandment of the Other emerges from pride, imperialism, and self-positing of the subject *within* the drama of substitution and, in this sense, is thus inscribed within responsibility: irresponsibility as refusal or avoidance of responsibility within responsibility, such that the shamelessness of irresponsibility would be an avoidance of shame, an intoxication, within its accusation.[72] But, in this alternative, we would ascribe evil as "contemporaneity" with the Good and thus commit what Levinas calls the Luciferian Lie—namely, admitting a self-affirming and self-creating ego *within* the drama of substitution rather than endorsing its original disruption and interpolation through the drama of substitution. Or, in the other alternative, deafness to the commandment of the Other is secondary and thus attests to, in its irresponsibility and indifference, the original binding of oneself to the Other in responsibility. But, in this alternative, it would seem that we have unwittingly reverted to a notion of evil as "derivative" or "derived," as a privation of sorts.

Where, in other words, does the moment of "deafness" find its place within the drama of substitution?[73] Is deafness not hearing, through suppression or amplification, what cannot not be heard and hence an original instance of bad faith? Or, is deafness the counterforce of an overlay voice that speaks over, and thus silences, a voice that becomes itself interrupted, snuffed in the midst of its own speaking, as if one shouted hatred at the heart of the world so as to silence the mute transcendence of the Good from the beginning? There is either the pretentious Lie that evil, as prideful rebellion against the Good, is contemporaneous with responsibility or the deceptive Lie of bad faith that I hear the voice of the Other in order not to have it be heard. In the first instance, we would risk admitting a Manichean bifurcation within the original drama of subjectivation as its veritable tragedy; in the second instance, we would risk reverting to a form of conceiving evil as *privatio boni* within the original drama of substitution as its veritable comedy. Both these alternatives, however, depend on ascribing the moment of deafness to the subject in some form or another: as pretentious lie or deceptive bad faith. In both these alternatives, it is the subject who is assumed to initiate its own deafness. It is revealing, however, that Levinas speaks of "a deafening trauma" and "an echo of sound that would precede the resonance of this sound." Moreover, Levinas insists that the Good is "before good and evil," where good and evil are understood here as a function of freedom, of having chosen for either good or evil.[74] On the other hand, the incitement to murder is traced upon the face of the Other in its assignment and accusation. The "evil" of this incitement cannot in this regard be categorized as an "evil" one would choose against the Good. Implied with such expressions, noted above, is that the commandment is itself *deafening*, sonically imprinted with the intrigue of the face's enigma as prohibition and incitement that speaks in tongues, requiring, that is, a *translation*— "transfer"—that would disambiguate, in enduring its trial, the enigma of the Good without the promise of any final resolution or reconciliation that would leave no scars behind: the trace of the Face itself.

Exposed to the nudity of the face and its commandment Thou shall not kill, I am ashamed, not for the nudity of the Other but for oneself. Sourced from shame, as the affect that opens oneself to the Other as oneself for the Other, one stands exposed to one's own unjustifiable existence. Shame, however, carries the imprint of the enigma of the face as prohibition and incitement. In shame for one's freedom, the subject is incited to take flight from this exposure and outrage in claiming for itself its own justification and place in the sun by clothing and armoring oneself "with purely borrowed being, which masks its nameless singularity by conferring on it a role," where the locus of this standing and support is the personal pronoun I.[75] This strategy of evasion, which in the same gesture attests to an irrecusable responsibility *and* its abandonment, as marked by the bad faith of the question "Am I the Other's keeper?", does not represent the only intrigue lurking within the outrage of persecution and the pitiless tonality in which the Other pursues me in their assignment and accusation. Instead of evasion, the subject can also be incited to becoming enraged against the Good, not as an evasion of an unavoidable responsibility but, more stridently, in a rebounding binding back against itself through the summoning forth of the destructive goblin of an original and irresistible force called Rage. As the countertransfer to the transfer from outrage to responsibility, we pass here from outrage from the Other to rage against the Other.

In contrast to guilt and consciousness of failure, what distinguishes shame is its recalcitrance to suppression or dispelling by means of one's own effort, judgment, or capacity. I might regret my shame but cannot thereby also forgive myself—that is, offer repentance for it—since, as Montaigne points out, "repentance does not apply to the things that are not in my power."[76] In the existential plunge of shame at one's own freedom, the spontaneity of freedom is interrupted; the unspooling thread of consciousness in its temporal self-constitution becomes "cut" from within, thus rendering the subject helpless and without recourse toward its own shame. In the accusation without foundation, shame renders oneself powerless to overcome one's shame. Shame is a source of both impotence (I am unable to recover myself from my shame) and inertia (I remain ashamed without end). Shame, in these terms, cannot be localized within a phenomenological frame of reference. Strictly speaking, shame is not caused by the Gaze of the Other (as with Sartre) but affected by myself in my exposure to the Other's "nudity"—the sheerness and absoluteness of their face. The manifestation of shame attests in this regard to the nonphenomenality of the Other's face that becomes imprinted within the shame of my own freedom. As a nonspecific exposure (the shame, that I am), shame does not stem from anything that I have done nor reflect some particular trait of my being (in this context of consideration). If shame, in contrast to guilt, is thus not tethered to anything specific that I have done or failed to do, there is by extension no specific act that can expiate my shame from me. What can be termed "shame forgiveness" in contrast to "guilt forgiveness" must be continual and unbearable in this twofold sense: because I cannot expiate my own shame and because any expiation of my shame remains without end.[77]

In the midst of this predicament of shame, the drama of substitution becomes compounded, folding itself back upon and turning against itself, given that, in Levinas's characterization, I am ashamed of my own freedom, not in the eyes of the Other (as with Sartre's account of the gaze of the Other in *Being and Nothingness*) but with regard to myself. In shame, one easily becomes incited to becoming ashamed at one's own shame and so inhibits this redoubled shame by inverting it into an unbridled rage against the Other. Whereas I can *attempt* to hide myself from the Other's gaze in Sartre's conception, with the shame involved in the exposure to the Other's face in the drama of substitution, there is no escaping the shame that I am, since I am unable to escape from myself nor from the Good that beholds, in exposing, me. It is not, however, that I am riveted to myself but rather that I am expelled from the armor of my pronoun to find myself in the "nonplace," in between myself and the Other, as oneself for the Other. Unable to hide from the shame that oneself is in this irrecusable openness to the Other, shame doubles upon itself into being ashamed at one's own shame. In this doubling, the subject doubles down on itself. The drama of shame overtakes, as it were, the drama of substitution: in becoming ashamed at my own shame, there becomes fueled an amplification of outrage into rage against the Other's persecution but, by the same token, an amplification of one's own impotence with regard to oneself. As with Michael Kohlhaas, rage implicitly avows to a binding against which it struggles in vain; responsibility for others undergoes a subverting countertransfer (or "counterexpiation") into rage against others. As with Kohlhaas, the religiosity of rage, its burning fervor, is the absoluteness of the pursuit of expiation by other, contorted means. It is as if the redoubling of shame against oneself became expelled in rebounding the outrage undergone from the Other into a rage launched against the Other. Rather than tend my cheek in shame to the smiter, I smite the smiter as a way to avoid bearing the shame at my own existence I cannot bear. In this rage against Goodness there is the inhibition of any passage from "outrage undergone" to "responsibility undertaken," the transfer from suffering to expiation. Rather than expiate, I exterminate. The Other becomes *unforgivable*—it is unforgivable that the Other is unforgiving toward me in Goodness. Unlike the case of Kohlhaas, however, the rebounding of outrage into rage in the drama of substitution, its subversion, is not predicated on anything having been done against me nor, as with the Underground Man, is the rebounding of shame into rage a function of an unbearable shame *at being forgiven,* and hence as caused by forgiveness. In the context of the drama of substitution, shame is caused by *being* unforgiven: unbearable shame at the shame of one's unjustifiable existence.

In the context of these considerations, rage against the Other, against the Good, is predicated on a mistranslation of the enigma of the face, or, as it were, a mishearing of its *deafening* commandment. Rage does not become incited by the Other's "malice" and "hatred" because of fear or anxiety nor because of an experience of limitation. Rage does not burst forth from frustration or failure. Rebounded as rage against the Other from the outrage undergone by their persecution, the enraged subject seeks to identify the source of its accusation and *master* the source of its trauma, thus embracing a double mistake. The Other's face is misidentified as the source of my shame, thus masking that I am the source itself, insofar as I am exposed in shame for my *own* virility. The subject thus projects a source for its shame outside itself in the Other, even as it is the Other who affects the subject to shame within itself. Unlike in Sartre, where the source of my shame is the Other's gaze, thus inciting me to destroy the Other as the source of my shame, in this context of consideration it is not the Gaze of the Other that is the source of my shame but oneself, as affected by the Other's commandment Thou shall not kill. And yet, unable to accept oneself as the source of one's own shame, I seek to see the Other as the source of my own shame and thus seek to exterminate the Other in the hope of expiating my own shame. In rage, there is thus a twofold misreading, of oneself as well as of the Other. As exemplified in the doubled characters of Ivan and Smerdyakov in *The Brothers Karamazov*, the enraged self cannot be understood as the manifestation of an unbridled pride or will to power. Rage is not anger (see chapter 7). In its self-consuming and decentering vortex, rage displaces the subject from its own axis of agency, thus undercutting from within itself any possibility of absolute self-constitution through rage despite the absoluteness of its intransigence. Enraged, the self does not constitute itself but, on the contrary, deconstitutes itself. *Who* is the subject of rage, its animating agency, becomes conflated in its self-consuming and self-destructive conflagration, much as *what* is the target of its rage (as with Lear's rage [see chapter 5] but also Kohlhaas). Enraged against the Good in the epiphany of the face, unleashing violence against the Other's face, it is as if one attempted to "forgive oneself" for one's inextirpable shame at one's "unforgiven" existence. In this salient sense, there is the attempt to become self-creating through the ruse of being self-forgiving for one's shameful and unjustifiable existence in the promise of extricating myself (as opposed to evading) any beholdenness to the Good and responsibility for the Other. As with the imposture of forgiveness in the delirious self-forgiveness of Jean-Claude Romand, the conceit of being absolutely self-creating *from nothing and hence for nothing* is the shameless dream of being absolutely self-forgiving for one's own shameful existence.

The Anarchy of Forgiveness

There is no outside or beyond the Good, even as the Good is beyond Being. The significance of the statement "There is no outside or beyond the Good, even as the Good is otherwise and beyond Being" can be genuinely measured only by the enigma that evil itself is not outside or beyond the Good without thereby being contemporaneous, or equal, with the Good. It is not "the very precariousness of Other [that] would produce for me a temptation to kill," as thinks Judith Butler.[78] It is the trauma of the Good itself as traced upon the enigmatic epiphany of the face of the Other. In the seduction of irresponsibility *and* the impossibility of escaping responsibility, the Good is impossible in two crosscurrent senses: impossible to escape and impossible not to be tempted to deface. Rather than place the incitement of rage against the Good in Being outside the Good, Goodness itself *incites* evil even as, in this rebounding, evil in turn always misses its target. As with the words that Abraham hears from God, commanding him to murder his son, God's words are *misheard* as the Adversary's incitement, thus placing Abraham in a double bind that puts his faith, or trust, to the test within an original entrustment of responsibility for the Other. The significance of this trial—the drama of substitution—consists in passing *through* this murderous temptation of oneself so as to discover behind, as it were, the enigma of what was heard, commanded, the true voice of the Other, of God's love (in this biblical narrative), which had always guided Abraham to the anarchic nonplace of responsibility held open in the *non-lieu* of murder.[79]

To murder in the Night. The misreading, or mistranslation ("countertransfer"), of the enigma of the face as prohibition and incitement, played out within the redoubling of shame and rebounding of outrage against the Good, remains beholden to the misreading of murder itself. For as Levinas writes, "Murder exercises power over what escapes power."[80] In the inscription of the face as prohibition and temptation, there comes into enigmatic tension the forked significance of impossibility: impossibility of murder as the prohibition of murder and impossibility of murder as the temptation for a murder that always misses its mark and, in this sense, fails to destroy the Other. For what is sought in the murder of the Other is not just the destruction of the Other in their being. Through this real destruction, murder aims at the *transcendental* destruction of the Other's face as the commandment Thou shall not kill. In murder, one seeks implicitly to unbind oneself from a responsibility not to murder that can be unbound, violated, only on the condition that one is already and always bound to it. Murder, in this regard, is a real possibility predicated on an ethical impossibility. As Levinas remarks, "For in reality murder is possible, but it is possible only when one has not looked the Other in the face. The impossibility of killing is not real, but moral."[81] Or, as provocatively stated in Blanchot's formulation, obliquely traced in the face of the Other "man is the indestructible, and this means that there is no limit to the destruction of man."[82] As with Améry's *ressentiment*, this "suffocated" speech, voiced from beyond "the living" and "the dead," cannot but insist, tactlessly, on the indestructible assignment and accusation, which survives even when the instinct for survival has itself been annihilated in the transfiguration of the lived-body and its constitutive "I can" into meat, or what Améry termed, provocatively, *Verfleischlichung*. Speaking from this nonplace and dead time of a "disjointed" or "deported knowledge," akin to what Anne-Lise Stern dubbed *le savoir-déporté*, Améry's *ressentiment* holds out against the unforgivable the enduring beholdenness of others to an originary responsibility for others in holding against forgiveness its unforgivable blasphemy.[83]

The ruse of murder, refracted in the ruse of rage as "expiation," consists in the misreading of the Other's unforgiving commandment as a "power" or "force" imposed against and upon me, against which, enraged, one revolts in the exercise of a presumed *greater force*. Caught in the trauma of the Other's assignment and accusation, the outrage undergone must disabuse itself of taking this pitiless tone of accusation and assignment as *hostility*, as issuing from a "freedom" opposite to mine or an authority that commands without opening itself, in forgiveness, to my hospitality (as with Markel's pronouncement). The operative misreading at play here, obscured in the blindness of rage, is "that one does not see the face of the other, one sees the other's freedom as a force; one identifies the absolute character of the other with this force."[84] As Blanchot astutely writes, "The absolute distance that 'measures' the relation of *autrui* to me is what calls forth in man the exercise of absolute power: the power to give death. Cain killing Abel is the self that, coming up against the transcendence of *autrui* . . . attempts to confront it by resorting to the transcendence of murder."[85] Enraged against the Other, one can be said not to *approach* the Other in murder (contrary to the intention of murder to grasp, in making disappear, the presence of the Other) but, on the contrary, to exonerate and extricate oneself backward, as it were, in reverse, from a responsibility to which one can only but be bound, for murder to rebound against it. The Other becomes *seen*, or phenomenalized, into a mask that does not properly belong to them, as barring the movement by which the Good, in its infinite beholding, approaches, against which one's murderous intention becomes proclaimed and aimed. But, in Blanchot's words, "as soon as this presence closes around *autrui* as a property of *autrui* established in the world, as soon as it ceases to give rise to speech, the earth ceases to be vast enough to contain at the same time *autrui* and myself, and it is necessary that one of the two reject the other—absolutely."[86] In the countertransfer of rage, murder substitutes the face of the Other with a mask, or pronoun, or identity not through an act of speech but in an act of violence.[87] There is no possibility of violence against someone other without a fascination that, by dint of its imaginative prowess, substitutes for the Other an image we have fashioned for ourselves, self-servingly, in order not to be seized in obsession and exposed in shame as oneself for the Other. The Other is hated into a realness that thereby can be killed in the fantasy of retaliation for its misread, or misheard, *forceful*—and not salvific—commandment.[88] Evil is essentially pornographic *and* abstraction (as exemplified with Ivan Karamazov).

"In the trauma of persecution, it is to pass from the outrage undergone to the responsibility for the persecutor, and, in this sense, from suffering to expiation."[89] In this transfer from outrage to responsibility, what is required of me is endurance and patience. I must atone for this "hatred" of me in forgiving the unforgiving. In bearing an unbearable responsibility towards the Other, I atone for the Other's unforgiving persecution of me. The persecution of the Good, its remorseless and pitiless tonality, becomes forgiven; in this forgiveness of the unforgiving Good, forgiveness itself becomes possible, as the Good, in the disposition to forgive, in patience and endurance, to the limit, and into the infinite, again and again. Yet the scene of original forgiveness in the drama of forgiveness is at the same time crystallized in the endurance of the postponement of my own murderous being in beseeching forgiveness for wanting to murder, *so to speak*, the Other, for in the accusation of my "unforgiven" and "unjustified" existence, there lurks the intrigue of having to pass through and survive the seduction of my own rebounding rage against the Good. As with Lear's twofold character of his "insane impartiality" with regard to himself as "unforgivable" for his murderous existence and with regard to "thou art the real thing" of Poor Tom, the tempest of his rage becomes broken—"Come not between the Dragon and his wrath" (1.1.123–24)—in his awakening to the touching proximity of the Other in *their* destitution.

In this sense, when Levinas writes, "We should think of all the murder there is in death: every death is a murder, is premature, and there is the responsibility of the survivor," survivor and guiltiness must be understood as imbued with a double significance.[90] As expressed in Levinas's talismanic citation, responsibility remains impossible to disentangle from culpability, as exposed in the shame for one's existence. The culpability of the survivor as witness to their death, as standing in the face of the Other, cannot be understood in terms of either "fault" or "failure" in the sense of failing to prevent or annul that the Other dies. If, as François-David Sebbah writes, the Other shall die and there is nothing I can do about it, such that their death obsesses and haunts me, then "fault" or "guiltiness" cannot carry here the meaning of a failure to do what should or could have been done.[91] It is impossible for me to substitute myself for the Other's mortality; at issue in the trial of substitution is, in other words, not a question of putting oneself in the place of the Other, sacrificing oneself for the Other so as to spare them from death, or embracing the Other in superlative compassion or caring. The death of the Other is unbearable for me; any compassion becomes summarily exasperated and exhausted.[92] The irreducibility of my fault lies precisely in that the Other dies not despite my effort to save her, and hence on account of my failure to save her, but on account of my murderous freedom. To Philippe Nemo's question "But if one fears for the Other and not for oneself, can one even live?" Levinas responds, "This is in fact the question one must ultimately pose. Should I be dedicated to being? By being, by persisting in being, do I not kill?"[93] Can one even live through—that is, survive—the entanglement of responsibility and culpability? The meaning of surviving is not in my failure to save the Other from their death but in surviving oneself from my own murderous being with regard of the Other. Responsibility is entangled anarchically with culpability not on account of its failure but in its culpable inhibiting of the passage of substitution from "outrage" to "responsibility." In interrupting one's own inhibiting of passage as the dramatic trial of substitution, there is not only expiation for the persecution inflicted upon oneself by the Other (I am "liable to answer," or atone, for the Other) but also, as befitting the enigma of prohibition *and* incitement, a beseeching of forgiveness for this inhibition, or, in other words, the countertransfer from outrage to rage. I welcome the Other in beseeching forgiveness for this rage against the Good in the shame at the shame of my murderous being. Standing in the posture of original forgiveness for my murderous being, the subject incessantly interrupts itself, never enough and always too late, from its doubling down on itself and its rebounding rage; caught in the act, as it were, evil becomes arrested in the throes of its own passage. Inscribed within the drama of substitution, original forgiveness in this forked sense—expiation for the Other, atonement for oneself; that is, forgiving and beseeching forgiveness—does not unbind oneself from the irreversibility of the past, after injury, but, on the contrary, opens oneself toward the approach of the Other in welcome. Conversely, insofar as "to undergo from the Other" in outrage and persecution to responsibility must "already be for-the-Other," in succumbing to rage against the Good, evil manifests itself most originally as blasphemy and betrayal—to wit, as rage and revolt against original forgiveness. As with Ivan's cornering of Alyosha, his rage against the Good (against God) and "torture" of his brother, the manifestation of the unforgivable, betrays his original responsibility for his brother in its blasphemy against standing *already* forgiven for his murderous being by his brother. This original blasphemy against original forgiveness becomes orchestrated into the Underground Man's refusal to be forgiven by Lizaveta. In being forgiven for what he has done, the Underground Man stands unbearably before himself ashamed, and in rebounding his shame at his shame into rage against Lizaveta, the original intrigue of shame's redoubling within the trial of substitution becomes replayed in the encounter with the question of forgiveness.

In a fleeting evocation of forgiveness in *Existence and Existents*, Levinas speaks of "forgiveness" (*pardon*) as "the most radical rupture of the very categories of the I, for it is for me to be somewhere else than myself"—otherwise than being.[94] As he writes, "it is to be pardoned, not to be a definite existence." When inscribed within the configuration of substitution, original forgiveness is not an initiation of a new beginning in the aftermath of injury, a repentance that incurs back into the past (to adopt here Max Scheler's formulation), or an unbinding of oneself from the irreversibility of something done in the past. In original forgiveness, beseeching forgiveness for one's murderous being entails an infinite postponement of one's own murderous being and rebounding rage in the patience, and hence trust, for the Other in my entrusted responsibility for them. Culpability is thereby not "forgotten" and also not "forgiven," and yet the subject becomes released from its burden in the shame of its own existence.[95] One's own shame becomes expiated in an original forgiveness, not for what I have done nor for who I am but for that I am. The entanglement of responsibility and culpability remains unyielding much as the enigma of the Good in the epiphany of the face as prohibition and temptation remains merciless.[96] Am I forgiven for my place in the sun?—this is the unbearable patience of time itself that subtends any standing in the world and entering into encounters with others.

In the anarchy of original forgiveness, I stand to be forgiven for this original rage against a responsibility entrusted to me as well as forgive the Other for their unforgiving assignment and accusation. To declare, "Here I am" is to stand in forgiveness for wanting to kill you, so to speak, in surviving—postponing—my own rebounding rage against the Good, not as an afterthought but as the anarchic setting for an infinite patience required to endure your merciless, and hence unforgiving, entrustment of responsibility (without consent or recourse) to me. As with the brothers Ivan and Alyosha, the mysteriousness of the Good is at the same time the mysteriousness of evil, both sourced from within a confounding anarchy of all beginnings. This mystery is the anarchy of Goodness: to be entrusted with the responsibility of wanting to die for the Other whom you yourself would want to murder, where, in an original forgiveness, we abide within an infinite patience for the Other as well as an infinite postponement of our own murderous being.

Afterwords

Sparse in its telling, Maurice Sendak's *Outside Over There* is the story of responsibility and rage in answer to the question "Am I the Other's keeper?" It is the story of bearing responsibility for all others, for some other, more than others, in response to the betrayal of the Other in rage against the Good. It is the story of the passage of the subjectivity of the subject as substitution in outrage and expiation, or, in other words, *original forgiveness.* As Sendak once remarked about his masterly children's book, "It was the story of me and my sister, basically. She's Ida and her vexation, if not rage, in having to take care of me."[1] The story begins before the story has begun, outside over there on the title page, before a page has been turned and any adventure begun. We see an image of a young girl, in blue, diligently and carefully aiding her little sister, in pink, to walk—that most human trait of freedom (standing upright and moving about the world, much as Cordelia lifts up her child-changed father to walk) emerging through an entrustment of responsibility for the Other such that freedom can become my freedom, their freedom. Alongside a fence lined with sunflowers—mysteriously grand—there sits, ominously, an apparition, cloaked and faceless, lurking and waiting. In the next frame, a second title page, and thus still outside over there with regard to inside the narrative proper, still yet to begin, the same scene has become enlarged to find the girl, apprehensive, holding her sister, equally concerned, in her arms, with a yellow bonnet. From either side of the fence, a group of apparitions—cloaked and faceless—approaches, armed with ladder and a French horn. Now the sunflowers appear ragged and have imperceptibly changed in composure with this change in scene. In the next scene, still before, or behind, the launch of the story, the girl carries the child away in the direction of the story, the subsequent page, with her back turned toward us, as a single apparition stealthily follows her as well.

When Papa was away at sea. The story begins, as do so many stories, with the departure of the father. Ida holds her sister standing next to her mother; both are facing the departing ship, while her sister looks in our direction but not at us, somewhat apprehensive, her eyes turned to her right in the direction of two apparitions who are also looking, with backs turned toward us, toward the sea.

And Mama in the arbor. The mother sits dejected and abandoned in the arbor with a faithful German shepherd; both look in the direction of the two apparitions walking off to the left of our image with a raised ladder in hand. Ida holds her crying sister, who, as evidenced by her bonnet lying on the ground, is visibly shaken. With the absence of the father and abandonment of the mother, Ida is now responsible for her sister. The assignment is hers alone. She has become hostage to her sister.

Ida played her wonder horn to rock the baby still—but never watched. Elected and entrusted, Ida alone bears responsibility for her sister, more than anyone, including even her mother. This assignment is "immemorial," since it began before the story in the sequence of images in the title pages. Ida enters onto the stage of the world—the narrative—with her sister, carrying her, and to find herself alone with this responsibility. She enters the narrative in the absence of the father and abandoned by the mother, who, evidently dejected by the departure of her husband, has forsaken her responsibility for her children. Ida plays the wonder horn "to rock the baby still." This is an ambiguous phrase vis-à-vis responsibility and rage. She plays the wonder horn to lull the baby (note: not "her sister" but "the baby") to sleep, and yet she faces away and "never" watched over the baby, not even from the beginning. It is an odd attitude and position, since we rock a baby to sleep in the paradigmatic situation of entrustment—the child must trust that we will be there when she awakes—and we look at the baby, reassuring it, into her sleep, lulling the baby to sleep in the kind nursery of our care. And yet Ida *never watched.* Moreover, we have seen the horn she plays "to rock the baby still" before: prior to the narrative, in the title page, in the hands of the creeping apparitions. The wonder horn "lulls the baby to sleep" in calling on the apparitions to steal the baby away from under Ida's negligent and indifferent care. She does not bear witness and remains inattentive to the baby; instead, she plays the wonder horn. For what purpose? "To rock the baby still" hits a decidedly ominous note: to murder the baby, her sister. The wonder horn, in this dark light, summons two apparitions in the window, one with a clawing hand to steal the baby away. The baby is evidently not falling asleep but is entranced by the wonder horn, ignorant of the murder that awaits her.

In the next scene, Ida continues to play her wonder horn as the sunflowers have crept farther through the window into the bedroom. Quickly, two apparitions have stolen the baby, who cries out looking and longingly toward Ida, whose back remains turned: it happened behind her back even as her horn would appear to have summoned the apparitions to "rock the baby still"—that is, to the exercise of violence in the night. Unbeknownst to her, the goblins—we now know them to be goblins—have swapped the baby with a pale-looking ice baby. The ice baby appears as does a corpse: it has the bonnet on, has eyes staring wide open, and is propped up in the crib. In the next scene, Ida, "never knowing, hugged the changeling and she murmured: 'How I love you.'" The object of her love is the replacement of love with hate. She loves a dead baby. Unbeknownst to her, love has become the desire to murder in her rage at this responsibility and entrustment. The sunflowers have protruded even farther into the room through the window. Throughout this story, from the title page the sunflowers have mirrored the working through of Ida's ambivalence. She hugs the baby and declares that she loves her, not realizing that she hugs a changeling made of ice. She hugs both in love and in death, for the baby she hugs in love is the baby she wants to kill. Embedded in the notion of rocking the baby still is the anarchic antinomy of absolute responsibility and absolute rage. As she hugs the changeling, the "ice thing only dripped and stared," and Ida now realizes that the goblins—her demons—had been there. The five goblins who have murdered her sister *are* Ida's rage personified and projected within her.[2] In the background, we at first see a ship at sea, and we then see the ship capsized at sea by a storm. Ida's rage is rage at having been left alone, at being a survivor entrusted with responsibility in the absence of the father and the mother.

Ida, in the next scene, is angry and declares that the goblins have stolen her sister away to be "a nasty goblin's bride." In stealing away the baby to become a bride, the baby becomes entrusted to someone else's responsibility but, more significantly, not Ida's and no one other. In a hurry, she takes her mother's yellow rain cloak, brings along her horn, but then "makes a serious mistake." The mistake is to have "climbed backwards out her window into outside over there." She makes the passage into outside over there *backward*—not facing outside over there but backward, still facing the room from which she is exiting. Because of this, "foolish Ida never looking" whirls about without ever seeing the goblin's cave where her sister is kept. As she floats helplessly and lost above the world, the world below is depicted in a somber hue of colors. We see the baby abandoned in a cave, her mother still lost in her mourning in the arbor, and a mysterious pair of sailors, evidently bored, sitting on rocks.[3] She would still be looking in vain, backward, were it not for hearing a call "from off the sea"—she hears her sailor Papa's song: *If Ida backwards in the rain would only turn around again and catch those goblins with a tune she'd spoil their kidnap honeymoon!* Ida finds herself in the midst of a wedding. The goblins "hollered and kicked" and morphed into babies themselves. Armed with her wonder horn, Ida "charmed them with a captivating tune" and caused the goblins to dance in a wild frenzy, against their will, and ever faster until they could no longer breathe. Ida continued to play her "frenzied jig" until the goblin babies danced so fiercely that they churned into a dancing stream. Ida's frenzied playing of her wonder horn expiates her shame for her rage against the entrustment of her sister to her responsibility.[4]

In churning the goblin babies back into a stream, thereby releasing her sister and redeeming herself, Ida expiates the demons within her; for if the goblins at first exchanged her sister with the ice-baby changeling, Ida undoes this confusion, in changing—churning—the goblin babies (the demons of rage within her), thus allowing her to bear the responsibility for her sister. All the babies have been churned back into nothing, except Ida's sister, who sits there "crooning and clapping as a baby should" in an eggshell. Ida now hugs "baby tight," knowing that this is not a changeling ice baby, and heads home, back to the arbor, where Mama is still sitting with the faithful dog. Mama has a letter in hand from Papa, which reads, *I'll be home one day, and my brave, bright little Ida must watch the baby and her Mama for her Papa, who loves her always.* That waiting is presumably unending—as unending as the patience endured in the entrustment of the Other. In the final image, we see Ida holding her sister by the hands, helping her walk, next to the fence lined with sunflowers, this time with her demons expelled. At times protruding and invasive, at times embracing Ida's sister, the sunflowers (and other flora) set her narrative against a natural world within which she must undertake her ethical ordeal. Mystery pervades—the mystery of creation, as symbolized by Ida's discovery of her sister in an eggshell, newly born—this natural world, as woven figuratively into Sendak's landscapes.[5] This mystery is the anarchy of Goodness: to be entrusted with the responsibility of wanting to die for the Other whom you yourself would want to murder, where, in an original forgiveness, we abide in an infinite patience for the Other as well as an infinite postponement of our own murderous being.

Notes

Chapter 1

A shorter version of this chapter appeared as "Trust" in *The Routledge Handbook of Phenomenology of Emotion*, ed. Thomas Szanto and Hilge Landweer (London: Routledge, 2020).

1. See Martin Hartmann, *Die Praxis des Vertrauens* (Berlin: Suhrkamp, 2011).

2. Jay Bernstein, *Torture and Dignity: An Essay on Moral Injury* (Chicago: University of Chicago Press, 2015), 230, states, "Trust is subject to rational correction and modification but not to rational installation; reason is the caretaker of trust, not its creator (or ground)." Likewise, Annette Baier, *Moral Prejudices: Essays on Ethics* (Cambridge, Mass.: Harvard University Press, 1995), 96, argues, "Morality requires trust."

3. See Lars Hertzberg, "On the Attitude of Trust," *Inquiry* 31 (1988): 307–22.

4. Barbara Misztal, *Trust in Modern Societies: The Search for the Bases of Social Order* (Cambridge: Polity Press, 1996), 56, argues that Max Weber's four forms of social action are amenable to recasting into four forms of trust.

5. Niklas Luhmann, *Trust and Power*, trans. H. Davies, J. Raffan, and K. Rooney (Cambridge: Polity Press, 2017), 5.

6. John Locke, "Letter to Tom (20 October 1659)," in *Political Writings*, ed. D. Wootton (Indianapolis: Hackett Publishing, 1993), 140.

7. Sissela Bok, *Lying* (New York: Vintage Books, 1999), 31; emphasis in original.

8. Locke, "Letter to Tom," 140.

9. Locke, "Letter to Tom," 140.

10. Jean-Paul Sartre, *Being and Nothingness*, trans. S. Richmond (London: Routledge, 2018), 87.

11. Locke, "Letter to Tom," 140.

12. See Max Scheler, "Führer und Vorbilder," in *Schriften aus dem Nachlass: Zur Ethik und Erkenntnislehre*, ed. Maria Scheler, 255–318 (Bern: Francke, 1957).

13. Max Scheler, *Die Formen des Wissens* (Bonn: F. Cohen, 1925), 106 ("Vorbilder sind nur Wegbereiter zum Hören des Rufes unserer Person. Sie sind nur anbrechende Morgenröte des Sonnentags unseres individuellen Gewissens und Gesetzes").

14. Quoted in Gary Lindberg, *The Confidence Man in American Literature* (Oxford: Oxford University Press, 1982), 6; emphasis in original.

15. Melville's final novel was itself first published in New York on April Fools' Day 1857.

16. See Dale Jones, "The Grotesque in Melville's *The Confidence-Man*," *Colby Quarterly* 19, no. 4 (1983): 194–205.

17. For this sentiment of imposture, this uneasiness within our skin and with any identity, however "sincere" and "genuine," see Belinda Cannone, *Le sentiment d'imposture* (Paris: Gallimard, 2005), 29.

18. Jason Wirth, "The Self without Character: Melville's *The Confidence-Man* and Murakami's *Kafka on the Shore*," *Humanities* 7, no. 25 (2018): 5.

19. Annette Baier, "Trust and Anti-Trust," in *Moral Prejudices*, 95–129.

20. Friedrich Nietzsche, *Menschliches, Allzumenschliches: Ein Buch für freie Geister* (Frankfurt: Insel, 2000), no. 311 ("Leute, welche uns ihr volles Vertrauen schenken, glauben dadurch ein Recht auf das unsrige zu haben. Dies ist ein Fehlschluß; durch Geschenke erwirbt man keine Rechte").

21. I omit, not from neglect but for reasons of prudence and time, trust in God (and deities) as well as trust in pets and domesticated animals. For an insightful discussion of trust in God and trusting as indispensable for human relations, see Sheela Pawar, *Trusting Others, Trusting God: Concepts of Belief, Faith, and Rationality* (Farnham, Surrey, U.K.: Ashgate Publishing, 2009).

22. Martin Heidegger, *Sein und Zeit* (Tübingen: Niemeyer, 2001), 86 ("Where-in Dasein in this manner always understands, it is originally familiar/intimate with" [*Being and Time*, trans. J. Stambaugh (Albany: State University of New York Press, 1996), 81]).

23. Peter Sloterdijk proposes that Heidegger's *Sein und Zeit* "contains an embryonically revolutionary treatise on being and space" (*Bubbles*, trans. W. Hoban [Cambridge, Mass.: MIT Press, 2011], 333).

24. Sloterdijk, *Bubbles*, 541. Emphasis added on the word "subject."

25. Richard Grathoff, *Milieu und Lebenswelt* (Frankfurt: Suhrkamp, 1989), 343.

26. Edmund Husserl, *Erfahrung und Urteil* (Hamburg: Felix Meiner, 1996), 33 ("an indeterminate general familiarity" *in which* "all further differences between familiarity and unfamiliarity flow").

27. Heidegger, *Sein und Zeit*, 86 (*Being and Time*, 81).

28. Heidegger, *Sein und Zeit*, 87 ("Dasein, in its trusted intimacy with meaningfulness, is the ontic condition of the possibility of the discoverability of being" [*Being and Time*, 81]).

29. Heidegger, *Sein und Zeit*, 88 (*Being and Time*, 82).

30. For a comparable view regarding trust as a means for the reduction of complexity, see Luhmann, *Trust and Power*.

31. For the importance of attestation and testimony for selfhood, see Paul Ricoeur, *Oneself as Another*, trans. K. Blamey (Chicago: University of Chicago Press, 1995).

32. Alfred Schutz, *Collected Papers II: Studies in Social Theory* (The Hague: Martinus Nijhoff, 1976), 155.

33. On the illocutionary force in promising and other acts of speech that

bind us to what we say, see J. L. Austin, *How to Do Things with Words* (Cambridge, Mass.: Harvard University Press, 1975).

34. Knud Ejler Løgstrup, *The Ethical Demand*, trans. H. Fink (Notre Dame, Ind.: University of Notre Dame Press, 1997), 14.

35. Løgstrup, *The Ethical Demand*, 17–18.

36. Georg Simmel, *The Philosophy of Money*, trans. D. Frisby (London: Routledge, 1978), 187.

37. For this conception of participation, see Nicolas de Warren, "Souls of the Departed: Toward a Phenomenology of the After-Life," *Metodo* 5, no. 1 (2017): 205–37.

38. For a classic sociological account of "trust networks," see Charles Tilly, *Trust and Rule* (Cambridge: Cambridge University Press, 2005).

39. For this notion of modal specification, see Anthony Steinbock, *Moral Emotions* (Evanston, Ill.: Northwestern University Press, 2014), 197. For a discussion of how trust is founded on reputation, see Misztal, *Trust in Modern Societies*, 120–39.

40. For this notion of symbolic form (influenced by Ernst Cassirer), see Geoffrey Hosking, *Trust: A History* (Oxford: Oxford University Press, 2014), 41.

41. Hosking, *Trust*, 110.

42. On this motif of gardens, see William Bottiglia, "Candide's Garden," *PMLA* 66 (1951): 718–33.

43. Following Annette Baier's insightful definition in "Trust and Anti-Trust."

44. For this notion of functional virtue, see Annette Baier, "Trust and Anti-Trust."

45. Annette Baier: "We inhabit a climate of trust as we inhabit an atmosphere and notice it as we notice air, only when it becomes scarce or polluted" (*Moral Prejudices*, 98). Sissela Bok: "Whatever matters to human beings, trust is the atmosphere in which it thrives" (*Lying: Moral Choice in Public and Private Life* [New York: Vintage, 2011], 69). For an insightful development of Bok's claim, see Jeffrey Courtright, "Is Trust Like an 'Atmosphere'? Understanding the Phenomenon of Existential Trust," *Journal for Philosophy in the Contemporary World* 20, no. 1 (Spring 2013): 39–51.

46. For an illuminating argument against trust as an emotion, see Hartmann, *Die Praxis des Vertrauens*, 151–71. Even Anthony Steinbock's case for considering trust as a "moral emotion" leaves his invoked notion of emotion fairly abstract: "By emotions, I understand those experiences that pertain to the domain of feelings (or what some would call the order of the 'heart'), but which take place or are enacted on the level of spirit" (*Moral Emotions*, 12).

47. For example, as argued by Karen Jones, "Trust as Affective Attitude," *Ethics* 107, no. 1 (October 1996): 4–25.

48. Erik Erikson, *Childhood and Society* (New York: Norton, 1963), 247. Trust versus mistrust is the first stage in Erikson's stages of child development. Feeding and responding to an infant's cries represented for Erikson the primary activities for the formation of basic trust in the mother-infant relationship. See also

John Bowlby, *A Secure Base: Parent-Child Attachment and Healthy Human Development* (London: Routledge, 1988), as well as his three-volume work *Attachment and Loss* (New York: Basic Books, 1982).

49. On infant crying as communicative appeal and address, see Joseph Soltis, "The Signal Functions of Early Infant Crying," *Behavioral and Brain Sciences* 27, no. 4 (2004): 443–90.

50. Erik Erikson, *Insight and Responsibility* (New York: Norton, 1994), 118.

51. Misztal, *Trust in Modern Societies*, 102.

52. Onora O'Neill, *A Question of Trust* (Cambridge: Cambridge University Press, 2002).

53. For the varieties of impostures, see Roland Breeur, *L.I.S.: Lies–Imposture–Stupidity* (Vilnius, Lith.: Jonas ir Jokūbas, 2019).

54. Emmanuel Carrère, *The Adversary*, trans. L. Coverdale (New York: Picador, 2000), 43. As Belinda Cannone also insightfully observes, "Il est possible qu'à l'origine, c'est-a-dire quand il a commence ses études de médecine, porté par le désir ardent de ses parents, il se soit senti *imposteur* . . . Ce qui tendrait à confirmer l'intuition: *l'imposteur* n'a pas de vrai problem avec les autres . . . c'est avec lui-même qu'il en a . . . Pour l'imposteur professionnel en revanche, les autres son *réellement* un problem" (*Le Sentiment d'imposture* [Paris: Calmann-Lévy, 2005], 60–61; emphasis in original). Here, then, the difference between the Confidence-Man (professional) and Romand. And here as well the founding significance of *shame* for selfhood: shame at being an impostor launches Romand into playing at being an impostor.

55. Carrère, *The Adversary*, 16.

56. Carrère, *The Adversary*, 51.

57. Carrère, *The Adversary*, 8.

58. Carrère, *The Adversary*, 9.

59. Carrère, *The Adversary*, 9.

60. Two years after the event, Luc and his family continued to live in apprehension. "Nothing is firm or dependable anymore" (Carrère, *The Adversary*, 161). Despite counseling for the children, their lives are still filled with apprehension.

61. Carrère, *The Adversary*, 18.

62. Carrère, *The Adversary*, 160.

63. Carrère, *The Adversary*, 158–59.

64. Carrère, *The Adversary*, 187.

65. Carrère, *The Adversary*, 171.

66. Carrère, *The Adversary*, 171.

67. Carrère, *The Adversary*, 191.

Chapter 2

A condensed version of this chapter appeared as "For the Love of the World: Redemption and Forgiveness in Arendt," in *Phenomenology and Forgiveness*, ed. Marguerite La Caze (London: Rowman and Littlefield, 2018).

1. Charles Griswold, *Forgiveness: A Philosophical Exploration* (Cambridge:

Cambridge University Press, 2007). Griswold identifies a set of conditions for the forgiving person as well as the person to be forgiven. For discussion of Griswold's account of forgiveness, see William Meninger, "Why Unconditional Forgiveness IS Needed," *Tikkun* 23, no. 2 (March/April 2008): 62–63; Michele Moody-Adams, "Reply to Griswold, *Forgiveness: A Philosophical Exploration*," *Philosophia* 38 (2010): 429–37; Charles Griswold, "Unconditional Forgiveness? Reply to Father Meninger," *Tikkun* 23, no. 2 (March/April 2008): 63–64; Charles Griswold, "Forgiveness, Secular and Religious: A Reply to My Critics," *Proceedings of the American Catholic Philosophical Association* 82 (2009): 303–13; Charles Griswold, "Debating Forgiveness: A Reply to My Critics," *Philosophia* 38 (2010): 457–73.

2. Margaret Holmgren, *Forgiveness and Retribution* (Cambridge: Cambridge University Press, 2012), 74; see also Margaret Holmgren, "Forgiveness and the Intrinsic Value of Persons," *American Philosophical Quarterly* 30, no. 4 (1993): 341–52.

3. Holmgren, *Forgiveness and Retribution*, 98.

4. As Griswold himself, impatiently and without nuance, recognizes, "J. Derrida asks: 'is this [the unforgivable] not, in truth, the only thing to forgive?' . . . He assumes, without argument, an affirmative answer; whence the paradoxical air of his assertions throughout (e.g., forgiveness is the 'madness of the impossible,'). By contrast, I answer this question in the negative" (*Forgiveness*, 90).

5. Jacques Derrida, "To Forgive: The Unforgivable and the Imprescriptible," trans. E. Rottenberg, in *Questioning God*, ed. J. Caputo, M. Dooley, and M. Scanlon (Bloomington: Indiana University Press, 2001), 48.

6. "If there is such a thing."

7. For a discussion of self-forgiveness, see Peter Goldie, *The Mess Inside: Narrative, Emotion, and the Mind* (Oxford: Oxford University Press, 2012), 98–117.

8. Karen Pagani, "Quotable Arendt: Toward a Properly Arendtian Account of Forgiveness," *New German Critique* 43, no. 1 (2016): 141; emphasis in original.

9. Pagani, "Quotable Arendt," 142.

10. As noted in Paul Ricoeur in *Memory, History, Forgetting*, trans. K. Blamey and D. Pellauer (Chicago: University of Chicago Press, 2004), 486.

11. For a cursory sketch of this "unlearning" of Christian forgiveness in Arendt's writings, see Marie Luise Knott, *Unlearning with Hannah Arendt*, trans. D. Dollenmayer (London: Granta, 2011), 63.

12. As Pagani notes, "Arendt's account of action bestows a certain urgency on any inquiry into the meaning of forgiveness in secular ethics that, to my knowledge, had yet to be so forcefully articulated in modern times prior to Arendt's contribution" ("Quotable Arendt," 145).

13. As noted in Margaret Canovan, *Hannah Arendt: A Reinterpretation of Her Political Thought* (Cambridge: Cambridge University Press, 1992), 111.

14. Elisabeth Young-Bruehl, "Hannah Arendt on Forgiveness," in *Considering Forgiveness*, ed. A. Wagner and C. Kuoni (New York: Vera List Center for Art and Politics, 2009), 53.

15. Canovan, *Hannah Arendt*, 101. For a similar view, see Roger Berkovitz, "Reconciling Oneself to the Impossibility of Reconciliation: Judgment and Worldliness in Hannah Arendt's Politics," in *Artifacts of Thinking: Reading Arendt's Denktagebuch*, ed. R. Berkowitz and I. Storey, 9–26 (New York: Fordham Uni-

versity Press), and Maguerite La Caze, "Promising and Forgiveness," in *Hannah Arendt: Key Concepts*, ed. P. Hayden, 209–21 (London: Acumen Publishing, 2014).

16. Canovan, *Hannah Arendt*, 102.

17. For phenomenological readings of Arendt, see Sophie Loidolt, *Phenomenology of Plurality: Hannah Arendt on Political Intersubjectivity* (London: Routledge, 2017), and Marieke Borren, *Amor Mundi: Hannah Arendt's Political Phenomenology of World* (Amsterdam: F & N Eigen Beheer, 2010).

18. Søren Kierkegaard, *The Present Age: On the Death of Rebellion*, trans. A. Dru (New York: HarperPerennial, 1962), 50.

19. For a reading of Arendt's "weak messianism" in *The Human Condition* within a tradition of Jewish messianic thought that does not, however, "concern itself with the restoration of the Davidic kingdom," present "any images of utopian peace," or "seek to universalize the messianic promise by converting it into some form of revolutionary socialism," see Susannah Young-ah Gottlieb, *Regions of Sorrow: Anxiety and Messianism in Hannah Arendt and W. H. Auden* (Stanford, Calif.: Stanford University Press, 2003), 139.

20. Hannah Arendt, *The Human Condition* (Chicago: University of Chicago Press, 1998), 236.

21. Arendt, *The Human Condition*, 236.

22. Hannah Arendt, *Denktagebuch: Erster Band, 1950–1973* (Munich: Piper, 2016), 417 ("Seen from the 'vita contemplativa,' all forms of non-thinking activity become essentially identical, because all of them appear to be for the sake of something").

23. Arendt, *Denktagebuch*, 496 ("in *praxis* there is neither *telos* nor Idea").

24. As Emerson observes, "I know that the world I converse with in the city and in the farms is not the world *I think*. I observe that difference, and shall observe it. One day I shall know the value and law of this discrepance" ("Experience," in *The Essential Writings of Ralph Waldo Emerson*, ed. B. Atkinson [New York: Modern Library, 2000], 326; emphasis in original).

25. Arendt, *The Human Condition*, 236.

26. Arendt, *The Human Condition*, 237.

27. For the importance of Arendt's analysis of totalitarianism for this insight, see Canovan, *Hannah Arendt*, 113: "Whereas totalitarianism is a realm of fiction and illusion, a politically free public sphere in which everything can appear and be discussed is necessary for the disclosure of reality." See also Seyla Benhabib, "Hannah Arendt and the Redemptive Power of Narrative," *Social Research* 57, no. 1 (1990): 175: "This totally fabricated universe reflects the ideological impulse of totalitarian regimes to create a universe of meaning which is wholly self-consistent and also curiously devoid of reality and immune to proof by it."

28. Hannah Arendt, *The Life of the Mind* (New York: Harcourt, 1978), 19.

29. Arendt, *Life of the Mind*, 20.

30. Arendt, *Life of the Mind*, 29; emphasis in original.

31. Arendt, *Life of the Mind*, 26.

32. Arendt, *Life of the Mind*, 46.

33. For this difference with Heidegger, see Canovan, *Hannah Arendt*, 112.

34. Arendt, *Life of the Mind*, 15; emphasis in original.

35. In Kantian terms, reason (*Vernunft*) attests to meaning in view of an Idea, whereas understanding (*Vernunft*), or "cognition"/"intellect," judges what is through the synthetic unison of concepts and intuitions.

36. Arendt, *Life of the Mind*, 176. As she continues, "To a certain extent, this is what Nietzsche did." See also Hannah Arendt, "On Humanity in Dark Times: Thoughts about Lessing," in *Men in Dark Times*, 3–32 (New York: Harvest Books, 1970).

37. Arendt, *Life of the Mind*, 185.

38. Arendt, *Life of the Mind*, 191.

39. For this emphasis on narrative for Arendt's conception of human life, see Julia Kristeva, *Hannah Arendt: Life Is a Narrative*, trans. F. Collins (Toronto: University of Toronto Press, 2001).

40. Arendt, *Men in Dark Times*, 24–25.

41. Arendt, *Denktagebuch*, 470.

42. On this theme of the afterlife, see Nicolas de Warren, "Souls of the Departed: Toward a Phenomenology of the After-Life," *Metodo* 5, no. 1 (2017): 205–37.

43. Arendt, *The Human Condition*, 97.

44. Arendt, *The Human Condition*, 324.

45. As Arendt writes in *The Life of the Mind*, "The very capacity for beginning is rooted in *natality*, and by no means in creativity, not in a gift but in the fact that human beings, new men, again and again appear in the world by virtue of birth" (217; emphasis in original). Forgiveness: that the same person can appear again and again by virtue of rebirth. The person who betrayed me is dead to me; in forgiveness, I give that person new life and standing once again as friend and stranger.

46. Arendt, *Denktagebuch*, 3 ("The wrong that one has done is the burden on the shoulders, something which one bears, because one has laden it upon oneself").

47. Joseph Butler, *Fifteen Sermons and Other Writings on Ethics* (Oxford: Oxford University Press, 2017), sermons 8 and 9.

48. See Peter Strawson, "Freedom and Resentment," *Proceedings of the British Academy*, 48 (1962): 1–25. Strawson defines *ressentiment* as a reactive attitude toward injury or indifference. As Stephen Darwall defines moral resentment, "It is, then, a response that helps constitute our sense of ourselves as having certain rights, our sense of others as possessing particular responsibilities, and our sense of a moral community that is premised on a recognition of equality" (*The Second-Person Standpoint: Morality, Respect, and Accountability* [Cambridge, Mass.: Harvard University Press, 2006], 17). See also Adam Smith, *The Theory of Sentiments* (Carmel, Ind.: Liberty Fund, 1985), and Charles Griswold, *Adam Smith and the Virtues of Enlightenment* (Cambridge: Cambridge University Press, 1999).

49. See Nicolas de Warren, "The Forgiveness of Time and Consciousness," in *The Oxford Handbook of Contemporary Phenomenology*, ed. D. Zahavi, 502–24 (Oxford: Oxford University Press, 2012).

50. As argued in Jeffrey Murphy, *Getting Even: Forgiveness and Its Limits* (New York: Oxford University Press, 2003), 16. On different roles and notions of anger

in contrast to the generosity of forgiveness, see Martha Nussbaum, *Anger and Forgiveness* (Oxford: Oxford University Press, 2018).

51. Letter to W. H. Auden, February 14, 1960, https://memory.loc.gov/mss/mharendt_pub/02/020030/0001d.jpg.

52. In this Arendtian sense, Griswold speaks of the "synchronization of narratives" in the work of forgiveness. Ashraf Rushdy likewise observes that "a crucially important reason that the *account* is so important in the dynamic of forgiveness is that the whole exchange between forgiver and forgiven is fraught with the possibility of misunderstanding" (*After Injury: A Historical Anatomy of Forgiveness, Resentment, and Apology* [New York: Oxford University Press, 2018], 92; emphasis in original).

53. For the notion "place forging" as well as for an elaboration of Arendtian forgiveness (and promising) as a political ethos, see Melissa Orlie, *Living Ethically, Acting Politically* (Ithaca, N.Y.: Cornell University Press, 1997), chapter 7.

54. *Jane Eyre* (chapter 27):

"Well, Jane! not a word of reproach? Nothing bitter—nothing poignant? Nothing to cut a feeling or sting a passion? You sit quietly where I have placed you, and regard me with a weary, passive look."

"Jane, I never meant to wound you thus. If the man who had but one little ewe lamb that was dear to him as a daughter, that ate of his bread and drank of his cup, and lay in his bosom, had by some mistake slaughtered it at the shambles, he would not have rued his bloody blunder more than I now rue mine. Will you ever forgive me?"

"Reader, I forgave him at the moment and on the spot. There was such deep remorse in his eye, such true pity in his tone, such manly energy in his manner; and besides, there was such unchanged love in his whole look and mien—I forgave him all: yet not in words, not outwardly; only at my heart's core."

55. As Christopher Allers remarks, "Forgiveness does not make the offender innocent; it makes the offender forgiven" ("Undoing What Has Been Done: Arendt and Levinas on Forgiveness," in *Forgiveness in Perspective*, ed. C. Allers and M. Smit [Amsterdam: Rodopi, 2010], 28).

56. John Milbank, *Being Reconciled: Ontology and Pardon* (London: Routledge, 2003), 187.

57. As Jean Hampton also argues in chapter 2 of *Forgiveness and Mercy* (Cambridge: Cambridge University Press, 1988), as well as Nicholas Wolterstorff: "I suggest that forgiveness—overcoming one's anger at the doer while continuing to condemn the deed—is possible only if one believes that there was then, or that there is now, a space, a distance, between the doer and the deed" ("Jesus and Forgiveness," in: *Jesus and Philosophy*, ed. P. Moser, 194–214 [Cambridge: Cambridge University Press, 2009], 205).

58. Arendt, *The Human Condition*, 241.

59. Hannah Arendt, *The Origins of Totalitarianism* (New York: Harcourt, Brace, Jovanovich, 1973), 459.

60. Arendt, *The Human Condition*, 242. As Arendt writes in her letter to Auden of February 14, 1960, "You talk about charity as though it were love, and it is true that love will forgive everything because of its utter commitment to the beloved person."

61. F. LeRon Shults and Steven J. Sandage, *The Faces of Forgiveness: Searching for Wholeness and Salvation* (Grand Rapids, Mich.: Baker Academic, 2003), 211.

62. Although it was Jesus of Nazareth, as Arendt claims (crucially, she does not write "Jesus Christ"), who "discovered the role of forgiveness in the realm of human affairs," this world-historical event nonetheless remains essentially *secular* in its enduring significance, despite its original "religious context" and "religious language" of discovery (*The Human Condition*, 238). For an insightful critique of Arendt's claim, see Nicholas Wolterstorff, "Jesus and Forgiveness," in *Jesus and Philosophy*, ed. P. Moser, 194–214 (Cambridge: Cambridge University Press, 2009). For a defense of Arendt's claim, see Rushdy, *After Injury*, 44: "Arendt was right" in her judgment that interpersonal forgiveness was inaugurated with Jesus, whose sayings in the New Testament became eclipsed by a Pauline conception of forgiveness. For Jesus, "human forgiveness is a condition of God's forgiveness," whereas for Paul, "human forgiveness imitates God's forgiveness."

63. In Bishop Butler's terms.

64. For this insight, see Pagani, "Quotable Arendt."

65. As Arendt remarks, "Forgiveness is the only reaction that acts in an unexpected way and thus retains, through being a reaction, something of the original character of action" (*The Human Condition*, 241).

66. As Pagani puts it, "Quotable Arendt," 166.

67. Arendt, *Life of the Mind*, 95.

68. This meaning of "impossibility" thus contrasts, on the one hand, with what Arendt herself calls the unforgivable—namely, a wrongdoing that exceeds the human capacity for forgiveness and commensurate punishment—and, on the other, with Derrida's conception, which he articulates as "when an impossible something happens or becomes possible *as* impossible" ("On Forgiveness: A Roundtable Discussion with Jacques Derrida," in: *Questioning God*, ed. J. Caputo, M. Dooley, and M. Scanlon [Bloomington: Indiana University Press, 2001], 53).

69. Paul Ricoeur observes an asymmetry between forgiving and promising: while there exists institutional forms of promising (and trusting), there are no institutional forms of forgiveness, and hence, in this view, no genuinely political institution of forgiveness (*Memory, History, Forgetting*, 459).

70. As Allers remarks ("Undoing," 25).

71. Arendt, *The Human Condition*, 245–46.

72. As argued by Alexander Hirsch, "The Promise of the Unforgiven: Violence, Power and Paradox in Arendt," *Philosophy and Social Criticism* 28, no. 1 (2012): 45–61.

73. Hirsch, "Promise of the Unforgiven," 57.

74. See Pagani, "Quotable Arendt," 144, 147: "Without respect, forgiveness is impossible; without forgiveness, respect cannot be resuscitated." "Is it not thus necessary to resuscitate genuine respect as a real and reliable possibility prior to

reinserting self-revelatory action . . . but respect and any variety of forgiveness garnered on behalf of such respect is not possible unless self-disclosure has already been achieved through action."

75. Arendt, *The Human Condition*, 240. This moment of recognition implies continued trust, that a basic fabric of human relations has not been destroyed; trust and recognition in the trustworthiness of the person who asks forgiveness; and sincerity in their remorse. Trust in the person must have survived the wrongdoing, and endured, despite my indignation and resentment and anger at the other.

76. As noted by Gottlieb, *Regions of Sorrow*, 156, "Only if one trusts others to relieve one of one's trespasses can anyone—oneself or others—be entrusted ever again with the power to act. A trust that entrusts is, therefore, the absolute condition of life 'going on.'"

77. Once bitten, twice shy: even a cautious attitude toward the forgiven person does not abrogate my availability to forgiveness, for however wary I might be, I cannot, in Arendt's account, promise never to be forgiven again once I have forgiven, or once I have been wronged again after having once forgiven.

78. Arendt, *Denktagebuch*, 470.

79. This quote is not found, however, in the Gospels but in Isaiah 9:6. For this *lapsus* on Arendt's part, see Gottlieb, *Regions of Sorrow*, 137.

Chapter 3

A few paragraphs of this chapter originally appeared in "The Forgiveness of Time and Consciousness," in *The Oxford Handbook of Contemporary Phenomenology*, ed. Dan Zahavi (Oxford: Oxford University Press, 2012). Reproduced with permission of the Licensor through PLSclear.

1. Simon Wiesenthal, *The Sunflower*, trans. H. A. Pichler (New York: Schocken Books, 1998), 9.

2. According to Hella Pick, "Christians believe in the resurrection, but for a Jew, the grave is his last and also his perpetual home. That is why Wiesenthal always stresses that, for a Jew, the significance of his sunflower image is so important" (*Simon Wiesenthal: A Life in Search of Justice* [Boston: Northeastern University Press, 1996], 78).

3. Sigmund Freud, "The Uncanny," in *The Standard Edition of the Complete Psychological Works of Sigmund Freud: Volume 17* (London: Hogarth Press, 1975), 219–56.

4. According to *Encyclopedia Britannica*, "These flies commonly infest carrion or excrement."

5. Wiesenthal, *The Sunflower*, 37.

6. This kind of brutal scene of killing in Karl's story is vividly portrayed in all its horror in the masterpiece of a film Elem Klimov's *Come and See* (1985)—its title taken from the Apocalypse of John: "And when he had opened the fourth seal, I heard the voice of the fourth beast say, Come and see! And I looked, and behold a pale horse: and his name that sat on him was Death, and Hell followed

with him. And power was given unto them over the fourth part of the earth, to kill with sword, and with hunger, and with death, and with the beasts of the earth."

7. Wiesenthal, *The Sunflower*, 55.

8. Wiesenthal, *The Sunflower*, 66.

9. Wiesenthal, *The Sunflower*, 67.

10. Wiesenthal, *The Sunflower*, 68.

11. See Peter Banki, *The Forgiveness to Come: The Holocaust and the Hyper-Ethical* (New York: Fordham University Press, 2018), 44: "In a prophetic manner, he [Wiesenthal] announces *the survival of the question*, which he gambles will not be resolved by future generations . . . Not as the agency of the world or of history, but as a painful and disturbing question, an open wound, 'forgiveness' will—Simon Wiesenthal affirms—survive not only the war but also the trials and testimonies of the war's aftermath" (emphasis in original).

12. Wiesenthal, *The Sunflower*, 82. For the Hebrew name "Simon" or "Shimon" and reference to Genesis, see Banki, *The Forgiveness to Come*, 48. As Ulrich Baer insightfully comments, "Even the most humble and commendable discussions of atonement, guilt, and forgiveness—whether they concern spiritual atonement, material reparations, or restitution in general—are necessarily haunted and threatened by the unstated presumption that the other side is capable of participating and listening" ("The Hubris of Humility: Günther Grass, Peter Schneider, and German Guilt after 1989," *Germanic Review* 80 [Winter 2005]: 50). This "presumption" in the case of Wiesenthal is not a presumption but a pity, and hence there is no presumption of hubris in listening; there is no presumption here of the possibility of forgiveness, even as he makes himself available, without presumption, to the possibility or impossibility of forgiveness. In such listening, he avails himself in a manner not unforgiving even as nothing is, or can, be forgiven.

13. Banki likewise stresses the forgiveness inherent to listening and testimony in Wiesenthal's narrative. As he writes, "He [Wiesenthal] will have planted a sunflower for this repentant Nazi in the form of a testimony, to remember him and connect him with the living—even to remember a part of his name (Karl). Perhaps this is forgiveness, if forgiveness means a new beginning without a definitive end or closure of the past. One can say that listening is the 'yes,' or more precisely, the 'yes, perhaps' of forgiving" (*The Forgiveness to Come*, 48). On the contrary, as argued above, listening, as neither condescension nor magnanimity, is neither already "the yes" or "yes, perhaps" of forgiving but the already forgiving availability to forgiveness as either yes, perhaps, or no, perhaps.

14. Wiesenthal, *The Sunflower*, 106.

15. For a discussion of these responses, see John K. Roth, "Who Needs Forgiveness?," in *Anti-Semitism: The Generic Hatred; Essays in Honor of Simon Wiesenthal*, ed. M. Fineberg, 165–76 (London: Vallentine Mitchell, 2007).

16. Wiesenthal, *The Sunflower*, 106.

17. Améry praises instead Wiesenthal's tireless effort to bring Nazi criminals to legal justice.

18. Wiesenthal, *The Sunflower*, 106.

19. The English translation inexplicably and misleadingly has Améry's title

as "Resentiments," thus losing the significant specificity of the French term *ressentiments*; Jean Améry, *At the Mind's Limits*, trans. S. Rosenfeld and S. Rosenfeld (Bloomington: Indiana University Press, 2009), 64. I have also corrected the poor translation ("retrospective grudge") of Améry's *reactive Groll.*

20. Améry, *At the Mind's Limits*, 63.

21. Adam Smith speaks of the "wild beast" of unreasonable and unyielding resentment.

22. However, as Griswold observes, "Butler is regularly misquoted as defining forgiveness as the 'forswearing of resentment.' Butler actually claims that forgiveness is the forswearing of *revenge*" (*Forgiveness: A Philosophical Exploration* [Cambridge: Cambridge University Press, 2007], 20).

23. For an extended analysis, see Nicolas de Warren, "The Forgiveness of Time and Consciousness," chapter 24 in *The Oxford Handbook of Contemporary Phenomenology*, ed. D. Zahavi (Oxford: Oxford University Press, 2012).

24. As Peter Sloterdijk notes, "At the beginning of the first sentence of the European tradition, in the first verse of the *Iliad*, the word 'rage' occurs" (*Rage and Time*, trans. M. Wenning [New York: Columbia University Press, 2010], 1).

25. As Rushdy astutely observes, "We can perhaps say that the sites for representing resentment fall into two categories—places of isolation and places of judgment. Dostoevsky chose the former, the underground, to suggest how an actual subterranean place can help augment the depiction of subterranean feelings. Likewise, Sophocles chose an island . . . the other place is the courtroom" (*After Injury: A Historical Anatomy of Forgiveness, Resentment, and Apology* [New York: Oxford University Press, 2018], 121). A third site for the representation of resentment can be seen with its transfiguration into an outward expansion of *rage* into and against the world.

26. The latter form, as brilliantly portrayed in Raduan Nassar's *A Cup of Rage.*

27. As Vladimir Jankélévitch observes, "The person who forgives . . . does not profit from the advantageous position that his innocence confers upon him, he does not keep from himself this privilege of alone being infallible, impeccable and irreproachable, and he renounces every monopoly that he may have upon this position, he sacrifices therefore a very brief and precarious superiority which perhaps is due to chance" (*Forgiveness*, trans. A. Kelley [Chicago: University of Chicago Press, 2005], 162).

28. Heinrich von Kleist, *Selected Prose of Heinrich von Kleist*, trans. P. Wortsman (New York: Archipelago Books, 2010), 143.

29. Kleist, *Selected Prose*, 151.

30. Kleist, *Selected Prose*, 168.

31. Kleist, *Selected Prose*, 181.

32. Améry's harsher tone with respect to Primo Levi: "I received from quite a different quarter a document in which he [Primo Levi] spoke of my book *At the Mind's Limits* without any understanding at all, and showed himself disposed to drown everything in ontological jargon. Unlike Levi, I am not a man to forgive and have no sympathy for the gentlemen who belonged to the 'management staff' of IG Auschwitz" (Irène Heidelberger-Leonard, *The Philosopher of Auschwitz:*

Jean Améry and Living with the Holocaust [London: I. B. Taurus, 2010], 70). As he writes in his essay "Ressentiments": "I can't keep up with the lofty ethical flights that a man like the French publicist André Neher propounds to us victims. We victims of persecution, the high-soaring man says, ought to internalize our past suffering and bear it in emotional asceticism, as our torturers should do with their guilt" (*At the Mind's Limits*, 69).

33. For an analysis of what is distinctive of *ressentiment* in Améry with regard to the philosophical tradition, see Thomas Brudholm, *Resentment's Virtue: Jean Améry and the Refusal to Forgive* (Philadelphia: Temple University Press, 2009). As Dania Hückmann notes, "By differentiating his position from both his notion of the Allies' *Realpolitik* and from that of *ius talionis*, Améry has in a sense already moved past the terminology of guilt and redemption, and even beyond that of justice and revenge" ("Beyond Law and Justice: Revenge in Jean Améry," *Germanic Review* 89 [2014]: 235).

34. Améry, *At the Mind's Limits*, 68. As W. G. Sebald remarks, "The issue, then, is not to resolve but to reveal the conflict. The spur of resentment which Améry conveys to us in his polemic demands recognition of the *right* to resentment, entailing no less than a programmatic attempt to sensitize the consciousness of a people 'already rehabilitated by time'" (*On the Natural History of Destruction*, trans. A. Bell [New York: Modern Library, 2004], 158).

35. In his novel *Lefeu oder der Abbruch* (*Lefeu or the Cancellation*), (Stuttgart: Klett-Cotta, 1974), Améry explored the theme of rage and revenge in its self-devouring conflagration.

Chapter 4

The core of this chapter appeared as "Torture and Trust in the World," *Phänomenologische Forschungen* (2015): 83–99.

1. http://www.breendonk.be/en/index.asp?ID=Virtual. Alain Resnais's *Night and Fog* includes a shot of Fort Breendonk's distinctive watchtower.

2. W. G. Sebald, *Austerlitz*, trans. A. Bell (New York: Modern Library, 2002), 20.

3. See Max Pensky, "Three Kinds of Ruin: Heidegger, Benjamin, Sebald," *Poligrafi* 16, no. 61/62 (2011): 65–89.

4. In Will Stone's elegant phrase, "This uniquely preserved room, its funereal stillness somehow mocking the existence of those rowdy Bavarian cellars devoured by Hitler's dark insistence, stands in triumphant indiscretion only a stone's throw from the torture chamber" ("At Risk of Interment: WG Sebald in Terezin and Breendonk," https://www.closeupfilmcentre.com/vertigo_magazine/volume-4-issue-3-summer-2009/at-risk-of-interment-wg-sebald-in-terezin-and-breendonk/).

5. Sebald, *Austerlitz*, 25.

6. Améry, *At the Mind's Limits*, 21.

7. For the notion of *lieux de mémoire*, see Pierre Nora, ed., *Realms of Memory: Rethinking the French Past* (Chicago: University of Chicago Press, 1998).

8. "There it happened to me: torture," or, alternatively, "There it happened to me: the ordeal of torture."

9. "Die Tortur ist das fürchterlichste Ereignis, das ein Mensch in sich bewahren kann."

10. Jean Améry, *On Aging: Revolt and Resignation,* trans. J. Barrow (Bloomington: Indiana University Press, 1994). As Irène Heidelberger-Leonard observes, "Strictly speaking, Améry's treatise on aging is a pendant to this essay on torture, this time outside the historical context" (*The Philosopher of Auschwitz: Jean Améry and Living with the Holocaust,* trans. A. Bell [London: I. B. Tauris, 2010], 174).

11. "So it was written and so it will occur."

12. Améry, *At the Mind's Limits,* 25.

13. Jean-Paul Sartre, *Being and Nothingness,* trans. S. Richmond (London: Routledge, 2018), 531; emphasis in original.

14. Sartre, *Being and Nothingness,* 681; emphasis in original.

15. For an illuminating discussion, see John Ireland, "Sartre and Scarry: Bodies and Phantom Pain," *Revue internationale de philosophie,* no. 231 (January 2005): 86. According to Simone de Beauvoir, Sartre was obsessed with the question "How would I hold up under torture?" As he writes in *What Is Literature?* "'Suppose I were tortured, what would I do?' And this question alone carried us to the very frontiers of ourselves and the human. We oscillated between the no-man's-land where mankind denies itself and the barren desert from which it surges and creates itself" (180–81). It is a question that he explores in *Men without Shadows* (*Mort sans sepulture*) but also, as a "photographic negative" of the former, in *No Exit* (Ireland, "Sartre and Scarry," 99).

16. My reading here of Sartre's story differs from Elaine Scarry, *The Body in Pain* (Oxford: Oxford University Press, 1987), 31–32.

17. Denis Hollier, "I've Done My Act: An Exercise in Gravity," *Representations,* no. 4 (1983): 88–100. See also Ireland, "Sartre and Scarry," 101.

18. As Sartre imagines in *What Is Literature?* "Whatever the sufferings that have been endured, it is the victim who decides, as a last resort, what the moment is when they are unbearable and when he must talk . . . But, on the other hand, most of the résistants, though beaten, burned, blinded and broken, did not speak. They broke the circle of Evil and reaffirmed the human—for themselves, for us and for their very torturers" (*"What Is Literature?" and Other Essays,* trans. B. Frechtman [Cambridge, Mass.: Harvard University Press, 1988], 180).

19. Améry raises the question of who and how a person has the strength for moral and physical resistance. The capacity of resistance, he argues, is entirely unpredictable and variable. No disposition or training prepares one for the ordeal of torture; it is not merely an issue of physical constitution but also a matter of faith and mental resoluteness (*At the Mind's Limits,* 69).

20. For the phenomenon of "ordinary faces" committing extraordinary atrocities during the Third Reich, see the classic study by Christopher Browning, *Ordinary Men: Reserve Police Battalion 101 and the Final Solution in Poland* (New York: Harper Perennial, 1998). For a discussion of the normalization of violence in the form of policing, see Nicolas de Warren, "From Protection to Predation: Policing as the Pursuit of War by Other Means in the Third Reich," in *The Ethics*

of Policing, ed. E. Mendieta and B. Jones (New York: New York University Press, forthcoming 2021).

21. As Améry remarks, "For there is no 'banality of evil,' and Hannah Arendt, who wrote about it in her Eichmann book, knew the enemy of mankind only from hearsay, saw him only through the glass cage" (*At the Mind's Limits,* 25).

22. Améry, *At the Mind's Limits,* 27.

23. See Ireland, "Sartre and Scarry." As J. M. Coetzee notes, "The fact that the torture room is a site of extreme human experience, accessible to no one save the participants, is a second reason why the novelist in particular should be fascinated by it" ("Into the Dark Chamber: The Novelist and South Africa," *New York Times,* January 12, 1986). Sartre, however, offers a cautionary lesson of how easy it is to fall into the trap of the torture chamber's "dark fascination" for a writer's imagination.

24. For the comparison between torture and rape, suggested by Améry himself, see Susan Brison, *Aftermath: Violence and the Remaking of a Self* (Princeton, N.J.: Princeton University Press, 2002), 46. See also the extended discussion in Jay Bernstein, *Torture and Dignity* (Chicago: University of Chicago Press, 2015), 154–61, as well as Louise du Toit, *A Philosophical Investigation of Rape: The Making and Unmaking of the Feminine Self* (London: Routledge, 2009). For an examination of rape in the employment of torture and the challenges of therapy and testimony, see Pierre Duterte, *Terres inhumaines: Un médecin face à la torture* (Paris: JC Lattès, 2007).

25. As Améry writes in his essay "Ressentiments," "Sometimes it happens that in the summer I travel through a thriving land. It is hardly necessary to tell of the model cleanliness of its large cities, of its idyllic towns and villages, to point out the quality of the goods to be bought there, the unfailing perfection of its handicrafts, or the impressive combination of cosmopolitan modernity and wistful historical consciousness that is evidenced everywhere . . . I feel uncomfortable in this peaceful, lovely land, inhabited by hardworking, efficient, and modern people" (*At the Mind's Limits,* 63).

26. Françoise Sironi, *Bourreaux et victimes: Psychologie de la torture* (Paris: Odile Jacob, 1999), 57–64. The weaponization of words in torture has long been recognized by clinical psychologists. As Scarry insightfully puts it, "The prisoner's body . . . is, like the prisoner's voice, made a weapon against him, made to betray him on behalf of the enemy, made to be the enemy" (*The Body in Pain,* 48).

27. Sironi, *Bourreaux et victimes,* 68.

28. As Scarry writes, "In confession, one betrays oneself and all those aspects of the world—friend, family, country, cause—that the self is made up of" (*The Body in Pain,* 29). The sources of human creativity, as Scarry argues, become destroyed in the inventiveness of torture's infliction of linguistic and physical suffering. For Améry, *writing* becomes the desperate means to survive in a world in which it has become impossible to breathe, and hence to speak. Drowning becomes salvaged, if at all, through, in Blanchot's terms, the writing of the disaster, but such writing does not guard against despair (contrary to Albert Camus's pronouncement that a "literature of despair is a contradiction in terms") but, on the contrary, communicates it unforgivingly. As Simone Weil observes, "As

for those who have been struck the kind of blow which leaves the victim writhing on the ground like a half-crushed worm, they have no words to describe what is happening to them . . . compassion for the afflicted is an impossibility. When it is really found, it is a more astounding miracle than walking on water, healing the sick, or even raising the dead" (*Waiting for God*, trans. E. Craufurd [London: Routledge, 2010], 67). For Camus's celebrated statement, see *Lyrical and Critical Essays*, trans. E. Kennedy (New York: Vintage, 1970), 160; see also the concluding discussion in this chapter.

29. Scarry, *The Body in Pain*, 47.

30. See Gaston Bachelard, *The Poetics of Space*, trans. M. Jolas (Boston: Beacon Press, 1964). As Scarry notes, "in normal contexts, the room, the simplest form of shelter, expresses the most benign potential of human life" (*The Body in Pain*, 38).

31. For multiple references to the metaphor of skin in contemporary architectural theory, see Claudia Benthien, *Skin: On the Cultural Border Between Self and the World*, trans. T. Dunlap (New York: Columbia University Press, 2002), 24.

32. This brutalization of the world in the exposure to arbitrariness of violence and absolute power, as essential for the evisceration of trust in the world, played an equally critical role in the organization of Nazi concentration camps; see Wolfgang Sofsky, *The Order of Terror: The Concentration Camp*, trans. W. Templer (Princeton, N.J.: Princeton University Press, 1997), 130.

33. Améry, *At the Mind's Limits*, 58.

34. In the words of Mansoor Adayfi, a victim of American torture at Guantánamo Bay Naval Base, "I am still trying to escape" ("Did We Survive Torture?," in *Witnessing Torture: Perspectives of Torture Survivors and Human Rights Workers*, ed. A. Moore and E. Swanson [London: Palgrave Macmillan, 2018], 231.

35. Améry, *At the Mind's Limits*, 114; emphasis in original ("The experience of persecution was, in the final analysis, that of extreme loneliness"). On the connection between the traumatic effect of the disavowal of a traumatic event and sense of isolation of the suffering individual, see Sándor Ferenczi, "Confusion of the Tongues Between the Adults and the Child—(*The Language of Tenderness and of Passion*)," *International Journal of Psychoanalysis* 30, no. 4 (1949): 225–30. For an elaboration of this insight taken directly from Améry, see Jill Stauffer, *Ethical Loneliness: The Injustice of Not Being Heard* (New York: Columbia University Press, 2015). For the sufferer's isolation in pain, see also Scarry, *The Body in Pain*, 161.

36. As Améry writes, "Whoever might come to help, a wife, a mother, a brother or a friend, here they cannot enter"—and likewise: the appeal for assistance cannot find them and make contact: cannot be heard, and this means: no witnesses. It is, of course, important that Améry evokes here the figures of "wife, mother, brother, and friend," or, in other words, those figures whose relationship are paradigmatically—and with the mother, for many, like Erikson, foundationally—forged in trust. What becomes frightfully real with this first blow is the "expectation of assistance," which is not an expectation that is formed, or a social norm, but more a "material a priori" for relationships and trust in the

world: that I am entrusted to others, and that others stand as both my witness and keeper in times of need and suffering (*At the Mind's Limits*, 113).

37. Contrary to Sartre (but also contrary to Bernstein, *Torture and Dignity*, 109), Améry does *not* consider torture as a confrontation of master and slave or "la lute à mort de deux consciences."

38. As Vivaldi Jean-Marie justly remarks, "The discussion of Améry's refusal to forgive, in existing literature, is not sensitive to the sensory logic of the tortured self. Améry's refusal to forgive is a by-product of the sensory logic of the tortured self; it is the unavoidable outcome of trauma" (*Reflections on Jean Améry: Torture, Resentment, and Homelessness as the Mind's Limits* [Cham, CH: Palgrave Macmillan, 2018], 53). Jean-Marie, however, draws the incorrect consequence that "the inability to forgive" here "eventually kindles the urge for revenge." As he wrongly claims, "The sensory logic of torture culminates in revenge instead of torture" (53).

39. Améry, *At the Mind's Limits*, 56.

40. Elias Canetti, *Crowds and Power*, trans. C. Stewart (New York: Farrar, Straus and Giroux, 1962).

41. In *Literature or Life*, Jorge Semprún recounts his final moments in the presence of Maurice Halbwachs's death in Buchenwald: "I placed a hand (lightly, gently) on the emaciated shoulder of Maurice Halbwachs." Seized with panic at the impossibility of response in the face of Halbwachs's dying, Semprún becomes aware of the need for prayer but does not recite the Kaddish but spontaneously recalls and recites Baudelaire's poem:

> *Ô Mort, vieux capitaine, il est temps! levons l'ancre!*
> *Ce pays nous ennuie, ô Mort! Appareillons!*
> *Si le ciel et la mer sont noirs comme de l'encre,*
> *Nos coeurs que tu connais sont remplis de rayons!*
> *Verse-nous ton poison pour qu'il nous réconforte!*
> *Nous voulons, tant ce feu nous brûle le cerveau,*
> *Plonger au fond du gouffre, Enfer ou Ciel, qu'importe?*
> *Au fond de l'Inconnu pour trouver du nouveau!*

As he speaks the line *Nos coeurs que tu connais sont remplis de rayons!*, a "delicate tremor" passes over Halbwachs's lips: "Dying, he smiled, gazing at me like a brother" ("Il sourit, mourant, son regard sur moi, fraternel"). In this availability for the Other in the hour of their death, as acutely experienced in Buchenwald, Semprún speaks (implicitly against Heidegger) of *Mit-Sein-zum-Tod* (*Literature or Life*, trans. L. Coverdale [New York: Viking Press, 1997], 18, 23).

42. For these two formulas in historical semantics of skin, see Benthien, *Skin*, 23.

43. Didier Anzieu, *The Skin-Ego*, trans. N. Segal (London: Karnac Books, 2016), 40. Although this idea cannot be developed here, skin is also a critical element in the thinking of Michel Serres ("Nothing is deeper in man than his skin"), for whom skin is not merely a surface or envelope but also an environment in which, or through which, comes into contact ("through the skin, the world

and the body touch, defining their common border"). See *Le cinq sens* (Paris: Hachette, 1998), 97. For a wide-ranging and informative examination of skin in philosophy, science, art, and literature, see Steven Connor, *The Book of Skin* (Ithaca, N.Y.: Cornell University Press, 2004).

44. Anzieu identifies three basic functions of the skin-self: "sack," "sieve," and "screen." Though in later writings, Anzieu expands these functions to nine: support, container, excitation screen, individuation, intersensoriality, medium for sexual excitation, libidinal recharge, inscription of tactile traces, toxic function.

45. Améry, *At the Mind's Limits*, 28.

46. Jorge Ulnik, *Skin in Psychoanalysis* (London: Karnac Books, 2007), 51.

47. Edmund Husserl, *Ideen II* (The Hague: Martinus Nijhoff, 1952), 147.

48. For a comparative phenomenology of skin, see Rudolf Bernet, "Deux interprétations de la vulnérabilité de la peau (Husserl et Levinas)," *Revue philosophique de Louvain* 95, no. 3 (1997): 437–56. Bernet's unfortunate characterization of the skin as "une surface tordue" (a "twisted" or "contorted surface") is glaringly apparent when contrasted with the *tortured* body as genuinely "tordue" in the manner described by Améry: "My own body weight caused luxation; I fell into a void and now hung by my dislocated arms, which had been torn high from behind and were now twisted over my head. Torture, from Latin *torquere*, to twist. What visual instruction in etymology!" (*At the Mind's Limits*, 32). There is, strictly speaking, no "inside" of the skin but only an outside as the inside, since sensitivity of the skin is registered on its surface. Wounding of intimacy of one's sense of self ("its inside") occurs in the touching of the skin, its "outside."

49. Améry, *At the Mind's Limits*, 63 ("His [the victim's] meat realizes itself completely in self-negation").

50. Likewise, as proposed by Marcelo Vinar, "any intentional disposition whatever methods are used that has for its aim the destruction of beliefs and convictions of the victim for the purpose of skinning or stripping [*dépouiller*] the identity constellation that constitutes the victim as person." As quoted by Sironi, who discusses torture as deliberate destruction of psychological and social identity, *Bourreaux et victimes*, 12.

51. On this aspect of complicity for the specificity of torture's moral harm, see David Sussman, "What's Wrong with Torture?," *Philosophy and Public Affairs* 33, no. 1 (Winter 2005): 1–33, and Marcelo Vinar, "The Specificity of Torture as Trauma," *International Journal of Psychoanalysis* 86 (2005): 311–33.

52. Gilles Deleuze, *Francis Bacon: Logique de la sensation* (Paris: Seuil, 2002), 30.

53. "But only in torture does the meatification of the human being become complete: Howling with pain is the human being."

54. For this expression of "ghosting," see Elisabeth Weber, "'Torture Was the Essence of National Socialism': Reading Jean Améry Today," in *Speaking About Torture*, ed. J. Carlson and E. Weber (New York: Fordham University Press, 2012), 91. As Semprún describes his own condition of "survival" after his ordeal at Buchenwald, "I have not escaped death, but passed through it. Rather, it has passed through me. That I have, in a way, lived through it. That I have come back from it the way you return from a voyage that has transformed and—perhaps—

transfigured you . . . I have not really survived death. I have not avoided it. I have not escaped it. I have, instead, crossed through it, from one end to the other. I have wandered along its paths, losing and finding my way in this immense land streaming with absence. All things considered, I am a ghost" (*Literature or Life*, 15).

55. Martin Heidegger, *Sein und Zeit* (Tübingen: Niemeyer, 2001), 238 (*Being and Time*, trans. J. Stambaugh [Albany: State University of New York Press, 1996], 221). Although embodiment is conspicuously absent from *Sein und Zeit*, Heidegger addresses embodiment in the *Zollikon Seminars*, where he speaks of "the bodying forth of the body [*das Leiben des Leibes*]" (*Zollikon Seminars: Protocols–Conversations–Letters*, ed. Medard Boss, trans. F. Mayr and R. Askay [Evanston, Ill.: Northwestern University Press, 2001], 231).

56. Améry, *At the Mind's Limits*, 65.

57. Dumitru Bacu, *The Anti-Humans: Student Re-education in Romanian Prisons* (Stockholm: Logik Förlag, 2016), 9.

58. Jean-François Lyotard, *Le différend* (Paris: Minuit, 1983), 148–49.

59. Benthien, *Skin*, 119

60. As Walter Benjamin writes, "His [Kafka] gestures of terror are given scope by the marvelous *margin* which the catastrophe will not grant us. But his experience was based solely on the tradition to which Kafka surrendered; there was no far-sightedness or 'prophetic vision.' Kafka listened to tradition, and he who listens hard does not see" (*Illuminations: Essays and Reflections*, trans. H. Zohn [New York: Schocken Books, 1968], 143; emphasis in original). For an illuminating historical contextualization, see Walter Müller-Seidel, *Die Deportation des Menschen: Kafkas Erzählung "In der Strafkolonie" im europäischen Kontext* (Stuttgart: Fischer, 1987).

61. Améry, *At the Mind's Limits*, 32.

62. For this insight into the reader's interpellation and the claim of ironic slippage, see Marianne Hirsch, "The First Blow: Torture and Close Reading," *Proceedings of the Modern Language Association* 121, no. 2 (2006): 366. As W. G. Sebald remarks, "Even Améry's description of his torture is in a tone emphasizing the monumental madness of the procedure inflicted on him rather than the emotional aspect of his suffering" (*On the Natural History of Destruction*, trans. A. Bell [New York: Random House, 2003], 151).

63. As Améry observes, the feeling of pain "marks the limit of the capacity of language to communicate" (*At the Mind's Limits*, 33).

64. See Michel de Certeau, "Corps tortures, paroles capturées," in *Michel de Certeau*, ed. Luce Giard, 19–70 (Paris: Centre Georges Pompidou, 1987).

65. Franz Kafka, *The Complete Stories* (New York: Schocken Books, 1983), 165–66.

66. Améry, *At the Mind's Limits*, 61 ("They used torture, but more fervently still, they served torture" or "they served at the mercy of torture").

67. Georg Bataille, *Erotism*, trans. M. Dalwood (San Francisco: City Light Books, 1986), 174.

68. Maurice Blanchot, *Lautréamont and Sade*, trans. S. Kendall and M. Kendall (Stanford, Calif.: Stanford University Press, 2004), 26.

69. Blanchot, *Lautréamont and Sade*, 28.

70. Blanchot, *Lautréamont and Sade*, 37.

71. Marquis de Sade, *Juliette*, trans. A. Wainhouse (New York: Grove Press, 1968), 35.

72. Certeau, "Corps tortures, paroles capturées," 62. See also Michel de Certeau, "The Institution of Rot," in *Heterologies: Discourse on the Other*, trans. B. Massumi, 35–46 (Minneapolis: University of Minnesota Press, 1986): "The goal of torture, in effect, is to produce acceptance of a State discourse, through the confession of putrescence . . . The victim must be the *voice* of the filth, everywhere denied, that everywhere supports the *representation* of the regime's 'omnipotence,' in other words, the 'glorious image' of themselves the regime provides for its adherents through its recognition of them. The victim must therefore assume the position of the subject upon whom the theater of identifying power is performed" (41; emphasis in original). As Améry writes, "The power structure of the SS state towered up before the prisoner monstrously and insuperably, a reality that could not be escaped and that therefore finally seemed *reasonable*. No matter what his thinking may have been on the outside, in this sense he became a Hegelian: in the metallic brilliance of its totality the SS state appeared as a state in which the idea was becoming reality" (*At the Mind's Limits*, 12; emphasis in original).

73. Certeau, "Corps tortures, paroles capturées," 65: "une capacité de faire croire."

74. Hence the distinctiveness of modern state-sanctioned torture: its removal from public visibility and spectacle.

75. William Cavanaugh, *Torture and the Eucharist* (London: Blackwell Publishing, 1998), 56. The liturgical theatricality of torture was nowhere more extreme than with the "re-education" of university students in the Pitești Experiment between 1949 and 1951 in Romania—"the most terrible act of barbarism in the contemporary world," in the words of Aleksandr Solzhenitsyn. See Bacu, *The Anti-Humans*, and Arleen Ionescu, "Witnessing Horrorism: The Pitești Experiment," *Slovo* 32, no. 1 (2019): 53–74.

76. For torture as "perverse liturgy" where the body of the victim becomes the ritual site for the manifestation of state power, see Cavanaugh, *Torture and the Eucharist*, 30.

77. For the originality of Améry's use of *Verfleischlichung*, see Weber, "'Torture Was the Essence.'"

78. Cavanaugh, *Torture and the Eucharist*, 203.

79. Cavanaugh, *Torture and the Eucharist*, 261.

80. Améry, *At the Mind's Limits*, 36.

81. In this regard, Améry's implied understanding of "survivance" stands markedly distinct from the reflections on Celan's *Atemwende* and conception of finitude as "survivance" in Derrida. As Derrida writes, "I shall say that this finitude is *survivance*. Survivance in a sense of survival that is neither life nor death pure and simple, a sense that is not thinkable on the basis of the opposition between life and death" (*The Beast and the Sovereign, Volume II*, trans. G. Bennington [Chicago: University of Chicago Press, 2011], 130; emphasis in original). By contrast,

in Améry the "zombie" condition of "surviving" torture is neither a phantasm nor a primordial ground from which "life and death arise" but rather the fracture of finitude into which the distinction between life and death has fallen, never to be resurrected.

82. Améry, *At the Mind's Limits,* 113 ("But my *ressentiments* are here so that the crime may become a moral reality for the criminal, so that he may be torn into the truth of his atrocity").

83. For an extended comparison, see Régine Waintrater, "Des lumières à l'obscurité . . . : Robert Antelme et Jean Améry, deux itinéraires," *Topiques* 92, no. 3 (2005): 95–110, whose thesis I follow: "J'émettrai l'hypothèse que le monde d'Antelme est un monde où la honte est assumée par le groupe, alors que le monde d'Améry est un monde où l'individu se retrouve seul face à la sienne."

84. Améry, *At the Mind's Limits,* 81. As Améry writes, "Wer der Folter erlag, kann nicht mehr heimisch werden in der Welt . . . die eingestürzte Weltvertrauen wird nicht widergewonnen" (73).

85. W. G. Sebald, *On the Natural History of Destruction,* trans. A. Bell (New York: Random House, 2003), 163.

86. Améry's essay on suicide speaks of "free death" or "dying freely" in contrast to "murdering oneself" or "self-murder." In German, both words, *Freitod* and *Selbstmord,* mean "suicide." See *Hand an sich Legen: Diskurs über den Freitod* (Stuttgart: Klett Cotta, 1976).

87. Cited in Heidelberger-Leonard, *The Philosopher of Auschwitz,* 256.

Chapter 5

1. Martin Buber, *I and Thou,* trans. W. Kaufmann (New York: Simon and Schuster, 1996), 62 ("Alles wirkliche Leben ist Begegnung").

2. In Buber's words, "Those who experience do not participate in the world. For the experience is 'in them' and not between them and the world" (Buber, *I and Thou,* 56).

3. In modified echo of Stanley Cavell's fine formulation, "It [the present-ness of the world] vanishes exactly with the effort to *make* it present" (*Must We Mean What We Say?* [Cambridge: Cambridge University Press, 2002], 323; emphasis in original).

4. "I loved her most, and thought to set my rest / On her kind nursery" (I.1.123–24).

5. *Coleridge: Lectures on Shakespeare (1811–1819),* ed. A. Roberts (Edinburgh: Edinburgh University Press, 2016), 167.

6. "Thou hast her, France; let her be thine, for we / Have no such daughter, nor shall ever see / That face of hers again" (I.1.264–65).

7. For this alternative between to speak and to kill, see Maurice Blanchot, *The Infinite Conversation,* trans. S. Hanson (Minneapolis: University of Minnesota Press, 1993).

8. In Goethe's harsh judgment, "In this scene Lear seems so absurd that we are not able, in what follows, to ascribe to his daughters the entire guilt. We are

sorry for the old man, but we do not feel real pity for him" (Johann Wolfgang von Goethe, "Shakespeare ad Infinitum," in *The Permanent Goethe*, ed. T. Mann [New York: Dial Press, 1953], 585).

9. As S. L. Goldberg remarks, "Anyone who sets out to say what he makes of *King Lear* is soon likely to start wondering at his rashness" (*An Essay on Lear* [Cambridge: Cambridge University Press, 1974], 1).

10. Søren Kierkegaard, *Journals and Papers*, ed. and trans. H. Hong and E. Hong (Bloomington: Indiana University Press, 1970), 2:29.

11. Stanley Cavell, "The Avoidance of Love," in *Must We Mean What We Say?*, 246–321. Insensitive to the sincerity of Lear's demand in its foolishness, A. D. Nuttall speaks of the "uncritical simplicity" of Lear's state of thinking (*Shakespeare the Thinker* [New Haven, Conn.: Yale University Press, 2007], 304). For an engaging examination of shame in *King Lear*, see Alba Montes Sánchez, "Shame, Recognition and Love in Shakespeare's *King Lear*," *Azafea* 16 (2014): 73–93.

12. Roberts, *Coleridge*, 167.

13. G. Wilson Knight, *The Wheel of Fire* (London: Routledge, 1989), 182 ("profoundly comic and profoundly pathetic").

14. Knight, *The Wheel of Fire*, 198.

15. Dan Brayton speaks of a "cartography of dispossession" ("Angling in the Lake of Darkness: Possession, Dispossession, and the Politics of Discovery in *King Lear*," *ELH* 70, no. 2 [2003]: 399–426).

16. For a reading of *King Lear* in the shadow of Beckett, see Jan Kott, "*King Lear* or Endgame," in *Shakespeare Our Contemporary*, trans. B. Taborski (New York: Doubleday, 1966), 105: "The theme of *King Lear* is the decay and the fall of the world."

17. For a comparable view, albeit without this crucial inflection on the volatile vitality of trust for the human condition, see Sam Gilchrist Hall, *Shakespeare's Folly: Philosophy, Humanism, Critical Theory* (London: Routledge, 2017), 155.

18. Edgar represents another figure of availability in his relationship to his father, the Earl of Gloucester.

19. Roberts, *Coleridge*, 167.

20. For this reading, see Paul Kahn, *Law and Love: The Trials of* King Lear (New Haven, Conn.: Yale University Press, 2000), 14.

21. Kierkegaard, *Journals and Papers*, 29. Kierkegaard remarks, however, that such an impious demand is "tolerable in an erotic relationship (when the lover asks the beloved how much she loves him), although," as he observes, "even here it is pandering." One might wonder whether Lear's specific demand to Cordelia betrays a motif of incest and an unconscious (or deliberate?) subversion of her betrothal; see Elizabeth Boyce, "The Trouble of Incest in Shakespeare's Late Plays: *King Lear* and *Pericles*," *Paper Shell Review* (Spring 2015), http://www.english .umd.edu/psr/7193.

22. See Jean-Paul Sartre, *Being and Nothingness*, trans. S. Richmond (London: Routledge, 2018), 109.

23. Joyce Carol Oates, "'Is This the Promised End?' The Tragedy of *King Lear*," *Journal of Aesthetics and Art Criticism* (1974): 19–32; 24.

24. Oates, "'Is This the Promised End?,'" 25.

25. The self-performing contradiction of which is exposed by Cordelia in her cutting observation that her sisters have husbands: "Why have my sisters husbands, if they say / They love you all?" (I.1.99–100). As Stanley Cavell remarks, Goneril's charade of love, and hence truthful speaking, manifests her contempt for human speech as such ("The Interminable Shakespearean Text," in *Philosophy the Day after Tomorrow* [Cambridge, Mass.: Harvard University Press, 2005], 56).

26. Buber, *I and Thou*, 61.

27. Buber, *I And Thou*, 83 ("Du kannst ohne sie nicht im Leben beharren, ihre Zuverlässigkeit erhält dich, aber stürbest du in sie hinein, so wärst du im Nichts begraben").

28. "Nur die Teilnahme am Sein der seienden Wesen erschliesst den Sinn im Grunde des eigenen Seins."

29. Buber, *I and Thou*, 68. Lear's confusion expresses itself in his intention to retain a retinue of men after his abdication of power and title.

30. For this reading of Buber's dialogical thinking in contrast to (and as critique of) transcendental philosophy as well as Heideggerian fundamental ontology, see Michael Theunissen, *Der Andere: Studien zur Sozialontologie der Gegenwart* (Berlin: Walter de Gruyter, 1965). For an insightful response to Theunissen's critique of the philosophy of dialogue, which he casts as effective in its oppositional character against transcendental yet falling short in grasping "the complete reality of the Thou" (496), see Joel Backström, *The Fear of Openness: An Essay on Friendship and the Roots of Morality* (Helsinki: Åbo Akademi University Press, 2007), 504. For an extended response to Theunissen from a Husserlian framework, see Bernhard Waldenfels, *Das Zwischenreich des Dialogs: Sozialphilosophische Untersuchungen in Anschluss an Edmund Husserl* (The Hague: Martinus Nijhoff, 1971).

31. In the same vein, as Annette Baier remarks, "Our actual motivation, in situations where trust comes into play, is not very helpfully seen as a mixture of egoistic and nonegoistic unless we can be fairly sure which strands are egoistic, which altruistic. But many of our motives resist easy classification in these terms. Is parental concern egoistic or nonegoistic?" (*Moral Prejudices: Essays on Ethics* [Cambridge, Mass.: Harvard University Press, 1995], 156).

32. Baier, *Moral Prejudices*, 98.

33. Baier, *Moral Prejudices*, 99, 187, 341.

34. For the pathology of overtrust, see chapter 1.

35. Baier, *Moral Prejudices*, 101.

36. Edmund Husserl, *Grenzprobleme der Phänomenologie: Analysen des Unbewusstseins und der Instinkte; Metaphysik; Späte Ethik; Texte aus dem Nachlass (1908–1937)* (Dordrecht: Springer, 2014), Hua XXXXII, 304. On the importance of self-esteem within recognition (valuing and honoring oneself as a rational and ethical agent), see Alex Honneth, *The Struggle for Recognition: The Moral Grammar of Social Conflicts*, trans. J. Anderson (Cambridge, Mass.: MIT Press, 1995), and Victoria McGeer, "Developing Trust," *Philosophical Explorations* 5 (2002): 21–38, which likewise underlines that trust requires "recognizing the other's acknowledgment of oneself as the source of self-determined action, hence as a reflectively self-conscious person with reactive attitudes toward other people and the world" (33).

37. As Bakhtin elaborates, "Understanding itself enters as a dialogic element in the dialogic system and somehow changes its total sense. The person who understands inevitably becomes a *third* party in the dialogue . . . but the dialogical position of this third party is a quite special one. Any utterance always has as its addressee . . . whose responsive understanding the author of the speech work seeks and surpasses. This is the second party . . . But in addition to this addressee (the second party), the author of the utterance, with a greater or lesser awareness, presupposes a higher *superaddressee* (third), whose absolutely just responsive understanding is presumed, in some metaphysical distance or in distant historic time" (*Speech Genres and Other Late Essays*, trans. V. McGee [Austin: University of Texas Press, 1986], 126; emphasis in original). On this notion of "self-understanding," see Hans-Georg Gadamer, "On the Problem of Self-Understanding," in *Philosophical Hermeneutics*, trans. D. Linge, 44–58 (Berkeley: University of California Press, 2008).

38. In Buber's dyadic form of the I-Thou relationship, the Eternal Thou functions in a Bakhtinian sense as the "third"—namely, as an invisibly third party, or Thou. In dialogical terms Bakhtin understands "the Fascist torture chamber" as "*absolute lack of being heard, as the absolute absence of a third party*" (Bakhtin, *Speech Genres*, 126; emphasis in original), and, to wit, as examined in chapter 4, as absence of the Thou *or* the I.

39. In *King Lear*, Edmund seizes the position of the third in his betrayal of his brother, Edgar, as well as with the betrayal of his father.

Chapter 6

1. In "Appartenance et disponibilité," poorly translated into English as "Belonging and Disposability"; Gabriel Marcel, *Creative Fidelity*, trans. R. Rosthal (New York: Fordham University Press, 2002), 38. As Otto Friedrich Bollnow observes, "The concept of availability played no previous role in the history of philosophy . . . it constitutes a genuine discovery by Marcel, who was the first to recognize the fundamental significance of the concept and elaborate on it" ("Marcel's Concept of Availability," in *The Philosophy of Gabriel Marcel*, Library of Living Philosophers, vol. 17 [Carbondale, Ill.: Open Court, 1984], 182).

2. Helen Tattum rightly characterizes Marcel as an "unplaced French philosopher." The "scattered," "unsystematic," and "inchoate" style of Marcel's thinking is frequently recognized and just as much bemoaned. Helen Tattam, *Time in the Philosophy of Gabriel Marcel* (London: Modern Humanities Research Association, 2013).

3. Before its uptake in Marcel's thinking, *disponibilité* was an integral element in Gide's moral thought, where it designated the value of openness through which an individual could expand beyond the given confines of her society, culture, and historical present. In a Nietzschean vein, *disponibilité* in Gide designates an insatiable curiosity toward different possibilities, all of which are to be embraced in a self-fashioning fullness of one's own existence. In the face of the new, one is to maintain an attitude of complete availability in order to become

one's own source of freedom. In Marcel, this Nietzschean emphasis on self-empowerment becomes inverted: *disponibilité* no longer designates openness and availability to otherness (the "new") for the sake of oneself but rather the giving of oneself in freedom and responsibility for the sake of the other. See Henri Freyburger, *L'évolution de la disponibilité gidienne* (Paris: A.-G. Nizet, 1970), and Stephen Kern, *Modernism After the Death of God: Christianity, Fragmentation, and Unification* (London: Routledge, 2017), chapter 5.

4. As she declares, "Good my lord, / You have begot me, bred me, loved me. I / Return those duties back as are right fit, / Obey you, love you and most honour you" (I.1.95–99).

5. For this insight, see Adriana Menassé, "*King Lear*: Los abismos del lenguaje," *La palabra y el hombre*, no. 100 (1996): 197–204. "Es posible que todos los personajes [in *King Lear*] estén equivocados respecto a la palabra; o por el contrario: tal vez cada uno pueda encontrar razones suficientes para sostener su postura frente a ese misterio inagotable que es el lenguaje" (204).

6. Marcel, *Creative Fidelity*, 49.

7. Marcel, *Creative Fidelity*, 135.

8. Niklas Luhmann, *Trust and Power*, trans. H. Davies, J. Raffan, and K. Rooney (Cambridge: Polity Press, 2017), 12.

9. Luhmann, *Trust and Power*, 17. This affordance of complexity, sustained in my availability for the Other in trust, is not entirely synonymous with (but does not exclude) the "tolerance of ambiguity" through trust. See chapter 1 for a comparable insight into the contraction of complexity into manageable forms of presencing in Heidegger's *Being and Time*.

10. On this contraction function of habit, see Henri Bergson, *Matter and Memory*, trans. N. Paul and W. Palmer (Cambridge: Zone Books, 1990).

11. See Helen Tattum, *Time in the Philosophy of Gabriel Marcel* (London: Modern Humanities Research Association, 2013), 132. For an analysis of Marcel's theater, see Katharine Hanley, *Dramatic Approaches to Creative Fidelity: A Study in the Theater and Philosophy of Gabriel Marcel (1889–1973)* (Lanham, Md.: University Press of America, 1987).

12. "Creative fidelity," "creative trustworthiness," or "creative faithfulness" might all justifiably provide English translations of this rich term. For Marcel's conception, see Brian Treanor, *Aspects of Alterity: Levinas, Marcel, and the Contemporary Debate* (New York: Fordham University Press, 2006). For different arguments and assessments that fidelity, or trustworthiness, is irreducible to social conventions and institutions and underlies social practices and reason-giving rationality, see David Hume, *A Treatise of Human Nature* (Oxford: Clarendon Press, 1978); for Hume, fidelity is a natural virtue. See also Annette Baier, "Sustaining Trust," chapter 8 in *Moral Prejudices* (Cambridge, Mass.: Harvard University Press, 1995). For a discussion of fidelity and trust in Hume, see Annette Baier, *A Progress of Sentiments* (Cambridge, Mass.: Harvard University Press, 1991), 244–50.

13. Marcel, *Creative Fidelity*, 152.

14. For this notion of hope as affirmation of the improbable, freely adopted here in an improbable manner from its original source, see Yves Bonnefoy, *L'improbable* (Paris: Mercure de France, 2016).

15. The distinction between "being" and "having" is central to Marcel's thinking; see Gabriel Marcel, *The Mystery of Being,* trans. G. S. Fraser (South Bend, Indiana: St. Augustine Press, 2001), as well as his metaphysical journals, Gabriel Marcel, *Being and Having,* trans. K. Farrer (New York: Harper and Row, 1965).

16. Marcel, *Creative Fidelity,* 134. As he stresses again, "We should note at once that this is an essentially mysterious act."

17. On the decisive historical shift in the semantics of "faith" from an ontological condition of "holding dear" and "prizing" (*credo*) to an opinion that one possesses, as in having a belief (*opinio*), see Wilfred Cantwell Smith, *Believing—An Historical Perspective* (Oxford: Oneworld Publications, 1998). For the etymology of "credit" as *credo* from "I set my heart" and "he believes," see p. 41.

18. Josiah Royce, *The Philosophy of Loyalty* (Middleton, Del.: SophiaOmni Press, 2017), 49. Royce's lectures on loyalty played a significant role in the formation of Marcel's reflections on *fidélité créatrice* (along with its evident Bergsonian resonances from *The Two Sources of Morality and Religion*). See Gabriel Marcel, *Royce's Metaphysics,* trans. V. and G. Ringer (Chicago: Henry Regnery, 1956).

19. Baier, *Moral Prejudices,* 184.

20. For Tillich's notion of ontological courage, see Paul Tillich, *The Courage to Be* (New Haven, Conn.: Yale University Press, 2014).

21. Baier, *Moral Prejudices,* 181.

22. Marcel, *Creative Fidelity,* 28 (translation modified). For a comparable view on the underwriting significance of hope for trust, without, however, Marcel's emphasis on hope in the Other as availability, see Victoria McGeer, "Trust, Hope and Empowerment," *Australasian Journal of Philosophy* 86, no. 2 (2008): 237–54.

23. Marcel, *Creative Fidelity,* 29.

24. Marcel, *Creative Fidelity,* 113. In George Eliot's *Middlemarch,* Harriet Bulstrode forgives her banker husband as an expression of her unconditional faithfulness to him. As Nicholas sits bent in shame and guilt before her, "a movement of new compassion and old tenderness went through her like a wave," and as she puts one hand on the chair, the other on his shoulder, in the benediction of forgiveness, she "solemnly, but kindly" says, "Look up, Nicholas." It is an exemplary instance of Marcel's understanding of how the unconditionality of creative faithfulness is a sign of God's presence ("went through her like a wave"). In looking up to the forgiving wife, the encounter of forgiveness gives sign to God's unconditional love. Martha Nussbaum quips, however, "Is there forgiveness in this scene? I can't find it" (*Anger and Forgiveness: Resentment, Generosity, Justice* [Oxford: Oxford University Press, 2016], 120). What Nussbaum fails to find, "struggle with angry emotion," in her perception that Harriet Bulstrode's unconditional love "gets ahead of the angry response," resides plainly before her eyes. An attentive reading would recognize that the sign of God's grace passing through Harriet's hands *is at the same time* the working through of her angry response, which, only through forgiveness, passes through her like a wave in expiation.

25. For Marcel's response, see Erin Tremblay Ponnou-Delaffon, "'Ni haine ni pardon': Gabriel Marcel and Robert Antelme on the Limits of the Human," *French Forum* 40, no. 2 (2015): 33–46.

26. These lines are taken from Shelley: "To suffer woes which Hope thinks

infinite; / To forgive wrongs darker than Death or Night; / To defy Power, which seems Omnipotent; / To love, and bear; to hope, till Hope creates / From its own wreck the thing it contemplates" (*Prometheus Unbound*, IV.570–75).

27. Jean-Luc Marion, *Negative Certainties*, trans. S. Lewis (Chicago: University of Chicago Press, 2015), 140–47. See also Jean-Luc Marion, "What Love Knows," in *Love and Forgiveness for a More Just World*, ed. H. de Vries and N. Schott, 27–35 (New York: Columbia University Press, 2015). For a discussion of Marion's reading of Lear in the context of *Negative Certainties*, see Christina Gschwandtner, *Degrees of Givenness: On Saturation in Jean-Luc Marion* (Bloomington: Indiana University Press, 2014), 134–37.

28. For Marion's extended and engaging deconstruction of economies of the gift and logics of givenness, see his *The Reason of the Gift*, trans. S. Lewis (Charlottesville: University of Virginia Press, 2011), as well as *Being Given: Toward a Phenomenology of Givenness*, trans. J. Kossky (Stanford, Calif.: Stanford University Press, 2002).

29. As Marion writes, "Between forgiveness and justice there lies the same gulf that exists between justice and exchange" (*Negative Certainties*, 140).

30. On the complex resonances in Cordelia's silence, see Małgorzata Grzegorzewska, "The War of 'Nothings' in *The Tragedy of King Lear*," in *Shakespeare and Conflict: A European Perspective*, ed. C. Dente and S. Soncini, 55–67 (London: Palgrave Macmillan, 2013).

31. Marion, *Negative Certainties*, 143.

32. Marion, *Negative Certainties*, 143 ("aucun pardon ne peut intervenir sinon à partir d'un don préalable").

33. To note in passing: if forgiveness thus renders present the presentness of love's gift as well as the one who gives to the beneficiary, sacrifice, according to Marion, renders present the presentness of the gift to the one who gives. As he writes, "In this way, forgiveness and sacrifice answer each other, making the phenomenality of givenness appear through the doubling redounding of the gift, whether starting from the recipient, or from the giver" (*Negative Certainties*, 153).

34. Marion, *Negative Certainties*, 151.

35. Marion, *Negative Certainties*, 153.

36. As Marion thinks, "God hence gives himself to see inasmuch as he gives in an originary fashion, inasmuch as he shows that all gifts come from him" (*Negative Certainties*, 147).

37. "Forgiveness supposes the gift, because it consists in its redundancy."

38. Whereas the English word "connivance" carries negative connotations (connivance in wrongdoing), Marcel's use of the French term is meant to affirm the opposite meaning of "connivance in the doing good."

39. Marcel, *Creative Fidelity*, 29.

40. See Ponnou-Delaffon, "'Ni haine ni pardon.'"

41. Marion, *Negative Certainties*, 147. See also Jean-Luc Marion, "Nothing Is Impossible for God," in *Believing in Order to See*, trans. C. Gschwandtner, 87–101 (New York: Fordham University Press, 2017).

42. Marion, *Negative Certainties*, 231: "La puissance de Dieu, qui peut tout, même pardonner, ne consiste donc que dans sa bonté."

43. As with Saint Paul, interhuman forgiveness is grounded in God's forgiveness.

44. A. C. Bradley, *Shakespearean Tragedy*, (London: Penguin, 1991), 286. For Bradley, *King Lear* "presents the world as a place where heavenly good grows side by side with evil, where extreme evil cannot long endure, and where all that survives the storm is good, if not great" (271–72). For another form of Christian reading of Cordelia's death as redemption, see Robert Speaight, *Nature in Shakespearean Tragedy* (New York: Collier, 1962), 89–129.

45. For this distinction between "optimistic" and "hopeful" readings in the service of defending a Christian frame of interpretation, see R. V. Young, "Hope and Despair in *King Lear*," in King Lear*: New Critical Essays*, ed. J. Kahan, 253–77 (London: Routledge, 2008).

46. As exemplary of this approach, see Jan Kott, *Shakespeare Our Contemporary*, trans. B. Taborski (New York: Doubleday, 1966).

47. For a historical assessment of the multivocal composition of *King Lear*, see William R. Elton, King Lear *and the Gods* (Lexington: University Press of Kentucky, 2014).

48. "Real despair means death, the grave or the abyss. If despair prompts speech or reasoning, and above all if it results in writing, fraternity is established, natural objects are justified, love is born. A literature of despair is a contradiction in terms" (Albert Camus, "The Enigma," in *Lyrical and Critical Essays*, trans. E. Kennedy [New York: Vintage Books, 1970], 160).

49. For Edgar's point, see Terry Eagleton, *Hope without Optimism* (Charlottesville: University of Virginia Press, 2015), 124. For a critique of readings of "aesthetic redemption" in *King Lear*, see Sam Gilchrist Hall, *Shakespeare's Folly* (London: Routledge, 2017), 156–57.

50. For this formulation, see Maurice Blanchot, *The Infinite Conversation*, trans. S. Hanson (Minneapolis: University of Minnesota Press, 1993), 131.

51. As pointed out in Hall, *Shakespeare's Folly*, 160.

52. As Chesterton wryly remarks, "Those who leave out the context really leave out the conception. They have a mysterious power of making the world weary of a few fixed and disconnected words, and yet leaving the world entirely ignorant of the real meaning of those words." G. K. Chesterton, *The Spice of Life and Other Essays* (Beaconsfield: Darwen Finlayson, 1964); "The Tragedy of King Lear," http://www.gkc.org.uk/gkc/books/Spice_Of_Life.html. For a historically erudite and interpretatively astute dismantling of any Christian promise or dimension in *King Lear*, arguing instead for its subversive destruction of Christian optimism and providential faith, see the classic study Elton, *King Lear and the Gods*. In William Empson's judgment, "The attempts to fit Christian sentiments into it [*King Lear*] seem to me to falsify the play" (*The Structure of Complex Words* [London: Chatto and Windus, 1977], 8). Echoing Empson, Stanley Cavell writes, "Is this a Christian play? The question is very equivocal. When it is answered affirmatively, Cordelia is viewed as a Christ figure whose love redeems nature and transfigures Lear. So far as this is intelligible to me, I find it false both to the experience of the play and to the fact that it is a play" (*Must We Mean What We Say?* [Cambridge: Cambridge University Press, 2002], 250). For the continuing

debate regarding Christian allusions and the purported Christian theme of forgiveness in Lear, see Jessica Vanden Berg, "Grace, Consequences, and Christianity in *King Lear*," *Italics*: 2000, no. 1, article 3; Reuben Brower, *Hero and Saint: Shakespeare and the Graeco-Roman Heroic Tradition* (Oxford: Oxford University Press, 1972); and Nathan Lefler, "The Tragedy of King Lear: Redeeming Christ?," *Literature and Theology* 24, no. 3 (2010): 211–26. For a critique of Elton's argument based on drawing a distinction between a false conception of Christian "optimism" and true Christian conception of hope, see Young, "Hope and Despair."

53. Marion, *Negative Certainties*, 148: "How can we avoid recognizing an inverted paradigm of *King Lear*, where three daughters (in fact, two and one) face a similar division of an inheritance?"

54. For a discussion of the emergence of a secular conception of forgiveness in the seventeenth century with reference to Shakespeare, see David Konstan, *Before Forgiveness: The Origins of a Moral Idea* (Cambridge: Cambridge University Press, 2010), 150: "It would appear, then, that interpersonal forgiveness, in a form at least resembling the modern idea, was available as a theme at the time when Molière was writing, in the middle of the seventeenth century. It may have had a function in drama even earlier, in the works of Shakespeare, for example, although it seems to be illustrated there in rather a perfunctory way, and perhaps scarcely counts as true forgiveness." For the theme of forgiveness in Shakespeare's plays, see Sarah Beckwith, *Shakespeare and the Grammar of Forgiveness* (Stanford, Calif.: Stanford University Press, 2011), and William Matchett, *Shakespeare and Forgiveness* (Santa Barbara, Calif.: Fithian Press, 2002). Neither of these two works deals extensively with *King Lear*. My proposed interpretation of Cordelia's originality places its significance outside any opposition between "pagan" and "Christian," as developed through a historical contextualization in Elton, King Lear *and the Gods*.

55. For Cordelia's diction, see Elton, King Lear *and the Gods*, 75.

56. In terms of historical contextualization, for the erosion of religious belief during the Elizabethan and Jacobean eras, see Elton, King Lear *and the Gods*, and Jonathan Dollimore, *Radical Tragedy: Religion, Ideology, and Power in the Drama of Shakespeare and His Contemporaries* (Durham, N.C.: Duke University Press, 2004).

57. Richard van Oort, *Shakespeare's Big Men: Tragedy and the Problem of Resentment* (Toronto: University of Toronto Press, 2016), proposes a reading of five Shakespearian tragedies through the framework of René Girard's anthropological theory of mimetic rivalry and resentment, without any consideration of *King Lear*, however. For Girard's conception of Christ's mercy, see *Things Hidden Since the Foundation of the World*, trans. S. Bann and M. Metteer (Stanford, Calif.: Stanford University Press, 1987), 180–223.

58. As Edwin Martínez Pulido justly remarks, "In a play where mothers are conspicuously absent or where the references to motherhood are mingled with allusions to sterility and adultery, or even to disturbances of the body, Cordelia comes to embody the ultimate manifestation of motherly love when it is she who reassures 'this child-changed father' (4, 7, 17) concerning his lost identity: 'How does my royal Lord? How fares your majesty?' (4, 7, 44)" ("The Transformation of the Protagonist's Personality in the Tragedy of *King Lear*," *Matices en lenguas*

extranjeras, no. 4 [2010], https://revistas.unal.edu.co/index.php/male/article/view/30141/32007).

59. G. K. Chesterton, "The Tragedy of *King Lear*," in *The Spice of Life and Other Essays* (London: Darwen Finlayson, 1964), http://www.gkc.org.uk/gkc/books/Spice_Of_Life.html.

60. As Chesterton remarks, "The Fool juggles with time and space and to-morrow and yesterday, as he says soberly at the end of his rant: 'This prophecy Merlin shall make; for I live before his time.' This is one of the Shakespearian shocks or blows that take the breath away," "The Tragedy of King Lear," http://www.gkc.org.uk/gkc/books/Spice_Of_Life.html.

61. Dan Brayton speaks of the "evacuation of the social" ("Angling in the Lake of Darkness: Possession, Dispossession, and the Politics of Discovery in *King Lear*," *ELH* 70, no. 2 [2003]: 406).

62. "Lear. . . . They flattered me like a dog, and told me I had the white hairs in my beard ere the black ones were there. To say 'ay' and 'no' to every thing that I said! 'Ay' and 'no' too was good divinity . . . Go to, they are not men o' their words: they told me I was every thing; 'tis a lie, I am not ague-proof" (IV.6.97–106).

63. Chesterton, "The Tragedy of *King Lear*."

64. Blanchot, *The Infinite Conversation*, 130.

65. Blanchot, *The Infinite Conversation*, 77.

66. As Blanchot writes, "When through oppression and terror man falls as though outside of himself, there where he loses every perspective, every point of reference, and every difference and is thus handed over to a time without respite that he endures as the perpetuity of an indifferent present, he has one last possibility. At this moment when he becomes the unknown and the foreign, when, that is, he becomes a fate for himself, his last recourse is to know that he has been struck not by the elements, but by me, and to give the name *man* to everything that assails him" (*The Infinite Conversation*, 131; emphasis in original).

67. In the words of Blanchot (speaking of Levinas), "We are called upon to become responsible for what philosophy essentially is, by entertaining precisely the idea of the Other in all its radiance and in the infinite exigency that are proper to it, that is to say, the relation with *autrui*" (*The Infinite Conversation*, 51–52).

68. For the interpretative challenges posed by the offstage decision of Cordelia's return, see Richard Knowles, "Cordelia's Return," *Shakespeare Quarterly* 50, no. 1 (Spring 1999): 33–50.

69. Whereas Goneril's steward, Oswald, behaves without honor, good Kent acts honorably and trustingly. Kent is not a henchman or a lackey.

70. Pray, do not mock me:

> I am a very foolish fond old man,
>
> Fourscore and upward, not an hour more nor less;
>
> And, to deal plainly,
>
> I fear I am not in my perfect mind.
>
> Methinks I should know you, and know this man;
>
> Yet I am doubtful for I am mainly ignorant
>
> What place this is; and all the skill I have

> Remembers not these garments; nor I know not
> Where I did lodge last night. Do not laugh at me;
> For, as I am a man, I think this lady
> To be my child Cordelia.
> Act IV,viii, 58-68

71. Hall calls attention to this deliberate and hence significant doubling of "no cause" by Shakespeare. In *King Lear*, Cordelia forgives Lear thus: "O grieve not you, my Lord, you have no cause" (*Shakespeare's Folly*, 172).

72. The speech act of pledging myself to the Other would itself be based on an original availability for the Other.

73. Hannah Arendt, *Denktagebuch: Erster Band, 1950–1973* (Munich: Piper, 2016), 470.

Chapter 7

1. Michaël de Saint Cheron, *Conversations with Emmanuel Levinas, 1983–1984*, trans. G. Mole (Pittsburgh: Duquesne University Press, 2010), 27.

2. Emmanuel Levinas, *Totality and Infinity*, trans. A. Lingis (Pittsburgh: Duquesne University Press, 1987), 233.

3. Emmanuel Levinas, *Of God Who Comes to Mind*, trans. B. Bergo (Stanford, Calif.: Stanford University Press, 1998), 71.

4. As Levinas writes, "*For it remains incomprehensible to me that another concerns me*: 'Who is Hecuba to me?' Stated otherwise, 'Am I my brother's keeper?' Such questions are incomprehensible within being" (*God, Death, and Time*, trans. B. Bergo [Stanford, Calif.: Stanford University Press, 2000], 175; emphasis in original). In the same vein, who I am for the Other. "What's Hecuba to him or he to Hecuba / That he should weep for her?" (*Hamlet*, II.2.516–18).

5. I'll forgo here any commentary on this intriguing detail that God favors *meat* rather than *fruit*. For a debate regarding whether these two gifts should be seen as equivalent or not in the light of God's preference, see the discussion between Levinas and André Neher in *La conscience juive: Données et débats*, ed. Éliane Amado Lévy-Valensi and Jean Halpérin, 34–53 (Paris: Presses universitaires de France, 1963).

6. On the figure of the elder son in biblical fraternal relationships, see Jill Robbins, *Prodigal Son/Elder Brother: Interpretation and Alterity in Augustine, Petrarch, Kafka, Levinas* (Chicago: University of Chicago Press, 1991).

7. For this distinction between guilt and shame, see Rein Nauta, "Cain and Abel: Violence, Shame and Jealousy," *Pastoral Psychology* 58, no. 1 (2009): 65–71.

8. For this insight, see Maurice Blanchot, *The Infinite Conversation*, trans. S. Hanson (Minneapolis: University of Minnesota Press, 1993), 61.

9. Thomas Nagel, "Death," in *The Metaphysics of Death*, ed. J. Fischer, 61–69 (Stanford, Calif.: Stanford University Press, 1993).

10. And even if I *had* murdered a person, in what sense is the murder of the Other, *any* Other, "murder"?

11. Emmanuel Levinas, *Otherwise Than Being*, trans. A. Lingis (Pittsburgh: Duquesne University Press, 2008), 6.

12. *Otherwise Than Being* is dedicated to "the memory of those who were closest among the six million assassinated by the National Socialists, and of the millions on millions of all confessions and all nations, victims of the same hatred of the other man, the same anti-semitism."

13. As Derrida notes, "The thematic development of *Totality and Infinity* is neither purely descriptive nor purely thematic" but "proceeds with incessant insistence of waves pounding on the shore." Jacques Derrida, *Writing and Difference*, trans. Alan Bass (Chicago: University of Chicago Press, 1978), 312.

14. For a discussion of these two scenes of discourse and the "interruption" of the ethical within the ontological, see Robert Bernasconi, "'Only the Persecuted . . .': Language of the Oppressor, Language of the Oppressed," in *Ethics as First Philosophy*, ed. A. Peperzak, 77–86 (London: Routledge, 1995), as well as Robert Bernasconi, "Rereading *Totality and Infinity*," in *The Question of the Other*, ed. A. Dallery and C. Scott, 23–40 (Albany: State University of New York Press, 1989).

15. Rudi Visker, *The Inhuman Condition: Looking for Difference After Levinas and Heidegger* (Pittsburgh: Duquesne University Press, 2004), 99.

16. Levinas, *Of God*, 88–89. For an insightful treatment of Levinas's style of writing, see Didier Franck, *L'un-pour-l'autre* (Paris: Presses universitaires de France, 2008), chapter 2.

17. As with the opening of *King Lear*, the narrative launches into its dramatic unfolding through a grotesquely botched attempt at ensuring an equitable resolution of disputed inheritance.

18. This abandonment of the son is more violently manifest with Fyodor's refusal to accept Smerdyakov—his bastard progeny with Lizaveta. Smerdyakov becomes adopted by Fyodor's loyal servant.

19. Dostoevsky, *The Brothers Karamazov*, trans. Richard Pevear and Larissa Volokhonsky (New York: Farrar, Straus and Giroux, 2002), 774.

20. For the layered dialogism of Dostoevsky's poetics, see Mikhail Bakhtin, *Problems of Dostoevsky's Poetics*, trans. C. Emerson (Minneapolis: University of Minnesota Press, 1984), and Michael Holquist, *Dostoevsky and the Novel* (Princeton, N.J.: Princeton University Press, 1977).

21. As in *King Lear*, the absence of the mother figures prominently in the lives of these three sons in relation to their father.

22. Dostoevsky, *The Brothers Karamazov*, 49.

23. To overintellectualize this affect of the grieving mother would be to think that such an affect presupposed a belief in the afterlife, when, in fact, this original affect testifies to the impossibility of an afterlife without us, the living, participating in the death of the Other. See Nicolas de Warren, "Souls of the Departed: Toward a Phenomenology of the After-Life," *Metodo* 5, no. 1 (2017): 205–37.

24. In a letter to his wife, Dostoevsky writes, "I am reading Job and it puts me into a state of painful ecstasy; I leave off reading and I walk about the room almost crying . . . This book, dear Anna, it's strange, it was one of the first to impress me in my life. I was still practically an infant" (cited in Joseph Frank, *Dostoevsky: A Writer in His Time* [Princeton, N.J.: Princeton University Press, 2012], 789). The

book of Job is invoked again in the lessons from the life of the Elder Zosima—I do not discuss this here, nor the contrast with Ivan's narrative.

25. As Jan Patočka remarks, "Dostoevsky takes the antinomy of reason more seriously even than Kant, if that is possible, because he does not see in it the conflict between an illusionary world of the sense and the world of true reality, but rather as the conflict between two realities, two worlds" ("Masaryk's Philosophy of Religion," in *La crise du sens: Comte, Masaryk, Husserl*, trans. E. Abrams [Brussels: OUSIA, 2000], 38). Patočka echoes Shestov's insight: "Yet, if ever a 'Critique of Pure Reason' was written, it is to Dostoevsky that we must go seek it" (Lev Shestov, "The Conquest of the Self-Evident," in *In Job's Balances* [Athens: Ohio University Press, 1975], 21). For Patočka's reading of Dostoevsky, see Nicolas de Warren, "The Gift of Eternity," in *The New Yearbook for Phenomenology and Phenomenological Philosophy*, vol. 14, ed. James Dodd and Ludger Hagedorn (London: Routledge, 2015), 161–80. For the confrontation between Kant and Dostoevsky, albeit without any reference to Patočka, see Evgenia Cherkasova, *Dostoevsky and Kant: Dialogues on Ethics* (Amsterdam: Rodopi, 2009).

26. Dostoevsky, *The Brothers Karamazov*, 236.

27. Dostoevsky, *The Brothers Karamazov*, 236.

28. Dostoevsky, *The Brothers Karamazov*, 238. However, as Robin Feuer Miller does well to note, "Although it is customary and correct to emphasize Ivan's horror at the suffering of children, in all of his examples *parents* are involved as well—emblems of infinite love, or tormentors, or perhaps as both" (*The Brothers Karamazov* [New York: Twayne, 1992], 61; emphasis in original).

29. J. M. Coetzee, *Elizabeth Costello* (New York: Viking, 2003), 160.

30. Dostoevsky, *The Brothers Karamazov*, 243 (note Ivan's use of the diminutive for his little brother).

31. Whether the natural evil of death is considered along theological lines (as with Zosima's position) or secular lines (as with, for example, of Nagel's deprivation argument).

32. Alyosha's transformation in the novel is inscribed within the novel's arc of forgetting to remembrance. When we are introduced to Alyosha, we are told of his peculiar character and "inner preoccupation"—his spiritual idiocy—which caused him, even in his devout love for humankind (and not standing in judgment of others), "to forget others." His own spiritual awakening turns on the axis of remembering others—that is, accepting his calling as his brother's keeper.

33. As Victor Terras notes, Dostoevsky's novel is centered on the fundamental moral conflict between these two statements, "Am I my brother's keeper?" and "Every one of us is guilty before everyone for everyone, and I more than others" (*A Karamazov Companion: Commentary on the Genesis, Language, and Style of Dostoevsky's Novel* [Madison: University of Wisconsin Press, 2002]). Cain's question is also spoken by Smerdyakov and Rakitin.

34. As the Elder Zosima speaks, "His face [the older brother Markel] is like a reminder and prophecy to me. At the dawn of my life, when I was still a very small boy, I had an older brother who died in his youth, before my eyes, when he was only seventeen. And later, in the course of my life, I realized that this brother was like a sign to me, like a message from above . . . And now the face that first

appeared to me in my childhood has made a second appearance as I near the end of my life, as if it were a reminder," 343.

35. Jill Robbins, *Altered Reading* (Chicago: University of Chicago Press, 1999), 67.

36. Dostoevsky, *Brothers Karamazov*, 29. "Election" should not to be confused with any "expectation" and "obligation." After the Elder Zosima has sanctified his election of and assignment to Alyosha, he dies; there is the expectation among his devoted followers, including Alyosha, that, given the Elder's saintliness, his body won't rot after his death. Alyosha shares in this expectation of visible evidence for the Elder's spiritual purity. A few days later, Zosima's body begins to smell, thus throwing Alyosha into a spiritual crisis of self-doubt about his own vocation, election, and assignment.

37. For an insightful analysis of this quotation from Dostoevsky's novel (with particular emphasis on book 6) in Levinas's writings, see Alain Toumayan, "'I more than the others': Dostoevsky and Levinas," in "Encounters with Levinas," ed. Thomas Trezise, special issue, *Yale French Studies* 104 (2004): 55–66. As Toumayan notes, "The reference to Cain's answer to God could plausibly be characterized as the other side of the coin of Levinas's favorite quotation from *The Brothers Karamazov*" (59). For Levinas's reading of Dostoevsky and, more generally, the importance of literature for his ethical thinking, see Robbins, *Altered Reading*, 147–50. Robbins counts "nearly a dozen" instances of this citation in Levinas's writings (147). For a Levinasian-inspired reading of Dostoevsky's novels, see Jacques Rolland, *Dostoïevski: La question de l'autre* (Paris: Verdier, 1982).

38. Levinas, *Of God*, 84. Marie-Anne Lescourret considers this recurring saying from Dostoevsky's novel to be Levinas's "citation fétiche" (*Emmanuel Levinas* [Paris: Flammarion, 1994], 47).

39. Jill Robbins, ed., *Is It Righteous to Be? Interviews with Emmanuel Levinas* (Stanford, Calif.: Stanford University Press, 2001), 28; for his favorite citation, see 72–73.

40. Emmanuel Levinas, "God and Philosophy," in *Collected Philosophical Papers*, trans. A. Lingis (Dordrecht: Martinus Nijhoff, 1987), 168, 169; emphasis in original. "The recurrence in awakening is something one can describe as a shudder of incarnation through which *giving* takes on meaning, as the primordial dative of the *for another*, in which a subject becomes a heart, a sensibility, and hands which give" (169; emphasis in original).

41. Robbins, *Is It Righteous to Be?*, 133. Elsewhere Levinas remarks, "You know, as concerns the relation with the other, I always come back to my phrase from Dostoevsky" (56). "My point of departure is in Dostoevsky in the phrase I quote to you" (72).

42. Levinas, *God, Death, and Time*, 117.

Chapter 8

1. As Alasdair MacIntyre, for example, writes, "What difference to moral philosophy would it make, if we were to treat the facts of vulnerability and afflic-

tion and the related facts of dependence as central to the human condition?" (*Dependent Rational Animals* [Chicago: Open Court, 1999], 4). According to Mac-Intyre's argument, virtues of independent rational agency and autonomy require for their adequate exercise what he calls virtues of acknowledged dependence and vulnerability. Even as this proposal speaks to the created condition of human existence, it nonetheless remains bound to the natural assumption of determining essentially the significance of our begotten condition in terms of a sense of being—in this instance, our animal condition in its vulnerability and affliction. As MacIntyre writes, "An acknowledgement of anything like the full extent of that dependence and of the ways in which it stems from our vulnerability and our afflictions is generally absent" (4).

2. Emmanuel Levinas, *Otherwise Than Being*, trans. A. Lingis (Pittsburgh: Duquesne University Press, 2008), 110.

3. Levinas, *Otherwise Than Being*, 116.

4. Levinas, *Otherwise Than Being*, 56.

5. For the connection between remorse and the intrinsic mysteriousness of the affectivity of the Good, see Raimond Gaita, *Good and Evil: An Absolute Conception* (London: Routledge, 2004), chapters 4 and 9. Though there is much that resonates in Gaita's conception of good with Levinas, Gaita loosens the bond between responsibility and culpability in a manner that runs counter to Levinas's tightening.

6. Emmanuel Levinas, *Of God Who Comes to Mind*, trans. B. Bergo (Stanford, Calif.: Stanford University Press, 1998), 90; emphasis in original.

7. When the child was a child
   it was the time of these questions:
   Why am I me, and why not you?
   Why am I here, and why not there?
   When did time begin, and where does space end?
   Isn't life under the sun just a dream?
   Isn't what I see, hear, and smell
   only the illusion of a world before the world?
   Does evil actually exist,
   and are there people who are really evil?
   How can it be that I, who am I,
   didn't exist before I came to be
   and that someday
   the one who I am
   will no longer be the one I am?

8. When the child was a child
   It didn't know it was a child.
   Everything was full of life, and all life was one.

(https://www.babelmatrix.org/works/de/Handke%2C_Peter-1942/Lied_Vom _Kindsein/en/42791-Song_of_Childhood)

9. Without developing further this essential conception, the temporality of what Levinas calls "recurrence" and "diachrony," in contrast to the temporality

of "repetition and identity," or "chronology," both of which, in fact, cannot be disentangled from each other, is structured in terms of three moments of creation, revelation, and redemption, each of which cannot be understood "ecstatically," as with the threefold temporalization of Heidegger's Dasein nor in terms of the threefold imbrication of retention, original presentation, and protention of Husserl's inner time consciousness.

10. As Levinas writes, "The uniqueness of the responsible me is possible only *in* being obsessed by another, in the trauma suffered prior to any auto-identification, in an unrepresentable *before*. The one affected by the other is an anarchic trauma, or an inspiration of the one by the other, and not a causality striking mechanically a matter subject to its energy" (*Otherwise Than Being*, 123; emphasis in original). For a discussion of the "two times" of trauma as *Nachträglichkeit* in Levinas, see Rudi Visker, *The Inhuman Condition: Looking for Difference After Levinas and Heidegger* (Pittsburgh: Duquesne University Press, 2004), 99. In a strictly psychoanalytic context, see Jean Laplanche, *Après-coup*, trans. J. House and L. Thurston (New York: The Unconscious in Translation, 2017).

11. Emmanuel Levinas, *Collected Philosophical Papers* (Dordrecht: Martinus Nijhoff, 1987), 159, 166.

12. *The Brothers Karamazov*, trans. Richard Pevear and Larissa Volokhonsky (New York: Farrar, Straus and Giroux, 2002), 776.

13. Emmanuel Levinas, *Nine Talmudic Readings*, trans. A. Aronowicz (Bloomington: Indiana University Press, 1990), 42. As Michael Fagenblat emphasizes, "In Levinas's secular version of covenantal faith, the idea is that *we live in trust*, in ordinary but absolutely indispensable, numberless ways" (*A Covenant of Creatures* [Stanford, Calif.: Stanford University Press, 2010], 154; emphasis in original).

14. For this interplay between "too late" and "too early," see François-David Sebbah, *Levinas: Ambiguïtés de l'altérité* (Paris: Les Belles Lettres, 2000).

15. For this intrinsic prophetic dimension (without the clarity of any prophecy), see Stéphane Mosès, "Histoire et paternité, *Philosophie*, no. 72 (2001): 71–87.

16. For this formulation, see Maurice Blanchot, *The Infinite Conversation*, trans. S. Hanson (Minneapolis: University of Minnesota Press, 1993), 134.

17. Emmanuel Levinas, *Outside the Subject*, trans. M. Smith (Stanford, Calif.: Stanford University Press, 1993), 149.

18. Levinas, *Collected Philosophical Papers*, 165.

19. As Levinas says, "These negative qualifications [unsayable, unjustifiable] of the subjectivity of the oneself do not consecrate some ineffable mystery" (*Otherwise Than Being*, 107).

20. As significantly, "substitution" cannot be deemed "phenomenological," in concept or method, but stands instead, as Levinas writes, "equal to the paradox which phenomenological description enters when, starting with the disclosure, the appearing of a neighbor, it reads it in its trace, which orders the face according to a diachrony which cannot be synchronized in representation" (*Otherwise Than Being*, 193).

21. Levinas, *Otherwise Than Being*, 19 (translation modified).

22. Franz Rosenzweig, *Philosophical and Theological Writings*, trans. P. Franks and M. Morgan (Indianapolis: Hackett Publishing, 2000), 116.

23. Levinas, *Otherwise Than Being*, 125.

24. Levinas, *Otherwise Than Being*, 14.

25. Emmanuel Levinas, *Autrement qu'être, ou au-dela de l'essence* (Paris: Livre du Poche, 1991), 29–30.

26. "Fully," for the word "expiation" has already been spoken, already in the "Argument" section—"It is a substitution for another, one in the place of another, expiation" (Levinas, *Otherwise Than Being*, 15); and not "completely," since there is no finality to the pronouncement of substitution as expiation.

27. Levinas, *Otherwise Than Being*, 118, 120, 125, 145, 146.

28. Levinas, *Autrement qu'être*, 187; emphasis added. As Levinas remarks, "In order to explain the notion of substitution, it is necessary that I say more, that I use hyperbole" (*Of God*, 91).

29. Levinas, *Otherwise Than Being*, 14–15; emphasis added.

30. Levinas, *Otherwise Than Being*, 102.

31. Levinas, *Of God*, 92.

32. Levinas, *Of God*, 92.

33. Levinas, *Of God*, 92.

34. Emmanuel Levinas, *Ethics and Infinity*, trans. R. Cohen (Pittsburgh: Duquesne University Press, 1985), 52.

35. Levinas, *Otherwise Than Being*, 100.

36. Levinas, *Otherwise Than Being*, 88.

37. Levinas, *Otherwise Than Being*, 101.

38. Levinas, *Otherwise Than Being*, 106.

39. Levinas, *Otherwise Than Being*, 102.

40. Levinas, *Otherwise Than Being*, 129.

41. Richard A. Cohen, ed., *Face to Face with Levinas* (Albany: State University of New York Press, 1986), 23.

42. Levinas, *Nine Talmudic Readings*, 10.

43. Levinas, *Ethics and Infinity*, 90.

44. This "curious doubleness" of the Face is frequently noted. As Robert Bernasconi remarks, "The face is ambiguous, two-faced, Janus-headed, both inviting and yet forbidding violence" ("The Violence of the Face," *Philosophy and Social Criticism* 23, no. 6 [1997]: 87). For this formulation of the Face as the alternative "to speak or to kill," see Blanchot, *The Infinite Conversation*, 62: "Man facing man has no choice but to speak or to kill."

45. Levinas, *Difficult Freedom. Essays on Judaism*, trans. Seán Hand (Baltimore: John Hopkins University Press, 1997), 8.

46. Emmanuel Levinas, *Basic Philosophical Writings*, ed. A. Peperzak, S. Critchley, R. Bernasconi (Bloomington: Indiana University Press, 1996), 167.

47. Levinas, *Otherwise Than Being*, 109.

48. Revealingly, the etymology of the word "guilt," from the Old English *gylt* (crime, sin, moral defect, failure of duty), is of unknown origin.

49. Emmanuel Levinas, *Totality and Infinity*, trans. A. Lingis (Pittsburgh: Duquesne University Press, 1987), 99. On the implicit demand of truthfulness and responsibility that underlies the meaningfulness of speaking to one another, see chapter 1.

50. Levinas, *Otherwise Than Being*, 109; emphasis in original. For the incarnation of time, see Danielle Cohen-Levinas, "The Corporeal Meaning of Time: Phenomenology and Literature; Lévinas, Reader of Proust," trans. Lena Taub Robles, *CR: The New Centennial Review* 17, no. 2 (Fall 2017): 25–42.

51. Levinas, *Otherwise Than Being*, 106.

52. As Diane Perpich observes, "Skin is the exemplary site of the ambiguity of the face" (*The Ethics of Emmanuel Levinas* [Stanford, Calif.: Stanford University Press, 2008], 116).

53. Levinas, *Otherwise Than Being*, 111.

54. Levinas, *Otherwise Than Being*, 111; emphasis added.

55. Levinas, *Totality and Infinity*, 84. As Levinas writes, "Morality begins when freedom, instead of being justified by itself, feels itself to be arbitrary and violent."

56. Levinas, *Ethics and Infinity*, 129.

57. Levinas, *Ethics and Infinity*, 129. As Robert Bernasconi notes, the Hegelian fear of one's own death at the hands of the Other becomes inverted into the fear of the Other's death by one's own hands.

58. Levinas, *Totality and Infinity*, 85.

59. Levinas, *Totality and Infinity*, 83. As Visker remarks, shame is "the philosophical cornerstone on which Lévinas' ethics rests" and the affective basis for openness toward the Other (*The Inhuman Condition*, 130).

60. Levinas, *Basic Philosophical Writings*, 50; emphasis in original.

61. Levinas, *Otherwise Than Being*, 113.

62. Much as evil targets me in particular without it ever just being about me in particular. Hence Job's incredulity, "Why me?" as the despair of evil. For this understanding of evil as targeting and pursuing me, see Levinas, "Transcendence and Evil," *Collected Philosophical Papers*, 175–86.

63. Levinas, *Otherwise Than Being*, 111 (my emphasis).

64. Or rather, he *predominantly* speaks of expiation. In the crucial chapter 4, "Substitution," in *Otherwise Than Being*, Levinas does on occasion speak of "sacrifice"—"The approach, inasmuch as it is a sacrifice, confers a sense on death" (129). Expiation, however, nonetheless remains, it is the contention here, the initializing concept for understanding what "sacrifice" must mean in this context. Admittedly, as with the nexus of the biblical terms "atonement," "expiation," "sacrifice," and "forgiveness," the complexity of these differentiations, relationships, and overlaps are substantial indeed.

65. Levinas, *Otherwise Than Being*, 111; emphasis added. "This accusation can be reduced to the passivity of the self only as a persecution, but a persecution that turns into an expiation" (112). "There is substitution for another, expiation for another" (125).

66. Levinas, *Otherwise Than Being*, 118. "The self as an expiation is prior to activity and passivity" (116).

67. For this analysis, see Alain Toumayan, "'I more than others': Dostoevsky and Levinas," in "Encounters with Levinas," ed. Thomas Trezise, special issue, *Yale French Studies* 104 (2004): 55–66.

68. Levinas, *Otherwise Than Being*, 111 (my emphasis).

69. Levinas, *Otherwise Than Being*, 117.

70. For a discussion of the Levinas understanding of evil in his earlier writings, see Nicolas de Warren, "Darkness Over the Deep: Levinas and the Evil of Being," *Journal for Cultural and Religious Theory* 17, no. 2 (2018): 415–31. For Levinas's most developed treatment of evil, see "Transcendence and Evil," where the seminal configuration of substitution underpins the passage from "one's suffering in evil" to "suffering oneself for the suffering of all others," or what Levinas calls the "reversal of evil" into a discovery, or theophany, of the transcendence of the Good: "That in the evil that pursues me the evil suffered by the other man afflicts me, that it touches me, as though from the first the other was calling to me, putting into question my resting on myself and my *conatus essendi*, as though before lamenting over my evil here below, I had to answer for the other—is this not a breakthrough of the Good in the 'intention' of which I am in my woe so exclusively aimed at? . . . The horror of evil that aims at me becomes horror over evil in the other man. Here is a breakthrough of the Good which is not a simple inversion of Evil, but an elevation" (*Collected Philosophical Papers*, 184–85). For a lucid discussion of the problem of evil in Levinas, see Visker, *The Inhuman Condition*, chapter 5, to which my own discussion quietly and admiringly responds. See also the extensive treatment given to this topic in Catherine Chalier, *La persévérance du mal* (Paris: Cerf, 1987). For her own discussion of forgiveness, see *Mémoire et pardon* (Paris: François Bourin, 2018).

71. For this formulation, see Visker, *The Inhuman Condition*, 128.

72. Following Visker's formulation, *The Inhuman Condition*, 129.

73. For a useful discussion of the evolution of Levinas's understanding of the "deafness" of the subject in his writings, see Perpich, *Ethics of Emmanuel Levinas*, chapter 3.

74. Levinas, *Otherwise Than Being*, 122.

75. Levinas, *Otherwise Than Being*, 106.

76. Michel de Montaigne, "On Repentance," 610–21 in *Essais: The Complete Works* (New York: Everyman's Library, 2003), 617.

77. For these insights into shame in contrast to guilt as well as the distinction between "shame forgiveness" and "guilt forgiveness," I am indebted to Basil Vassilicos.

78. Judith Butler, *Precarious Life* (London: Verso, 2006), 134–35.

79. See Stéphane Mosès, *Le sacrifice d'Abraham* (Paris: Declée de Brouwer, 2002), 29. As Mosès writes, "Les paroles qu'Abraham entend au début du récit, et qui lui demandent de sacrifier son fils, ne seraient donc pas celles du Dieu de bonté et d'amour qu'il avait connu jusque-là, mais, nous le dit le commentaire talmudique, celles d'une instance démoniaque dont les injonctions inhumaines se seraient glissées, *comme par un effet de citation*, dans le discours divin" (26; emphasis in original).

80. Levinas, *Totality and Infinity*, 198.

81. Levinas, *Difficult Freedom*, 10.

82. Blanchot, *The Infinite Conversation*, 133. For a discussion of this Blanchotian thought in conversation with Levinas, see Christopher Fynsk, "Blanchot's 'The Indestructible,'" in *After Blanchot: Literature, Criticism, Philosophy*, ed. L. Hill, B. Nelson, and D. Vardoulakis, 100–122 (Newark: University of Delaware Press,

2005). For a profound reflection on this formulation, see Sarah Kofman, *Paroles suffoquées* (Paris: Galilée, 1987).

83. Anne-Lise Stern, *Le savoir-déporté* (Paris: Seuil, 2004).

84. Levinas, *Collected Philosophical Papers*, 19.

85. Blanchot, *The Infinite Conversation*, 61.

86. Blanchot, *The Infinite Conversation*, 61.

87. As Jill Robbins, who follows on this point of Blanchot's, observes, "Thus the one who murders is caught in a substitutive structure; he is like a man who must aim at his target (infinity) over and over again and always miss it" (*Altered Reading*, 66).

88. For an interesting psychoanalytic take on this fantasy of one's murderous impulse that suggestively draws on the function of "holding" and "containment," and hence implicitly trust ("basic trust"; see chapter 1), see Simone Drichel, "'A forgiveness that remakes the world': Trauma, Vulnerability, and Forgiveness in the Work of Emmanuel Levinas," in *Phenomenology and Forgiveness*, ed. M. La Caze, 43–63 (London: Rowman and Littlefield, 2018).

89. Levinas, *Otherwise Than Being*, 111.

90. Levinas, *God, Death, and Time*, 72. "In the guiltiness of the survivor, the death of the other is my affair. *My* death is in my *part* in the death of the other, and in my death I die the death that is my fault" (39; emphasis in original).

91. François-David Sebbah, *The Ethics of the Survivor*, trans. M. Laferté-Coutu, 37. Published in *Levinas Studies* 12 (2018): 3–60.

92. Sebbah, *Ethics of the Survivor*, 37–38.

93. Levinas, *Ethics and Infinity*, 120. As Levinas further remarks, "In society such as it functions one cannot live without killing, or at least without taking the preliminary steps for the death of someone" (120).

94. Levinas, *Existence and Existents*, trans. Alphonso Lingis (Pittsburgh: Duquesne University Press, 2001), 85. For this futurity of forgiveness, see Verena Rauen, *Die Zeitlichkeit des Verzeihens* (Stuttgart: Fink, 2015).

95. See Robert Bernasconi, "Hegel and Levinas on Forgiveness," *Archivio di filosofia* 54 (1986): 325–46.

96. See Colin Davis, "Levinas on Forgiveness; or, The Intransigence of Rav Hanina," *PMLA* 117, no. 2 (2002): 302.

Afterwords

1. As Sendak also once remarked, "And that's the situation in *Outside Over There*: a baby is taken care of by an older child named Ida, who both loves and hates the newcomer" (quoted in Jonathan Cott, *There's a Mystery There: The Primal Vision of Maurice Sendak* [New York: Doubleday, 2017], 122).

2. For a connection between these five goblins and the five wild things in Sendak's *Where the Wild Things Are*, see Cott, *There's a Mystery There*, 121.

3. As Stephen Roxburgh observes, "In this picture, Sendak depicts the three strands of his narrative, showing each character [the baby, the mother,

Ida] in their context" ("A Picture Equals How Many Words? Narrative Theory and Picture Books for Children," *The Lion and the Unicorn* 7, no. 8 [1983–1984]: 28).

4. See Jane Doonan, "*Outside Over There*: A Journey in Style," part 1 in *Signal* 50 (1986): 92–103; part 2 in *Signal* 51 (1986): 172–87.

5. For the influence of German Romantic painters, especially Philipp Otto Runge (compare, for example, Runge's painting *The Hülsenbeck Children*), see Doonan, "*Outside Over There*," 99: "Within the Northern Romantic tradition the sunflower is charged with associated meaning . . . In *Outside Over There* it may be said to symbolize Ida's negative and positive feelings about her sister. While the sunflowers may thrust and tower in the living room, elsewhere they are content to embrace the baby. And as Ida floats through them, they appear strong, healthy, belonging to the natural world she must leave in order to undertake her quest."

Index

abandonment, 10–11

absence, 109

absolute helplessness, 107–8

absolute sadism, 118–19

absolute sovereignty, 120

abuse, 39–40, 110

Abuser of Trust, 145

acceptance, 84–86, 142–43, 150–51

accountability, 60, 64–65, 82

acting: anarchy and, 53; human agency for, 64; narration and, 54–62; ontological performance, 65–66; potentiality and, 66–67; risk and, 50; self-awareness in, 71

action, 22, 26–27, 35, 99–100, 260n76

Adversary, The (Carrère), 8, 36–42

affordance, 149–50

agency, 261n11

aging, 98–99, 114–15

ambiguity, 82–83

ambivalence, 79–80

Améry, Jean, 9–10, 262n32; boundaries for, 109–13; family for, 266n36; *Hilfserwartung* for, 106–9; human experience for, 121–22; responsibility for, 209–10; ressentiment for, 123–25, 242, 265n25; skin, 225; survival for, 84–86, 103–6; survivance for, 270n81; "Torture" by, 96–102; torture for, 117–19, 264n19; unforgivability for, 93–94; *Vernichtungsvollzug* for, 104, 113–16

anarchy: acting and, 53; of forgiveness, 176–77, 213–14, 231–32, 245–46; of Goodness, 13; of potentiality, 72–73

anger, 90–92, 135–36, 238–43, 245–50, 258n57

animals, 50–54

Antelme, Robert, 86, 124–25, 209

anxiety, 34

Anzieu, Didier, 10, 110–11, 267n43, 268n44

Apemantus, 132

appearance, 57, 59–60, 68, 134

Arendt, Hannah, 8, 178–79, 256n27; being-in-the-world for, 55–62; ethics of, 255n12; forgiveness for, 62–69, 123; *The Human Condition*, 43, 47–54, 256n19, 260n75; morality for, 73; *The Origins of Totalitarianism*, 69; religion for, 259n62; strangers for, 74–75; temporality for, 72

assumptions, 2, 35

assurances, 157–58

atonement, 82, 92–94

attitude, 27–28, 43–44, 63–64

Austerlitz (Sebald), 95–96

authenticity, 98–99, 116

authorship, 61–62

autonomy, 143–44

autri, 242–43

availability: conceptions of, 274n1; encounter and, 160; faith and, 161–62; in family, 173–74; to forgiveness, 159, 163–64, 172, 175, 179, 260n77; for the Good, 171; in human existence, 148–49, 151–58, 168, 170, 176–78; original, 132. See also *disponibilité*

Baier, Annette, 141–42, 156, 158, 253n45, 273n31

Bakhtin, Mikhail, 144–45, 274n37

Bataille, Georges, 119

Baudelaire, Charles, 267n41

Being and Nothingness (Sartre), 17, 239

Being and Time (Heidegger), 23, 216